DASH DIET COOKBOOK FOR BEGINNERS

650 LOW-SODIUM RECIPES TO LIVE A HEALTHY LIFE.
21-DAY DASH DIET MEAL PLAN TO LOSE WEIGHT
AND LOWER YOUR BLOOD PRESSURE

© Copyright 2025 - All rights reserved.

The content contained within this book may not be reproduced, duplicated or transmitted without direct written permission from the author or the publisher.

Under no circumstances will any blame or legal responsibility be held against the publisher, or author, for any damages, reparation, or monetary loss due to the information contained within this book. Either directly or indirectly.

Legal Notice:

This book is copyright protected. This book is only for personal use. You cannot amend, distribute, sell, use, quote or paraphrase any part, or the content within this book, without the consent of the author or publisher.

Disclaimer Notice:

Please note the information contained within this document is for educational and entertainment purposes only. All effort has been executed to present accurate, up to date, and reliable, complete information. No warranties of any kind are declared or implied. Readers acknowledge that the author is not engaging in the rendering of legal, financial, medical or professional advice. The content within this book has been derived from various sources. Please consult a licensed professional before attempting any techniques outlined in this book.

By reading this document, the reader agrees that under no circumstances is the author responsible for any losses, direct or indirect, which are incurred as a result of the use of information contained within this document, including, but not limited to, errors, omissions, or inaccuracies.

Table of Contents

INTRODUCTION 10
1. Why the DASH Diet Still Matters Today 10
2. The Truth About Sodium: What You're Really Eating 10
3. Stress, Sleep Salt – The Hidden Connection 11
4. How to Make Healthy Eating Stick (Even If You've Tried Before) 12
5. The Power of Small Wins: Your First 10 Days 12

CHAPTER 1
THE DIETARY APPROACH TO STOP HYPERTENSION (DASH) BASICS 14
Who Should Follow This Diet? 14
The Improved DASH Diet Plan 14
Beginning the DASH Diet 15
Does It Work for Everyone? 15
What to Eat on DASH Diet? 16
What Foods and Drinks Should Be Avoided? 17
FAQs on DASH Diet 17
The Bottom Line 17

CHAPTER 2
BENEFITS OF DASH DIET 18
More Nutritious Meals 18
Healthier Kidneys 18
Cardiovascular Health 18
Helpful for Patients with Diabetes 18
Weight Reduction 18
21-Days Meal Plan 19

CHAPTER 3
WEEKLY SHOPPING LIST 23
The Pantry 23
The Refrigerator 23
The Freezer 23

CHAPTER 4
BREAKFAST 24
Blueberry Waffles 24
Apple Pancakes 24
Super-Simple Granola 24
Savory Yogurt Bowls 24
Energy Sunrise Muffins 25
Spinach, Egg, And Cheese Breakfast Quesadillas 25
Simple Cheese and Broccoli Omelets 25
Creamy Avocado and Egg Salad Sandwiches 26
Breakfast Hash 26
Hearty Breakfast Casserole 26
Creamy Apple-Avocado Smoothie 27
Strawberry, Orange, and Beet Smoothie 27
Blueberry-Vanilla Yogurt Smoothie 27
Greek Yogurt Oat Pancakes 27
Scrambled Egg and Veggie Breakfast Quesadillas 27
Stuffed Breakfast Peppers 28
Sweet Potato Toast Three Ways 28
Apple-Apricot Brown Rice Breakfast Porridge ... 28
Carrot Cake Overnight Oats 29
Steel-Cut Oatmeal with Plums and Pear 29
French Toast with Applesauce 29
Banana-Peanut Butter and Greens Smoothie ... 29
Baking Powder Biscuits 29
Oatmeal Banana Pancakes with Walnuts 30
Creamy Oats, Greens Blueberry Smoothie 30
Banana Cinnamon Oatmeal 30
Bagels Made Healthy 30
Cereal with Cranberry-Orange Twist 31
No Cook Overnight Oats 31
Avocado Cup with Egg 31
Mediterranean Toast 31
Instant Banana Oatmeal 31
Almond Butter-Banana Smoothie 32
Brown Sugar Cinnamon Oatmeal 32
Buckwheat Pancakes with Vanilla Almond Milk .. 32
Salmon and Egg Scramble 32
Pumpkin Muffins 32
Sweet Berries Pancake 33
Zucchini Pancakes 33
Breakfast Banana Split 33
Easy Veggie Muffins 33
Carrot Muffins 34
Pineapple Oatmeal 34
Spinach Muffins 34
Chia Seeds Breakfast Mix 34
Breakfast Fruits Bowls 34
Pumpkin Cookies 35
Veggie Scramble 35
Mushrooms and Turkey Breakfast 35
Mushrooms and Cheese Omelet 35
Egg White Breakfast Mix 36
Pesto Omelet 36
Quinoa Bowls 36
Strawberry Sandwich 36
Apple Quinoa Muffins 36
Very Berry Muesli 37
Veggie Quiche Muffins 37
Turkey Sausage and Mushroom Strata 37
Bacon Bits 37

Steel Cut Oat Blueberry Pancakes 38
Spinach, Mushroom, and Feta Cheese
Scramble 38
Red Velvet Pancakes with Cream Cheese
Topping 38
Peanut Butter Banana Breakfast Smoothie 39
No-Bake Breakfast Granola Bars 39
Mushroom Shallot Frittata 39
Jack-o-Lantern Pancakes 39
Fruit Pizza 40
Flax Banana Yogurt Muffins 40
Tasty Cucumber Bites 40
Sweet Potatoes with Coconut Flakes 40
Fruity Tofu Smoothie 40
Banana-Peanut Butter 'n Greens Smoothie 41
Raspberry Yogurt 41
Southwest Tofu Scramble 41

CHAPTER 5
SOUPS AND SALADS 42
Tofu Soup 42
Vichyssoise 42
Pumpkin and Rosemary Soup 42
Mangetout Soup 42
Niçoise Salad 43
Black Bean Soup 43
Chicken and Dill Soup 43
Cheese Soup with Crispy Bacon 43
Cherry Stew 43
Raspberry and Cranberry Soup 44
Sirloin Carrot Soup 44
Classical Wonton Soup 44
Pumpkin and Coconut Soup 44
Kale And Spinach Soup 44
Onion Soup 45
Vegetarian Soup in a Crock Pot 45
Rhubarb Stew 45
Gazpacho 45
Mixed Beans Soup 45
Beef Stew 46
Homemade Turkey Soup 46
Meatball Soup 46
Sorrel Soup 47
Mexican Pozole 47
Carrot and Ginger Soup 47
Minestrone Soup 47
Brussels Soup 47
Crab and Watermelon Soup 48
Garlic Tomato Soup 48
Lobster Bisque 48
Eggplant Soup 48
Sweet Potato Soup 49
Organic Chicken Thigh Soup 49
Butternut Squash Soup 49
Soup a la Kiev 49
Summer Strawberry Stew 49
Blueberry Stew 50
Chipotle Chicken Chowder 50
Peach Stew 50
Summer Tomato Soup 50
Summer Tomato Sorbet 50
Carrot and Coriander Soup 51
Pappa al pomodoro 51
Zucchini Cream Soup 51
Salmon and Vegetable Soup 51
Mango Salad 51
Tomato and Cucumber Salad 52
Fresh Fruit Salad 52
Green Papaya Salad 52
Quinoa and Fruit Salad 52
Shrimp and Veggie Salad 52
Salmon and Spinach Salad 53
Fattoush Salad 53
Broccoli Salad 53
Baby Spinach Salad 53
Classic Tuna Salad 54
Greek Salad 54
Delicious Tuna Salad 54
Yogurt and Cucumber Salad 54
Tasty Eggplant Salad 54
Potato Octopus Salad 55
Balsamic Beet Salad 55
Squash Garden Salad 55
Beet and Walnut Salad 55
Steamed Saucy Garlic Greens 56
Daikon Radish Salad 56
Calamari Salad 56
Chicken Raisin Salad 56
Pickled Onion Salad 56
Pickled Grape Salad with Pear, and Cheese 57
Tuna and Potato Salad 57
Spinach Parmesan Dip 57

CHAPTER 6
RECIPES FOR LUNCH 58
Homogenized Rabbit With Courgettes (For
Children) 58
Brussels Sprouts In Salad 58
Sandwich With Ham And Tomato 58
Shrimp Cocktail 58
Pumpkin Cream 58
Salad With Tomatoes And Gorgonzola 59
Cream Of Pumpkin Soup With Cheese
Croutons 59
Corn And Bean Tortilla 59
Quinoa And Peas 59
Pepper Salad 59
Bean Mix 59
Egg Salad 60
Garnish Of Carrots And Peas 60
Goat Cheese Sandwich With Tomato And Salad 60
Triumph Of Chicken And Spinach 60

Scrambled Eggs With Mushroom Garnish............60
Salmon Omelette..60
Turkey And Cauliflower 61
Side Dish Of Sauteed Peas..................................61
Cauliflower In A Pan 61
Salmon Salad...61
Chicken And Tomato Mix 61
Salmon And Olive Salad 61
Shrimp Salad 62
Turkey Tortillas 62
Bean Soup..62
Avocado Salad...62
Fillet of Beef..62
Beef Stew With Thyme, Potatoes And Tomatoes...62
Risotto With Chives 63
Shrimp And Spinach Salad 63
Shrimp Salad With Raspberries And Tomatoes.. 63
Cod tacos...63
Fried zucchini..63
Pea soup..63
Lemon Chicken Salad..64
Asparagus salad 64
Beef stew with tomato 64
Pork chops 64
Shrimp salad with balsamic vinegar 64
Tomato and eggplant soup 64
Turkey stew with lime...65
Beans salad 65
Zucchini and peppers stew 65
Cabbage and pepper stew 65
Zucchini soup..65
Almond and shrimp salad...................................65
Baked chicken with potatoes 66
Stew Chicken 66
Carrot and turkey soup.......................................66
Chicken and lentil soup 66
Baked pork ribs with potatoes 66
Trout soup 66
Pea and mint salad..67
Turkey stew...67
Potato soup...67
Spicy Chicken Soup 67
Salmon fillet in a pan..67
Potato and spinach salad....................................67
Velvety Broccoli...68
Shrimp and rocket salad.....................................68
Pasta salad 68
Cauliflower soup..68
Pork soup...68
Shrimp salad with olives and mint 68
Mixed fish soup...68
Spinach and tomato soup...................................69
Pork flavored with oregano 69
Salmon and mushroom salad 69
Sautéed peas...69
Spiced chicken mix 69
Lentils with vegetables 69
Mussel and clam soup..70
Grilled cod 70
Hake salad 70
Baked hake with zucchini salad..........................70
Scrambled eggs with green salad.......................70
Chicken with peppers 70
Turkey salad 71
Vegetables and eggs 71
Turkey bites with raisins and pine nuts 71
Chicken with balsamic vinegar and cauliflower..71
Tomato soup..72
Carrot soup..72
Avocado humus...72
Shrimp with cucumbers, avocado, tomatoes and apples 72
Pao de Valencia 72
Sicilian cod with marinated courgettes..............72
Hake and soy soup with vegetables 73
Spelled with broccoli and peas...........................73
Spelled burger...73
Turkey salad, bean cream and vinegared shallots...73
Chicken in coconut milk and lime juice 74
Salmon mousse...74
Salmon with butter sauce and capers 74
Fresh Robiola with courgette side dish 74
Chicken Kabobs...74
Curried Chicken Parcels......................................75
Tuna Salad-Stuffed Tomatoes with Arugula 75
Herbed Seafood Casserole..................................75
Shrimp Pasta Primavera 76
Fajita Chicken Wraps..76
Curried Pork Tenderloin in Apple Cider 76
Honey Crusted Chicken.......................................77

CHAPTER 7
SIDE DISHES..78
Turmeric Endives 78
Parmesan Endives...78
Lemon Asparagus..78
Lime Carrots 78
Garlic Potato Pan 79
Balsamic Cabbage...79
Chili Broccoli...79
Hot Brussels Sprouts..79
Paprika Brussels Sprouts....................................79
Creamy Cauliflower Mash...................................80
Avocado, Tomato, and Olives Salad....................80
Radish and Olives Salad.....................................80
Spinach and Endives Salad.................................80
Basil Olives Mix 80
Arugula Salad..81
Spanish Rice 81
Sweet Potatoes and Apples................................81
Roasted Turnips..81

No-Mayo Potato Salad 82
Zucchini Tomato Bake 82
Creamy Broccoli Cheddar Rice 82
Smashed Brussels Sprouts 82
Cilantro Lime Rice 83
Corn Salad with Lime Vinaigrette 83
Mediterranean Chickpea Salad 83
Italian Roasted Cabbage 84
Tex-Mex Cole Slaw 84
Roasted Okra 84
Brown Sugar Glazed Carrots 84
Oven-Roasted Beets with Honey Ricotta 85
Easy Carrots Mix 85
Tasty Grilled Asparagus 85
Roasted Carrots 85
Oven Roasted Asparagus 85
Baked Potato with Thyme 86
Spicy Brussels Sprouts 86
Baked Cauliflower with Chili 86
Baked Broccoli 86
Slow Cooked Potatoes with Cheddar 87
Squash Salad with Orange 87
Colored Iceberg Salad 87
Fennel Salad with Arugula 87
Corn Mix 87
Persimmon Salad 88
Avocado Side Salad 88
Spiced Broccoli Florets 88
Lima Beans Dish 88
Soy Sauce Green Beans 89
Butter Corn 89
Stevia Peas with Marjoram 89
Pilaf with Bella Mushrooms 89
Parsley Fennel 89
Sweet Butternut 90
Mushroom Sausages 90
Parsley Red Potatoes 90
Jalapeno Black-Eyed Peas Mix 90
Sour Cream Green Beans 91
Cumin Brussels Sprouts 91
Peach and Carrots 91
Baby Spinach and Grains Mix 91
Quinoa Curry 91
Lemon and Cilantro Rice 92
Chili Beans 92
Bean Spread 92
Stir-Fried Steak, Shiitake, and Asparagus 92
Chickpeas and Curried Veggies 93
Brussels Sprouts Casserole 93
Tasty Cauliflower 93
Artichoke and Spinach Dip 93
Apple Salsa 94

CHAPTER 8
RECIPES FOR DINNER 95
Broccoli au gratin 95
Summer tomato salad 95
Tyrolean side dish in avocado sauce 95
Curried chicken wings with carrot cream
and yogurt 95
Hash brown 95
Risotto with mushrooms 96
Lemon marinated chicken 96
Roasted turkey in tuna sauce 96
Chicken with walnut pesto and salad 96
Eggs and zucchini 97
Raw ham with pumpkin puree for children 97
Tuna salad 97
Cream cheese with zucchini 97
Mountain dish 97
Side dish in avocado sauce 97
Curried Chicken Wings with Cream of
Potatoes and Yogurt 98
Pork skewer with grilled peppers 98
Summer dish 98
Hash brown potato casserole 98
Rice and mushrooms 98
Chicken with walnut pesto and red salad 99
Pasta with cabbage and black olives 99
Rice with cabbage and red wine 99
Spicy cabbage cream 99
Pork ribs with mushroom sauce 99
Buckwheat with rocket pesto and tomatoes 100
Sirloin steak in a bed of rocket 100
Chicken in Green Sauce 100
lasagna 100
Pasta with walnut pesto 100
Sea bream with red wine and onion 101
Chicken salad with sesame 101
Chunks of salmon and bacon 101
Eggplant parmigiana 101
Salmon escalope with pink pepper 101
Tagliatelle with cream and ham 102
Buckwheat spaghetti with prawns 102
Chicken breast with red onion and cabbage ... 102
Salmon with turmeric 102
Rosbeef cooked at a low temperature 103
Beef with red onions 103
Chicken in red wine 103
Chilli with beef 103
Smoked salmon roll 104
Pasta Alla Carrettiera 104
Penne pasta with arrabbiata sauce 104
Baked chillies with herbs and capers 104
Salmon skewers in sweet and sour sauce 104
Grilled salmon fillet with chili and avocado
puree 105
Falafel with yogurt sauce 105
Sweet and sour onions 105
Risotto with broccoli and chilli 105
Marinated cod with green beans and sesame .. 106
Cod with cherry tomatoes, olives and capers ... 106
Baked sea bream 106

Roasted veal curry with spring onions 106
Fusilli with cherry tomatoes, capers and
crispy crumbs 107
Onion pie 107
Neapolitan cod 107
Steamed sea bass 107
Salmon and bacon rolls 108
Sliced beef with artichokes 108
Baked squid and potatoes 108
Salmon and leek quiche 108
Hake fillets with quinoa salad 109
Turkey bites with apple sauce 109
Baked sea bass 109
Fish balls 109
Baked chicken thighs 109
Chicken Cacciatore 110
Mini quiche with mozzarella, sausages and
broccoli 110
Fried chicken with spiced beans 110
Shrimp and chicken skewers with lemon
and avocado sauce 110
Beef burger with lettuce and carrot salad 111
Stuffed eggs 111
Potatos pizza 111
Chicken burger with lime marinade 111
Grilled squid stuffed with beans and pecorino ... 112
Fried eggplant in a pan with olives and capers .. 112
Chicken escalope in white wine 112
Roast pork with beer and onions 113
Pepperoni pizza 113
Pork sausage with fennel salad garnish 113
Tomato cream with crispy capers 113
Calamarata with squid, capers and lemon 113
Mackerel fillets with roasted peppers 114
Smoked salmon croutons with green beans 114
Fresh salmon escalope with pink pepper 114
Salmon with red wine and broccoli 114
Pork sausage with fennel 114
Ham and melon 115
Chicken with curry 115
Turkey skewer and beer sausages 115
Oats kichdi 115
Toasted vegetables 116
Spicy asparagus 116
Omelette 116
Sausage and turkey skewers in beer 116
Asian Beef and Noodles 116
Beef Kabobs with Grilled Pineapple Salsa 117
Pork Medallions with Pear-Maple Sauce 117
Mexican Chicken 117
Sweet Potato Turkey Breast 117
Pesto Tilapia 118
Egg-Topped Rice Bowl 118
Chickpea Burgers 118
Beef Stroganoff 119

CHAPTER 9
SNACKS AND DESSERTS 120
Hearty Chia And Blackberry Pudding 120
Special Cocoa Brownies 120
Nutmeg Nougats 120
Apple And Almond Muffins 121
Sweet Potatoes and Apples Mix 121
Sautéed Bananas with Orange Sauce 121
Caramelized Apricot 121
Rhubarb Pie 122
Berry Bars 122
Chocolate Avocado Pudding 122
Pomegranate Mix 122
Blueberry Cream 122
Mocha Ricotta Cream 122
Mango Sweet Mix 123
Ginger Peach Pie 123
Berries Mix 123
Coconut Cream 123
Coconut Figs 123
Cinnamon Apples 124
Green Apple Bowls 124
Pecan Granola 124
Banana Sashimi 124
Creamy Peanuts with Apples 124
Maple Malt 125
Walnut Green Beans 125
Cheese Stuffed Apples 125
Green Tea Cream 125
Fresh Figs With Walnuts And Ricotta 125
Coconut Mousse 125
Rice Pudding with Oranges 126
Chickpeas and Pepper Hummus 126
Tortilla Chips 126
Kale Popcorn 126
Peas and Parsley Hummus 126
White Beans Hummus 127
Peanuts Snack Bar 127
Chickpeas Dip 127
Special Raspberry Chocolate Bombs 127
Cranberry Muffins 127
Broad Bean Hummus 128
Carrot Cake 128
Hearty Almond Bread 128
Apple Coffee Cake 128
Baked Apple Slices 128
Frosted Cake 129
Fruit Skewers with Yogurt Dip 129
Fudgy Fruit 129
Mousse Vanilla Banana 130
Oatmeal Cookies 130
Oven Fried Plantains 130
Mixed Fruits Freeze 130
Peach Apple Crisp 130
Peach Crumble 131
Peachy Pita 131
Peanut Butter Hummus 131

Rainbow Salad 131
Savory Grilled Fruit 132
Southern Banana Pudding 132
Tropical Fruit and Nut Snack Mix 132
Fruit Compote 132
Winter/Summer Crisp 132
Hearty Cashew And Almond Butter 133
Stylish Chocolate Parfait 133
Supreme Matcha Bomb 133
Pure Avocado Pudding 133
Sweet Almond and Coconut Fat Bombs 134
Simple Brownies 134
Grapefruit Granita 134
Banana Delight 134

CHAPTER 10
BROTHS, CONDIMENTS, AND SAUCES 135
Potato Vegetable Broth 135
Homemade Chicken Broth 135
Red Pepper Pesto 135
Basil Pesto 136
Greek Yogurt Mayonnaise 136
Fresh Vegetable Salsa 136
Chili Lime Marinade 136
Creamy Avocado "Alfredo" Sauce 136
Simple Tomato Sauce 137
Tzatziki Sauce 137
Honey Chipotle Sauce 137
Creamy Spinach-Artichoke Sauce 137

CHAPTER 11
NOURISHING DASH BOWLS 139
Mediterranean Chickpea Quinoa Bowl 139
Grilled Chicken Avocado Brown Rice Bowl 139
Vegan Buddha Bowl with Roasted Veggies 139
DASH Salmon Sweet Potato Bowl 139
Spicy Black Bean Corn Power Bowl 140
Tofu Teriyaki Edamame Bowl 140
Cauliflower Shawarma Bowl 140
Tuna Nicoise Grain Bowl 140
Lentil Kale Anti-Inflammatory Bowl 140
Turkey Cranberry Barley Bowl 141
Greek Lentil Feta Bowl 141
Spiced Quinoa Roasted Squash Bowl 141
DASH Chicken Gyro Bowl 141
Miso Mushroom Brown Rice Bowl 141
Rainbow Slaw Tofu Bowl 142
Harissa Chickpea Cauliflower Bowl 142
BBQ Tempeh Sweet Potato Bowl 142
DASH Falafel Couscous Bowl 142
Grilled Shrimp Avocado Bowl 142
DASH Chicken Caesar Grain Bowl 143
Roasted Pepper Hummus Bowl 143
DASH Veggie Chili Rice Bowl 143
Asian Noodle Edamame Bowl 143
DASH Kimchi Egg Grain Bowl 143
DASH Caprese Barley Bowl 144
DASH Zoodle Roasted Tomato Bowl 144
Roasted Butternut Farro Bowl 144
DASH Pesto Quinoa Bowl 144
Grilled Veggie Halloumi Bowl 144
DASH Southwestern Bean Corn Bowl 145
DASH Avocado Lentil Bowl 145
DASH Italian Chickpea Bowl 145
DASH Tofu Avocado Lime Bowl 145
DASH Sweet Corn Tomato Bowl 145
DASH Spicy Turkey Wild Rice Bowl 146
DASH Mango Black Bean Bowl 146
DASH Curry Veggie Bowl 146
DASH Roasted Eggplant Tahini Bowl 146
DASH Sauteed Greens Potato Bowl 146
DASH Peanut Noodle Bowl 146
DASH Sweet Potato Kale Bowl 147
DASH Carrot Ginger Wild Rice Bowl 147
DASH Tomato Cucumber Bulgar Bowl 147
DASH Baked Falafel Grain Bowl 147
DASH Garlic Mushroom Spinach Bowl 147
Spicy Tofu Sweet Potato Skillet 148
Sheet Pan Turkey Sausage Peppers 148
Baked Eggplant Tomato Parmesan 148
DASH Pesto Chicken Thighs Carrots 148
Cinnamon-Spiced Roasted Root Veggies 148
DASH Honey Mustard Chicken Tray Bake 149
Garlic Shrimp Asparagus Sheet Pan 149
Roasted Cauliflower Chickpeas 149
One-Pan Spinach Feta Turkey Burgers 149
DASH Herb-Crusted Pork with Apples 149
Sheet Pan Tempeh Stir-Fry 150
Maple Dijon Chicken with Green Beans 150
Roasted Brussels with Balsamic Tofu 150
DASH BBQ Chicken Sweet Potato Tray 150
Sheet Pan Sausage, Squash Onion 150
DASH Ginger Chicken Broccoli 151
Mediterranean Stuffed Peppers Bake 151
DASH Zucchini Mushroom Bake 151
Teriyaki Tofu Edamame Rice Tray 151
DASH Baked Haddock with Leeks 151
DASH Roasted Veggie Fajitas 152
Honey Lime Chicken Cauliflower 152
DASH One-Pot Cabbage Stir-Fry 152
DASH Baked Portobello Spinach 152
Sheet Pan Chickpea Tikka Masala 153
DASH Butternut Squash Red Onion Bake 153
DASH Garlic Chicken Rainbow Veggies 153
DASH Spicy Sweet Potato Hash 153
Sheet Pan Ratatouille 153
DASH One-Pan Pasta Primavera 153
DASH Broccoli Tofu Stir-Fry Tray 154
Baked Lemon Chicken Brown Rice 154
DASH Roasted Kale Lentil Mix 154
DASH Cajun Tilapia Veggie Sheet 154
Roasted Garlic Shrimp with Peppers 154
DASH Pesto Salmon with Zoodles 155

Sheet Pan Vegan Stir-Fry with Peanuts 155
DASH Mushroom Green Bean Bake 155
DASH Apple Chicken Skillet 155
DASH Spiced Squash Chickpea Bake 155
Sheet Pan Bruschetta Chicken 156
DASH Roasted Beets Carrot Casserole 156
DASH Sweet Chili Tofu Snap Peas 156
DASH Tray Bake with Beans Tomato Jam 156
DASH Mustard Chicken Veggie Roast 156
DASH Mac Cheese with Butternut Squash Sauce 157
Low-Sodium Chicken Pot Pie 157
Baked Turkey Meatloaf with Oat Crust 157
DASH Cauliflower Mashed Bowl with Gravy 157
Lightened Shepherd's Pie with Lentils 157
DASH Tex-Mex Casserole 157
Sweet Potato Lasagna 158
Crispy Baked Zucchini Fries 158
DASH Alfredo Pasta with Spinach 158
DASH Sloppy Joes with Ground Chicken 158
DASH Chicken Alfredo Casserole 158
DASH Turkey Chili Mac 159
Light Chicken and Dumplings 159
Sweet Corn Black Bean Enchilada Bake 159
DASH Low-Sodium Meatball Stew 159
Butternut Mac and Cheese Cups 159
DASH Baked Fish and Chips 159
Creamy Mushroom Lentil Pot Pie 160
DASH Chicken Veggie Enchiladas 160
Cauliflower Gratin with Whole Grain Crumbs ... 160
DASH Baked Eggplant Parmesan 160
DASH Tuna Noodle Casserole 160
DASH Sausage Peppers Flatbread 161
Creamy Polenta Roasted Tomatoes 161
DASH Mini Chicken Pot Pies 161
DASH Baked Chicken Wild Rice 161
Baked Spaghetti Zucchini Nest 161
DASH Shepherd's Pie with Turkey 161
DASH Vegan Lentil Meatballs 162
DASH Mushroom Sweet Potato Bake 162
DASH Creamy Vegetable Bake 162
Light BBQ Pulled Chicken Sliders 162
DASH Veggie Tamale Pie 162
DASH Low-Sodium Baked Burritos 162
Roasted Broccoli Cheddar Quiche 163
DASH Chicken Zoodle Alfredo 163
DASH Tuna Bean Melt 163
DASH Eggplant and Chickpea Bake 163
DASH Sweet Potato Black Bean Tacos 163
DASH Chicken Cornbread Casserole 163
DASH Zucchini Noodle Lasagna 164
DASH Chickpea Stew with Root Veggies 164
DASH Mozzarella Tomato Flatbreads 164
DASH Cheesy Broccoli Quinoa Bake 164
DASH Baked Chicken Nuggets 164
DASH Low-Sodium Jambalaya 164
DASH Turkey Spinach Stuffed Shells 165
DASH Sloppy Lentil Joes 165
DASH Cajun Pasta with Turkey Sausage 165

APPENDICES 166
Weekly Meal Planner 166
28 Days Meal Plan 167

INTRODUCTION

1. Why the DASH Diet Still Matters Today

Two decades after the original NIH-funded trials revealed that a carefully balanced menu could lower blood pressure as effectively as first-line medication, the Dietary Approaches to Stop Hypertension (DASH) pattern remains at the center of serious nutrition science. Its staying power begins with physiology: elevated pressure inside arteries is driven not just by genetics but by a constellation of modifiable factors—excess sodium, deficient potassium, refined carbohydrate overload, sedentary habits, and chronic inflammation. DASH was constructed to address all of them simultaneously through whole foods that supply potassium, calcium, magnesium, fiber, and protective phytonutrients in the very proportions human kidneys, vessels, and microbiota evolved alongside.

Since 2020, systematic reviews have confirmed that people who follow the diet closely show a 20–30 percent lower risk of stroke, heart failure, and chronic kidney disease progression. Emerging evidence now links DASH adherence to improved insulin sensitivity, reduced visceral fat, and greater microbial diversity in the gut—mechanisms that help explain why the approach lowers C-reactive protein and other inflammatory markers. In an era when cardiometabolic conditions frequently overlap, a template that treats shared upstream drivers is more valuable than ever.

Relevance also comes from flexibility. Unlike elimination protocols or celebrity cleanses, DASH prescribes daily and weekly targets for food groups rather than forbidding entire cuisines. Lean poultry can be swapped for tofu; berries can be fresh, frozen, or lightly sweetened; and seasoning can rely on citrus, smoked paprika, or a miso drizzle instead of the saltshaker. That adaptability has allowed researchers to test Mediterranean-style, vegetarian, low-glycemic, and budget-constrained versions without losing the blood-pressure benefit, showing that the core principles travel well across cultures and income levels.

Sustainability is another modern imperative. Because the plan emphasizes plants, moderate portions of animal protein, and minimal ultra-processing, its greenhouse-gas footprint and fresh-water use are markedly lower than the typical Western diet. Younger generations who evaluate health choices through a climate lens can adopt DASH without moral tradeoffs.

Finally, the diet keeps pace with busy lives. Smartphone apps let users photograph meals to track servings, grocery delivery platforms stock low-sodium staples, and air fryers or multicookers transform raw ingredients into DASH-friendly dinners in under 20 minutes. The practical hurdles that once discouraged adherence—meal-prep time, flavor fatigue, and confusing nutrition labels—are shrinking each year.

Hypertension continues to be the world's leading preventable cause of death, claiming more than ten million lives annually. Far from being a relic, the DASH template meets twenty-first-century challenges head-on: it works synergistically with current medications, dovetails with climate-smart agriculture, and meshes with digital tools for self-monitoring. Whether you are newly diagnosed, genetically predisposed, or simply committed to aging well, the case for DASH is stronger—not weaker—than when it was first unveiled.

2. The Truth About Sodium: What You're Really Eating

Ask a typical diner how much salt they consume in a day and you will almost always hear an underestimate. That is because sodium hides in plain sight, woven into breads, breakfast cereals, flavored coffee creamers, and vegan "meats" as surely as in chips or deli ham. The average intake in North America hovers around 3,400 milligrams—roughly 1½ teaspoons of table salt—far above the 1,500–2,300 milligram ceiling recommended for people concerned about blood pressure. Even if you never touch the saltshaker, nine of every ten dollars spent on food goes to items made outside the home, and commercial kitchens rely on sodium for flavor, texture, and shelflife.

Physiologically, sodium's main job is to help regulate fluid balance and nerve conduction. The trouble starts when chronic excess pulls water into the bloodstream, stretching arterial walls and forcing the heart to pump harder. Over time that mechanical stress stiffens vessels, scars kidneys, and thickens the heart muscle, paving the way for stroke, blindness, and heart failure. Yet individual sensitivity varies: genetics, age, insulin resistance, and hormone status all influence how aggressively the body retains salt. That is why DASH does not treat sodium reduction as a onesizefitsall mandate but pairs it with abundant potassiumrich produce, which encourages renal excretion of excess sodium and relaxes vascular smooth muscle.

Understanding hidden sources is Step One. "Organic" canned soups, cottage cheese, baking soda in muffins, and bottled salad dressings can each deliver 200–400 milligrams per modest serving. Restaurant entrées regularly top 2,000 milligrams before a single dessert bite. Reading the Nutrition Facts label helps, but so does scanning the ingredient list for synonyms such as sodium phosphate, baking powder, disodium inosinate, and sodium benzoate. Step Two is label literacy: "reduced sodium" means 25 percent less than the original version, which could still be very high; "no salt added" items can contain up to 140 milligrams per serving; only "sodiumfree" guarantees fewer than 5 milligrams.

Step Three involves culinary strategy. Rinsing canned beans cuts sodium by roughly 40 percent, choosing unsalted nuts saves another 80 milligrams per ounce, and substituting acid (lemon, vinegar, tamarind) or umamirich spices (smoked paprika, nutritional yeast) adds brightness without the bloat. Gradual reduction retrains taste buds in two to three weeks, while potassium chloride blends can bridge the transition for people who miss a salty snap.

Finally, remember the numbers. Cutting 1,000 milligrams of sodium daily drops systolic blood pressure by an average of 5 points—similar to a firstline medication—while simultaneously reducing urinary calcium loss, an overlooked contributor to osteoporosis. When you see sodium as more than what you sprinkle on fries, you gain the knowledge and leverage to reclaim vascular health bite by bite.

3. Stress, Sleep Salt – The Hidden Connection

Blood pressure does not rise in a vacuum. Psychological stress, erratic sleep, and dietary salt form a selfreinforcing triad that can sabotage even the most wellintentioned meal plan. Under stress, the adrenal cortex releases cortisol and aldosterone, hormones that instruct kidneys to conserve sodium and water in preparation for a "fightorflight" scenario. Heart rate accelerates, vessels constrict, and the body stands ready for action that never arrives in the boardroom or traffic jam. If highsalt convenience food is your coping mechanism, you pour gasoline on the biochemical fire, pushing plasma volume still higher.

Sleep deprivation intensifies the cycle. Fewer than seven hours of quality rest disrupts circadian rhythms in the reninangiotensinaldosterone system and ramps up sympathetic nervous activity, both of which increase overnight bloodpressure "nondipping." Meanwhile, fatigue blunts executive function, making impulse control at the pantry door weaker the next day. Studies show that just one week of restricted sleep boosts appetite for salty and highcarbohydrate snacks by 45 percent. The resulting sodium surge further fragments sleep through nocturia (nighttime urination) and heightened ventilatory drive, creating a vicious loop.

DASH offers a nutritional counterbalance but must be paired with lifestyle tweaks to break the feedback. Mindful breathing and progressive muscle relaxation attenuate sympathetic outflow within minutes, lowering heart rate variability in real time. Evening routines that dim screens, cool bedroom temperature, and anchor bedtime within a 30minute window restore melatonin release and stabilize endocrine patterns that govern fluid regulation. Magnesiumrich DASH staples—spinach, almonds, black beans—add an extra edge by promoting parasympathetic tone and improving sleep efficiency.

Tracking also helps. A short nightly journal that scores stress on a 1–10 scale and logs hours slept makes invisible patterns visible. If highstress days correlate with restaurant takeout, you can preemptively stock lowsodium freezer meals or set a calendar reminder for a fiveminute boxbreathing break before the commute home. Wearable devices that capture heartrate variability and nocturnal bloodpressure cuffs provide objective feedback, turning big, abstract health goals into manageable experiments.

Remember: stress management and sleep hygiene are not optional accessories to a lowsodium agenda; they are upstream levers with power equal to, or greater than, the food on your plate. When you quiet the nervous system and honor circadian biology, the same DASH framework delivers outsized benefits because the kidneys and vasculature are finally able to listen to the dietary cues you are sending.

4. How to Make Healthy Eating Stick (Even If You've Tried Before)

Most people fail to change their diet not because they lack information but because they underestimate the friction of everyday life. Sustainable behavior change hinges on three pillars: clarity, convenience, and emotional reward. Clarity begins with translating the broad DASH prescription—six to eight servings of grains; four to five of vegetables; two to three of lowfat dairy—into visual cues. A labeled pantry shelf, prechopped produce in transparent containers, and a phone wallpaper showing a simple plate model serve as onthespot reminders. Implementationintention research shows that when a goal is paired with a "when–then" statement ("When I make coffee, then I'll slice fruit for a midmorning snack"), followthrough doubles.

Convenience is next. Weekend batch cooking of quinoa or lentils, bagged salad kits, and frozen preportioned fish reduce the cognitive load at 6 p.m. when willpower is exhausted. A slow cooker or multicooker can turn ten minutes of morning prep into a balanced dinner that awaits your return. Digital grocery lists shared with household members keep staples stocked, while subscription spice blends remove guesswork from flavor. Each microoptimization trims seconds from healthy choices and adds seconds to lesshealthy alternatives—exactly the friction gradient habits researchers say predicts longterm adoption.

Emotional reward must also be present. Celebrate nonscale victories such as steadier energy at work, deeper sleep, or a shrinkingly small antihypertensive prescription. Use a habittracking app to streakcount vegetable servings, or move a paperclip from one jar to another every time you meet a sodium target. The brain releases dopamine for completed tasks, and small, repeated hits are more motivating than an abstract promise of "better health someday." Social reinforcement matters, too. Share wins in a group chat, recruit a friend for Sunday meal prep, or post a colorful DASH plate on social media. External accountability supplements internal resolve.

When setbacks occur—and they will—frame them as data, not failure. A salty takeout binge reveals a gap in stressmanagement, a skipped grocery run, or unrealistic expectations about cooking time. Adjust your environment rather than blaming willpower. Finally, review progress monthly. If breakfast is consistently on autopilot but lunches are chaotic, shift planning energy accordingly. Studies show that a 10minute reflective audit can reinvigorate adherence for another month.

In short, making DASH stick is less about heroic discipline and more about engineering surroundings, routines, and social scaffolding so that the healthiest option becomes the path of least resistance. Treat habitbuilding as a design project and success moves from probable to inevitable.

5. The Power of Small Wins: Your First 10 Days

Big transformations begin with tiny victories, and the opening ten days on the DASH program are tailormade for compounding success. Day 1 starts with observation, not overhaul: log everything you eat without judgment to expose sodium hotspots and produce gaps. Awareness itself often cuts 200–300 milligrams of hidden salt. Day 2 targets breakfast—replace processed cereal with overnight oats topped with berries and a tablespoon of slivered almonds, delivering potassium, magnesium, and fiber before work emails intrude.

Day 3 adds one extra serving of vegetables at lunch, perhaps baby carrots beside a sandwich. Day 4 tackles beverages: swap the 20ounce soda or sweetened latte for sparkling water with citrus slices, trimming up to 250 calories and 40 grams of sugar. On Day 5, bring flavor back by experimenting with a saltfree spice blend or fresh herbs in a simple tomatocucumber salad. A pleasant sensory hit reduces the fear that "healthy" must be bland.

The weekend—Days 6 and 7—focuses on infrastructure. Batchcook a grain, roast mixed vegetables, and portion unsalted nuts into singleserve bags. Set an automated grocery order for lowsodium canned beans, frozen fruit, and lowfat yogurt so the next workweek begins stocked. Day 8 introduces movement synergy: a brisk 20minute walk after dinner primes insulin sensitivity and aids nighttime bloodpressure dipping. Day 9 invites reflection; jot down three improvements you feel—clearer thinking, lighter ankles, or quieter snoring—to cement intrinsic motivation.

Day 10 is celebration and recalibration. Prepare a colorful DASHcompliant meal you genuinely love—think grilled salmon with mangoavocado salsa and broccoli sautéed in garlic—and eat it mindfully, acknowledging each small victory that brought you here. Then set one new microgoal for the next ten days, such as reducing restaurant meals from four to two per week or adding a potassiumrich banana to your afternoon routine. Neuroscience shows that immediate recognition of progress releases dopamine, increasing the likelihood of repeating the behavior; setting the next modest challenge keeps the motivational flywheel turning.

By the end of this short sprint you will have removed roughly 1,500 milligrams of average daily sodium, replaced 1012 ounces of refined grains with wholegrains, added 15 servings of produce, and banked at least 200 minutes of light exercise—all without drastic sacrifice. More importantly, you will have concrete evidence that change is possible, and a replicable blueprint for layering new habits. Those early wins are not trivial; they are psychological downpayments that create momentum for the deeper, structural shifts—consistent meal planning, advanced culinary skills, sustained stress management—that lead to enduring cardiovascular health. Start small, finish strong.

Chapter 1
The Dietary Approach to Stop Hypertension (DASH) Basics

Unlike the regular diets out there, DASH is a tad bit different. It means Dietary Approaches to Stop Hypertension. Yes, you read that right. Finally, a diet that focuses on one of the greatest killers of the 21st century- hypertension. According to recent studies, one out of three adults suffers from hypertension or high blood pressure. It keeps increasing with age, with almost two-thirds of the population suffering from it from the age of 65. High blood pressure is not a single stroke disease- it brings heart trouble, kidney diseases, and even diabetes.

Our sedentary lifestyles, coupled with unhealthy eating habits, have fueled several hypertension-related diseases. Most can be corrected by following a healthy diet, which is what DASH aims at. This diet comprises foods and recipes that promote lower sodium levels and higher potassium, calcium, fiber, and magnesium levels in the body. It also helps lower the overall blood pressure to an optimum level without harming the body processes. When this happens, disorders related to hypertension disappear, such as osteoporosis, diabetes, and kidney failure.

The original diet plan aimed to lower blood pressure through natural foods and without medication aid. It was sponsored and endorsed by the US National Institute of Health. When the trials of the first DASH diet came out, it was found that lowering the blood pressure helped maintain the level even with some excess sodium in the blood. Not only this, but the diet was also found to be beneficial in keeping the extra pounds off and prevent many disorders related to hypertension.

Who Should Follow This Diet?

Is the diet for me? Or is it only for people with existing hypertension problems? According to the Dietary Guidelines for Americans, the DASH diet is a healthy eating model that anyone can follow. Of course, since the diet's primary objective is to lower blood pressure, people suffering from hypertension become the primary beneficiaries of the diet. But anyone who wishes to get healthy and scientifically lose weight can follow it, children included.

This diet works while other diets fail miserably because the body is kept full with the required nutrition. The fundamental nutrients, such as calcium, magnesium, and potassium, are elevated in the body through a wholesome diet plan, and sodium levels are also kept in control. And it is all done in a controlled, scientific, and disciplined manner without any crashes or spikes in the metabolism, ensuring a healthier you.

The Improved DASH Diet Plan

When research into diet plans for hypertension began, they did not focus too much on weight loss. They were more concerned with getting the blood pressure levels regulated. But soon, the researchers realized that healthy weight loss was the need of the hour, and therefore there were an additional need to create a systematic weight loss plan and reduced blood pressure levels. So, after a lot of deliberation, the DASH diet for weight loss was also formulated, including nuts, cereals, whole fruits and vegetables, and seeds.

Unlike other flyby diets, which are more word of mouth than scientific, the DASH diet is primarily based on scientific principles of good health. The research on DASH diets indicates that it is not merely a tool for reducing your blood pressure by eating a low sodium diet. The plan is designed for each person, keeping their specific needs in mind, and comprises wholesome foods, such as fruits, vegetables, grains, fresh produce, etc. which keeps the body in fighting fit condition. Top rung research institutes such as the American Heart Association, Dietary Guidelines for Americans, the National Heart, Lung, and Blood Institute- all endorse this diet plan.

Several more corroborating research reports after, the DASH diet was further improved to optimize health and reduce hypertension by increasing the protein intake and cutting down on empty carbs and bad fats. The DASH diet's primary hypothesis is based on sound scientific principles of attainable and sustainable weight loss. The meals and snacks prescribed in the diet plan comprise bulky, fibrous foods, which keep you filled for hours and do not let you snack mindlessly. They are designed to keep your blood sugar levels regulated, instead of the spike and crash cycles, as seen with other diets. By following this diet, you keep your blood sugar levels on an even keel, defeat other diseases like diabetes, reduce your triglycerides, melt your stubborn belly fat, lower your LDL, improve your HDL numbers, and generally feel healthier on average. Of course, a significant portion of the diet is protein-rich, so you build your muscle and lose body fat, and in the process, you avoid slowing your metabolism, which aids in sustaining your current weight.

Even if you're is not suffering from hypertension, you can adopt the DASH diet to keep your internal systems healthy and robust. In this part of your journey, you will learn how you can make this diet work for you.

Rome wasn't built in a day. Similarly, your body will not take too kindly to change if you do it suddenly. It will protest, and you will soon return to square one. To avoid that discomfort, take baby steps. Do not jump into the diet headlong. Try the meal plan for two days a week, then increase it to three times, and when you are comfortable with it, adopt it ultimately. You might already be eating some DASH diet foods and snacks and not be aware of it. Make a list and see which food items correspond to the diet's meal plan. And do not be under the impression that the DASH diet goes for a toss while dining out. There are plenty of options and strategies you can adopt while eating out. You need to be careful and select healthy choices.

Beginning the DASH Diet

Now that you are supplied with the necessary background information on the DASH diet let us see first what it entails. This meal plan is rich in vegetables, fruits, dairy products, whole grains, lean meats, poultry, fish, and legumes such as peas and beans. Additionally, it contains low fat from natural sources and high fiber from sweet potatoes, cabbage, and leafy vegetables. It adheres to the US guidelines about the sodium and potassium content. It is a flexible eating plan designed to meet the needs of a variety of people and keeps in mind their food preferences. There is a healthy alternative to almost any kind of food craving. It is what a typical DASH diet comprises:

TYPE OF FOOD	NUMBER OF SERVINGS (1600-3000 CALORIE PLAN)	NUMBER OF SERVINGS (1500-2000 CALORIE PLAN)
Whole grains or meals made out of whole grains	6-12	7-9
Fresh fruits (not fruit juice)	4-5	4-6
Farm fresh vegetables (try avoiding store bought ones)	4-6	4-6
Dairy products (low fat)	3-4	2-4
Poultry, fish, lean meats	2-3	3-4
Legumes, seeds and nuts	3-5	4-5
Desserts, natural fats	2-3	2

Does It Work for Everyone?

Many people may benefit from the DASH diet, but even so, the best results were seen in individuals that already have high blood pressure. With that in mind, if your blood pressure is within normal levels, the chances are that you may not see any significant results. Some doctors also suggest that several categories of people should exercise caution when undergoing the DASH diet. While the diet is safe and healthy for most people, those who have chronic liver disease, kidney disease, or those who have been prescribed renin-angiotensin-aldosterone system (RAAS) inhibitors should be careful. Ideally, discussions with your physician should be due. Certain modifications of the DASH diet may also be necessary in case the person has chronic heart failure, lactose intolerance, Mellitus type 2, and celiac disease. This is why you may want to keep in touch with your healthcare provider, to be certain that the diet is your best choice. Depending on the circumstances, you may as well need to make some modifications to the diet.

What to Eat on DASH Diet?

Both DASH diet versions, no matter if you are going for the standard or the lower sodium option, include pretty much the same types of vegetables. The only difference is in the quantities and number of servings.

The DASH diet is quite variable, as you can eat almost anything you want aside from processed, fatty meat and sugary food (although sweets are still allowed in small amounts, and the same thing goes for red meat).

With that in mind, here are the foods that you may eat during the DASH diet, along with the recommended servings per day for an average 2,000 calorie diet. You're not going to eat from all of them, but you may choose which ones you want that day, as long as you do not go over the daily serving size.

You may adjust them according to your desired calorie intake, but you may still want to discuss matters with your healthcare provider. Starving yourself to lose weight is not an option either.

Grains (6-8 servings a day)

During the DASH diet, grains should be an important part of your meals. Here, you have plenty of options, including pasta, rice, and cereal. Focus on whole grain rather than the refined kind, as it has more nutrients. Also, since grains are naturally very low in fats, avoid putting them in dishes that include cream, butter, and sauces.

Vegetables (4-8 servings a day)

Vegetables such as carrots, tomatoes, sweet potatoes, broccoli, greens, and other veggies are packed with a variety of nutrients. Not only are they high in vitamins and fiber, but they are also rich in magnesium and potassium, the centerpieces of the DASH diet.

Fruits (4-5 servings a day)

Except for coconut, fruits are very low in fat and make for great snacks. Plus, they are rich in magnesium, potassium, and fiber, but whenever possible, you might also want to consume them together with the edible peel. Canned fruit is also acceptable, but make sure it doesn't have sugar.

Dairy (2-3 servings a day)

Yogurt, milk, cheese, and other dairy products are a great source of calcium, another centerpiece of the DASH diet. However, make sure that you go for low-fat or even fat-free options. This applies mostly to cheese, as the high-fat ones are often packed with sodium.

Lean Meat, Fish and Poultry (6 one-ounce servings or less a day)

Meat is packed with B vitamins, protein, zinc, and iron. You may want to focus on lean meat and healthy fish, and you may also want to make sure you trim the skin away.

Legumes, Seeds, and Nuts (4-5 servings a week)

Now and again, you may add sunflower seeds, almonds, kidney beans, peas, lentils, and other foods from this category in your diet. They are high in potassium, magnesium, and protein, making them a great choice. However, since they are high in fat, you should make sure you only consume them a few times a week.; Fats and Oils (2-3 servings a day); Fat: is necessary for you to absorb the vitamins, but too much of it increases the risk of heart disease. This is why you should get at most 30% of your calories from fat, and make sure those fats are monounsaturated.

Sweets (5 servings a week or fewer)

While you don't have to say goodbye entirely to sweets, you might want to keep them under 5 servings a week. Plus, when you DO consume them, make sure they are as low fat as possible. Some good examples can be sorbet, low-fat cookies, and fruit ices. You can find more ideas in my DASH diet cookbook.

What Foods and Drinks Should Be Avoided?

Certain foods and drinks should also be avoided when you are following the DASH diet. Ideally, you should steer clear of foods that are packed in sugar, salt, and high fat such as:

- Cookies
- Candy
- Chips
- Sodas
- Salted nuts
- Pastries
- Sugary beverages
- Snacks
- Meat dishes
- Soups
- Pizza
- Salad dressings
- Rice dishes
- Prepackaged pasta
- High-fat cheese
- Cured meats and cold cuts
- Rolls and bread
- Sauces and gravies
- Sandwiches
- Salt substitutes will help you improve the taste of certain dishes and will often come with a high concentration of potassium. This can help lower your blood pressure even further.

FAQs on DASH Diet

Can I have eggs on a DASH diet?

There is a myth going around that eggs raise your cholesterol levels, and therefore, your blood pressure. That being said, with the DASH diet, you are also encouraged to consume lean protein, something that eggs are very rich in. This is why they are a great addition to your DASH diet.

Is it difficult to follow a DASH diet?

It's very easy to follow the DASH diet, as the ingredients are available at every grocery store. The only issue is that since processed food is not allowed, you need to cook things yourself. You can find some good ideas by going through my DASH diet cookbook.

Is exercise necessary while following the DASH diet?

While it's not mandatory (you can lower your blood pressure just as well with the diet alone), it does not mean that you shouldn't pair this plan with some moderate exercising. It will help you lose weight more efficiently if that's your goal, and it may also help your blood pressure issues. After all, you'll be losing the fat that's pressing on your organs.

When will I see results?

The DASH diet works quite fast, and usually, people see results within the first two weeks. This will also depend on how efficient you are in sticking to the diet.

Can I follow the DASH diet even if I don't have high blood pressure? Yes, while this diet was made specifically for those with high blood pressure, this does not mean that someone with normal blood pressure cannot use it. After all, the diet focuses on healthy foods, so it's not lacking in nutrients.

The Bottom Line

The DASH diet can prove very useful for those struggling with hypertension. It can bring your body back on track, ensuring you get your nutrition while watching what you eat. To make things tastier and not feel like you are on a diet, you may want to check my DASH diet cookbook and prepare some delicious recipes for your next meal.

Chapter 2
Benefits of Dash Diet

Hypertension affects millions of people around the world. Therefore, switching to the DASH Diet can help many people live healthier lives. It is not very difficult to follow this diet because it is not restrictive. All you need to do is consume more vegetables and fruits while having red meat and sugary foods in moderation.

More Nutritious Meals

Eliminating processed foods and incorporating more fresh foods gives you healthy meals which are beneficial for every aspect of your wellbeing. Adjusting may take some effort at first, especially if you're accustomed to fast foods, but the results will be well worth the effort. You will reduce the chances of health issues throughout your lifetime and enjoy a largely vibrant, pain-free life.

Healthier Kidneys

The nutrients found in the DASH eating plan, including potassium, calcium, magnesium, and fiber, nourish every part of the body, and the kidneys are no exception. The lower consumption of sodium as recommended, further favor the kidneys, allowing them to filter blood efficiently.

Cardiovascular Health

The DASH Diet decreases your consumption of refined carbohydrates by increasing your consumption of foods high in potassium and dietary fiber (fruits, vegetables, and whole grains). It also lessens your consumption of saturated fats. Therefore, the DASH Diet has a positive effect on your lipid profile and glucose tolerance, which reduces the prevalence of metabolic syndrome (MS) in post-menopausal women.

Reports state that a diet limited to 500 calories favors a loss of 17% of total body weight in 6 months in overweight women. This reduces the prevalence of metabolic syndrome by 15%.

However, when this diet follows the patterns of the DASH Diet, while triglycerides decrease similarly, the reduction in weight and blood pressure is even greater.

It also reduces blood sugar and increases HDL (high-density lipoprotein cholesterol), which decreases the prevalence of MS in 35% of women. These results contrasted with those of other studies, which have reported that the DASH Diet alone, i.e., without caloric restriction, does not affect HDL and glycemia. This means that the effects of the DASH Diet on MS are associated mainly with the greater reduction in BP (Blood Pressure) and that, for more changes, the diet would be required to be combined with weight loss.

Helpful for Patients with Diabetes

The DASH Diet helps reduce inflammatory and coagulation factors (C-reactive protein and fibrinogen) in patients with diabetes. These benefits are associated with the contribution of antioxidants and fibers, given the high consumption of fruits and vegetables that the DASH Diet requires. In addition, the DASH Diet has been shown to reduce total cholesterol and LDL (low-density lipoprotein cholesterol), which reduces the estimated 10-year cardiovascular risk. Epidemiological studies have determined that women in the highest quintile of food consumption, according to the DASH Diet, have a 24% to 33% lower risk of coronary events and an 18% lower risk of a cerebrovascular event. Similarly, a meta-analysis of six observational studies has determined that the DASH Diet can reduce the risk of cardiovascular events by 20%.

Weight Reduction

Limited research associates the DASH Diet, in isolation, with weight reduction. In some studies, weight reduction was greater when the subject was on the DASH Diet as compared to an isocaloric controlled diet. This could be related to the higher calcium intake and lower energy density of the DASH Diet. The American guidelines for the treatment of obesity emphasize that, regardless of diet, a caloric restriction would be the most important factor in reducing weight.

However, several studies have made an association between greater weight and fat loss in diets and caloric restriction and higher calcium intake. Studies have also observed an inverse association between dairy consumption and body mass index (BMI). In obese patients, weight loss has been reported as being 170% higher after 24 weeks on a hypocaloric diet with high calcium intake.

In addition, the loss of trunk fat was reported to be 34% of the total weight loss as compared to only 21% in a control diet. It has also been determined that a calcium intake of 20 mg per gram has a protective effect in overweight middle-aged women. This would be equivalent to 1275 mg of calcium for a western diet of 1700 kcal.

Despite these reports, the effect that diet-provided calcium has on women's weight after menopause is a controversial subject. An epidemiological study has noted that a sedentary lifestyle and, to a lesser extent, caloric intake is associated with post-menopausal weight gain and calcium intake is not associated with it. The average calcium intake in this group of women is approximately 1000 mg, which would be low, as previously stated. Another study of post-menopausal women shows that calcium and vitamin D supplementation in those with a calcium intake of less than 1200 mg per day decreases the risk of weight gain by 11%.

In short, the DASH Diet has positive impacts, both in weight control and in the regulation of fatty tissue deposits, due to its high calcium content (1200 mg/day). The contribution of calcium plays a vital role in the regulation of lipogenesis.

21-Days Meal Plan

An example of a 21-day food plan is presented in this short chapter. I suggest you follow the letter for the first cycle, take a week off, and start again with the second. During the second cycle, if you do not want to repeat it as it is, you can change some foods, but always keeping the quantities and macronutrients (eg. If the plan includes salmon, you can replace it with another type of fish, but certainly not with a pizza).

Fruits and vegetables in general are extremely important foods not only in diets, but in the diet in the broad sense, because thanks to their vitamins and antioxidants are able to capture the free radicals present in the body, slow the aging process and thus improve overall health.

That said, there are some perticular varieties of vegetables whose beneficial effects are particularly important: cabbage in all its forms, caarote, cucumber, salad, mushrooms, asparagus and green beans are extremely rich sources of vitamins and antioxidants.

All weights are intended on raw foods. Try to always drink AT LEAST 2 liters of water per day. The quantities of vegetables are approximate, you can increase the quantities as long as the dressing is always the same.

DAY 1

Breakfast: 1 slice of wholemeal bread with sugar-free jam, 150 ml of orange juice

Snack: 15 g of dried fruit

Lunch: 100 g brown rice with vegetables

Snack: 200 g seasonal fruit

Dinner: 200 g turkey, 50 g wholemeal bread and 200 g seasonal vegetables

DAY 2

Breakfast: 4 tablespoons porridge with 1 tablespoon honey

Snack: 100 g carrots

Lunch: 100 g wholemeal pasta with seasonal vegetables and 1 tablespoon of oil

Snack: 200 g seasonal fruit

Dinner: 200 g fresh ricotta cheese with 1 slice of wholemeal bread and 200 g seasonal vegetables

DAY 3

Breakfast: 170 g Greek yogurt and 1 tablespoon peanut butter

Snack: 15 g of dried fruit

Lunch: 100 g spelt salad, seasoned with fresh vegetables and 1 tablespoon of oil

Snack: 200 g seasonal fruit

Dinner: 200 g grilled fish with 150 g potatoes

DAY 4

Breakfast: 200 ml of whole milk with 25 g of cornflakes without added sugar

Snack: 150 g fresh fruit

Lunch: 2 sandwiches with 50 g of ham each, tomatoes and salad

Snack: 150 g of fresh carrots

Dinner: 100 g legume soup with salad and 1 slice of whole wheat bread

DAY 5

Breakfast: 1 slice of wholemeal bread with 1 tablespoon of honey

Snack: 150 g Greek yogurt

Lunch: 100 g brown rice with 100 g shrimp and vegetables

Snack: 150 g fresh fruit

Dinner: 250 g vegan burgers with green salad

DAY 6

Breakfast: 170 g Greek yogurt with 100 g fresh fruit

Snack: 150 g of fennel

Lunch: 100 g wholemeal pasta with tomato and grated Parmesan cheese

Snack: 15 g of dried fruit

Dinner: 200 g chicken with 1 slice of whole wheat bread and vegetables

DAY 7

Breakfast: 200 ml of whole milk with 25 g of cornflakes without added sugar

Snack: 150 g fresh fruit

Lunch: 100 g of pearl barley with vegetables of your choice

Snack: 150 g Greek yogurt

Dinner: 200 g of salmon with 1 slice of wholemeal bread and vegetables

DAY 8

Breakfast: 150 grams of yogurt, 1 slice of wholemeal bread with jam, 150 ml of pineapple juice with no added sugar

Snack: 150 g fresh fruit

Lunch: 150 g of beef burgers, 1 slice of wholemeal bread and vegetable side dish of your choice

Snack: 150 g of fresh carrots

Dinner: 100 g legume soup with salad and 1 slice of whole wheat bread and 100 g of fresh spinach

DAY 9

Breakfast: 120 g low-fat yogurt, 1 banana

Snack: 15 g of dried fruit

Lunch: 1 serving of 150 g lasagna, 100 g fresh tomatoes as a side dish

Snack: 3 kiwis

Dinner: 150 g baked trout, with 150 g of vegetables of your choice

DAY 10

Breakfast: 150 ml of skimmed milk, 1 banana

Snack: 170 g Greek yogurt

Lunch: 2 slices of wholemeal bread with 50 g of turkey breast and a mixed salad with 100 g of green salad, 100 g of carrots and 1 medium tomato

Snack: 150 g fresh fruit

Dinner: 200 g of sea bass and 200 g of spinach

DAY 11

Breakfast: 200 ml of whole milk with 25 g of cornflakes without added sugar

Snack: 150 g fresh fruit

Lunch: 2 sandwiches with 50 g of ham each, tomatoes and salad

Snack: 150 g of fresh carrots

Dinner: 100 g legume soup with salad and 1 slice of whole wheat bread

DAY 12

Breakfast: One low-fat yogurt, 2 slices of wholemeal biscuits with 2 tablespoons of jam

Snack: 150 g fresh fruit

Lunch: 2 sandwiches with 50 g of prociutto each, spreadable cheese, tomato and lettuce

Snack: 15 almonds

Dinner: 100 g wholemeal pasta with vegetables

DAY 13

Breakfast: 200 ml of whole milk with 25 g of cornflakes without added sugar

Snack: 150 g fresh fruit

Lunch: 80 g wholemeal pasta with tomato and grated Parmesan cheese

Snack: 15 g of dried fruit

Dinner: 200 g turkey breast with seasonal vegetables per side dish

DAY 14

Breakfast: 170 g of whole yogurt, 1 apple and 4 whole wheat biscuits

Snack: 15 g of dried fruit

Lunch: 1 serving of 150 g lasagna, 100 g fresh tomatoes as a side dish

Snack: 150 g of fresh carrots

Dinner: 150 g of salmon, with 150 g of baked potatoes as a side dish

DAY 15

Breakfast: 200 ml of whole milk with 25 g of cornflakes

Snack: 1 low fat yogurt

Lunch: 80 g brown rice and 120 g artichokes

Snack: 1 apple and 5 almonds

Dinner: 150 g mozzarella, side dish of eggplant, peperoni and zucchini seasoned with 1 tablespoon olive oil

DAY 16

Breakfast: 200 ml of whole milk with 30 g of cornflakes, 150 ml of fruit juice

Snack: 150 g fresh fruit

Lunch: 80 g wholemeal pasta with tomato sauce

Snack: 170 g Greek yogurt

Dinner: 150 g chicken breast with seasonal vegetables per side dish

DAY 17

Breakfast: 4 rusks with 2 tablespoons of sugar-free jam

Snack: 150 g fresh fruit

Lunch: 150 g fresh tuna, for green side dish seasoned with 1 tablespoon of oil

Snack: 1 low fat yogurt

Dinner: 80 g lentils, 1 slice of whole-wheat bread and 150 g zucchini

DAY 18

Breakfast: 150 ml of milk, 3 whole-wheat biscuits and 1 kiwi

Snack: A lean yogurt

Lunch: 70 g brown rice with tomato sauce

Snack: 7 walnuts

Dinner: 150 g chicken breast with 60 g boiled potatoes and 150 g seasonal vegetables

DAY 19

Breakfast: 200 ml of whole milk with 30 g of cornflakes

Snack: A lean yogurt

Lunch: 150 g swordfish and 200 g broccoli, 1 slice of wholemeal bread

Snack: 1 apple

Dinner: 60 g wholemeal pasta with 100 g shrimp and 5 almonds before going to sleep

DAY 20

Breakfast: 150 ml of skimmed milk, 1 banana

Snack: 170 g Greek yogurt

Lunch: 2 slices of wholemeal bread with 50 g of turkey breast and a mixed salad with 100 g of green salad, 100 g of carrots and 1 medium tomato

Snack: 150 g fresh fruit

Dinner: 200 g of sea bass and 200 g of spinach

DAY 21

Breakfast: 170 g of whole yogurt, 1 apple and 4 whole wheat biscuits

Snack: 15 g of dried fruit

Lunch: 1 serving of 150 g lasagna, 100 g fresh tomatoes as a side dish

Snack: 150 g of fresh carrots

Dinner: 150 g of salmon, with 150 g of baked potatoes as a side dish

Chapter 3
Weekly Shopping List

The Pantry

- Brown rice
- Quinoa
- Whole-wheat pasta
- Ready-to-eat whole-grain cereals (shredded wheat, toasted oat, bran flakes)
- Oatmeal (whole oats or quick-cooking, not instant)
- 100% whole-wheat bread (small slice) and pita pockets
- Flour (unbleached and whole-wheat)
- Cornstarch or arrowroot
- Baking powder (aluminium-free) and baking soda
- Beans (dried and/or canned)
- Canned tuna (packed in water, not oil)
- Canned tomatoes (preferably no-salt-added)
- Unsweetened apple sauce
- Dried fruit and nuts
- Vegetable oil spray
- Olive and canola oils
- Low-calorie salad dressings
- Low-sodium chicken, beef, and/or vegetable broth Salsa
- Reduced-sodium tomato sauce
- Brown sugar
- Vinegar (balsamic and white wine)
- Reduced-sodium ketchup, deli mustard, "lite" mayonnaise
- Low-fat granola bars
- Pretzels (unsalted)
- Low-fat whole-wheat snack crackers.

The Refrigerator

- Fruit (an assortment)
- More fresh vegetables (a variety)
- Fresh-pack salad greens
- Onions
- Garlic
- Low-fat or non-fat milk
- Low-fat and non-fat yoghurt (an assortment)
- Low-fat cottage cheese
- Low-fat cheese (an assortment)
- Reduced-fat string cheese (mozzarella) sticks
- Trans-fat-free margarine
- Eggs and/or egg substitute
- Reduced-fat, low-sodium deli meat, such as sliced turkey breast
- Natural peanut butter
- Tortillas, whole-wheat or corn (could be frozen, too)
- Bottled lemon juice
- Reduced-sodium soy sauce and teriyaki sauce.

The Freezer

- Frozen vegetables (plain vegetables; no sauces or salt)
- Frozen fruit (without added sugar; such as blueberries, strawberries, raspberries)
- Liver organ (skinless chicken breasts, low-fat cuts of beef, pork)
- Fish
- Low-calorie frozen desserts (frozen juice bars, non-fat frozen yogurt).

Chapter 4
Breakfast

BLUEBERRY WAFFLES

Preparation Time: 15 minutes
Cooking Time: 15 minutes
Servings: 8

INGREDIENTS:

- 2 cups whole wheat flour
- 1 tablespoon baking powder
- 1 teaspoon ground cinnamon
- 2 tablespoons sugar
- 2 large eggs
- 3 tablespoons unsalted butter, melted
- 3 tablespoons nonfat plain Greek yogurt
- 1½ cups 1% milk
- 2 teaspoons vanilla extract
- 4 ounces blueberries
- Nonstick cooking spray
- ½ cup maple almond butter

DIRECTIONS:

» Preheat waffle iron. Mix the flour, baking powder, cinnamon, plus sugar in a large bowl. Mix the eggs, melted butter, yogurt, milk, and vanilla in a small bowl. Combine well. Put the wet fixing to the dry mix and whisk until well combined. Do not over whisk; it's okay if the mixture has some lumps. Fold in the blueberries. Oiled the waffle iron with cooking spray, then cook 1/3 cup of the batter until the waffles are lightly browned and slightly crisp. Repeat with the rest of the batter.

» Place 2 waffles in each of 4 storage containers. Store the almond butter in 4 condiment cups. To serve, top each warm waffle with 1 tablespoon of maple almond butter.

Nutrition: Calories: 647 Fat: 37g; Carbohydrates: 67g Protein: 22g; Sodium: 156mg

APPLE PANCAKES

Preparation Time: 15 minutes
Cooking Time: 5 minutes
Servings: 16

INGREDIENTS:

- ¼ cup extra-virgin olive oil, divided
- 1 cup whole wheat flour
- 2 teaspoons baking powder
- 1 teaspoon baking soda
- 1 teaspoon ground cinnamon
- 1 cup 1% milk
- 2 large eggs
- 1 medium Gala apple, diced
- 2 tablespoons maple syrup
- ¼ cup chopped walnuts

DIRECTIONS:

» Set aside 1 teaspoon of oil to use for greasing a griddle or skillet. In a large bowl, stir the flour, baking powder, baking soda, cinnamon, milk, eggs, apple, and the remaining oil.
» Warm griddle or skillet on medium-high heat and coat with the reserved oil. Working in batches, pour in about ¼ cup of the batter for each pancake. Cook until browned on both sides.
» Place 4 pancakes into each of 4 medium storage containers and the maple syrup in 4 small containers. Put each serving with 1 tablespoon of walnuts and drizzle with ½ tablespoon of maple syrup.

Nutrition: Calories: 378; Fat: 22g; Carbohydrates: 39g; Protein: 10g; Sodium: 65mg

SUPER-SIMPLE GRANOLA

Preparation Time: 15 minutes
Cooking Time: 25 minutes
Servings: 8

INGREDIENTS:

- ¼ cup extra-virgin olive oil
- ¼ cup honey
- ½ teaspoon ground cinnamon
- ½ teaspoon vanilla extract
- ¼ teaspoon salt
- 2 cups rolled oats
- ½ cup chopped walnuts
- ½ cup slivered almonds

DIRECTIONS:

» Preheat the oven to 350°F. Mix the oil, honey, cinnamon, vanilla, and salt in a large bowl. Add the oats, walnuts, and almonds. Stir to coat. Put the batter out onto the prepared sheet pan. Bake for 20 minutes. Let cool.

Nutrition: Calories: 254; Fat: 16g; Carbohydrates: 25g; Fiber: 3.5g; Protein: 5g; Potassium: 163mg; Sodium: 73mg

SAVORY YOGURT BOWLS

Preparation Time: 15 minutes
Cooking Time: 0 minutes
Servings: 4

INGREDIENTS:

- 1 medium cucumber, diced
- ½ cup pitted Kalamata olives, halved
- 2 tablespoons fresh lemon juice

- 1 tablespoon extra-virgin olive oil
- 1 teaspoon dried oregano
- ¼ teaspoon freshly ground black pepper
- 2 cups nonfat plain Greek yogurt
- ½ cup slivered almonds

DIRECTIONS:

» In a small bowl, mix the cucumber, olives, lemon juice, oil, oregano, and pepper. Divide the yogurt evenly among 4 storage containers. Top with the cucumber-olive mix and almonds.

Nutrition: Calories: 240; Fat: 16g; Carbohydrates: 10g; Protein: 16g; Potassium: 353mg; Sodium: 350mg

ENERGY SUNRISE MUFFINS

Preparation Time: 15 minutes
Cooking Time: 25 minutes
Servings: 16

INGREDIENTS:

- Nonstick cooking spray
- 2 cups whole wheat flour
- 2 teaspoons baking soda
- 2 teaspoons ground cinnamon
- 1 teaspoon ground ginger
- ¼ teaspoon salt
- 3 large eggs
- ½ cup packed brown sugar
- 1/3 cup unsweetened applesauce
- ¼ cup honey
- ¼ cup vegetable or canola oil
- 1 teaspoon grated orange zest
- Juice of 1 medium orange
- 2 teaspoons vanilla extract
- 2 cups shredded carrots
- 1 large apple, peeled and grated
- ½ cup golden raisins
- ½ cup chopped pecans
- ½ cup unsweetened coconut flakes

DIRECTIONS:

» If you can fit two 12-cup muffin tins side by side in your oven, then leave a rack in the middle, then preheat the oven to 350°F.
» Coat 16 cups of the muffin tins with cooking spray or line with paper liners. Mix the flour, baking soda, cinnamon, ginger, and salt in a large bowl. Set aside.
» Mix the eggs, brown sugar, applesauce, honey, oil, orange zest, orange juice, and vanilla until combined in a medium bowl. Add the carrots and apple and whisk again.
» Mix the dry and wet ingredients with a spatula. Fold in the raisins, pecans, and coconut. Mix everything once again, just until well combined. Put the batter into the prepared muffin cups, filling them to the top.
» Bake within 20 to 25 minutes, or until a wooden toothpick inserted into the middle of the center muffin comes out clean (switching racks halfway through if baking on 2 racks). Cool for 5 minutes in the tins, then transfers to a wire rack to cool for an additional 5 minutes. Cool completely before storing in containers.

Nutrition: Calories: 292 Fat: 14g; Carbohydrates: 42g; Protein: 5g Sodium: 84mg

SPINACH, EGG, AND CHEESE BREAKFAST QUESADILLAS

Preparation Time: 15 minutes
Cooking Time: 15 minutes
Servings: 4

INGREDIENTS:

- 1½ tablespoons extra-virgin olive oil
- ½ medium onion, diced
- 1 medium red bell pepper, diced
- 4 large eggs
- 1/8 teaspoon salt
- 1/8 teaspoon freshly ground black pepper
- 4 cups baby spinach
- ½ cup crumbled feta cheese
- Nonstick cooking spray
- 4 (6-inch) whole-wheat tortillas, divided
- 1 cup shredded part-skim low-moisture mozzarella cheese, divided

DIRECTIONS:

» Warm-up oil over medium heat in a large skillet. Add the onion and bell pepper and sauté for about 5 minutes, or until soft.
» Mix the eggs, salt, and black pepper in a medium bowl. Stir in the spinach and feta cheese. Put the egg batter in the skillet and scramble for about 2 minutes, or until the eggs are cooked. Remove from the heat.
» Coat a clean skillet with cooking spray and add 2 tortillas. Place one-quarter of the spinach-egg mixture on one side of each tortilla. Sprinkle each with ¼ cup of mozzarella cheese. Fold the other halves of the tortillas down to close the quesadillas and brown for about 1 minute.
» Turnover and cook again in a minute on the other side. Repeat with the remaining 2 tortillas and ½ cup of mozzarella cheese. Cut each quesadilla in half or wedges. Divide among 4 storage containers or reusable bags.

Nutrition: Calories: 453 Fat: 28g; Carbohydrates: 28g; Fiber: 4.5g; Protein: 23g; Potassium: 205mg; Sodium: 837mg

SIMPLE CHEESE AND BROCCOLI OMELETS

Preparation Time: 15 minutes
Cooking Time: 10 minutes
Servings: 4

INGREDIENTS:

- 3 tablespoons extra-virgin olive oil, divided
- 2 cups chopped broccoli
- 8 large eggs
- ¼ cup 1% milk
- ½ teaspoon freshly ground black pepper
- 8 tablespoons shredded reduced-fat Monterey Jack cheese, divided

DIRECTIONS:

» In a nonstick skillet, heat 1 tablespoon of oil over medium-high heat. Add the broccoli and sauté, occasionally stirring, for 3 to 5 minutes, or until the broccoli turns bright green. Scrape into a bowl.
» Mix the eggs, milk, plus pepper in a small bowl. Wipe out the skillet and heat ½ tablespoon of oil. Add one-quarter of the egg mixture and tilt the skillet to ensure an even layer. Cook for 2 minutes and then add 2 tablespoons of cheese and one-quarter of the broccoli. Use a spatula to fold into an omelet.
» Repeat step 3 with the remaining 1½ tablespoons of oil, remaining egg mixture, 6 tablespoons of cheese, and remaining broccoli to make a total of 4 omelets. Divide into 4 storage containers.

Nutrition: Calories: 292 Fat: 23g; Carbohydrates: 4g; Fiber: 1g; Protein: 18g; Potassium: 308mg; Sodium: 282mg

CREAMY AVOCADO AND EGG SALAD SANDWICHES

Preparation Time: 15 minutes
Cooking Time: 15 minutes
Servings: 4

INGREDIENTS:

- 2 small avocados, halved and pitted
- 2 tablespoons nonfat plain Greek yogurt
- Juice of 1 large lemon
- ¼ teaspoon salt
- ½ teaspoon freshly ground black pepper
- 8 large eggs, hardboiled, peeled, and chopped
- 3 tablespoons finely chopped fresh dill
- 3 tablespoons finely chopped fresh parsley
- 8 whole wheat bread slices (or your choice)

DIRECTIONS:

» Scoop the avocados into a large bowl and mash. Mix in the yogurt, lemon juice, salt, and pepper. Add the eggs, dill, and parsley and combine.
» Store the bread and salad separately in 4 reusable storage bags and 4 containers and assemble the night before or serving. To serve, divide the mixture evenly among 4 of the bread slices and top with the other slices to make sandwiches.

Nutrition: Calories: 488 Fat: 22g; Carbohydrates: 48g Fiber: 8g; Protein: 23g Potassium: 469mg; Sodium: 597mg

BREAKFAST HASH

Preparation Time: 15 minutes
Cooking Time: 25 minutes
Servings: 4

INGREDIENTS:

- Nonstick cooking spray
- 2 large sweet potatoes, ½-inch cubes
- 1 scallion, finely chopped
- ¼ teaspoon salt
- ½ teaspoon freshly ground black pepper
- 8 ounces extra-lean ground beef (96% or leaner)
- 1 medium onion, diced
- 2 garlic cloves, minced
- 1 red bell pepper, diced
- ¼ teaspoon ground cumin
- ¼ teaspoon paprika
- 2 cups coarsely chopped kale leaves
- ¾ cup shredded reduced-fat Cheddar cheese
- 4 large eggs

DIRECTIONS:

» Oiled a large skillet with cooking spray and heat over medium heat. Add the sweet potatoes, scallion, salt, and pepper. Sauté for 10 minutes, stirring often.
» Add the beef, onion, garlic, bell pepper, cumin, and paprika. Sauté, frequently stirring, for about 4 minutes, or until the meat browns. Add the kale to the skillet and stir until wilted. Sprinkle with the Cheddar cheese.
» Make four wells in the hash batter and crack an egg into each. Cover and let the eggs cook until the white is fully cooked and the yolk is to your liking. Divide into 4 storage containers.

Nutrition: Calories: 323; Fat: 15g; Carbohydrates: 23g; Fiber: 4g; Protein: 25g; Potassium: 676mg; Sodium: 587mg

HEARTY BREAKFAST CASSEROLE

Preparation Time: 15 minutes
Cooking Time: 30 minutes
Servings: 4

INGREDIENTS:

- Nonstick cooking spray
- 1 large green bell pepper, diced
- 8 ounces cremini mushrooms, diced
- ½ medium onion, diced
- 3 garlic cloves, minced
- 1 large sweet potato, grated
- 1 cup baby spinach
- 12 large eggs
- 3 tablespoons 1% milk
- 1 teaspoon mustard powder
- 1 teaspoon paprika
- 1 teaspoon freshly ground black pepper
- ½ teaspoon salt
- ½ cup shredded reduced-fat Colby-Jack cheese

DIRECTIONS:

» Preheat the oven to 350°F. Oiled at a 9-by-13-inch baking dish with cooking spray. Coat a large skillet with cooking spray and heat over medium heat. Add the bell pepper, mushrooms, onion, garlic, and sweet potato.
» Sauté, frequently stirring, for 3 to 4 minutes, or until the onion is translucent. Add the spinach and continue to sauté while stirring, until the spinach has wilted. Remove, then set aside to cool slightly.
» Mix the eggs, milk, mustard powder, paprika, black pepper, and salt in a large bowl. Add the sautéed vegetables. Put the batter into the prepared baking dish.
» Bake for 30 minutes. Remove from the oven, sprinkle with the Colby-Jack cheese, return to the oven, and bake again within 5 minutes to melt the cheese. Divide into 4 storage containers.

Nutrition: Calories: 378; Fat: 25g; Carbohydrates: 17g Fiber: 3g; Protein: 26g; Potassium: 717mg; Sodium: 658mg

CREAMY APPLE-AVOCADO SMOOTHIE

Preparation Time: 15 minutes
Cooking Time: 0 minutes
Servings: 2

INGREDIENTS:

- ½ medium avocado, peeled and pitted
- 1 medium apple, chopped
- 1 cup baby spinach leaves
- 1 cup nonfat vanilla Greek yogurt
- ½ to 1 cup of water
- 1 cup ice
- Freshly squeezed lemon juice (optional)

DIRECTIONS:

» Blend all of the fixing using a blender, and blend until smooth and creamy. Put a squeeze of lemon juice on top if desired, and serve immediately.

Nutrition: Calories: 200 Fat: 7g; Sodium: 56mg Potassium: 378mg; Carbohydrates: 27g; Fiber: 5g; Sugars: 20g; Protein: 10g

STRAWBERRY, ORANGE, AND BEET SMOOTHIE

Preparation Time: 5 minutes
Cooking Time: 0 minutes
Servings: 2

INGREDIENTS:

- 1 cup nonfat milk
- 1 cup of frozen strawberries
- 1 medium beet, cooked, peeled, and cubed
- 1 orange, peeled and quartered
- 1 frozen banana, peeled and chopped
- 1 cup nonfat vanilla Greek yogurt
- 1 cup ice

DIRECTIONS:

» In a blender, combine all of the fixings, and blend until smooth. Serve immediately.

Nutrition: Calories: 266 Fat: 0g Cholesterol: 7mg; Sodium: 104mg Carbohydrates: 51g Fiber: 6g; Sugars: 34g; Protein: 15g

BLUEBERRY-VANILLA YOGURT SMOOTHIE

Preparation Time: 5 minutes
Cooking Time: 0 minutes
Servings: 2

INGREDIENTS:

- 1½ cups frozen blueberries
- 1 cup nonfat vanilla Greek yogurt
- 1 frozen banana, peeled and sliced
- ½ cup nonfat or low-fat milk
- 1 cup ice

DIRECTIONS:

» In a blender, combine all of the fixing listed, and blend until smooth and creamy. Serve immediately.

Nutrition: Calories: 228; Fat: 1g; Sodium: 63mg; Potassium: 470mg; Carbohydrates: 45g; Fiber: 5g; Sugars: 34g; Protein: 12g

GREEK YOGURT OAT PANCAKES

Preparation Time: 15 minutes
Cooking Time: 10 minutes
Servings: 2

INGREDIENTS:

- 6 egg whites (or ¾ cup liquid egg whites)
- 1 cup rolled oats
- 1 cup plain nonfat Greek yogurt
- 1 medium banana, peeled and sliced
- 1 teaspoon ground cinnamon
- 1 teaspoon baking powder

DIRECTIONS:

» Blend all of the listed fixing using a blender. Warm a griddle over medium heat. Spray the skillet with non-stick cooking spray.
» Put 1/3 cup of the mixture or batter onto the griddle. Allow to cook and flip when bubbles on the top burst, about 5 minutes. Cook again within a minute until golden brown. Repeat with the remaining batter.
» Divide between two serving plates and enjoy.

Nutrition: Calories: 318 Fat: 4g; Sodium: 467mg; Potassium: 634mg; Carbohydrates: 47g; Fiber: 6g Sugars: 13g; Protein: 28g

SCRAMBLED EGG AND VEGGIE BREAKFAST QUESADILLAS

Preparation Time: 15 minutes
Cooking Time: 15 minutes
Servings: 2

INGREDIENTS

- 2 eggs
- 2 egg whites

- 2 to 4 tablespoons nonfat or low-fat milk
- ¼ teaspoon freshly ground black pepper
- 1 large tomato, chopped
- 2 tablespoons chopped cilantro
- ½ cup canned black beans, rinsed and drained
- 1½ tablespoons olive oil, divided
- 4 corn tortillas
- ½ avocado, peeled, pitted, and thinly sliced

DIRECTIONS:

» Mix the eggs, egg whites, milk, and black pepper in a bowl. Using an electric mixer, beat until smooth. To the same bowl, add the tomato, cilantro, and black beans, and fold into the eggs with a spoon.
» Warm-up half of the olive oil in a medium pan over medium heat. Add the scrambled egg mixture and cook for a few minutes, stirring, until cooked through. Remove from the pan.
» Divide the scrambled-egg mixture between the tortillas, layering only on one half of the tortilla. Top with avocado slices and fold the tortillas in half.
» Heat the remaining oil over medium heat, and add one of the folded tortillas to the pan. Cook within 1 to 2 minutes on each side or until browned. Repeat with remaining tortillas.
» Serve immediately.

Nutrition: Calories: 445; Fat: 24g; Sodium: 228mg; Potassium: 614mg; Carbohydrates: 42g; Fiber: 11g; Sugars: 2g; Protein: 19g

---

STUFFED BREAKFAST PEPPERS

Preparation Time: 15 minutes
Cooking Time: 45 minutes
Servings: 4

INGREDIENTS:

- 4 bell peppers (any color)
- 1 (16-ounce) bag frozen spinach
- 4 eggs
- ¼ cup shredded low-fat cheese (optional)
- Freshly ground black pepper

DIRECTIONS:

» Preheat the oven to 400°F. Line a baking dish with aluminum foil. Cut the tops off the pepper, then discard the seeds. Discard the tops and seeds. Put the peppers in the baking dish, and bake for about 15 minutes.
» While the peppers bake, defrost the spinach and drain off the excess moisture. Remove the peppers, then stuff the bottoms evenly with the defrosted spinach.
» Crack an egg over the spinach inside each pepper. Top each egg with a tablespoon of the cheese (if using) and season with black pepper to taste. Bake within 15 to 20 minutes, or until the egg whites are set and opaque.

Nutrition: Calories: 136 Fat: 5g; Sodium: 131mg Potassium: 576mg; Carbohydrates: 15g Protein: 11g

---

SWEET POTATO TOAST THREE WAYS

Preparation Time: 15 minutes
Cooking Time: 2 5 minutes
Servings:

INGREDIENTS:

- 1 large sweet potato, unpeeled
- Topping Choice #1:
- 4 tablespoons peanut butter
- 1 ripe banana, sliced
- Dash ground cinnamon
- Topping Choice #2:
- ½ avocado, peeled, pitted, and mashed
- 2 eggs (1 per slice)
- Topping Choice #3:
- 4 tablespoons nonfat or low-fat ricotta cheese
- 1 tomato, sliced
- Dash black pepper

DIRECTIONS:

» Slice the sweet potato lengthwise into ¼-inch thick slices. Place the sweet potato slices in a toaster on high for about 5 minutes or until cooked through.
» Repeat multiple times, if necessary, depending on your toaster settings. Top with your desired topping choices and enjoy.

Nutrition: Calories: 137 Fat: 0g Sodium: 17mg; Potassium: 265mg Carbohydrates: 32g; Fiber: 4g; Sugars: 0g; Protein: 2g

---

APPLE-APRICOT BROWN RICE BREAKFAST PORRIDGE

Preparation Time: 15 minutes
Cooking Time: 8 minutes
Servings: 4

INGREDIENTS:

- 3 cups cooked brown rice
- 1¾ cups nonfat or low-fat milk
- 2 tablespoons lightly packed brown sugar
- 4 dried apricots, chopped
- 1 medium apple, cored and diced
- ¾ teaspoon ground cinnamon
- ¾ teaspoon vanilla extract

DIRECTIONS:

» Combine the rice, milk, sugar, apricots, apple, and cinnamon in a medium saucepan. Boil it on medium heat, lower the heat down slightly and cook within 2 to 3 minutes. Turn it off, then stir in the vanilla extract. Serve warm.

Nutrition: Calories: 260; Fat: 2g; Sodium: 50mg; Potassium: 421mg; Carbohydrates: 57g; Fiber: 4g; Sugars: 22g; Protein: 7g

CARROT CAKE OVERNIGHT OATS

Preparation Time: overnight
Cooking Time: 2 minutes
Servings: 1

INGREDIENTS:

- ½ cup rolled oats
- ½ cup plain nonfat or low-fat Greek yogurt
- ½ cup nonfat or low-fat milk
- ¼ cup shredded carrot
- 2 tablespoons raisins
- ½ teaspoon ground cinnamon
- 1 to 2 tablespoons chopped walnuts (optional)

DIRECTIONS:

» Mix all of the fixings in a lidded jar, shake well, and refrigerate overnight. Serve.

Nutrition: Calories: 331; Fat: 3g; Sodium: 141mg; Carbohydrates: 59g; Fiber: 8g; Sugars: 26g; Protein: 22g

STEEL-CUT OATMEAL WITH PLUMS AND PEAR

Preparation Time: 15 minutes
Cooking Time: 25 minutes
Servings: 4

INGREDIENTS:

- 2 cups of water
- 1 cup nonfat or low-fat milk
- 1 cup steel-cut oats
- 1 cup dried plums, chopped
- 1 medium pear, cored, and skin removed, diced
- 4 tablespoons almonds, roughly chopped

DIRECTIONS:

» Mix the water, milk, plus oats in a medium pot and bring to a boil over high heat. Reduce the heat and cover. Simmer for about 10 minutes, stirring occasionally.
» Add the plums and pear, and cover. Simmer for another 10 minutes. Turn off the heat and let stand within 5 minutes until all of the liquid is absorbed. To serve, top each portion with a sprinkling of almonds.

Nutrition: Calories: 307; Fat: 6g; Sodium: 132mg; Potassium: 640mg; Carbohydrates: 58g; Fiber: 9g; Sugars: 24g; Protein: 9g

FRENCH TOAST WITH APPLESAUCE

Preparation Time: 5 minutes
Cooking Time: 5 minutes
Servings: 6

INGREDIENTS:

- ¼ c. unsweetened applesauce
- ½ c. skim milk
- 2 packets Stevia
- 2 eggs
- 6 slices whole-wheat bread
- 1 tsp. ground cinnamon

DIRECTIONS:

» Mix well applesauce, sugar, cinnamon, milk, and eggs in a mixing bowl. Soak the bread into the applesauce mixture until wet. On medium fire, heat a large non-stick skillet.
» Add soaked bread on one side and another on the other side. Cook in a single layer within 2-3 minutes per side on medium-low fire or until lightly browned. Serve and enjoy.

Nutrition: Calories: 122.6 Fat:2.6 g; Carbs: 18.3 g Protein:6.5 g; Sugars:14.8 g Sodium: 11mg

BANANA-PEANUT BUTTER AND GREENS SMOOTHIE

Preparation Time: 5 minutes
Cooking Time: 0 minutes
Servings: 1

INGREDIENTS:

- 1 c. chopped and packed Romaine lettuce
- 1 frozen medium banana
- 1 tbsp. all-natural peanut butter
- 1 c. cold almond milk

DIRECTIONS:

» In a heavy-duty blender, add all ingredients. Puree until smooth and creamy. Serve and enjoy.

Nutrition: Calories: 349.3; Fat:9.7 g; Carbs: 57.4 g Protein:8.1 g; Sugars:4.3 g; Sodium:18 mg

BAKING POWDER BISCUITS

Preparation Time: 5 minutes
Cooking Time: 5 minutes
Servings: 1

INGREDIENTS:

- 1 egg white
- 1 c. white whole-wheat flour
- 4 tbsps. Non-hydrogenated vegetable shortening
- 1 tbsp. sugar
- 2/3 c. low-Fat milk
- 1 c. unbleached all-purpose flour
- 4 tsp.
- Sodium-free baking powder

DIRECTIONS:

» Warm oven to 450°F. Put the flour, sugar, plus baking powder into a mixing bowl and mix. Split the shortening into the batter using your fingers until it resembles coarse crumbs. Put the egg white plus milk and stir to combine.
» Put the dough out onto a lightly floured surface and

knead 1 minute. Roll dough to ¾ inch thickness and cut into 12 rounds. Place rounds on the baking sheet. Bake 10 minutes, then remove the baking sheet and place biscuits on a wire rack to cool.

Nutrition: Calories: 118; Fat:4 g; Carbs: 16 g; Protein:3 g; Sugars:0.2 g; Sodium: 6 mg

OATMEAL BANANA PANCAKES WITH WALNUTS

Preparation Time: 15 minutes
Cooking Time: 5 minutes
Servings: 8

INGREDIENTS:

- 1 finely diced firm banana
- 1 c. whole wheat pancake mix
- 1/8 c. chopped walnuts
- ¼ c. old-fashioned oats

DIRECTIONS:

» Make the pancake mix, as stated in the directions on the package. Add walnuts, oats, and chopped banana. Coat a griddle with cooking spray. Add about ¼ cup of the pancake batter onto the griddle when hot.
» Turn pancake over when bubbles form on top. Cook until golden brown.
» Serve immediately.

Nutrition: Calories: 155; Fat:4 g; Carbs: 28 g; Protein:7 g; Sugars:2.2 g; Sodium:16 mg

CREAMY OATS, GREENS BLUEBERRY SMOOTHIE

Preparation Time: 4 minutes
Cooking Time: 0 minutes
Servings: 1

INGREDIENTS:

- 1 c. cold
- Fat-free milk
- 1 c. salad greens
- ½ c. fresh frozen blueberries
- ½ c. frozen cooked oatmeal
- 1 tbsp. sunflower seeds

DIRECTIONS:

» Blend all ingredients using a powerful blender until smooth and creamy. Serve and enjoy.

Nutrition: Calories: 280; Fat:6.8 g; Carbs: 44.0 g; Protein:14.0 g; Sugars:32 g; Sodium:141 mg

BANANA CINNAMON OATMEAL

Preparation Time: 5 minutes
Cooking Time: 0 minutes
Servings: 6

INGREDIENTS:

- 2 c. quick-cooking oats
- 4 c. Fat-free milk
- 1 tsp. ground cinnamon
- 2 chopped large ripe banana
- 4 tsp. Brown sugar
- Extra ground cinnamon

DIRECTIONS:

» Place milk in a skillet and bring to boil. Add oats and cook over medium heat until thickened, for two to four minutes.
» Stir intermittently. Add cinnamon, brown sugar, and banana and stir to combine. If you want, serve with the extra cinnamon and milk. Enjoy!

Nutrition: Calories: 215 Fat:2 g; Carbs: 42 g Protein:10 g; Sugars:1 g Sodium:40 mg

BAGELS MADE HEALTHY

Preparation Time: 5 minutes
Cooking Time: 40 minutes
Servings: 8

INGREDIENTS:

- 1 ½ c. warm water
- 1 ¼ c. bread flour
- 2 tbsps. Honey
- 2 c. whole wheat flour
- 2 tsp. Yeast
- 1 ½ tbsps. Olive oil
- 1 tbsp. vinegar

DIRECTIONS:

» In a bread machine, mix all ingredients, and then process on dough cycle. Once done, create 8 pieces shaped like a flattened ball. Create a donut shape using your thumb to make a hole at the center of each ball.
» Place donut-shaped dough on a greased baking sheet then covers and let it rise about ½ hour. Prepare about 2 inches of water to boil in a large pan.
» In boiling water, drop one at a time the bagels and boil for 1 minute, then turn them once. Remove them and return to the baking sheet and bake at 350oF for about 20 to 25 minutes until golden brown.

Nutrition: Calories: 228 Fat:3.7 g; Carbs: 41.8 g Protein:6.9 g; Sugars:0 g Sodium:15 mg

CEREAL WITH CRANBERRY-ORANGE TWIST

Preparation Time: 5 minutes
Cooking Time: 0 minutes
Servings: 1

INGREDIENTS:

- ½ c. water
- ½ c. orange juice
- 1/3 c. oat bran
- ¼ c. dried cranberries
- Sugar
- Milk

DIRECTIONS:

» In a bowl, combine all ingredients. For about 2 minutes, microwave the bowl, then serve with sugar and milk. Enjoy!

Nutrition: Calories: 220; Fat:2.4 g; Carbs: 43.5 g; Protein:6.2 g; Sugars:8 g; Sodium:1 mg

NO COOK OVERNIGHT OATS

Preparation Time: 5 minutes
Cooking Time: 0 minutes
Servings: 1

INGREDIENTS:

- 1 ½ c. low-fat milk
- 5 whole almond pieces
- 1 tsp. chia seeds
- 2 tbsps. Oats
- 1 tsp. sunflower seeds
- 1 tbsp. Craisins

DIRECTIONS:

» In a jar or mason bottle with a cap, mix all ingredients. Refrigerate overnight. Enjoy for breakfast.

Nutrition: Calories: 271; Fat:9.8 g; Carbs: 35.4 g; Protein:16.7 g; Sugars:9; Sodium:103 mg

AVOCADO CUP WITH EGG

Preparation Time: 5 minutes
Cooking Time: 0 minutes
Servings: 4

INGREDIENTS:

- 4 tsp. parmesan cheese
- 1 chopped stalk scallion
- 4 dashes pepper
- 4 dashes paprika
- 2 ripe avocados
- 4 medium eggs

DIRECTIONS:

» Preheat oven to 375 0F. Slice avocadoes in half and discard the seed. Slice the rounded portions of the avocado to make it level and sit well on a baking sheet.
» Place avocadoes on a baking sheet and crack one egg in each hole of the avocado. Season each egg evenly with pepper and paprika. Bake within 25 minutes or until eggs is cooked to your liking. Serve with a sprinkle of parmesan.

Nutrition: Calories: 206 Fat:15.4 g; Carbs: 11.3 g Protein:8.5 g; Sugars:0.4 g; Sodium:21 mg

MEDITERRANEAN TOAST

Preparation Time: 10 minutes
Cooking Time: 0 minutes
Servings: 2

INGREDIENTS:

- 1 ½ tsp. reduced-Fat crumbled feta
- 3 sliced Greek olives
- ¼ mashed avocado
- 1 slice good whole wheat bread
- 1 tbsp. roasted red pepper hummus
- 3 sliced cherry tomatoes
- 1 sliced hardboiled egg

DIRECTIONS:

» First, toast the bread and top it with ¼ mashed avocado and 1 tablespoon hummus. Add the cherry tomatoes, olives, hardboiled egg, and feta.
» To taste, season with salt and pepper.

Nutrition: Calories: 333.7; Fat:17 g; Carbs: 33.3 g; Protein:16.3 g; Sugars:1 g; Sodium:19 mg

INSTANT BANANA OATMEAL

Preparation Time: 1 minute
Cooking Time: 2 minutes
Servings: 1

INGREDIENTS:

- 1 mashed ripe banana
- ½ c. water
- ½ c. quick oats

DIRECTIONS:

» Measure the oats and water into a microwave-safe bowl and stir to combine. Place bowl in microwave and heat on high for 2 minutes. Remove the bowl, then stir in the mashed banana and serve.

Nutrition: Calories: 243; Fat:3 g; Carbs: 50 g; Protein:6 g; Sugars:20 g; Sodium:30 mg

ALMOND BUTTER-BANANA SMOOTHIE

Preparation Time: 5 minutes
Cooking Time: 0 minutes
Servings: 1

INGREDIENTS:

- 1 tbsp. Almond butter
- ½ c. ice cubes
- ½ c. packed spinach
- 1 peeled and a frozen medium banana
- 1 c. Fat-free milk

DIRECTIONS:

- Blend all the listed fixing above in a powerful blender until smooth and creamy.
- Serve and enjoy.

Nutrition: Calories: 293; Fat:9.8 g; Carbs: 42.5 g; Protein:13.5 g; Sugars:12 g; Sodium:40 mg

BROWN SUGAR CINNAMON OATMEAL

Preparation Time: 1 minute
Cooking Time: 3 minutes
Servings: 4

INGREDIENTS:

- ½ tsp. ground cinnamon
- 1 ½ tsp pure vanilla extract
- ¼ c. light brown sugar
- 2 c. low- Fat milk
- 1 1/3 c. quick oats

DIRECTIONS:

- Put the milk plus vanilla into a medium saucepan and boil over medium-high heat.
- Lower the heat to medium once it boils. Mix in oats, brown sugar, plus cinnamon, and cook, stirring 2–3 minutes. Serve immediately.

Nutrition: Calories: 208; Fat:3 g; Carbs: 38 g; Protein:8 g; Sugars:15 g; Sodium:33 mg

BUCKWHEAT PANCAKES WITH VANILLA ALMOND MILK

Preparation Time: 10 minutes
Cooking Time: 10 minutes
Servings: 1

INGREDIENTS:

- ½ c. unsweetened vanilla almond milk
- 2-4 packets natural sweetener
- 1/8 tsp salt
- ½ cup buckwheat flour
- ½ tsp. double-acting baking powder

DIRECTIONS:

- Prepare a nonstick pancake griddle and spray with the cooking spray, place over medium heat. Whisk the buckwheat flour, salt, baking powder, and stevia in a small bowl and stir in the almond milk after.
- Onto the pan, scoop a large spoonful of batter, cook until bubbles no longer pop on the surface and the entire surface looks dry and (2-4 minutes). Flip and cook for another 2-4 minutes. Repeat with all the remaining batter.

Nutrition: Calories: 240; Fat:4.5 g; Carbs: 2 g; Protein:11 g; Sugars:17 g; Sodium:38 mg

SALMON AND EGG SCRAMBLE

Preparation Time: 15 minutes
Cooking Time: 4 minutes
Servings: 4

INGREDIENTS:

- 1 teaspoon of olive oil
- 3 organic whole eggs
- 3 tablespoons of water
- 1 minced garlic
- 6 Oz. Smoked salmon, sliced
- 2 avocados, sliced
- Black pepper to taste
- 1 green onion, chopped

DIRECTIONS:

- Warm-up olive oil in a large skillet and sauté onion in it. Take a medium bowl and whisk eggs in it, add water and make a scramble with the help of a fork. Add to the skillet the smoked salmon along with garlic and black pepper.
- Stir for about 4 minutes until all ingredients get fluffy. At this stage, add the egg mixture. Once the eggs get firm, serve on a plate with a garnish of avocados.

Nutrition: Calories: 120 Carbs: 3g; Fat: 4g Protein: 19g; Sodium: 898 mg Potassium: 129mg

PUMPKIN MUFFINS

Preparation Time: 15 minutes
Cooking Time: 20 minutes
Servings: 4

INGREDIENTS:

- 4 cups of almond flour
- 2 cups of pumpkin, cooked and pureed
- 2 large whole organic eggs
- 3 teaspoons of baking powder
- 2 teaspoons of ground cinnamon
- 1/2 cup raw honey
- 4 teaspoons almond butter

DIRECTIONS:

- Preheat the oven at 400-degree F. Line the muffin paper on the muffin tray. Mix almond flour, pumpkin

puree, eggs, baking powder, cinnamon, almond butter, and honey in a large bowl.
- » Put the prepared batter into a muffin tray and bake within 20 minutes. Once golden-brown, serve, and enjoy.

Nutrition: Calories: 136; Carbs: 22g; Fat: 5g; Protein: 2g; Sodium: 11 mg; Potassium: 699 mg

SWEET BERRIES PANCAKE

Preparation Time: 15 minutes
Cooking Time: 15 minutes
Servings: 4

INGREDIENTS:
- 4 cups of almond flour
- Pinch of sea salt
- 2 organic eggs
- 4 teaspoons of walnut oil
- 1 cup of strawberries, mashed
- 1 cup of blueberries, mashed
- 1 teaspoon baking powder
- Honey for topping, optional

DIRECTIONS:
- » Take a bowl and add almond flour, baking powder, and sea salt. Take another bowl and add eggs, walnut oil, strawberries, and blueberries mash. Combine ingredients of both bowls. Heat a bit of walnut oil in a cooking pan and pour the spoonful mixture to make pancakes. Once the bubble comes on the top, flip the pancake to cook from the other side. Once done, serve with the glaze of honey on top.

Nutrition: Calories: 161; Carbs: 23g; Fat: 6g; Protein: 3g; Cholesterol: 82 mg; Sodium: 91 mg; Potassium: 252mg

ZUCCHINI PANCAKES

Preparation Time: 15 minutes
Cooking Time: 10 minutes
Servings: 4

INGREDIENTS:
- 4 large zucchinis
- 4 green onions, diced
- 1/3 cup of milk
- 1 organic egg
- Sea Salt, just a pinch
- Black pepper, grated
- 2 tablespoons of olive oil

DIRECTIONS:
- » First, wash the zucchinis and grate it with a cheese grater. Mix the egg and add in the grated zucchinis and milk in a large bowl. Warm oil in a skillet and sauté onions in it.
- » Put the egg batter into the skillet and make pancakes. Once cooked from both sides. Serve by sprinkling salt and pepper on top.

Nutrition: Calories: 70; Carbs: 8g; Fat: 3g; Protein: 2g

Cholesterol: 43 mg; Sodium: 60 mg; Potassium: 914mg

BREAKFAST BANANA SPLIT

Preparation Time: 15 minutes
Cooking Time: 0 minutes
Servings: 3

INGREDIENTS:
- 2 bananas, peeled
- 1 cup oats, cooked
- 1/2 cup low-fat strawberry yogurt
- 1/3 teaspoon honey, optional
- 1/2 cup pineapple, chunks

DIRECTIONS:
- » Peel the bananas and cut lengthwise. Place half of the banana in each separate bowl. Spoon strawberry yogurt on top and pour cooked oats with pineapple chunks on each banana. Serve immediately with a glaze of honey of liked.

Nutrition: Calories: 145; Carbs: 18g; Fat: 7g; Protein: 3g; Sodium:2 mg; Potassium: 380 mg

EASY VEGGIE MUFFINS

Preparation Time: 10 minutes
Cooking Time: 40 minutes
Servings: 4

INGREDIENTS:
- ¾ cup cheddar cheese, shredded
- 1 cup green onion, chopped
- 1 cup tomatoes, chopped
- 1 cup broccoli, chopped
- 2 cups non-fat milk
- 1 cup biscuit mix
- 4 eggs
- Cooking spray
- 1 teaspoon Italian seasoning
- A pinch of black pepper

DIRECTIONS:
- » Grease a muffin tray with cooking spray and divide broccoli, tomatoes, cheese, and onions in each muffin cup.
- » In a bowl, combine green onions with milk, biscuit mix, eggs, pepper, and Italian seasoning, whisk well and pour into the muffin tray as well.
- » Cook the muffins in the oven at 375 degrees F for 40 minutes, divide them between plates, and serve.

Nutrition: Calories: 80; Carbs: 3g; Fat: 5g; Protein: 7g; Sodium: 25 mg

CARROT MUFFINS

Preparation Time: 10 minutes
Cooking Time: 30 minutes
Servings: 5

INGREDIENTS:

- 1 and ½ cups whole wheat flour
- ½ cup stevia
- 1 teaspoon baking powder
- ½ teaspoon cinnamon powder
- ½ teaspoon baking soda
- ¼ cup natural apple juice
- ¼ cup olive oil
- 1 egg
- 1 cup fresh cranberries
- 2 carrots, grated
- 2 teaspoons ginger, grated
- ¼ cup pecans, chopped
- Cooking spray

DIRECTIONS:

» Mix the flour with the stevia, baking powder, cinnamon, and baking soda in a large bowl. Add apple juice, oil, egg, cranberries, carrots, ginger, and pecans and stir well.
» Oiled a muffin tray with cooking spray, divide the muffin mix, put in the oven, and cook at 375 degrees F within 30 minutes. Divide the muffins between plates and serve for breakfast.

Nutrition: Calories: 34; Carbs: 6g Fat: 1g; Protein: 0g; Sodium: 52 mg

PINEAPPLE OATMEAL

Preparation Time: 10 minutes
Cooking Time: 25 minutes
Servings: 4

INGREDIENTS:

- 2 cups old-fashioned oats
- 1 cup walnuts, chopped
- 2 cups pineapple, cubed
- 1 tablespoon ginger, grated
- 2 cups non-fat milk
- 2 eggs
- 2 tablespoons stevia
- 2 teaspoons vanilla extract

DIRECTIONS:

» In a bowl, combine the oats with the pineapple, walnuts, and ginger, stir and divide into 4 ramekins. Mix the milk with the eggs, stevia, and vanilla in a bowl and pour over the oats mix. Bake at 400 degrees F within 25 minutes. 4. Serve for breakfast.

Nutrition: Calories: 200 Carbs: 40g; Fat: 1g; Protein: 3g; Sodium: 275 mg

SPINACH MUFFINS

Preparation Time: 10 minutes
Cooking Time: 30 minutes
Servings: 6

INGREDIENTS:

- 6 eggs
- ½ cup non-fat milk
- 1 cup low-fat cheese, crumbled
- 4 ounces spinach
- ½ cup roasted red pepper, chopped
- 2 ounces prosciutto, chopped
- Cooking spray

DIRECTIONS:

» Mix the eggs with the milk, cheese, spinach, red pepper, and prosciutto in a bowl. Grease a muffin tray with cooking spray, divide the muffin mix, introduce in the oven, and bake at 350 degrees F within 30 minutes.
» Divide between plates and serve for breakfast.

Nutrition: Calories: 112; Carbs: 19g; Fat: 3g; Protein: 2g; Sodium: 274 mg

CHIA SEEDS BREAKFAST MIX

Preparation Time: 8 hours
Cooking Time: 0 minutes
Servings: 4

INGREDIENTS:

- 2 cups old-fashioned oats
- 4 tablespoons chia seeds
- 4 tablespoons coconut sugar
- 3 cups of coconut milk
- 1 teaspoon lemon zest, grated
- 1 cup blueberries

DIRECTIONS:

» In a bowl, combine the oats with chia seeds, sugar, milk, lemon zest, and blueberries, stir, divide into cups and keep in the fridge for 8 hours. 2. Serve for breakfast.

Nutrition: Calories: 69 Carbs: 0g; Fat: 5g Protein: 3g Sodium: 0 mg

BREAKFAST FRUITS BOWLS

Preparation Time: 10 minutes
Cooking Time: 0 minutes
Servings: 2

INGREDIENTS:

- 1 cup mango, chopped
- 1 banana, sliced
- 1 cup pineapple, chopped
- 1 cup almond milk

DIRECTIONS:

» Mix the mango with the banana, pineapple, and almond milk in a bowl, stir, divide into smaller bowls, and serve.

Nutrition: Calories: 10 Carbs: 0g Fat: 1g; Protein: 0g Sodium: 0mg

PUMPKIN COOKIES

Preparation Time: 10 minutes
Cooking Time: 25 minutes
Servings: 6

INGREDIENTS:

- 2 cups whole wheat flour
- 1 cup old-fashioned oats
- 1 teaspoon baking soda
- 1 teaspoon pumpkin pie spice
- 15 ounces pumpkin puree
- 1 cup coconut oil, melted
- 1 cup of coconut sugar
- 1 egg
- ½ cup pepitas, roasted
- ½ cup cherries, dried

DIRECTIONS:

» Mix the flour the oats, baking soda, pumpkin spice, pumpkin puree, oil, sugar, egg, pepitas, and cherries in a bowl, stir well, shape medium cookies out of this mix, arrange them all on a baking sheet, then bake within 25 minutes at 350 degrees F. Serve the cookies for breakfast.

Nutrition: Calories: 150; Carbs: 24g; Fat: 8g; Protein: 1g; Sodium: 220 mg

VEGGIE SCRAMBLE

Preparation Time: 10 minutes
Cooking Time: 2 minutes
Servings: 1

INGREDIENTS:

- 1 egg
- 1 tablespoon water
- ¼ cup broccoli, chopped
- ¼ cup mushrooms, chopped
- A pinch of black pepper
- 1 tablespoon low-fat mozzarella, shredded
- 1 tablespoon walnuts, chopped
- Cooking spray

DIRECTIONS:

» Grease a ramekin with cooking spray, add the egg, water, pepper, mushrooms, and broccoli, and whisk well. Introduce in the microwave and cook for 2 minutes. Add mozzarella and walnuts on top and serve for breakfast.

Nutrition: Calories: 128; Carbs: 24g; Fat: 0g; Protein: 9g; Sodium: 86 mg

MUSHROOMS AND TURKEY BREAKFAST

Preparation Time: 10 minutes
Cooking Time: 1 hour and 5 minutes
Servings: 12

INGREDIENTS:

- 8 ounces whole-wheat bread, cubed
- 12 ounces turkey sausage, chopped
- 2 cups fat-free milk
- 5 ounces low-fat cheddar, shredded
- 3 eggs
- ½ cup green onions, chopped
- 1 cup mushrooms, chopped
- ½ teaspoon sweet paprika
- A pinch of black pepper
- 2 tablespoons low-fat parmesan, grated

DIRECTIONS:

» Put the bread cubes on a prepared lined baking sheet, bake at 400 degrees F for 8 minutes. Meanwhile, heat a pan over medium-high heat, add turkey sausage, stir, and brown for 7 minutes.
» In a bowl, combine the milk with the cheddar, eggs, parmesan, black pepper, and paprika and whisk well.
» Add mushrooms, sausage, bread cubes, and green onions stir, pour into a baking dish, bake at 350 degrees F within 50 minutes. 5. Slice, divide between plates and serve for breakfast.

Nutrition: Calories: 88; Carbs: 1g Fat: 9g; Protein: 1g; Sodium: 74 mg

MUSHROOMS AND CHEESE OMELET

Preparation Time: 10 minutes
Cooking Time: 15 minutes
Servings: 4

INGREDIENTS:

- 2 tablespoons olive oil
- A pinch of black pepper
- 3 ounces mushrooms, sliced
- 1 cup baby spinach, chopped
- 3 eggs, whisked
- 2 tablespoons low-fat cheese, grated
- 1 small avocado, peeled, pitted, and cubed
- 1 tablespoons parsley, chopped

DIRECTIONS:

» Add mushrooms, stir, cook them for 5 minutes and transfer to a bowl on a heated pan with the oil over medium-high heat.
» Heat-up the same pan over medium-high heat, add eggs and black pepper, spread into the pan, cook within 7 minutes, and transfer to a plate.
» Spread mushrooms, spinach, avocado, and cheese on half of the omelet, fold the other half over this mix, sprinkle parsley on top, and serve.

Nutrition: Calories: 136; Carbs: 5g; Fat: 5g; Protein: 16g; Sodium: 192 mg

EGG WHITE BREAKFAST MIX

Preparation Time: 10 minutes
Cooking Time: 10 minutes
Servings: 4

INGREDIENTS:

- 1 yellow onion, chopped
- 3 plum tomatoes, chopped
- 10 ounces spinach, chopped
- A pinch of black pepper
- 2 tablespoons water
- 12 egg whites
- Cooking spray

DIRECTIONS:

» Mix the egg whites with water and pepper in a bowl. Grease a pan with cooking spray, heat up over medium heat, add ¼ of the egg whites, spread into the pan, and cook for 2 minutes.
» Spoon ¼ of the spinach, tomatoes, and onion, fold, and add to a plate. 4. Serve for breakfast. Enjoy!

Nutrition: Calories: 31; Carbs: 0g; Fat: 2g; Protein: 3g; Sodium: 55 mg

PESTO OMELET

Preparation Time: 10 minutes
Cooking Time: 6 minutes
Servings: 2

INGREDIENTS:

- 2 teaspoons olive oil
- Handful cherry tomatoes, chopped
- 3 tablespoons pistachio pesto
- A pinch of black pepper
- 4 eggs

DIRECTIONS:

» In a bowl, combine the eggs with cherry tomatoes, black pepper, and pistachio pesto and whisk well. Add eggs mix, spread into the pan, cook for 3 minutes, flip, cook for 3 minutes more, divide between 2 plates, and serve on a heated pan with the oil over medium-high heat.

Nutrition: Calories: 240; Carbs: 23g; Fat: 9g; Protein: 17g; Sodium: 292 mg

QUINOA BOWLS

Preparation Time: 10 minutes
Cooking Time: 20 minutes
Servings: 2

INGREDIENTS:

- 1 peach, sliced
- 1/3 cup quinoa, rinsed
- 2/3 cup low-fat milk
- ½ teaspoon vanilla extract
- 2 teaspoons brown sugar
- 12 raspberries
- 14 blueberries

DIRECTIONS:

» Mix the quinoa with the milk, sugar, and vanilla in a small pan, simmer over medium heat, cover the pan, cook for 20 minutes and flip with a fork. Divide this mix into 2 bowls, top each with raspberries and blueberries and serve for breakfast.

Nutrition: Calories: 170; Carbs: 31g; Fat: 3g; Protein: 6g; Sodium: 120 mg

STRAWBERRY SANDWICH

Preparation Time: 10 minutes
Cooking Time: 0 minutes
Servings: 4

INGREDIENTS:

- 8 ounces low-fat cream cheese, soft
- 1 tablespoon stevia
- 1 teaspoon lemon zest, grated
- 4 whole-wheat English muffins, toasted
- 2 cups strawberries, sliced

DIRECTIONS:

» In your food processor, combine the cream cheese with the stevia and lemon zest and pulse well. Spread 1 tablespoon of this mix on 1 muffin half and top with some of the sliced strawberries. Repeat with the rest of the muffin halves and serve for breakfast. Enjoy!

Nutrition: Calories: 150; Carbs: 23g; Fat: 7g; Protein: 2g; Sodium: 70 mg

APPLE QUINOA MUFFINS

Preparation Time: 10 minutes
Cooking Time: 35 minutes
Servings: 4

INGREDIENTS:

- ½ cup natural, unsweetened applesauce
- 1 cup banana, peeled and mashed
- 1 cup quinoa
- 2 and ½ cups old-fashioned oats
- ½ cup almond milk
- 2 tablespoons stevia

- 1 teaspoon vanilla extract
- 1 cup of water
- Cooking spray
- 1 teaspoon cinnamon powder
- 1 apple, cored, peeled, and chopped

DIRECTIONS:

» Put the water in a small pan, bring to a simmer over medium heat, add quinoa, cook within 15 minutes, fluff with a fork, and transfer to a bowl.
» Add all ingredients, stir, divide into a muffin pan greases with cooking spray, introduce in the oven, and bake within 20 minutes at 375 degrees F. Serve for breakfast.

Nutrition: Calories: 241; Carbs: 31g; Fat: 11g; Protein: 5g; Sodium: 251 mg

VERY BERRY MUESLI

Preparation Time: 15 minutes
Cooking Time: 0 minutes
Servings: 2

INGREDIENTS:

- 1 c. Oats
- 1 c. Fruit flavored Yogurt
- ½ c. Milk
- 1/8 tsp. Salt
- ½ c dried Raisins
- ½ c. Chopped Apple
- ½ c. Frozen Blueberries
- ¼ c. chopped Walnuts

DIRECTIONS:

» Combine your yogurt, salt, and oats in a medium bowl, mix well, and then cover it tightly. Fridge for at least 6 hours. Add your raisins and apples the gently fold. Top with walnuts and serve. Enjoy!

DIRECTIONS:

Nutrition: Calories: 195; Protein 6g; Carbs: 31g; Fat: 4g; Sodium: 0mg

VEGGIE QUICHE MUFFINS

Preparation Time: 15 minutes
Cooking Time: 40 minutes
Servings: 12

INGREDIENTS:

- ¾ c. shredded Cheddar
- 1 c. chopped Green Onion
- 1 c. chopped Broccoli
- 1 c. diced Tomatoes
- 2 c. Milk
- 4 Eggs
- 1 c. Pancake mix
- 1 tsp. Oregano
- ½ tsp. Salt
- ½ tsp. Pepper

DIRECTIONS:

» Preheat your oven to 375 0F, and lightly grease a 12-cup muffin tin with oil. Sprinkle your tomatoes, broccoli, onions, and cheddar into your muffin cups.
» Combine your remaining ingredients in a medium, whisk to combine, then pour evenly on top of your veggies.
» Set to bake in your preheated oven for about 40 minutes or until golden brown. Allow to cool slightly (about 5 minutes), then serve. Enjoy!

Nutrition: Calories: 58.5; Protein 5.1 g; Carbs: 2.9 g; Fat: 3.2 g; Sodium: 340 mg

TURKEY SAUSAGE AND MUSHROOM STRATA

Preparation Time: 15 minutes
Cooking Time: 8 minutes
Servings: 12

INGREDIENTS:

- 8 oz. cubed Ciabatta bread
- 12 oz. chopped turkey sausage
- 2 c. Milk
- 4 oz. shredded Cheddar
- 3 large Eggs
- 12 oz. Egg substitute
- ½ c. chopped Green onion
- 1 c. diced Mushroom
- ½ tsp. Paprika
- ½ tsp. Pepper
- 2 tbsps. grated Parmesan cheese

DIRECTIONS:

» Set oven to preheat to 400 0F. Lay your bread cubes flat on a baking tray and set it to toast for about 8 min. Meanwhile, add a skillet over medium heat with sausage and cook while stirring, until fully brown and crumbled.
» Mix salt, pepper, paprika, parmesan cheese, egg substitute, eggs, cheddar cheese, and milk in a large bowl. Add in your remaining ingredients and toss well to incorporate.
» Transfer mixture to a large baking dish (preferably a 9x13-inch), then tightly cover and allow to rest in the refrigerator overnight. Set your oven to preheat to 3500F, remove the cover from your casserole, and set to bake until golden brown and cooked through. Slice and serve.

Nutrition: Calories: 288.2 Protein 24.3g; Carbs: 18.2g Fat: 12.4g; Sodium: 355 mg

BACON BITS

Preparation Time: 15 minutes
Cooking Time: 60 minutes
Servings: 4

INGREDIENTS:

- 1 c. Millet

- 5 c. Water
- 1 c. diced Sweet potato
- 1 tsp. ground Cinnamon
- 2 tbsps. Brown sugar
- 1 medium diced Apple
- ¼ c. Honey

DIRECTIONS:

» In a deep pot, add your sugar, sweet potato, cinnamon, water, and millet, then stir to combine, then boil on high heat. After that, simmer on low.
» Cook like this for about an hour, until your water is fully absorbed and millet is cooked. Stir in your remaining ingredients and serve.

Nutrition: Calories: 136; Protein 3.1g; Carbs: 28.5g; Fat: 1.0g; Sodium: 120 mg

STEEL CUT OAT BLUEBERRY PANCAKES

Preparation Time: 15 minutes
Cooking Time: 15 minutes
Servings: 4

INGREDIENTS:

- 1½ c. Water
- ½ c. steel-cut oats
- 1/8 tsp. Salt
- 1 c. Whole wheat Flour
- ½ tsp. Baking powder
- ½ tsp. Baking soda
- 1 Egg
- 1 c. Milk
- ½ c. Greek yogurt
- 1 c. Frozen Blueberries
- ¾ c. Agave Nectar

DIRECTIONS:

» Combine your oats, salt, and water in a medium saucepan, stir, and allow to come to a boil over high heat. Adjust the heat to low, and allow to simmer for about 10 min, or until oats get tender. Set aside.
» Combine all your remaining ingredients, except agave nectar, in a medium bowl, then fold in oats. Preheat your skillet, and lightly grease it.
» Cook ¼ cup of milk batter at a time for about 3 minutes per side. Garnish with Agave Nectar.

Nutrition: Calories: 257; Protein 14g; Carbs: 46g; Fat: 7g; Sodium: 123 mg

SPINACH, MUSHROOM, AND FETA CHEESE SCRAMBLE

Preparation Time: 15 minutes
Cooking Time: 4 minutes
Servings: 1

INGREDIENTS:

- Olive oil cooking spray
- ½ c. sliced Mushroom
- 1 c. chopped Spinach
- 3 Eggs
- 2 tbsps. Feta cheese
- Pepper

DIRECTIONS:

» Set a lightly greased, medium skillet over medium heat. Add spinach and mushrooms, and cook until spinach wilts.
» Combine egg whites, cheese, pepper, and whole egg in a medium bowl, whisk to combine. Pour into your skillet and cook, while stirring, until set (about 4 minutes). Serve.

Nutrition: Calories: 236.5; Protein 22.2g; Carbs: 12.9g; Fat: 11.4g; Sodium: 405 mg

RED VELVET PANCAKES WITH CREAM CHEESE TOPPING

Preparation Time: 15 minutes
Cooking Time: 10 minutes
Servings: 2

INGREDIENTS:

- Cream Cheese Topping:
- 2 oz. Cream cheese
- 3 tbsps. Yogurt
- 3 tbsps. Honey
- 1 tbsp. Milk
- Pancakes:
- ½ c. Whole wheat Flour
- ½ c. all-purpose flour
- 2¼ tsps. Baking powder
- ½ tsp. Unsweetened Cocoa powder
- ¼ tsp. Salt
- ¼ c. Sugar
- 1 large Egg
- 1 c. + 2 tbsps. Milk
- 1 tsp. Vanilla
- 1 tsp. Red paste food coloring

DIRECTIONS:

» Combine all your topping ingredients in a medium bowl, and set aside. Add all your pancake ingredients in a large bowl and fold until combined. Set a greased skillet over medium heat to get hot.
» Add ¼ cup of pancake batter onto the hot skillet and cook until bubbles begin to form on the top. Flip and cook until set. Repeat until your batter is done well. Add your toppings and serve.

Nutrition: Calories: 231; Protein 7g; Carbs: 43g; Fat: 4g; Sodium: 0mg

PEANUT BUTTER BANANA BREAKFAST SMOOTHIE

Preparation Time: 15 minutes
Cooking Time: 0 minutes
Servings: 1

INGREDIENTS:

- 1 c. Non-fat milk
- 1 tbsp. Peanut butter
- 1 Banana
- ½ tsp. Vanilla

DIRECTIONS:

» Place non-fat milk, peanut butter, and banana in a blender.
» Blend until smooth.

Nutrition: Calories: 295; Protein 133g; Carbs: 42g; Fat: 8.4g; Sodium: 100 mg

NO-BAKE BREAKFAST GRANOLA BARS

Preparation Time: 15 minutes
Cooking Time: 0 minutes
Servings: 18

INGREDIENTS:

- 2 c. Old fashioned oatmeal
- ½ c. Raisins
- ½ c. Brown sugar
- 2½ c. Corn rice cereal
- ½ c. Syrup
- ½ c. Peanut butter
- ½ tsp. Vanilla

DIRECTIONS:

» In a suitable size mixing bowl, mix using a wooden spoon, rice cereal, oatmeal, and raisins. In a saucepan, combine corn syrup and brown sugar. On a medium-high flame, continuously stir the mixture and bring to a boil.
» On boiling, take away from heat. In a saucepan, stir vanilla and peanut into the sugar mixture. Stir until very smooth.
» Spoon peanut butter mixture on the cereal and raisins into the mixing bowl and combine — shape mixture into a 9 x 13 baking tin. Allow to cool properly, then cut into bars (18 pcs).

Nutrition: Calories: 152 Protein 4g; Carbs: 26g Fat 4.3g; Sodium: 160 mg

MUSHROOM SHALLOT FRITTATA

Preparation Time: 15 minutes
Cooking Time: 25 minutes
Servings: 4

INGREDIENTS:

- 1 tsp. butter
- 4 chopped shallots
- ½ lb. chopped mushrooms
- 2 tsp. chopped parsley
- 1 tsp. dried thyme
- Black pepper
- 3 medium Eggs
- 5 large Egg whites
- 1 tbsp. Milk
- ¼ c. grated parmesan cheese

DIRECTIONS:

» Heat oven to 350 0F. In a suitable size oven-proof skillet, heat butter over medium flame. Add shallots and sauté for about 5 mins. or until golden brown. Add to pot, thyme, parsley, chopped mushroom, and black pepper to taste.
» Whisk milk, egg whites, parmesan, and eggs into a bowl. Pour mixture into the skillet, ensuring the mushroom is covered completely. Transfer the skillet to the oven as soon as the edges begin to set.
» Bake until frittata is cooked (15-20 mins). Should be served warm, cut into equal wedges (4 pcs).

Nutrition: Calories: 346; Protein 19.1g; Carbs: 48.3g; Fat: 12g; Sodium: 218 mg

JACK-O-LANTERN PANCAKES

Preparation Time: 15 minutes
Cooking Time: 5 minutes
Servings: 8

INGREDIENTS:

- 1 Egg
- ½ c. Canned pumpkin
- 1¾ c. Low-fat milk
- 2 tbsps. Vegetable oil
- 2 c. Flour
- 2 tbsps. Brown sugar
- 1 tbsp. Baking powder
- 1 tsp. Pumpkin pie spice
- 1 tsp. Salt

DIRECTIONS:

» In a mixing bowl, mix milk, pumpkin, eggs, and oil. Add dry ingredients to egg mixture. Stir gently. Coat skillet lightly with cooking spray and heat on medium.
» When the skillet is hot, spoon (using a dessert spoon) batter onto the skillet. When bubbles start bursting, flip pancakes over and cook until it's a nice golden-brown color.

Nutrition: Calories: 313; Protein 15g; Carbs: 28g; Fat: 16g; Sodium: 1 mg

FRUIT PIZZA

Preparation Time: 15 minutes
Cooking Time: 0 minutes
Servings: 2

INGREDIENTS:

- 1 English muffin
- 2 tbsps. Fat-free cream cheese
- 2 tbsps. sliced strawberries
- 2 tbsps. blueberries
- 2 tbsps. crushed pineapple

DIRECTIONS:

» Cut English muffin in half and toast halves until slightly browned. Coat both halves with cream cheese. Arrange fruits atop cream cheese on muffin halves. Serve soon after preparation. Any leftovers refrigerate within 2 hours.

Nutrition: Calories: 119; Protein 6g; Carbs: 23g; Fat: 1g; Sodium: 288 mg

FLAX BANANA YOGURT MUFFINS

Preparation Time: 15 minutes
Cooking Time: 20 minutes
Servings: 12

INGREDIENTS:

- 1 c. Whole wheat flour
- 1 c. Old-fashioned rolled oats
- 1 tsp. Baking soda
- 2 tbsps. Ground flaxseed
- 3 large ripe bananas
- ½ c. Greek yogurt
- ¼ c. Unsweetened applesauce
- ¼ c. Brown sugar
- 2 tsp. Vanilla extract

DIRECTIONS:

» Set oven at 355 0F and preheat. Prepare muffin tin, or you can use cooking spray or cupcake liners. Combine dry ingredients in a mixing bowl.
» In a separate bowl, mix yogurt, banana, sugar, vanilla, and applesauce. Combine both mixtures and mix. Do not over mix. The batter should not be smooth but lumpy. Bake for 20 mins, or when inserted, toothpick comes out clean.

Nutrition: Calories: 136; Protein 4g; Carbs: 30g; Fat: 2g; Sodium: 242 mg

TASTY CUCUMBER BITES

Preparation Time: 5 minutes
Cooking Time: 0 minutes
Servings: 4

INGREDIENTS:

- 1 (8 ounce) cream cheese container, low fat
- 1 tablespoon bell pepper, diced
- 1 tablespoon shallots, diced
- 1 tablespoon parsley, chopped
- 2 cucumbers
- Pepper to taste

DIRECTIONS:

» Take a bowl and add cream cheese, onion, pepper, parsley.
» Peel cucumbers and cut in half.
» Remove seeds and stuff with cheese mix.
» Cut into bite sized portions and enjoy!

Nutrition: Calories: 85 Fat: 4g Carbohydrates: 2g Protein: 3g

SWEET POTATOES WITH COCONUT FLAKES

Preparation Time: 15 minutes
Cooking Time: 1 hour
Servings: 2

INGREDIENTS:

- 16 oz. sweet potatoes
- 1 tbsp. maple syrup
- ¼ c.
- Fat-free coconut Greek yogurt
- 1/8 c. unsweetened toasted coconut flakes
- 1 chopped apple

DIRECTIONS:

» Preheat oven to 400 0F.
» Place your potatoes on a baking sheet. Bake them for 45 - 60 minutes or until soft.
» Use a sharp knife to mark "X" on the potatoes and fluff pulp with a fork.
» Top with coconut flakes, chopped apple, Greek yogurt, and maple syrup.
» Serve immediately.

Nutrition: Calories: 321, Carbs: 70 g Fat: 3 g Protein: 7 g Sodium: 3% Sugars: 0.1 g

FRUITY TOFU SMOOTHIE

Preparation Time: 5 minutes
Cooking Time: 0 minutes
Servings: 2

INGREDIENTS:

- 1 c. ice cold water
- 1 c. packed spinach
- ¼ c. frozen mango chunks
- ½ c. frozen pineapple chunks
- 1 tbsp. chia seeds
- 1 container silken tofu
- 1 frozen medium banana

DIRECTIONS:

» In a powerful blender, add all ingredients and puree until smooth and creamy.
» Evenly divide into two glasses, serve and enjoy.

Nutrition: Calories: 175, Carbs:33.3 g Fat:3.7 g Protein:6.0 g Sodium:1% Sugars:16.3 g

---

BANANA-PEANUT BUTTER 'N GREENS SMOOTHIE

Preparation Time: 5 minutes
Cooking Time: 0 minutes
Servings: 1

INGREDIENTS:

- 1 c. chopped and packed Romaine lettuce
- 1 frozen medium banana
- 1 tbsp. all-natural peanut butter
- 1 c. cold almond milk

DIRECTIONS:

» In a heavy-duty blender, add all ingredients.
» Puree until smooth and creamy.
» Serve and enjoy.

Nutrition: Calories: 349.3, Carbs:57.4 g Fat:9.7 g Protein:8.1 g g Sodium:18% Sugars:4.3

RASPBERRY YOGURT

Preparation Time: 5 min
Cooking Time: 0 minutes
Servings: 2

INGREDIENTS:

- ½ cup low-fat yogurt
- ½ cup raspberries
- 1 teaspoon almond flakes

DIRECTIONS:

» Mix up yogurt and raspberries and transfer them in the serving glasses.
» Top yogurt with almond flakes.

Nutrition: per serving: 77 calories,3.9g protein, 8.6g carbohydrates, 3.4g fat, 2.6g fiber, 4mg cholesterol, 32mg sodium, 192mg potassium.

SOUTHWEST TOFU SCRAMBLE

Preparation Time: 10 minutes
Cooking Time: 15 minutes
Servings: 1

INGREDIENTS:

- ½ tablespoon olive oil
- ½ red onion, chopped
- 2 cups chopped spinach
- 8 ounces firm tofu, drained well
- 1 teaspoon ground cumin
- ½ teaspoon garlic powder
- Optional for serving: sliced avocado, sliced tomatoes

DIRECTIONS:

» Heat the olive oil in a medium skillet over medium heat. Add the onion and cook until softened, about 5 minutes.
» Add the spinach and cover to steam for 2 minutes.
» Using a spatula, move the veggies to one side of the pan. Crumble the tofu into the open area in the pan, breaking it up with a fork. Add the garlic and cumin to the crumbled tofu and mix well. Sauté for 5 to 7 minutes until the tofu is slightly browned.
» Serve immediately with whole-grain bread, fruit, or beans. Top with sliced avocado and tomato, if using.

Nutrition: Calories: 267 Fat: 0g Carbohydrates: 13g Protein: 23g, Sodium: 75mg

Chapter 5
Soups and Salads

TOFU SOUP

Preparation Time: 10 mins
Servings: 8
Cooking Time: 10 mins

INGREDIENTS:

- 1 lb. cubed extra-firm tofu
- 3 diced medium carrots
- 8 cup low-sodium vegetable broth
- ½ tsp freshly ground white pepper
- 8 minced garlic cloves
- 6 sliced and divided scallions
- 4 oz sliced mushrooms
- 1-inch minced fresh ginger piece

DIRECTIONS:

» Pour the broth into a stockpot. Add all of the Ingredients, except for the tofu and last 2 scallions. Bring to a boil over high heat.
» Once boiling, add the tofu. Reduce heat to low, cover, and simmer for 5 mins.
» Remove from heat, ladle soup into bowls, and garnish with the remaining sliced scallions. Serve immediately.

Nutrition: Calories 91, Fat 3 g, Carbs 8 g, Protein 6 g

VICHYSSOISE

Preparation Time: 10 mins
Servings: 6
Cooking Time: 25 mins

INGREDIENTS:

- 1lb leeks, finely sliced
- 8 oz potatoes, peeled and sliced
- 1 tbsp olive oil
- 2 cup water
- 1 cup milk
- ¾ cup natural yoghurt

DIRECTIONS:

» Heat up a pot using the oil over medium heat, add the leeks and potatoes for 10 mins.
» Add the water, bring to the boil and simmer for about 20 mins, Cool and put in a blender. Stir in the milk and chill very well. Serve garnished with yoghurt.

Nutrition: Calories 131, Fat 8 g, Carbs 8 g, Protein 5 g

PUMPKIN AND ROSEMARY SOUP

Preparation Time: 10 mins
Servings: 4
Cooking Time: 25 mins

INGREDIENTS:

- 1lb pumpkin flesh
- 3 oz pumpkin seeds
- 5 garlic clove
- 2 onions
- 1 tbsp freshly chopped rosemary
- ½ cup olive oil
- 3 cup vegetable stock

DIRECTIONS:

» Cut the pumpkin in cubes. Peel the cloves of garlic and chop finely.
» Mix the pumpkin, garlic, onions, pumpkin seeds, rosemary, and olive oil and put everything on a baking tray on a baking sheet.
» Bake in a preheated oven (350 °F) for approx. 25 mins, stirring every 10 mins
» Then put everything in a large saucepan, mix roughly if necessary.
» Add broth little by little, bring back to boil and cook in small broths for another 5 mins.

Nutrition: Calories 125, Fat 8 g, Carbs 8 g, Protein 5 g

MANGETOUT SOUP

Preparation Time: 10 mins
Servings: 6
Cooking Time: 25 mins

INGREDIENTS:

- 1 onion finely chopped
- 4 oz yellow peas, soaked for 1 hour
- 1 tbsp olive oil
- 4 cup vegetable stock
- 9 oz mangetout

DIRECTIONS:

» Heat up a pot using the oil over medium heat, add the onions and cook for 5 mins. Add the split peas and stir to coat in the oil.
» Add the stock and bring to boil and simmer for 30 mins add the mangetout and continue to simmer for 5 mins. Cool a little and serve.

Nutrition: Calories 111, Fat 7 g, Carbs 8 g, Protein 4 g

NIÇOISE SALAD

Preparation Time: 10 mins
Servings: 4
Cooking Time: 25 mins

INGREDIENTS:

- Mesclun
- 1 big can of tuna
- Some anchovies
- 4 tomatoes
- Radish
- 2 peppers
- 1 cucumber (optional)
- 1 cup green beans (optional)
- 2 hard-boiled eggs
- 2 onions
- Black olives
- Basil
- Olive oil

DIRECTIONS:

» Wash and drain the mesclun.
» Wash and cut peppers into small cubes and mince the onions
» Wash and cut the tomatoes in quarters.
» Add tomatoes to salad, olives, boiled eggs, tuna, and anchovies.
» Make the vinaigrette with oil and basil and serve

Nutrition: Calories 125, Fat 9 g, Carbs 8 g, Protein 4 g

BLACK BEAN SOUP

Preparation Time: 10 mins
Servings: 4
Cooking Time: 20 mins

INGREDIENTS:

- 1 tsp. cinnamon powder
- 32 oz. low-sodium chicken stock
- 1 chopped yellow onion
- 1 chopped sweet potato
- 38 oz. no-salt-added, drained and rinsed canned black beans
- 2 tsps. organic olive oil

DIRECTIONS:

» Heat up a pot using the oil over medium heat, add onion and cinnamon, stir and cook for 6 mins.
» Add black beans, stock and sweet potato, stir, cook for 14 mins, puree utilizing an immersion blender, divide into bowls and serve for lunch.

Nutrition: Calories 221, Fat 3 g, Carbs 15 g, Protein 7 g

CHICKEN AND DILL SOUP

Preparation Time: 10 mins
Servings: 6
Cooking Time: 1 hour

INGREDIENTS:

- 1 cup chopped yellow onion
- 1 whole chicken - 1 lb. sliced carrots
- 6 cup low-sodium veggie stock
- ½ cup chopped red onion
- 2 tsps. chopped dill

DIRECTIONS:

» Put chicken in a pot, add water to pay for, give your boil over medium heat, cook first hour, transfer to a cutting board, discard bones, shred the meat, strain the soup, get it back on the pot, heat it over medium heat and add the chicken. Also add the carrots, yellow onion, red onion, a pinch of salt, black pepper and also the dill, cook for fifteen mins, ladle into bowls and serve.

Nutrition: Calories 202, Fat 6 g, Carbs 8 g, Protein 12 g

CHEESE SOUP WITH CRISPY BACON

Preparation Time: 10 mins
Servings: 6
Cooking Time: 35 mins

INGREDIENTS:

- 1 garlic clove
- 1 tsp olive oil
- 1 lb potatoes peeled and chopped
- 4 cup vegetable stock
- 6 rashers bacon, diced
- 4 oz cheddar cheese grated
- 1 large onion finely chopped

DIRECTIONS:

» In a pan, heat the oil and cook garlic and onion. Add potatoes, stock and bring to the boil. Simmer for about 20 mins. To garnish add crispy bacon.

Nutrition: Calories 257, Fat 15g, Carbs 11g, Protein 12g

CHERRY STEW

Preparation Time: 10 mins
Servings: 6

INGREDIENTS

- 2 cup water
- ½ cup powered cocoa
- ¼ cup coconut sugar
- 1 lb pitted cherries

DIRECTIONS:

» In a pan, combine the cherries with all the water, sugar

plus the hot chocolate mix, stir, cook over medium heat for ten mins, divide into bowls and serve cold.

Nutrition: Calories 207, Fat 1 g, Carbs 8 g, Protein 6 g

RASPBERRY AND CRANBERRY SOUP

Preparation Time: 10 mins
Servings: 6
Cooking Time: 15 mins

INGREDIENTS:

- 1 lb fresh or frozen raspberries
- 3 cup cranberry juice
- 3 tsp arrowroot
- 1 tbsp sugar

DIRECTIONS:

» Combine 2/3 of the raspberries with the cranberry juice. Bring to the boil in a saucepan. In a separate bowl mix the arrowroot and the tbsp of cranberry juice until smooth. Mix together and stir over a gentle heat until the soup has thickened.

Nutrition: Calories 157, Fat 1 g, Carbs 6 g, Protein 6 g

SIRLOIN CARROT SOUP

Preparation Time: 30-35 mins
Servings: 4 | **Cooking Time:** 20 mins

INGREDIENTS:

- 1 lb. chopped carrots and celery mix
- 32 oz. low-sodium beef stock
- 1/3 cup whole-wheat flour
- 1 lb. ground beef sirloin
- 1 tbsp olive oil
- 1 chopped yellow onion

DIRECTIONS:

» Heat up the olive oil in a saucepan over medium-high flame; add the beef and the flour.
» Stir well and cook to brown for 4-5 mins.
» Add the celery, onion, carrots, and stock; stir and bring to a simmer.
» Turn down the heat to low and cook for 12-15 mins.
» Serve warm.

Nutrition: Calories 140, Fat 4.5 g, Carbs 16 g, Protein 9 g

CLASSICAL WONTON SOUP

Preparation Time: 5 mins
Servings: 8
Cooking Time: 15 mins

INGREDIENTS:

- 4 sliced scallions
- ¼ tsp. ground white pepper
- 2 cup sliced fresh mushrooms
- 4 minced garlic cloves
- 6 oz. dry whole-grain yolk-free egg noodles
- ½ lb. lean ground pork
- 1 tbsp minced fresh ginger
- 8 cup low-sodium chicken broth

DIRECTIONS:

» Place a stockpot over medium heat. Add the ground pork, ginger, and garlic and sauté for 5 mins. Drain any excess fat, then return to stovetop.
» Add the broth and bring to a boil. Once boiling, stir in the mushrooms, noodles, and white pepper. Cover and simmer for 10 mins. Remove pot from heat. Stir in the scallions and serve immediately.

Nutrition: Calories 143, Fat 4 g, Carbs 14 g, Protein 12 g

PUMPKIN AND COCONUT SOUP

Preparation Time: 10 mins | **Servings:** 3
Cooking Time: 30 mins

INGREDIENTS:

- 1 cup pumpkin, canned
- 6 cups chicken broth
- 1 cup low fat coconut almond milk
- 1 tsp sage, chopped
- 3 garlic cloves, peeled
- Sunflower seeds and pepper to taste

DIRECTIONS:

» Take a stockpot and add all the Ingredients: except coconut almond milk into it.
» Place stockpot over medium heat.
» Let it bring to a boil.
» Reduce heat to simmer for 30 mins.
» Add the coconut almond milk and stir.

Nutrition: Calories 144.3, Fat 15.7 g, Carbs 15 g, Protein 3 g

KALE AND SPINACH SOUP

Preparation Time: 5 mins | **Servings:** 4
Cooking Time: 10 mins

INGREDIENTS:

- 3 oz coconut oil
- 8 oz kale, chopped
- 2 avocado, diced
- 4 and 1/3 cups coconut almond milk
- Sunflower seeds and pepper to taste

DIRECTIONS:

» Take a skillet and place it over medium heat
» Add kale and Sauté for 2-3 mins
» Add kale to blender
» Add water, spices, coconut almond milk and avocado to blender as well
» Blend until smooth and pour mix into bowl

Nutrition: Calories 145.3, Fat 13.7 g, Carbs 14 g, Protein 3 g

ONION SOUP

Preparation Time: 10 mins | **Servings:** 4
Cooking Time: 1 hour

INGREDIENTS:

- 2 tbsp avocado oil
- 5 yellow onions, cut into halved and sliced
- Black pepper to taste
- 5 cups beef stock
- 3 thyme sprigs
- 1 tbsp tomato paste

DIRECTIONS:

» Take a pot and place it over medium high heat
» Add onion and thyme and stir
» Lower down heat to low and cook for 30 mins
» Uncover pot and cook onions for 1 hour, stirring often
» Add tomato paste, stock and stir
» Simmer for 30 mins more
» Ladle soup into bowls and enjoy!

Nutrition: Calories 86, Fat 4 g, Carbs 7 g, Protein 5 g

VEGETARIAN SOUP IN A CROCK POT

Prep: 10 mins
Servings: 8
Cooking Time: 4 hours

INGREDIENTS:

- 2 chopped ribs celery
- 2 cubes low-sodium bouillon
- 8 cup water
- 2 cup uncooked green split peas
- 3 bay leaves
- 2 carrots
- 2 chopped potatoes

DIRECTIONS:

» In your Crock-Pot, put the bouillon cubes, split peas, and water. Stir a bit to break up the bouillon cubes.
» Next, add the chopped potatoes, celery, and carrots followed with bay leaves.
» Stir to combine well.
» Cover and cook for at least 4 hours on your Crock-Pot's low setting or until the green split peas are soft.
» Add a bit salt and pepper as needed.
» Before serving, remove the bay leaves and enjoy.

Nutrition: Calories 149, Fat 1 g, Carbs 30 g, Protein 7 g

RHUBARB STEW

Preparation Time: 10 mins
Servings: 3
Cooking Time: 5 mins

INGREDIENTS:

- 1 tsp. grated lemon zest
- 1 ½ cup coconut sugar
- Juice of 1 lemon
- 1 ½ cup water
- 4 ½ cup roughly chopped rhubarbs

DIRECTIONS:

» In a pan, combine the rhubarb while using water, fresh lemon juice, lemon zest and coconut sugar, toss, bring using a simmer over medium heat, cook for 5 mins, and divide into bowls and serve cold.

Nutrition: Calories 108, Fat 1 g, Carbs 8 g, Protein 5 g

GAZPACHO

Preparation Time: 10 mins
Servings: 6

INGREDIENTS:

- 4 cups tomato juice
- 1/2 medium onion, peeled and coarsely chopped
- 1 small green pepper, peeled, cored, seeded, and coarsely chopped
- 1 small cucumber, peeled, pared, seeded, and coarsely chopped
- 1/2 tsp Worcestershire sauce
- 1 clove garlic, minced
- 1 drop hot pepper sauce
- 1/8 tsp cayenne pepper
- 2 tbsp olive oil
- 1 large tomato, finely diced
- 2 tbsp minced chives or scallion tops
- 1 lemon, cut in 6 wedges

DIRECTIONS:

» Put 2 cups of tomato juice and all other ingredients except diced tomato, chives, and lemon wedges in the blender. Puree.
» Slowly add the remaining 2 cups of tomato juice to pureed mixture. Add chopped tomato. Chill.
» Serve icy cold in individual bowls garnished with chopped chives and lemon wedges.

Nutrition: Calories 87, Fat 5 g, Carbs 8 g, Protein 5 g

MIXED BEANS SOUP

Preparation Time: 10 mins
Servings: 8
Cooking Time: 1 hour

INGREDIENTS:

- 1/2 cup each dried pink beans, dried lentils, dried

- black beans, yellow split peas, dried kidney beans, and dried blackeye peas
- 8 cups water
- 1 smoked ham hock (about 1/2 lb)
- 1 tsp each dried basil, dried rosemary, dried marjoram, and crushed red chilies
- 1 bay leaf
- 1 cup chopped onion 1/2 cup chopped carrots 1/2 cup chopped celery
- 2 (141/2-ounce) cans no salt added diced tomatoes, undrained
- 1 (8-ounce) can tomato sauce

DIRECTIONS:

» Rinse dried beans and lentils under cold running water. Place them in a large bowl, then cover with water to 2 inches above the mixture. Cover and let stand 8 hours, then drain.
» Combine drained bean, lentil and pea mixture, water, and ham hock in a large pot; bring to a boil. Add spices, onion, carrots, celery, tomatoes, and tomato sauce. Uncover and cook 1 hour.
» Discard bay leaf. Remove ham hock from soup. Remove meat from bone; shred meat with 2 forks. Return meat to soup and serve.

Nutrition: Calories 346, Carbs 50 g, Fiber 16 g, Protein 22 g, Fat 9 g

---

BEEF STEW

Preparation Time: 10 mins
Servings: 6
Cooking Time: 1 hour and 30 mins

INGREDIENTS:

- 1 shredded green cabbage head
- 4 chopped carrots
- 2 ½ lbs. non-fat beef brisket
- 3 chopped garlic cloves
- Black pepper
- 2 bay leaves
- 4 cup low-sodium beef stock

DIRECTIONS:

» Put the beef brisket in a pot, add stock, pepper, garlic and bay leaves, provide your simmer over medium heat and cook for an hour.
» Add carrots and cabbage, stir, cook for a half-hour more, divide into bowls and serve for lunch.

Nutrition: Calories 271, Fat 8 g, Carbs 16 g, Protein 9 g

HOMEMADE TURKEY SOUP

Preparation Time: 10 mins
Servings: 4
Cooking Time: 1 hour and 30 mins

INGREDIENTS:

- 6 lbs turkey breast. It should have some meat (at least 2 cups) remaining on it to make a good, rich soup.
- 2 medium onions
- 3 stalks of celery
- 1 tsp dried thyme
- 1/2 tsp dried rosemary and sage
- 1 tsp dried basil
- 1/2 tsp dried tarragon
- 1/2 lb Italian pastina or pasta

DIRECTIONS:

» Place turkey breast in a large 6-quart pot. Cover with water, at least 3/4 full.
» Peel onions, cut in large pieces, and add to pot. Wash celery stalks, slice, and add to pot also.
» Simmer covered for about 1 hour.
» Remove carcass from pot. Divide soup into smaller, shallower containers for quick cooling in the refrigerator.
» While soup is cooling, remove remaining meat from turkey carcass. Cut into pieces.
» Add turkey meat to skimmed soup along with herbs and spices.
» Bring to a boil and add pastina. Continue cooking on low boil for about 20 mins until pastina is done. Serve at once or refrigerate for later reheating.

Nutrition: Calories 226, Fat 5 g, Carbs 19 g, Protein 9 g

MEATBALL SOUP

Preparation Time: 10 mins
Servings: 4
Cooking Time: 1 hour and 30 mins

INGREDIENTS:

- 6 cups water
- 1/3 cup brown rice
- 3 low-sodium beef- or chicken-flavored bouillon cubes or 1 tbsp low-sodium bouillon powder
- 4 sprigs fresh oregano, finely chopped or 1 tbsp dried oregano
- 8 oz lean ground beef, turkey, or chicken
- 1 tomato, finely chopped
- 1/2 onion, peeled and finely chopped
- 1 large egg
- 2 cups chopped fresh vegetables (carrots, celery, and broccoli)

DIRECTIONS:

» In a large pot, combine water, rice, bouillon cubes, and oregano. Bring to a boil over high heat. Stir to dissolve bouillon. Reduce heat to low and simmer.
» Meanwhile, in a large bowl, mix ground meat, tomato, onion, egg. Form into 12 large meatballs.
» Add meatballs to broth mixture and simmer 30 mins.
» Add vegetables. Cook 10 to 15 mins or until meatballs are cooked and rice and vegetables are tender. Serve hot.

Nutrition: Calories 196, Carbs 20 g, Fiber 4 g, Protein 16 g, Fat 6 g

SORREL SOUP

Preparation Time: 5 mins
Servings: 6
Cooking Time: 15 mins

INGREDIENTS:

- 4 cup vegetable stock1 tbsp olive oil
- 1 large onion, chopped
- 1 clove garlic finely chopped
- 80 oz fresh sorrel leaves
- 1 cup single cream

DIRECTIONS:

» In a large pot, heat oil and cook onion.
» Add the stock and bring to boil. Stir in the sorrel, cover and cook for 1 min. Put in a blinder. Serve hot or chilled.

Nutrition: Calories 68, Fat 6 g, Carbs 9,2 g, Protein 4g

MEXICAN POZOLE

Preparation Time: 10 mins
Servings: 10
Cooking Time: 35 mins

INGREDIENTS:

- 2 lbs lean beef, cubed
- 1 tbsp olive oil
- 1 large onion, chopped
- 1 clove garlic finely chopped
- 1/4 cup cilantro
- 1 can (15 ounce) stewed tomatoes
- 2 oz tomato paste
- 1 can (1 lb 13 ounce) hominy

DIRECTIONS:

» In a large pot, heat oil. Sauté beef.
» Add onion, garlic, salt, pepper, cilantro, and enough water to cover the meat. Cover pot and cook over low heat until meat is tender.
» Add tomatoes and tomato paste. Continue cooking for about 20 mins.
» Add hominy and continue cooking another 15 mins, stirring occasionally, over low heat. If too thick, add water for desired consistency.

Nutrition: Calories 253, Fat 10 g, Carbs 7 g, Protein 5 g

CARROT AND GINGER SOUP

Preparation Time: 15 mins |**Servings:** 4
Cooking Time: 40 mins

INGREDIENTS:

- 6 cups chicken broth
- ¼ cup full fat coconut milk, unsweetened
- ¾ lb carrots, peeled and chopped
- 1 tsp turmeric, ground
- 2 tsp ginger, grated
- 1 yellow onion, chopped
- 2 garlic cloves, peeled
- Pinch of pepper

DIRECTIONS:

» Take a stockpot and add all the Ingredients: except coconut milk into it.
» Place stockpot over medium heat.
» Let it bring to a boil.
» Reduce heat to simmer for 40 mins.
» Remove the bay leaf.
» Blend the soup until smooth by using an immersion blender.
» Add the coconut milk and stir.
» Serve immediately and enjoy!

Nutrition: Calories 80, Fat 6 g, Carbs 7 g, Protein 5 g

MINESTRONE SOUP

Preparation Time: 10 mins |**Servings:** 6
Cooking Time: 50 mins

INGREDIENTS:

- 1/4 cup olive oil
- 1 clove garlic, minced or 1/8 tsp garlic powder
- 1-1/3 cups coarsely chopped onion
- 1-1/2 cups coarsely chopped celery and leaves
- 1 can (6 oz) tomato paste
- 1 tbsp chopped fresh parsley
- 1 cup sliced carrots, fresh or frozen
- 4-3/4 cups shredded cabbage
- 1 can (1 lb) tomatoes, cut up
- 1 cup canned red kidney beans, drained and rinsed
- 1-1/2 cups frozen peas
- 1-1/2 cups fresh green beans
- dash hot sauce
- 11 cups water
- 2 cups uncooked, broken spaghetti

DIRECTIONS:

» Heat oil in a 4-quart saucepan.
» Add garlic, onion, and celery and sauté about 5 mins.
» Add all remaining ingredients except spaghetti, and stir until ingredients are well mixed.
» Bring to a boil. Reduce heat, cover, and simmer about 45 mins or until vegetables are tender.
» Add uncooked spaghetti and simmer 2-3 mins only.

Nutrition: Calories 153, Carbs 9,2 g, Protein 4g

BRUSSELS SOUP

Preparation Time: 10 mins |**Servings:** 4
Cooking Time: 20 mins

INGREDIENTS:

- 2 tbsp olive oil
- 1 yellow onion, chopped
- 2 lbs Brussels sprouts, trimmed and halved
- 4 cups chicken stock
- ¼ cup coconut cream

DIRECTIONS:

- » Take a pot and place it over medium heat
- » Add oil and let it heat up
- » Add onion and stir cook for 3 mins
- » Add Brussels sprouts and stir, cook for 2 mins
- » Add stock and black pepper, stir and bring to a simmer
- » Cook for 20 mins more
- » Use an immersion blender to make the soup creamy
- » Add coconut cream and stir well
- » Ladle into soup bowls and serve

Nutrition: Calories 66, Fat 4 g, Carbs 7 g, Protein 5 g

CRAB AND WATERMELON SOUP

Preparation Time: 10 mins | Servings: 4

INGREDIENTS:

- ¼ cup basil, chopped
- 2 lbs tomatoes
- 5 cups watermelon, cubed
- ¼ cup wine vinegar
- 2 garlic cloves, minced
- 1 zucchini, chopped
- Pepper to taste
- 1 cup crabmeat

DIRECTIONS:

- » Take your blender and add tomatoes, basil, vinegar, 4 cups watermelon, garlic, 1/3 cup oil, pepper and pulse well
- » Transfer to fridge and chill for 1 hour
- » Divide into bowls and add zucchini, crab and remaining watermelon

Nutrition: Calories 321, Fat 5 g, Carbs 28.1 g, Protein 3g

GARLIC TOMATO SOUP

Preparation Time: 15 mins | Servings: 4 | Cooking: 15 mins

INGREDIENTS:

- 8 Roma tomatoes, chopped
- 1 cup tomatoes, sundried
- 2 tbsp coconut oil
- 5 garlic cloves, chopped
- 14 oz coconut milk
- 1 cup vegetable broth
- Pepper to taste
- Basil, for garnish

DIRECTIONS:

- » Take a pot, heat oil into it.
- » Sauté the garlic in it for ½ minute.
- » Mix in the Roma tomatoes and cook for 8-10 mins.
- » Stir occasionally.
- » Add in the rest of the Ingredients: except the basil and stir well.
- » Cover the lid and cook for 5 mins.
- » Let it cool.
- » Blend the soup until smooth by using an immersion blender.
- » Garnish with basil.

Nutrition: Calories 315, Fat 5 g, Carbs 25.1 g, Protein 5g

LOBSTER BISQUE

Preparation Time: 10 mins | Servings: 4 | Cooking: 15 mins

INGREDIENTS:

- ¾ lb lobster, cooked and lobster
- 4 cups chicken broth
- 2 garlic cloves, chopped
- ¼ tsp pepper
- ½ tsp paprika
- 1 yellow onion, chopped
- 14 and ½ oz tomato, diced
- 1 tbsp coconut oil
- 1 cup low fat cream

DIRECTIONS:

- » Take a stockpot and add the coconut oil over medium heat.
- » Then sauté the garlic and onion for 3 to 5 mins
- » Add diced tomatoes, spices and chicken broth then bring them to boil.
- » Reduce to a simmer then simmer for about 10 mins.
- » Add the warmed heavy cream to the soup.
- » Blend the soup till creamy by using an immersion blender.
- » Stir in cooked lobster

Nutrition: Calories 315, Fat 8 g, Carbs 27.1 g, Protein 8g

EGGPLANT SOUP

Preparation Time: 10 mins
Servings: 4 | Cooking: 30 mins

INGREDIENTS:

- 2 tbsp no-salt-added tomato paste
- 1 tbsp olive oil
- 1 quart low-sodium veggie stock
- ¼ tsp. black pepper
- 1 chopped red onion
- 2 roughly cubed big eggplants
- 1 tbsp chopped cilantro

DIRECTIONS:

» Heat up a pot with the oil over medium heat, add the onion, stir and sauté for 5 mins.
» Add the eggplants and the other Ingredients, bring to a simmer over medium heat, cook for 25 mins, divide into bowls and serve.

Nutrition: Calories 335, Fat 14.4 g, Carbs 16.1 g, Protein 8.4 g

---

SWEET POTATO SOUP

Preparation Time: 10 mins
Servings: 6 | Cooking: 1 hour and 40 mins

INGREDIENTS:

- 28 oz. veggie stock
- 4 big sweet potatoes
- ¼ tsp. black pepper
- 1/3 cup low-sodium heavy cream
- ¼ tsp. ground nutmeg

DIRECTIONS:

» Arrange the sweet potatoes around the lined baking sheet, bake them at 350 0 F for 60 mins and 30, cool them down, peel, roughly chop them and put them inside the pot.
» Add stock, nutmeg, cream and pepper, pulse effectively utilizing an immersion blender, heat the soup over medium heat, cook for 10 mins, ladle into bowls and serve.

Nutrition: Calories 235, Fat 4 g, Carbs 16 g, Protein 18 g

ORGANIC CHICKEN THIGH SOUP

Preparation Time: 5 mins
Servings: 4 | Cooking: 50 mins

INGREDIENTS:

- 1 cup fresh pineapple chunks
- 1 tsp. cinnamon
- ½ cup chopped up green onion
- 2 tbsp coconut aminos
- 2 lbs. organic chicken thigh
- 1/8 tsp. flavored vinegar
- ½ cup coconut cream

DIRECTIONS:

» Set your pot to Sauté mode and add ghee
» Allow the ghee to melt and add diced up onion, cook for about 5 mins until the onions are caramelized
» Add pressed garlic, ham, broth and simmer for 2-3 mins
» Add thyme and asparagus and lock up the lid
» Cook on SOUP mode for 45 mins
» Release the pressure naturally and enjoy!

Nutrition: Calories 161, Fat 8 g, Carbs 16 g, Protein 6 g

BUTTERNUT SQUASH SOUP

Preparation Time: 10 mins
Servings: 6 | Cooking: 20 mins

INGREDIENTS:

- 2 cup diced apple
- 1/8 tsp. ground allspice
- 6 cup diced butternut squash
- 6 cup water
- ½ tsp. ground cinnamon
- 2 cup unsweetened apple juice

DIRECTIONS:

» Place diced squash and apple into a stockpot, add the water and apple juice, and bring to a boil over high heat. Once boiling, reduce heat to medium-low, cover, and simmer until tender, roughly 20 mins.
» Remove from heat. Add spices and stir to combine. Purée in a blender or food processor.

Nutrition: Calories 150, Fat 0 g, Carbs 38 g, Protein 3 g

SOUP A LA KIEV

Preparation Time: 31 mins
Servings: 8 | Cooking: 20 mins

INGREDIENTS:

- 1 cup brown sugar
- 1 cup favorite red wine
- 3 cup chopped strawberries
- 1 cup sour cream
- 4 c cold water

DIRECTIONS:

» In a food processor, blend the strawberries.
» Pour the mixture in a medium sauce pan.
» Stir in the brown sugar, sour cream, wine and water.
» Cook over low heat. Stir gently for 20 mins. Do not allow the soup to boil, just serve it warm.

Nutrition: Calories 37, Fat 0.9 g, Carbs 19 g, Protein 8 g

SUMMER STRAWBERRY STEW

Preparation Time: 10 mins
Servings: 6 | Cooking: 10 mins

INGREDIENTS:

- 2 tbsp water
- ¼ tsp. almond extract
- 2 tbsp fresh lemon juice
- 16 oz. halved strawberries
- 2 tbsp coconut sugar
- 2 tbsp cornstarch

DIRECTIONS:

» In a pot, combine the strawberries because of the water, sugar, fresh lemon juice, cornstarch and almond extract, toss well, cook over medium heat for ten mins, divide into bowls and serve.

Nutrition: Calories 160, Fat 2 g, Carbs 6 g, Protein 6 g

BLUEBERRY STEW

Preparation Time: 10 mins
Servings: 4 | **Cooking:** 10 mins

INGREDIENTS:

- 1 cup water
- 2 tbsp lemon juice
- 12 oz. blueberries
- 3 tbsp coconut sugar

DIRECTIONS:

» In a pan, combine the blueberries with the sugar and the other Ingredients; bring to a gentle simmer and cook over medium heat for 10 mins.
» Divide into bowls and serve.

Nutrition: Calories 122, Fat 0.4 g, Carbs 26.7 g, Protein 1.5 g

CHIPOTLE CHICKEN CHOWDER

Preparation Time: 10 mins | **Servings:** 4 | **Cooking:** 23 mins

INGREDIENTS:

- 1 medium onion, chopped
- 2 garlic cloves, minced
- 6 bacon slices, chopped
- 4 cups jicama, cubed
- 3 cups chicken stock
- 2 cups low-fat, cream
- 1 tbsp olive oil
- 2 tbsp fresh cilantro, chopped
- 1 and ¼ lbs chicken, thigh boneless, cut into 1 inch chunks
- ½ tsp pepper
- 1 chipotle pepper, minced

DIRECTIONS:

» Heat olive oil over medium heat in a large sized saucepan, add bacon.
» Cook until crispy, add onion, garlic, and jicama.
» Cook for 7 mins, add chicken stock and chicken.
» Bring to a boil and lower temperature to low.
» Simmer for 10 mins
» Add heavy cream and chipotle, simmer for 5 mins.
» Sprinkle chopped cilantro and serve, enjoy!

Nutrition: Calories 203, Fat 0.9 g, Carbs 51 g, Protein 2 g

PEACH STEW

Preparation Time: 10 mins
Servings: 6 | **Cooking:** 10 mins

INGREDIENTS:

- 3 tbsp coconut sugar
- 5 cup peeled and cubed peaches
- 2 cup water
- 1 tsp grated ginger

DIRECTIONS:

» In a pot, combine the peaches while using the sugar, ginger and water, toss, provide a boil over medium heat, cook for 10 mins, divide into bowls and serve cold

Nutrition: Calories 142, Fat 1.4 g, Carbs 7.7 g, Protein 2.5 g

SUMMER TOMATO SOUP

Preparation Time: 10 mins
Servings: 6 | **Cooking:** 20 mins

INGREDIENTS:

- 1 tbsp olive oil
- 1 medium onion, finely chopped
- 1 garlic clove
- a pinch of paprika
- 2 lb ripe tomatoes
- 1 tsp lemon juice
- 1 cup water
- 1 tbsp mil

DIRECTIONS:

» In a pot, heat olive oil and cook onion and garlic.
» Add paprika and tomatoes and cook for 10 mins
» Add lemon juice and water and simmer for 5 mins
» Cool a little and then put in a blinder. Serve garnished with basil leaves.

Nutrition: Calories 142, Fat 1.4 g, Carbs 7.7 g, Protein 2.5 g

SUMMER TOMATO SORBET

Preparation Time: 10 mins
Servings: 4 | **Cooking:** 10 mins

INGREDIENTS:

- 2 cups summer tomato soup
- 4 tbsp vodka
- 2 tsp sugar

DIRECTIONS:

» In a pot, mix together soup, vodka, sugar and seasoning.
» Put in a blender until is a soft-scoop consistency. Place in a freezer for 10 mins and then serve.

Nutrition: Calories 142, Fat 1.4 g, Carbs 7.7 g, Protein 2.5 g

CARROT AND CORIANDER SOUP

Preparation Time: 10 mins
Servings: 6 | **Cooking:** 30 mins

INGREDIENTS:

- 1 tbsp olive oil
- 1 medium onion, finely chopped
- 1 garlic clove
- 1 lb carrots roughly chopped
- 1 tbsp chopped fresh coriander
- fresh ground pepper
- 4 cup vegetable stock

DIRECTIONS:

- In a pot, heat olive oil and cook onion and garlic.
- Add the chopped carrots and stock and cover. Bring to the boil.
- Once the vegetables are tender cool a little and then put in a blender. Taste and serve.

Nutrition: Calories 121, Fat 1.4 g, Carbs 4.7 g, Protein 2.5 g

PAPPA AL POMODORO

Preparation Time: 10 mins
Servings: 6 | **Cooking:** 30 mins

INGREDIENTS:

- 1 cup olive oil
- 5 cup peeled and cubed peaches
- 4 garlic cloves
- 9 lb ripe tomatoes, skinned quarted and seeded
- bread
- 1 large bunch fresh basil
- 2 cup water

DIRECTIONS:

- In a pot, warm the oil and cook the garlic few mins. Add the tomatoes and simmer for 20 mins.
- Add water and bring to the boil
- Brake the bread in large pieces and add it to the tomato mixture and stir until the bread absorb the liquid.
- Add the basil leaves and the olive oil and serve

Nutrition: Calories 122, Fat 1.5 g, Carbs 9.7 g, Protein 2.5 g

ZUCCHINI CREAM SOUP

Preparation Time: 10 mins
Servings: 4 | **Cooking:** 20 mins

INGREDIENTS:

- 1 tbsp chopped dill
- 1 tbsp olive oil
- 32 oz. low-sodium chicken stock
- 1 tsp. grated ginger
- 1 lb. chopped zucchinis
- 1 cup coconut cream
- 1 chopped yellow onion

DIRECTIONS:

- Heat up a pot with the oil over medium heat, add the onion and ginger, stir and cook for 5 mins.
- Add the zucchinis and the other Ingredients; bring to a simmer and cook over medium heat for 15 mins.
- Blend using an immersion blender, divide into bowls and serve.

Nutrition: Calories 293, Fat 12.3 g, Carbs 11.2 g, Protein 6.4 g

SALMON AND VEGETABLE SOUP

Preparation Time: 10 mins | **Servings:** 4 | **Cooking:** 22 mins

INGREDIENTS:

- 2 tbsp extra-virgin olive oil
- 1 leek, chopped
- 1 red onion, chopped
- Pepper to taste
- 2 carrots, chopped
- 4 cups low stock vegetable stock
- 4 oz salmon, skinless and boneless, cubed
- ½ cup coconut cream
- 1 tbsp dill, chopped

DIRECTIONS:

- Take a pan and place it over medium heat, add leek, onion, stir and cook for 7 mins
- Add pepper, carrots, stock and stir
- Boil for 10 mins
- Add salmon, cream, dill and stir
- Boil for 5-6 mins
- Ladle into bowls and serve

Nutrition: Calories 200, Fat 3 g, Carbs 51 g, Protein 3 g

MANGO SALAD

Preparation Time: 5 mins
Servings: 2

INGREDIENTS:

- ½ seeded and minced jalapeño pepper
- 2 tbsp chopped fresh cilantro
- Juice of 1 lime
- 3 pitted and cubed ripe mangos
- 1 tsp minced red onion

DIRECTIONS:

- Combine all Ingredients: in a salad bowl.
- Toss well.

Nutrition: Calories 331, Fat 5 g, Carbs 28.1 g, Protein 1g

TOMATO AND CUCUMBER SALAD

Preparation Time: 10 mins | Serving: 4

INGREDIENTS:
- 1 minced garlic clove
- ¼ tsp freshly ground black pepper
- 1 tbsp olive oil
- 1 thinly sliced small onion
- 2 medium cucumbers
- 4 quartered ripe medium tomatoes
- ¼ cup chopped fresh basil
- 3 tbsp red wine vinegar

DIRECTIONS:
» Peel the cucumbers, slice in half lengthwise, and then use a spoon to gently scrape out the seeds.
» Slice the cucumber halves and place in a bowl. Add the tomatoes, onion, and basil.
» Place the remaining Ingredients: into a small bowl and whisk well to combine.
» Pour the dressing over the salad and toss to coat. Serve immediately or cover and refrigerate until ready to serve.

Nutrition: Calories 66, Fat 4 g, Carbs 7 g, Protein 1 g

FRESH FRUIT SALAD

Preparation Time: 15 mins
Servings: 3

INGREDIENTS:
- 1 halved and sliced ripe banana
- 170 g sliced and halved strawberries,
- 170 g julienned granny smith apples
- 340 g chopped ripe pineapple
- 170 g sliced and quartered kiwi
- 340 g chopped ripe mango

DIRECTIONS:
» Cut the mangoes and kiwis into small cubes to get that full burst of flavor.
» Slice the bananas about a centimeter thick and then halve them.
» Once you have all the fruits cut up, put them in a bowl, and top with salt.
» Stir it all together and you are ready to serve!

Nutrition: Calories 203, Fat 0.9 g, Carbs 51 g, Protein 2 g

GREEN PAPAYA SALAD

Preparation Time: 10 mins
Servings: 6

INGREDIENTS:
- 10 small shrimps, dried
- 2 small red Thai Chilies
- 1 garlic clove, peeled
- ¼ cup tamarind juice
- 1 tbsp Thai fish sauce, low sodium
- 1 lime, cut into 1 inch pieces
- 4 cherry tomatoes, halved
- 3 long beans, trimmed into 1 inch pieces
- 1 carrot, coarsely shredded
- ½ English cucumber, coarsely chopped and seeded
- 1/6 a small green cabbage, cored and thinly sliced
- 1 lb unripe green papaya, quartered, seeded and shredded using mandolin
- 3 tbsp unsalted roasted peanuts

DIRECTIONS:
» Take a mortar and pestle and crush your shrimp alongside garlic, chills
» Add tamarind juice, fish sauce and palm sugar
» Squeeze 3 quarts of lime pieces over the mortar
» Grind to make a dressing, keep the dressing on the side
» Take a bowl add the remaining Ingredients: (excluding the peanut), making sure to add the papaya last
» Use a spoon and stir in the dressing
» Mix the vegetable and fruit and coat them well
» Transfer to your serving dish
» Garnish with some peanuts and lime pieces

Nutrition: Calories 183, Fat 0.9 g, Carbs 51 g, Protein 2 g

QUINOA AND FRUIT SALAD

Preparation Time: 5 mins | **Servings:** 5 | **Cooking:** 10 mins

INGREDIENTS:
- 3 and ½ oz Quinoa
- 3 peaches, diced
- 1 and ½ oz toasted hazelnuts, chopped
- Handful of mint, chopped
- Handful of parsley, chopped
- 2 tbsp olive oil
- Zest of 1 lemon
- Juice of 1 lemon

DIRECTIONS:
» Take medium sized saucepan and add quinoa
» Add 1 and ¼ cups of water and bring it to a boil over medium-high heat
» Lower down the heat to low and simmer for 20 mins
» Drain any excess liquid
» Add fruits, herbs, Hazelnuts to the quinoa
» Allow it to cool and season
» Take a bowl and add olive oil, lemon zest and lemon juice
» Pour the mixture over the salad and gie it a mix

Nutrition: Calories 203, Fat 0.9 g, Carbs 51 g, Protein 2 g

SHRIMP AND VEGGIE SALAD

Preparation Time: 10 mins
Servings: 4

INGREDIENTS:
- 2 cup halved cherry tomatoes
- Cracked black pepper

- 12 oz trimmed fresh asparagus spears
- 16 oz frozen peeled and cooked shrimp
- Cracker bread
- 4 cup watercress
- ½ cup bottled light raspberry

DIRECTIONS:

» In a large skillet, cook asparagus, covered, in a small amount of boiling lightly salted water for 3 mins or until crisp-tender; drain in a colander. Run under cold water until cool.
» Divide asparagus among 4 dinner plates; top with watercress, shrimp, and cherry tomatoes. Drizzle with dressing.
» Sprinkle with cracked black pepper and serve with cracker bread.

Nutrition: Calories 155.5, Fat 1.4 g, Carbs 15 g, Protein 22 g

SALMON AND SPINACH SALAD

Preparation Time: 10 mins | Servings: 4

INGREDIENTS:

- 1 cup canned salmon, drained and flaked
- 1 tbsp lime zest, grated
- 1 tbsp lime juice
- 3 tbsp fat-free yogurt
- 1 cup baby spinach
- 1 tsp capers, drained and chopped
- 1 red onion, chopped
- Pinch of pepper

DIRECTIONS:

» Take a bowl and add salmon, zest, lime juice and other Ingredients:
» Toss well and serve

Nutrition: Calories 155.5, Fat 1.4 g, Carbs 15 g, Protein 22 g

- **Corn Salad**

Preparation Time: 10 mins
Servings: 6 | Cooking: 2 hours

INGREDIENTS:

- 2 oz prosciutto, cut into strips
- 1 tsp olive oil
- 2 cups corn
- 1/2 cup salt –free tomato sauce
- 1 tsp garlic, minced
- 1 green bell pepper, chopped

DIRECTIONS:

» Grease your Slow Cooker with oil
» Add corn, prosciutto, garlic, tomato sauce, bell pepper to your Slow Cooker
» Stir and place lid
» Cook on HIGH for 2 hours

Nutrition: Calories 158.5, Fat 1.4 g, Carbs 15 g, Protein 23 g

FATTOUSH SALAD

Preparation Time: 15 mins
Servings: 4 | Cooking: 2-3 mins

INGREDIENTS:

- 1 whole wheat pita bread
- 1 large English cucumber, diced
- 2 cup grape tomatoes, halved
- ½ of a medium red onion, finely diced
- ¾ cup of fresh parsley, chopped
- ¾ cup of mint leaves, chopped
- 1 clove of garlic, minced
- ¼ cup of fat free feta cheese, crumbled
- 1 tbsp of olive oil
- 1 tsp of ground sumac
- Juice from ½ a lemon

DIRECTIONS:

» Mist pita bread with cooking spray
» Season with salt
» Toast until the breads are crispy
» Take a large bowl and add the remaining Ingredients: and mix (except feta)
» Top the mix with diced toasted pita and feta

Nutrition: Calories 158.5, Fat 1.4 g, Carbs 15 g, Protein 23 g

BROCCOLI SALAD

Preparation Time: 5 mins
Servings: 1 | Cooking: 10 mins

INGREDIENTS:

- 10 broccoli florets
- 2 red onions, sliced
- 1 oz bacon, chopped into small pieces
- 1 cup coconut cream
- 1 tsp sesame seeds

DIRECTIONS:

» Cook bacon in hot oil until crispy
» Cook onions in fat left from the bacon
» Take a pan of boiling water and add broccoli florets, boil for a few mins
» Take a salad bowl and add bacon pieces, onions, broccoli florets, coconut cream and salt
» Toss well and top with sesame seeds

Nutrition: Calories 158.5, Fat 1.4 g, Carbs 15 g, Protein 23 g

BABY SPINACH SALAD

Preparation Time: 10 mins | Servings: 2

INGREDIENTS:

- 1 bag baby spinach, washed and dried
- 1 red bell pepper, cut in slices
- 1 cup cherry tomatoes, cut in halves
- 1 small red onion, finely chopped
- 1 cup black olives, pitted

- For dressing
- 1 tsp dried oregano
- 1 large garlic clove
- 3 tbsps red wine vinegar
- 4 tbsps olive oil
- Sunflower seeds and pepper to taste

DIRECTIONS:

» Prepare the dressing by blending in garlic, olive oil, vinegar in a food processor
» Take a large salad bowl and add spinach leaves, toss well with the dressing
» Add remaining Ingredients: and toss again, season with sunflower seeds and pepper and enjoy!

Nutrition: Calories 135.5, Fat 1.4 g, Carbs 12 g, Protein 25 g

CLASSIC TUNA SALAD

Preparation Time: 10 mins | Servings: 4

INGREDIENTS:

- 12 oz white tuna, in water
- ½ cup celery, diced
- 2 tbsp fresh parsley, chopped
- 2 tbsp low-calorie mayonnaise, low fat and low sodium
- ½ tsp Dijon mustard
- ½ tsp sunflower seeds
- ¼ tsp fresh ground black pepper

DIRECTIONS:

» Take a medium sized bowl and add tuna, parsley, and celery
» Mix well and add mayonnaise Season with pepper and sunflower seeds Stir and add olives, relish, chopped pickle, onion and mix well

Nutrition: Calories 155.5, Fat 1.4 g, Carbs 15 g, Protein 22 g

GREEK SALAD

Preparation Time: 10 mins | Servings: 6

INGREDIENTS:

- 2 cucumbers, diced
- 2 tomatoes, sliced
- 1 green lettuce, cut into thin strips
- 2 red bell peppers, cut
- ½ cup black olives pitted
- 3 and ½ oz feta cheese, cut
- 1 red onion, sliced
- 2 tbsp olive oil
- 2 tbsp lemon juice
- Sunflower seeds and pepper to taste

DIRECTIONS:

» Dice cucumbers and slice up the tomatoes
» Tear the lettuce and cut it up into thin strips
» De-seed and cut the peppers into strips
» Take a salad bowl and mix in all the listed vegetables, add olives and feta cheese (cut into cubes)
» Take a small cup and mix in olive oil and lemon juice, season with sunflower seeds and pepper. Pour mixture into the salad and toss well, enjoy!

Nutrition: Calories 155.5, Fat 1.4 g, Carbs 15 g, Protein 22 g

DELICIOUS TUNA SALAD

Preparation Time: 5-10 mins | Servings: 4

INGREDIENTS:

- 15 oz small white beans
- 6 oz drained chunks of light tuna
- 10 cherry tomatoes, quartered
- 4 scallions, trimmed and sliced
- 2 tbsp lemon juice

DIRECTIONS:

» Add all of the listed Ingredients: to a bowl and gently stir
» Season with sunflower seeds and pepper accordingly, enjoy!

Nutrition: Calories 135.5, Fat 2.4 g, Carbs 18 g, Protein 22 g

YOGURT AND CUCUMBER SALAD

Preparation Time: 5-10 mins | Servings: 4

INGREDIENTS:

- 5-6 small cucumbers, peeled and diced
- 1 (8 oz) container plain Greek yogurt
- 2 garlic cloves, minced
- 1 tbsp fresh mint, minced
- Sea sunflower seeds and fresh black pepper

DIRECTIONS:

» Take a large bowl and add cucumbers, garlic, yogurt, mint
» Season with sunflower seeds and pepper
» Refrigerate the salad for 1 hour and serve

Nutrition: Calories 135.5, Fat 1.4 g, Carbs 13 g, Protein 22 g

TASTY EGGPLANT SALAD

Preparation Time: 10 mins | Servings: 3 | Cooking: 30 mins

INGREDIENTS:

- 2 eggplants, peeled and sliced
- 2 garlic cloves
- 2 green bell paper, sliced, seeds removed
- ½ cup fresh parsley
- ½ cup mayonnaise, low fat, low sodium

- Sunflower seeds and black pepper

DIRECTIONS:

» Preheat your oven to 480°F
» Take a baking pan and add eggplants and black pepper in it
» Bake for about 30 mins
» Flip the vegetables after 20 mins
» Then, take a bowl and add baked vegetables and all the remaining ingredients

Nutrition: Calories 135.5, Fat 2.4 g, Carbs 18 g, Protein 22 g

POTATO OCTOPUS SALAD

Preparation Time: 10 mins
Servings: 6-8 |Cooking: 30 mins

INGREDIENTS:

- 2 lbs. octopus
- 2 crushed garlic cloves
- 1 bay leaf
- ½ tbsp peppercorns
- 2 lbs. potatoes
- 1 chopped parsley bunch
- 1 whole garlic cloves
- ½ cup olive oil
- 5 tbsp White wine vinegar

DIRECTIONS:

» Scrub the potatoes and place them in your pressure cooker. Pour in enough water to cover the potatoes halfway. Close and lock the lid of your pressure cooker. Cook on low pressure for 15 mins.
» Release the pressure using the quick release method and take the potatoes out of the pressure cooker. Don't discard the cooking liquid.
» Peel the hot potatoes; dice them into small cubes and place in a large mixing bowl.
» To cook the prepared octopus in the pressure cooker, pour enough water to almost cover it.
» Add the bay leaf, whole garlic clove, and peppercorns and bring to the boil. Then add the octopus.
» Close and lock the lid. Cook on low pressure for 15 mins. When the time is up, release the pressure using the quick release method.
» Once the octopus is done, take it out of the pressure cooker and remove any remaining skin.
» Add the octopus chunks to the bowl with the potatoes and mix well.
» To prepare the vinaigrette, combine all the Ingredients: in a jar and shake well to blend everything.
» Flood the octopus and potato chunks with the vinaigrette, garnish with the chopped parsley and serve.

Nutrition: Calories 119, Fat 0 g, Carbs 27 g, Protein 3 g

BALSAMIC BEET SALAD

Preparation Time: 5 mins
Servings: 4 |Cooking: 30 mins

INGREDIENTS:

- Extra virgin olive oil
- Kosher flavored vinegar
- 6 medium sized beets
- Freshly ground black pepper
- 1 cup water
- Balsamic vinegar

DIRECTIONS:

» Wash the beets carefully and trim them to ½ inch portions
» Add 1 cup of water to the pot
» Place a steamer on top and arrange the beets on top of the steamer
» Lock up the lid and cook on HIGH pressure for 1 minute
» Release the pressure naturally and allow the beet to cool
» Slice the top of the skin carefully
» Slice up the beets in uniform portions and season with flavored vinegar and pepper
» Add a splash of balsamic vinegar and allow them to marinate for 30 mins
» Add a bit of extra olive oil and serve!

Nutrition: Calories 120, Fat 7 g, Carbs 13 g, Protein 2 g

SQUASH GARDEN SALAD

Preparation Time: 15 mins
Servings: 2

INGREDIENTS:

- 1 pitted and cubed avocado
- 2 tbsp lemon juice
- 2 tbsp olive oil
- 8 oz. peeled and cubed summer squash
- 1 oz. chopped watercress

DIRECTIONS:

» Arrange all the vegetables in a salad bowl and dress with olive oil and lemon juice.
» Add the watercress leaves.

Nutrition: Calories 326, Fat 29.6 g, Carbs 3 g, Protein 3 g

BEET AND WALNUT SALAD

Preparation Time: 5 mins
Servings: 2

INGREDIENTS:

- 1 minced garlic clove
- 2 tbsp olive oil
- 10 chopped prunes
- 2 peeled and grated small beets
- 1 cup chopped walnuts

DIRECTIONS:

- Combine all the Ingredients: in a salad bowl.
- Dress with olive oil.

Nutrition: Calories 296, Fat 21 g, Carbs 26 g, Protein 3.6 g

STEAMED SAUCY GARLIC GREENS

Preparation Time: 5 mins
Servings: 4

INGREDIENTS:

- 1/8 tsp. flavored vinegar
- 1 peeled whole clove
- ¼ cup water
- 1 tbsp lemon juice
- 1 bunch leafy greens
- ½ cup soaked cashews
- 1 tsp. coconut aminos

DIRECTIONS:

- Make the sauce by draining and discard the soaking water from your cashew and add them cashew to blender
- Add fresh water, lemon juice, flavored vinegar, coconut aminos, and garlic
- Blitz until you have a smooth cream and transfer to bowl
- Add ½ cup of water to the pot
- Place the steamer basket to the pot and add the greens in the basket
- Lock up the lid and steam for 1 minute
- Quick release the pressure
- Transfer the steamed greens to strainer and extract excess water
- Place the greens into a mixing bowl
- Add lemon garlic sauce and toss

Nutrition: Calories 77, Fat 5 g, Carbs 0 g, Protein 2 g

DAIKON RADISH SALAD

Preparation Time: 5 mins
Servings: 2

INGREDIENTS:

- 2 tbsp lemon juice
- 2 peeled and grated small daikon
- 3 tbsp olive oil
- ¼ peeled and grated medium pumpkin
- 2 cup minced parsley

DIRECTIONS:

- Combine all the Ingredients: in a salad bowl.
- Sprinkle with olive oil and lemon juice.

Nutrition: Calories 237, Fat 2.6 g, Carbs 13.9 g, Protein 2.0 g

CALAMARI SALAD

Preparation Time: 15 mins
Servings: 2

INGREDIENTS:

- 1 peeled and sliced cucumber
- Lettuce leaves
- 3 ½ oz. washed, cleaned and sliced calamari fillets
- Fresh parsley
- 1 peeled, boiled and sliced potato
- 1 tbsp sour cream
- 1 peeled, cored and sliced apple

DIRECTIONS:

- Place the calamari into boiling salted water and cook for 5 min.
- Arrange lettuce leaves on the bottom of a salad bowl. Mix the apple and vegetable strips with the calamari. Dress with sour cream, place on the lettuce leaves, and garnish with the parsley.

Nutrition: Calories 468, Fat 8.5 g, Carbs 5.1 g, Protein 17.8 g

CHICKEN RAISIN SALAD

Preparation Time: 15-20 mins
Servings: 2

INGREDIENTS:

- 2 tbsp lemon juice
- 2 tbsp raisins
- 1 peeled, cored and cubed apple
- ¼ cup chopped celery
- 2 tbsp olive oil
- 3 ¼ cup skinless and sliced chicken meat

DIRECTIONS:

- In a saucepan or skillet, cook the cubed chicken meat in olive oil until golden.
- Transfer the cooked meat to a mixing bowl of medium-large size and add all other Ingredients. Stir to combine
- Serve while the chicken is warm.

Nutrition: Calories 382, Fat 16 g, Carbs 41 g, Protein 25.7 g

PICKLED ONION SALAD

Preparation Time: 1 hour
Servings: 4

INGREDIENTS:

- 4 chopped spring onions
- ½ cup chopped fresh cilantro
- 2 tbsp brown sugar
- 1 tbsp lime juice
- ½ cup cider vinegar
- 2 thinly sliced red onions
- 4 lettuce leaves
- 2 tsps. olive oil

DIRECTIONS:

» In a salad bowl combine the onions, vinegar, oil and sugar. Cover and refrigerate for 1 hr.
» Add cilantro and lime juice. Serve on lettuce leaves.

Nutrition: Calories 223, Fat 14.1 g, Carbs 20 g, Protein 1.8 g

---

PICKLED GRAPE SALAD WITH PEAR, AND CHEESE

Preparation Time: 15 mins| Servings: 3

INGREDIENTS:

- 200g sliced taleggio cheese
- 4 tbsp red wine vinegar
- 2 tbsp light brown sugar
- 2 handfuls fresh watercress
- 100g halved red grapes
- 1 wedged pear
- 50g halved walnut

DIRECTIONS:

» Heat a cast-iron skillet or frying pan and toast the walnut halves, until they are slightly brown and give off a lovely nutty aroma. Set aside to cool.
» Stir together the red wine vinegar and light brown sugar in a bowl, and leave for 5 mins to allow the sugar to dissolve.
» Add the grapes to this sweet and tangy mixture, and toss. Marinate for 10 mins while you work on the rest of the recipe.
» Scatter the watercress onto 3 plates or onto one large sharing platter, and then top evenly with the taleggio cheese and pear wedges.
» Drain the grapes from their marinade, but do not discard the marinade.
» Whisk 2 tbsp of olive oil into the pickling marinade.
» Scatter the pickled grapes all over the salad, and then drizzle over 3-4 tbsp of the dressing.
» Finish with the toasted walnut halves, and enjoy immediately.

Nutrition: Calories 421, Fat 28.4 g, Carbs 24.1 g, Protein 15.9 g

---

TUNA AND POTATO SALAD

Preparation Time: 10 mins |Servings: 4

INGREDIENTS:

- 1 lb baby potatoes, scrubbed, boiled
- 1 cup tuna chunks, drained
- 1 cup cherry tomatoes, halved
- 1 cup medium onion, thinly sliced
- 8 pitted black olives
- 2 medium hard-boiled eggs, sliced
- 1 head Romaine lettuce
- ¼ cup olive oil
- 2 tbsp lemon juice
- 1 tbsp Dijon mustard
- 1 tsp dill weed, chopped
- Pepper as needed

DIRECTIONS:

» Take a small glass bowl and mix in your olive oil, lemon juice, Dijon mustard and dill
» Add in the tuna, baby potatoes, cherry tomatoes, red onion, green beans, black olives and toss everything nicely
» Arrange your lettuce leaves on a beautiful serving dish to make the base of your salad
» Top them up with your salad mixture and place the egg slices
» Drizzle it with the previously prepared Salad Dressing
» Serve hot

Nutrition: Calories 142.5, Fat 2.4 g, Carbs 16 g, Protein 20 g

---

SPINACH PARMESAN DIP

Preparation Time: 45 mins |Servings: 6
Cooking Time: 25 mins

INGREDIENTS:

- 6 bacon slices
- 5 oz spinach
- ½ cup sour cream
- 8 oz soft cream cheese
- 1 tbsp garlic minced
- 1½ tbsp chopped parsley
- 5 oz parmesan
- 1 tbsp lemon juice

DIRECTIONS:

» Place a pan over medium heat then add bacon
» Saute until crispy then transfer to a plate lined with a paper towel
» Heat the leftover bacon grease and add spinach
» Stir cook for 2 mins then keep it in a bowl
» Whisk cream cheese, salt, pepper, parsley, sour cream and garlic in a separate bowl
» Add bacon, spinach and lemon juice and mix well
» Divide this mixture in the ramekins then bake for 25 mins at 350°F
» Switch the oven to broil settings and broil for 4 mins

Nutrition: Calories 345, Fat 12g, Fiber 3g, Carbs 6g, Protein 11 g

Chapter 6
Recipes for Lunch

HOMOGENIZED RABBIT WITH COURGETTES (FOR CHILDREN)

Servings: 1
Preparation Time: 5 min
Cooking Time: 10 min

INGREDIENTS

- 25 g baby food, 40 g courgettes, 1 tablespoon olive oil

DIRECTIONS

» Prepare this dish by carefully weighing all the ingredients. Wash the zucchini and steam for 10 minutes.
» Mash with a fork, add them to homogenized and season with a spoonful of olive oil.

BRUSSELS SPROUTS IN SALAD

Servings: 1
Preparation Time: 5 min
Cooking Time: 10 min

INGREDIENTS

- Brussels sprouts 30 g, Bell pepper 45 g, Black olives 10 g, Olive oil 1 tablespoon

DIRECTIONS

» Wash and clean well brussels sprouts; Boil them in water for about 10 minutes, until they are soft.
» Wash and cut the rest of the vegetables and add them stirring with 1 drizzle of oil.
» Serve at room temperature. You can also prepare this dish the day before.

SANDWICH WITH HAM AND TOMATO

Servings: 1
Preparation Time: 5 min
Cooking Time: -

INGREDIENTS

- Wholemeal bread 2 slices, Cooked ham 60 g, Salad tomatoes 90 g, Mayonnaise 20 g, Olive oil 1 tablespoon, Oregano to taste Directions
- Weigh the tomato salad, wash and cut into thin slices. Season with mayonnaise, olive oil and if you like, oregano.
- Prepare the sandwich with freshly seasoned tomatoes and slices of cooked ham.
- Let rest for 20 minutes to mix better flavors.

SHRIMP COCKTAIL

Servings: 1
Preparation Time: 5 min
Cooking Time: 15 min

INGREDIENTS

- Fresh shrimp 60 g, Lettuce 50 g, Avocado 60 g, Lard 15 g, Mayonnaise 1 tablespoon, Olive oil 1 tablespoon, Lemon juice 1 tablespoon (to taste)

DIRECTIONS

» Cooked version of the classic shrimp cocktail. Clean the shrimps well, peel them and remove the small central casing.
» Grill them over a high flame for about 30 seconds, together with lard. Once out of the fire cut them both into cubes coarsely. Season with salt and pepper to taste.
» Place the washed lettuce in thin strips on a low plate. Place on it the mixture of shrimp and lard.
» Emulsify mayonnaise and olive oil, add 1 tablespoon of lemon juice to taste and season the dish.

PUMPKIN CREAM

Servings: 1
Preparation Time: 15 min
Cooking Time: 15 min

INGREDIENTS

- Pumpkin 140 g, fresh cream 65 g, olive oil 2 tablespoons, grated Parmesan to taste, pepper to taste, ½ onion

DIRECTIONS

» Clean the pumpkin by removing the peel and seeds.
» In a non-stick pan, heat 1 tablespoon of oil and let the onion fry over low heat. After about 2 minutes of Cooking Time, add the pumpkin cut into coarse cubes, cover and let it dry.
» When the pumpkin is cooked, turn off the heat and blend it with a mixer. Add salt and pepper to the mixture.
» Put the soup back in the pan and add the cream. Let it warm up and serve in a bowl with grated Parmesan cheese.

SALAD WITH TOMATOES AND GORGONZOLA

Servings: 1
Preparation Time: 10 min
Cooking Time: -

INGREDIENTS

- Gorgonzola 40 g, Cherry tomatoes 80 g, Salad 80 g, Salt to taste, 1 tablespoon olive oil, 15 g sunflower seeds

DIRECTIONS

» Wash and cut the salad and cherry tomatoes into small pieces, placing them in a bowl. Add the finely chopped gorgonzola and sunflower seeds. Stir the mixture to blend it.
» Season with olive oil and salt to taste.

CREAM OF PUMPKIN SOUP WITH CHEESE CROUTONS

Servings: 1
Preparation Time: 10 min
Cooking Time: 20 min

INGREDIENTS

- 75 g pumpkin, 15 g cooking cream, 8 g butter, 1/2 chopped onion, 1 tablespoon of olive oil, grated Parmesan

DIRECTIONS

» Remove the skin from the pumpkin and steam it for 10 minutes.
» Heat the oil in a non-stick pan and fry the onion with the butter, after about 5 minutes add the pumpkin and let it go for another 5 minutes.
» Blend the mixture obtained, add the cream and fill a single portion bowl.
» Add the Parmesan cheese on top and finish grilling in the oven for another 10 minutes to get a succulent cheese crust.

CORN AND BEAN TORTILLA

Servings: 1
Preparation Time: 10 min
Cooking Time: 20 min

INGREDIENTS

- 1 cup cooked beans, 1 diced pepper, 1 diced carrot, 1 tablespoon olive oil, 1 chopped red onion, ½ cup cooked corn, 80 g cheddar, 6 tortillas

DIRECTIONS

» Pour the oil into a non-stick pan and heat for 2 minutes.
» When ready, add the onion, and let it sauté for 5 minutes. At this point you can put the rest of the Ingredients (except the cheddar). Cook for 5 minutes, turn off the heat and add the cheese.
» Fill the tortillas with the hot mixture and serve.

QUINOA AND PEAS

Servings: 1
Preparation Time: 2 min
Cooking Time: 10 min

INGREDIENTS

- 1/2 chopped onion, 1 tablespoon of olive oil, 25 g of peas, 150 ml of water, 80 g of quinoa, Salt to taste

DIRECTIONS

» Heat the oil and onion in a non-stick pan for 2 minutes.
» Add the rest of the Ingredients, stirring constantly to prevent sticking. When the water is completely absorbed, the dish is ready.

PEPPER SALAD

Servings: 1
Preparation Time: 2 min
Cooking Time: 10 min

INGREDIENTS

- 20 black olives, 1 tablespoon of olive oil, 1 chopped shallot, 2 diced peppers, ½ lemon peel, 1 lemon juice, 1 chopped parsley branch, 1 sliced salad tomato,

DIRECTIONS

» Put the oil and the shallot in a non-stick pan and cook over low heat for 2 minutes.
» Add the olives, the peppers and the restod he Ingredients. Cook over low heat for about 8 minutes and serve.
» You can also do it the day before to allow the flavors to blend better.

BEAN MIX

Servings: 1
Preparation Time: 5 min
Cooking Time: 20 min

INGREDIENTS

- 1 clove of minced garlic, 1 chopped onion, ½ diced avocado, 300 g of boiled beans, 1 finely chopped parsley branch, 1 tablespoon of olive oil

DIRECTIONS

» Grease a non-stick pan with oil and sauté the garlic and onion over low heat for 2 minutes. Add the restod he Ingredients and cook over low heat for another 15 minutes.
» Turn off and let it rest for a few minutes before serving.

EGG SALAD

Servings: 1
Preparation Time: 5 min
Cooking Time: 20 min

INGREDIENTS

- 2 diced carrots, 1 sliced onion, 1 sprig of chopped parsley, 2 tablespoons of olive oil, 4 hard-boiled eggs cut into slices, 1 tablespoon of white wine vinegar, 1 pinch of black pepper

DIRECTIONS

» In a bowl, mix all the ingredients and leave to flavor before serving.
» Season with salt if necessary.

GARNISH OF CARROTS AND PEAS

Servings: 1
Preparation Time: 5 min
Cooking Time: 20 min

INGREDIENTS

- 1 clove of minced garlic, 1 chopped onion, 1 tablespoon of olive oil, 1 carrot cut into slices, 1 tablespoon of balsamic vinegar, 120 g of peas, 1 sprig of chopped parsley

DIRECTIONS

» Heat a non-stick pan with a drizzle of oil and saute the onion and chopped garlic for 5 minutes.
» Add the rest of the Ingredients and let it go for 5 minutes.
» Serve as a side dish while still hot.

GOAT CHEESE SANDWICH WITH TOMATO AND SALAD

Servings: 1
Preparation Time: 5 min
Cooking Time: 5 min

INGREDIENTS

- 20 g of sliced tomato, 1 tablespoon of toasted pine nuts, 2 slices of wholemeal bread, chopped basil to taste, ½ sliced avocado, 40 g of fresh goat cheese, pepper to taste

DIRECTIONS

» In a bowl, mix all the ingredients and leave to flavor for 5 minutes. In the meantime, toast the slices of bread well and spread the goat cheese on top.
» Add the rest of the ingredients and enjoy.

TRIUMPH OF CHICKEN AND SPINACH

Servings: 1
Preparation Time: 5 min
Cooking Time: 10 min

INGREDIENTS

- 250 g of chicken breast, 1 sprig of chopped parsley, 300 g of spinach, ½ diced mango, 2 tablespoons of olive oil, thyme to taste, salt to taste, pepper to taste

DIRECTIONS

» Very simple dish, but at the same time fast and healthy.
» In a non-stick pan heat a little oil and start the Cooking Time of the chicken breast, it must cook 4 minutes per side, add the thyme to flavor.
» While cooking, wash the spinach, and mix it with the mango, a drizzle of oil, salt and pepper.
» When the chicken is ready, serve with the spinach as a side dish.

SCRAMBLED EGGS WITH MUSHROOM GARNISH

Servings: 1
Preparation Time: 5 min
Cooking Time: 10 min

INGREDIENTS

- 2 whole eggs, ½ tablespoon of curry powder, 1 tablespoon of olive oil, 100 g of finely chopped mushrooms, 1 sprig of chopped parsley

DIRECTIONS

» Heat the oil in a non-stick pan, after 2 minutes add the eggs (previously beaten with a whisk) and mix immediately to "scramble" them. Cook about 4 minutes, add the curry and serve hot.
» Separately, mix the mushrooms with oil, salt and chopped parsley and serve as a side dish.

SALMON OMELETTE

Servings: 1
Preparation Time: 5 min
Cooking Time: 10 min

INGREDIENTS

- 2 whole eggs, 100 g of smoked salmon, 20 g of capers, 20 g of rocket, 10 g of chopped parsley, 1 tablespoon of olive oil

DIRECTIONS

» Break the eggs into a bowl and mix with the minced salmon, capers, rocket and parsley.
» Heat the oil in a non-stick pan and add the mixture obtained. Cook about 3 minutes per side and the salmon omelette will be ready.

TURKEY AND CAULIFLOWER

Servings: 1
Preparation Time: 10 min
Cooking Time: 10 min

INGREDIENTS

- 150 g of turkey breast in chunks, 150 g of cauliflower, 40 g of red onion, 1 tablespoon of fresh ginger, 1 clove of garlic, 3 tablespoons of olive oil, 10 g of chopped parsley, 20 g of capers, Juice of ½ lemon

DIRECTIONS

» Clean the cauliflower and cook the tops in a pan with 1 tablespoon of olive oil, garlic, onion, ginger. Let it cook for a few minutes, then add the ginger and continue cooking for another 5 minutes.
» In another pan, cook the tacchio breast with the remaining oil, salt and pepper if you like.
» When it is cooked, combine all the ingredients, including the rest and leave to flavor for a few minutes.
» You can serve right away or prepare this dish the day before.

SIDE DISH OF SAUTEED PEAS

Servings: 1
Preparation Time: 5 min
Cooking Time: 15 min

INGREDIENTS

- 1 clove of minced garlic, 200 g of peas, 1 tablespoon of cumin, 1 tablespoon of olive oil, ½ chopped onion, 1 tablespoon of lemon juice, 1 sprig of chopped parsley

DIRECTIONS

» Let the oil heat for 1 minute in a non-stick pan, once ready add the garlic and onion and cook for 2 minutes. Pour the peas and the rest of the Ingredients and finish the Cooking Time on low heat for about 10 minutes. Add water if the pan gets too dry.
» Serve hot.

CAULIFLOWER IN A PAN

Servings: 2
Preparation Time: 5 min
Cooking Time: 10 min

INGREDIENTS

- 1 tablespoon of olive oil, 1 diced pepper, 1 cauliflower, 1 red onion, Salt to taste, Pepper to taste

DIRECTIONS

» In a non-stick pan, heat the oil for 1 minute, add the onion and cauliflower. Cover and simmer for 5 minutes, then add the rest of the Ingredients and let it go for another 5 minutes.
» Serve still warm or at room temperature.

SALMON SALAD

Servings: 1
Preparation Time: 5 min
Cooking Time: -

INGREDIENTS

- 100 g of smoked salmon, grated ½ lemon peel, 1 tablespoon of lemon juice, 1 tablespoon of Greek yogurt, 100 g of spinach, ½ chopped onion, 20 g of capers, Salt to taste, Pepper to taste, 2 tablespoons of oil olive

DIRECTIONS

» Combine all the ingredients in a bowl and leave to flavor. The ideal is to prepare this dish the night before and then enjoy it for lunch the next day.

CHICKEN AND TOMATO MIX

Servings: 1
Preparation Time: 5 min
Cooking Time: 10 min

INGREDIENTS

- 1 tablespoon of olive oil, 200 g of chicken breast in bite-sized pieces, 4 diced cherry tomatoes, 1/3 chopped onion, salt to taste

DIRECTIONS

» Heat the oil in a non-stick pan and cook the chicken breast over low heat for about 7 mionuti. Separately, cut the tomatoes and onion, mix and season with oil and salt. Serve the chicken still hot with the tomatoes for a side dish.

SALMON AND OLIVE SALAD

Servings: 1
Preparation Time: 5 min
Cooking Time: -

INGREDIENTS

- 200 g of smoked salmon, 1 tablespoon of wine vinegar, 1 chopped shallot, 20 g of black olives, 50 g of rocket, 1 tablespoon of olive oil

DIRECTIONS

» Combine all Ingredients in a bowl and season with salt if necessary.
» Let it rest in the refrigerator for at least 30 minutes before serving.

SHRIMP SALAD

Servings: 1
Preparation Time: 5 min
Cooking Time: 5 min

INGREDIENTS

- 150 g of peeled shrimp, 1 tablespoon of olive oil, 1 tablespoon of basil pesto, 120 g of rocket, 1 chopped carrot, 1 sliced cucumber

DIRECTIONS

» Heat the oil in a non-stick pan and cook the shrimp for 5 minutes. Once cooked, cut them into small pieces and incorporate all the Ingredients into a bowl.
» You can serve hot or leave to rest in the fridge.

TURKEY TORTILLAS

Servings: 2
Preparation Time: 5 min
Cooking Time: 15 min

INGREDIENTS

- 2 corn or whole wheat tortillas, 2 tablespoons mustard, 400 g turkey breast in bite-sized pieces, 1 tablespoon of olive oil, 1 diced red pepper, 1 chopped red onion

DIRECTIONS

» Heat a non-stick pan and cook the turkey meat and onion for 5 minutes.
» Add the pepper and continue the Cooking Time for another 10 minutes.
» Season the tortillas with the mustard and fill them with the meat.

BEAN SOUP

Servings: 2
Preparation Time: 5 min
Cooking Time: 25 min

INGREDIENTS

- 2 tablespoons of olive oil, 1 clove of garlic, 180 g of beans, 1 chopped onion, 2 diced tomatoes, 1 tablespoon of sweet paprika, 1 sprig of chopped parsley

DIRECTIONS

» Heat a pan with the oil and let the garlic and onion dry for 5 minutes.
» Add the beans, previously boiled for 60 minutes, and the rest of the Ingredients. Cook for 2o minutes.
» Serve still hot and decorate with the chopped basil.

AVOCADO SALAD

Servings: 1
Preparation Time: 5 min
Cooking Time: -

INGREDIENTS

- 1 sliced avocato, 2 tablespoons of balsamic vinegar, 5 g of chopped mint, 90 g of spinach, 1 sliced cucumber, 1 tablespoon of olive oil

DIRECTIONS

» Combine all Ingredients in a bowl and season with salt if necessary.
» Let it rest in the refrigerator for at least 30 minutes before serving.

FILLET OF BEEF

Servings: 1
Preparation Time: -
Cooking Time: 10 min

INGREDIENTS

- 250 g of beef fillet, 1 tablespoon of olive oil, salt to taste, 1 sprig of rosemary, 15 g of butter

DIRECTIONS

» Heat the non-stick pan and cook the meat 30 seconds per side to seal it.
» Once this is done, add the rest of the Ingredients and with a spoon wet the fillet with the fat that will form, in a nutshell "nappate" the fillet.
» Cook for about 8 minutes, let it rest and serve.

BEEF STEW WITH THYME, POTATOES AND TOMATOES

Servings: 2
Preparation Time: 5 min
Cooking Time: 45 min

INGREDIENTS

- 500 g of beef stew, 3 tablespoons of olive oil, 1 sliced onion, 2 potatoes, salt and pepper to taste, 1 sliced carrot, 2 diced tomatoes

DIRECTIONS

» Heat a pan with oil, add the onion and let it go for about 1 minute. At this point add the stew and the rest of the Ingredients, stirring occasionally and adding water if it gets too dry.
» Cover and cook over low heat for at least 45 minutes.

RISOTTO WITH CHIVES

Servings: 1
Preparation Time: 5 min
Cooking Time: 45 min

INGREDIENTS

- 80 g of rice, 25 g of chives, 1 tablespoon of oil, 20 g of butter, 400 ml of vegetable broth, grated Parmesan to taste

DIRECTIONS

» Heat the oil in a pan and fry the chives for a minute. Add the rice, stir and let it toast until the grains are lightly shiny. Add the broth a little at a time and continue the Cooking Time for at least 30 minutes.
» Turn off the heat, add the butter and the cheese for freezing. Let it rest for a minute and serve still hot.

SHRIMP AND SPINACH SALAD

Servings: 1
Preparation Time: 5 min
Cooking Time: 10 min

INGREDIENTS

- 1 cup of corn, 100 g of spinach, 150 g of shrimp, Juice of 1 lemon, 1 tablespoon of olive oil

DIRECTIONS

» Heat the oil in a pan and cook the prawns for 2 minutes per side. Let them cool, shell them and cut them into small pieces.
» Combine all the ingredients in a bowl, mix to blend the flavors and serve.

SHRIMP SALAD WITH RASPBERRIES AND TOMATOES

Servings: 1
Preparation Time: 5 min
Cooking Time: 10 min

INGREDIENTS

- 20 g of raspberries, 100 g of cherry tomatoes, 150 g of prawns, juice of 1 lemon, 1 tablespoon of olive oil

DIRECTIONS

» Heat the oil in a pan and cook the prawns for 2 minutes per side. Let them cool, shell them and cut them into small pieces.
» Combine all the ingredients in a bowl, mix to blend the flavors and serve.

COD TACOS

Servings: 2
Preparation Time: 5 min
Cooking Time: 10 min

INGREDIENTS

- 4 tacos, 1 tablespoon of mayonnaise, 2 cod fillets, 1 sprig of chopped rosemary, 1 tablespoon of olive oil, 2 green salad leaves, 1 diced salad tomato

DIRECTIONS

» Heat a non-stick pan and cook the cod for 5 minutes.
» While it cooks, cut all the Ingredients.
» Season the tortillas with the mayonnaise, the chopped vegetables and the diced peach.

FRIED ZUCCHINI

Servings: 2
Preparation Time: 10 min
Cooking Time: 10 min

INGREDIENTS

- 2 courgettes, 1 whole egg, Breadcrumbs to taste, Salt to taste, Sunflower oil to taste

DIRECTIONS

» Wash the courgettes and cut them into slices. Separately, beat the egg and add salt to taste. Pass the zucchini in the egg and then in the breadcrumbs.
» Heat some seed oil in a pan, when it is hot fry the courgettes for about 5 minutes, taking care to remove the excess oil with absorbent paper once cooked. Serve hot.

PEA SOUP

Servings: 2
Preparation Time: 5 min
Cooking Time: 25 min

INGREDIENTS

- 2 tablespoons of olive oil, 1 clove of garlic, 200 g of peas, 1 chopped onion, 2 diced tomatoes, 1 tablespoon of sweet paprika, 1 sprig of chopped parsley

DIRECTIONS

» Heat a pan with the oil and let the garlic and onion dry for 5 minutes.
» Add the peas, previously boiled for 60 minutes, and the rest of the Ingredients. Cook for 20 minutes.
» Serve still hot and decorate with the chopped basil.

LEMON CHICKEN SALAD

Servings: 1
Preparation Time: 5 min
Cooking Time: -

INGREDIENTS

- 1 tablespoon of olive oil, 20 g of chopped tomatoes, ½ chopped onion, 150 g of cooked chicken breast, 50 g of spinach, 2 tablespoons of lemon juice

DIRECTIONS

» Combine all the Ingredients in a salad bowl and let it rest in the fridge for at least 30 minutes before serving for lunch.

ASPARAGUS SALAD

Servings: 1
Preparation Time: 5 min
Cooking Time: 10 min

INGREDIENTS

- 1 clove of garlic, 2 tablespoons of olive oil, ½ chopped onion, 2 chopped carrots, 60 g of spinach, 120 g of asparagus

DIRECTIONS

» Heat the oil and garlic in a non-stick pan for 1 minute, when hot add the asparagus and cook for about 10 minutes.
» Once cooked, cut them into small pieces and mix them with the rest of the Ingredients.

BEEF STEW WITH TOMATO

Servings: 1
Preparation Time: 5 min
Cooking Time: 45 min

INGREDIENTS

- 500 g of beef stew, 3 tablespoons of olive oil, 1 sliced onion, salt and pepper to taste, 1 sliced carrot, 400 ml of tomato sauce, 200 ml of water

DIRECTIONS

» Heat a pan with oil, add the onion and let it go for about 1 minute. At this point add the stew and the rest of the Ingredients, stirring occasionally and adding water if it gets too dry.
» Cover and cook over low heat for at least 45 minutes.

PORK CHOPS

Servings: 1
Preparation Time: 5 min
Cooking Time: 180 min

INGREDIENTS

- 4 pork chops, 1 tablespoon of olive oil, 2 chopped shallots, 60 g of mushrooms, 1 tablespoon of chopped rosemary

DIRECTIONS

» Heat some oil in a pan and add all the Ingredients.
» Brown over low heat for about 3 hours. Once ctto let it rest over the heat for a few minutes and serve hot.

SHRIMP SALAD WITH BALSAMIC VINEGAR

Servings: 1
Preparation Time: 5 min
Cooking Time: 5 min

INGREDIENTS

- 20 ml of balsamic vinegar, 1 sprig of chopped parsley, 150 g of prawns, juice of 1 lemon, 1 tablespoon of olive oil

DIRECTIONS

» Heat the oil in a pan and cook the prawns for 2 minutes per side. Let them cool, shell them and cut them into small pieces.
» Combine all the ingredients in a bowl, mix to blend the flavors and serve.

TOMATO AND EGGPLANT SOUP

Servings: 1
Preparation Time: 5 min
Cooking Time: 20 min

INGREDIENTS

- 200 g of diced aubergines, 1 clove of garlic, 2 tablespoons of olive oil, ½ chopped onion, 1 tablespoon of sweet paprika, 200 g of peeled tomatoes, 2 leaves of fresh basil

DIRECTIONS

» Heat the oil in a non-stick pan and sauté the onion and garlic for 1 minute.
» Add the rest of the Ingredients and cook on a low flame for about 18 minutes.
» Serve hot.

TURKEY STEW WITH LIME

Servings: 1
Preparation Time: 5 min
Cooking Time: 25 min

INGREDIENTS

- 2 tablespoons of olive oil, 500 g of turkey breast in chunks, 200 ml of tomato sauce, 1 lime juice, 1 tablespoon of sweet paprika, 10 g of fresh ginger, 1 chopped onion

DIRECTIONS

» Heat the oil in a non-stick pan and sauté the onion and garlic for 1 minute.
» Add the rest of the Ingredients and cook on a low flame for about 25 minutes.
» Serve hot.

BEANS SALAD

Servings: 1
Preparation Time: 5 min
Cooking Time: -

INGREDIENTS

- 200 g of cooked beans, ½ chopped red onion, 1 diced salad tomato, 1 fresh basil leaf, 1 tablespoon of olive oil

DIRECTIONS

» Mix all the Ingredients in a salad bowl and leave to flavor in the refrigerator for at least 30 minutes before serving.

ZUCCHINI AND PEPPERS STEW

Servings: 1
Preparation Time: 5 min
Cooking Time: 20 min

INGREDIENTS

- 1 diced courgette, 1 sliced tomato, 1 tablespoon of olive oil, 2 yellow peppers, ½ glass of quinoa, 1 sprig of parsley

DIRECTIONS

» Heat the oil in a pan and let the onion soak for about 2 minutes.
» Add the rest of the Ingredients, and dilute with water in case they get too dry, to avoid burning them.
» Cook for 15 minutes and serve hot.

CABBAGE AND PEPPER STEW

Servings: 1
Preparation Time: 5 min
Cooking Time: 20 min

INGREDIENTS

- 200 g of sliced cabbage, 1 sliced tomato, 1 tablespoon of olive oil, 2 yellow peppers, ½ glass of quinoa, 1 sprig of parsley

DIRECTIONS

» Heat the oil in a pan and let the onion soak for about 2 minutes.
» Add the rest of the Ingredients, and dilute with water in case they get too dry, to avoid burning them.
» Cook for 15 minutes and serve hot.

ZUCCHINI SOUP

Servings: 1
Preparation Time: 5 min
Cooking Time: 15 min

INGREDIENTS

- 1 tablespoon of olive oil, 1 chopped onion, 1 tablespoon of ginger powder, 2 courgettes, 200 ml of tomato sauce

DIRECTIONS

» In a pan heat the oil and cook the onion and zucchini for 2 minutes. Add the rest of the Ingredients, dilute with a glass of water and continue the Cooking Time for 10 minutes over very low heat.
» Serve hot.

ALMOND AND SHRIMP SALAD

Servings: 1
Preparation Time: 5 min
Cooking Time: 5 min

INGREDIENTS

- 20 g of chopped almonds, 1 sprig of chopped parsley, 150 g of prawns, juice of 1 lemon, 1 tablespoon of olive oil

DIRECTIONS

» Heat the oil in a pan and cook the prawns for 2 minutes per side. Let them cool, shell them and cut them into small pieces.
» Combine all the ingredients in a bowl, mix to blend the flavors and serve.

BAKED CHICKEN WITH POTATOES

Servings: 4
Preparation Time: 5 min
Cooking Time: 45 min

INGREDIENTS

- 1 kg of chicken pieces, 3 tablespoons of olive oil, 2 onions cut in half, 400 g of peeled and chopped potatoes, 1 sprig of rosemary, Salt to taste

DIRECTIONS

» In an oven pan, roll out some Cooking Time paper and place all the Ingredients, taking care to distribute them evenly.
» Bake for 45 minutes at 200 °, turning Cooking Time halfway to form a homogeneous crust.

STEW CHICKEN

Servings: 1
Preparation Time: 5 min
Cooking Time: 20 min

INGREDIENTS

- 200 g chicken breast in bite-sized pieces, 1 chopped shallot, 1 tablespoon of olive oil, 1 diced eggplant, 1 tablespoon of lime juice, 1 sprig of chopped parsley

DIRECTIONS

» Heat the oil in a pan and let the shallot soak for about 2 minutes.
» Add the rest of the Ingredients, and dilute with water in case they get too dry, to avoid burning them.
» Cook for 15 minutes and serve hot.

CARROT AND TURKEY SOUP

Servings: 2
Preparation Time: 5 min
Cooking Time: 20 min

INGREDIENTS

- 500 g turkey breast in bite-sized pieces, 1 tablespoon of tomato paste, 1 chopped onion, 2 chopped carrots, Salt to taste, Pepper to taste, 200 ml of water

DIRECTIONS

» Heat the oil in a pan and let the onion soak for about 2 minutes.
» Add the rest of the Ingredients, and dilute with water in case they get too dry, to avoid burning them.
» Cook for 15 minutes and serve hot.

CHICKEN AND LENTIL SOUP

Servings: 2
Preparation Time: 5 min
Cooking Time: 20 min

INGREDIENTS

- 500 g of turkey breast in bite-sized pieces, 1 tablespoon of tomato paste, 1 chopped onion, 200 g of cooked lentils, Salt to taste, Pepper to taste, 200 ml of water, 1 sprig of chopped parsley

DIRECTIONS

» Heat the oil in a pan and let the onion soak for about 2 minutes.
» Add the rest of the Ingredients, and dilute with water in case they get too dry, to avoid burning them.
» Cook for 15 minutes and serve hot.

BAKED PORK RIBS WITH POTATOES

Servings: 4
Preparation Time: 5 min
Cooking Time: 45 min

INGREDIENTS

- 1 kg of pork in pieces, 3 tablespoons of olive oil, 2 onions cut in half, 400 g of peeled and chopped potatoes, 1 sprig of rosemary, Salt to taste

DIRECTIONS

» In an oven pan, roll out some Cooking Time paper and place all the Ingredients, taking care to distribute them evenly. Bake for 45 minutes at 200 °, turning Cooking Time halfway to form a homogeneous crust.

TROUT SOUP

Servings: 2
Preparation Time: 5 min
Cooking Time: 20 min

INGREDIENTS

- 1 chopped onion, 1 sliced carrot, 400 g of trout fillet, 50 g of diced tomatoes, Salt to taste, 1 sprig of parsley, 1 tablespoon of olive oil, 200 ml of water

DIRECTIONS

» In a pan heat the oil and cook the onion for a minute. Add the trout fillets, sear for 2 minutes and then the rest of the Ingredients. Cook for 15 minutes, covered and on low heat. Serve hot.

PEA AND MINT SALAD

Servings: 1
Preparation Time: 5 min
Cooking Time: -

INGREDIENTS

- 200 g of cooked peas, ½ chopped red onion, 1 sprig of chopped fresh mint, 1 fresh basil leaf, 1 tablespoon of olive oil

DIRECTIONS

» Mix all the Ingredients in a salad bowl and leave to flavor in the refrigerator for at least 30 minutes before serving.

TURKEY STEW

Servings: 1
Preparation Time: 5 min
Cooking Time: 20 min

INGREDIENTS

- 200 g turkey breast in bite-sized pieces, 1 chopped shallot, 1 tablespoon of olive oil, 1 diced eggplant, 1 tablespoon of lime juice, 1 sprig of chopped parsley

DIRECTIONS

» Heat the oil in a pan and let the shallot soak for about 2 minutes.
» Add the rest of the Ingredients, and dilute with water in case they get too dry, to avoid burning them.
» Cook for 15 minutes and serve hot.

POTATO SOUP

Servings: 1
Preparation Time: 5 min
Cooking Time: 35 min

INGREDIENTS

- 2 cups of vegetable broth, 4 papatas cut into cubes, 1 chopped onion, 1 clove of garlic, Pepper to taste, Salt to taste, 1 tablespoon of olive oil, 100 ml of tomato sauce

DIRECTIONS

» Heat the oil in a pan and let the onion soak for about 2 minutes.
» Add the rest of the Ingredients, and dilute with water in case they get too dry, to avoid burning them.
» Cook for 35 minutes and serve hot.

SPICY CHICKEN SOUP

Servings: 2
Preparation Time: 5 min
Cooking Time: 25 min

INGREDIENTS

- 300 ml of vegetable broth, 1 tablespoon of ginger powder, 1 chopped onion, 500 g of chicken, 150 g of sliced mushrooms, 2 tablespoons of olive oil, juice of ½ lemon, 1 sprig of parsley, 4 chillies spicy

DIRECTIONS

» Heat the oil in a pan and add the onion, ginger, chillies and meat. Let it brown for 5 minutes.
» Add the rest of the Ingredients, cover and cook over low heat for another 20 minutes before serving.

SALMON FILLET IN A PAN

Servings: 1
Preparation Time: -
Cooking Time: 10 min

INGREDIENTS

- 200 g of salmon, 1 tablespoon of oil, salt to taste

DIRECTIONS

» Heat the oil in a pan, when it is very hot start the Cooking Time of the salmon on the skin side. Let it cook for about 8 minutes, until the skin has become crunchy.
» Turn it over and continue on the meat side for another 2 minutes. Turn off the heat, add salt and let it rest for 1 minute.
» Serve your beautiful salmon fillet hot, crunchy on the outside and soft on the inside.

POTATO AND SPINACH SALAD

Servings: 1
Preparation Time: 5 min
Cooking Time: -

INGREDIENTS

- 2 boiled potatoes into small pieces, 200 g of spinach, 1 sliced salad tomato, ½ sliced avocado, 1 tablespoon of oil, Salt to taste

DIRECTIONS

» Mix all the Ingredients in a salad bowl and leave to flavor in the refrigerator for at least 30 minutes before serving.

VELVETY BROCCOLI

Servings: 1
Preparation Time: 5 min
Cooking Time: 10 min

INGREDIENTS

- 200 g of broccoli, 100 ml of water, 1 tablespoon of olive oil, Salt to taste, Pepper to taste

DIRECTIONS

» Wash the broccoli and cut it into small pieces. Steam it for about 10 minutes and blend it with the mixer.
» Add water to taste, it depends how much liquid you prefer the dish.
» Season with salt and pepper and serve with a drizzle of oil.

SHRIMP AND ROCKET SALAD

Servings: 1
Preparation Time: 5 min
Cooking Time: 5 min

INGREDIENTS

- 60 g of rocket, 1 sprig of chopped parsley, 150 g of prawns, 1 tablespoon of balsamic vinegar, 1 tablespoon of olive oil, ½ orange juice

DIRECTIONS

» Heat the oil in a pan and cook the prawns for 2 minutes per side. Let them cool, shell them and cut them into small pieces.
» Combine all the ingredients in a bowl, mix to blend the flavors and serve.

PASTA SALAD

Servings: 1
Preparation Time: 5 min
Cooking Time: -

INGREDIENTS

- 80 g of freshly cooked pasta, 50g of chopped cherry tomatoes, 20 g of capers, 10 chopped olives, 1 tablespoon of oil, 1 leaf of fresh basil

DIRECTIONS

» Mix all the Ingredients in a salad bowl and leave to flavor in the refrigerator for at least 30 minutes before serving.

CAULIFLOWER SOUP

Servings: 2
Preparation Time: 5 min
Cooking Time: 25 min

INGREDIENTS

- 300 ml of vegetable broth, 1 chopped onion, 500 g of chopped cauliflower, 150 g of chopped potatoes, 2 tablespoons of olive oil, 200 ml of tomato sauce, 1 sprig of parsley

DIRECTIONS

» Heat the oil in a pan and add the onion and cauliflower. Let it brown for 5 minutes.
» Add the rest of the Ingredients, cover and cook over low heat for another 20 minutes before serving.

PORK SOUP

Servings: 2
Preparation Time: 5 min
Cooking Time: 25 min

INGREDIENTS

- 300 ml vegetable broth, 1 chopped onion, 500 g chopped pork, 150 g chopped potatoes, 2 tablespoons of olive oil, 200 ml tomato sauce, 1 chopped spring onions

DIRECTIONS

» Heat the oil in a pan and add the onion and pork. Let it brown for 5 minutes.
» Add the rest of the Ingredients, cover and cook over low heat for another 40 minutes before serving.

SHRIMP SALAD WITH OLIVES AND MINT

Servings: 1
Preparation Time: 5 min
Cooking Time: 5 min

INGREDIENTS

- 60 g of rocket, 1 sprig of chopped mint, 150 g of prawns, 1 tablespoon of balsamic vinegar, 1 tablespoon of olive oil, ½ orange juice, 10 sliced olives

DIRECTIONS

» Heat the oil in a pan and cook the prawns for 2 minutes per side. Let them cool, shell them and cut them into small pieces.
» Combine all the ingredients in a bowl, mix to blend the flavors and serve.

MIXED FISH SOUP

Servings: 2
Preparation Time: 5 min
Cooking Time: 15 min

INGREDIENTS

- 300 ml of vegetable broth, 1 chopped onion, 150 g of prawns, 150 g of cod fillet, 50 g of clams, 150 g of chopped potatoes, 2 tablespoons of olive oil, 200 ml of tomato sauce

DIRECTIONS

» Heat the oil in a pan and add the onion and potatoes. Let it brown for 5 minutes.
» Add the rest of the Ingredients, cover and cook over low heat for another 10 minutes before serving.

SPINACH AND TOMATO SOUP

Servings: 1
Preparation Time: 5 min
Cooking Time: 15 min

INGREDIENTS

- 25 g of chopped tomatoes, 100 ml of tomato sauce, 200 g of spinach, 200 ml of water, ½ chopped onion, 1 clove of garlic, Salt to taste, 1 tablespoon of olive oil

DIRECTIONS

» Heat the oil in a pan and add the onion and garlic. Let it brown for 5 minutes.
» Add the rest of the Ingredients, cover and cook over low heat for another 10 minutes before serving.

PORK FLAVORED WITH OREGANO

Servings: 2
Preparation Time: 5 min
Cooking Time: 30 min

INGREDIENTS

- 500 g of pork stew, 1 chopped onion, 1 clove of garlic, 1 tablespoon of oregano, 1 tablespoon of olive oil

DIRECTIONS

» Heat the oil in a pan for 1 minute, add the onion and garlic and stew for 3 minutes. Add the pork and oregano and cook for another 20 minutes over low heat.
» Let it rest in the pot before serving still hot.

SALMON AND MUSHROOM SALAD

Servings: 1
Preparation Time: 5 min
Cooking Time: -

INGREDIENTS

- 80 g smoked salmon, 80 g sliced fresh mushrooms, ½ chopped shallot, 50 g rocket, 4 sliced cherry tomatoes, 1 tablespoon of oil, 1 tablespoon of balsamic vinegar

DIRECTIONS

» Mix all the Ingredients in a salad bowl and leave to flavor in the refrigerator for at least 30 minutes before serving.

SAUTÉED PEAS

Servings: 1
Preparation Time: 5 min
Cooking Time: 30 min

INGREDIENTS

- 2 tablespoons of olive oil, 300 g of peas, 1 sweet potato, 2 cloves of garlic, 1 chopped shallot, 100 g of peeled tomatoes, 1 tablespoon of coriander, 200 ml of vegetable broth, 1 tablespoon of lemon juice

DIRECTIONS

» Heat some oil in a pan over medium heat, add the shallot and garlic and let it go for 5 minutes.
» Add the peas, potatoes and immediately after all the other Ingredients. Continue cooking for another 25 minutes over low heat. Serve hot.

SPICED CHICKEN MIX

Servings: 1
Preparation Time: 5 min
Cooking Time: 20 min

INGREDIENTS

- 1 tablespoon of olive oil, 200 g of chicken breast, 1/2 chopped onion, 10 g of fresh ginger, 1 clove of garlic, 1 tablespoon of lemon juice, Salt to taste

DIRECTIONS

» Heat some oil in a pan over medium heat, add the onion, ginger and garlic and let it go for 5 minutes.
» Add the chicken and continue the Cooking Time for another 5 minutes.
» Add the rest of the Ingredients, lower the heat and complete at Cooking Time for another 10 minutes. Serve hot.

LENTILS WITH VEGETABLES

Servings: 2
Preparation Time: 5 min
Cooking Time: 60 min

INGREDIENTS

- 250 g of lentils, 1 diced green pepper, 1 chopped onion, 1 tablespoon of olive oil, 1 carrot, 2 peeled tomatoes, Salt to taste

DIRECTIONS

» Fill a pot with water, add the cold lentils and bring to a boil. Continue cooking for another 10 minutes and remove the lentils from the heat.
» Heat the oil in a pan, add the onion, carrot, diced pepper and cook for 5 minutes.
» Add the lentils and the rest of the Ingredients, cook for 10 minutes and serve hot.

MUSSEL AND CLAM SOUP

Servings: 1
Preparation Time: 20 min
Cooking Time: 15 min

INGREDIENTS

- Clams 50 g, Mussels 50 g, Olive oil 2 tablespoons, 1 clove of garlic, Parsley to taste, Salt to taste, White wine 50 ml

DIRECTIONS

» Wash the clams and mussels under running water, being careful to remove any impurities. In particular, in mussels, care must be taken to remove the central tendon near the opening of the shell.
» In a fairly large saucepan, heat the oil and garlic. Once hot, add the shellfish and blend with the white wine.
» When the alcohol has evaporated, lower the heat and cover with a lid. In 5 minutes all the shells will be opened and ready to be tasted.
» Serve in a pan with a sprinkling of parsley.

GRILLED COD

Servings: 1
Preparation Time: 5 min
Cooking Time: 15 min

INGREDIENTS

- Cod 200 g, Olive oil 1 tablespoon, Lard 5 g, Lemon to taste, Salt to taste, Curry to taste

DIRECTIONS

» Turn on the grill and when the embers are ready, place the fish on it with the lard on top. The Cooking Time depends on the intensity of the flame, usually 7-8 minutes per side are sufficient. As a general rule, when the skin is dry and peeling off easily, the fish is usually ready.
» Separately, make a sauce with oil, lemon juice, salt and curry. Use a sprig of parsley to wet the meat of the fish during the Cooking Time and prevent it from becoming too dry.
» Serve freshly cooked.

HAKE SALAD

Servings: 1
Preparation Time: 5 min
Cooking Time: -

INGREDIENTS

- 100 g of cooked plaice, 30 g of black olives, 20 g chopped almonds, 1 tablespoon olive oil, 1 salad tomato

DIRECTIONS

» Mix all the Ingredients in a salad bowl and leave to flavor in the refrigerator for at least 30 minutes before serving.

BAKED HAKE WITH ZUCCHINI SALAD

Servings: 1
Preparation Time: 5 min
Cooking Time: 20 min

INGREDIENTS

- Hake 150 g, Zucchini 100 g, Green olives 15 g, Butter 10 g, Olive oil 2 tablespoons, Salt to taste, Lemon juice to taste

DIRECTIONS

» Clean the hake and divide it into fillets. Place it in a pan with oil, lard, salt and lemon juice.
» Turn on the oven at 200 degrees and cook for about 20 minutes.
» While the fish is in Cooking Time, wash the courgettes and cut them very finely into julienne strips.
» Season them with salt, pepper and extra virgin olive oil, you can add fresh mint to your liking.

SCRAMBLED EGGS WITH GREEN SALAD

Servings: 1
Preparation Time: 5 min
Cooking Time: 3 min

INGREDIENTS

- 3 whole eggs, green salad 100 g, pumpkin seeds 10 g, hazelnuts 20 g, black olives 15 g, olive oil 2 tablespoons

DIRECTIONS

» Break the eggs and beat them with a fork to incorporate a good amount of air and make them fluffy in Cooking Time.
» Heat 1 tablespoon of oil in a non-stick pan and pour the mixture. Immediately move it with a spoon and cook them for about 3 minutes, always turning them.
» Separately wash the salad and cut it finely. Season it with salt, extra virgin olive oil, pumpkin seeds and coarsely chopped hazelnuts.

CHICKEN WITH PEPPERS

Servings: 1
Preparation Time: 10 min
Cooking Time: 15 min

INGREDIENTS

- Chicken breast 150 g, Peppers 70 g, Pork sausage 50 g, Lard 20 g, Olive oil 1 tablespoon, Salt to taste, Chopped almonds 20 g Directions
- In a non-stick pan, heat the oil and lard.
- Cut the chicken into thin strips and the sausage into even pieces. Once the oil is hot, add the meat to the pan along with the chopped almonds and a pinch of salt. After about 5 minutes, add the chopped peppers.

- Cook for another 10 minutes, just enough time for the meat to flavor and for the peppers to dry.
- Season with salt if needed and serve hot.
- **Legume soup**

Servings: 1
Preparation Time: 10 min
- Cooking Time: 60 min

INGREDIENTS

- Peas 60 g, Borlotti beans 60 g, Cannellini beans 60 g, ½ onion, Lard 20 g, Parmesan 20 g, Olive oil 1 tablespoon, Rosemary to taste

DIRECTIONS

» In a pan, heat the oil and add the onion and lard. Once the onion is wilted, add 2 liters of water and all the legumes. Cover and simmer for at least 60 minutes. Just before it is ready, add the rosemary and season with salt. Serve hot with a sprinkling of Parmesan cheese and a drizzle of raw oil if you want.

TURKEY SALAD

Servings: 3
Preparation Time: 60 min
Cooking Time: 15 min

INGREDIENTS

- 200 g dry white wine, 80 g mixed salad, 70 g honey, 40 g walnuts, 4 artichokes, 30 g sunflower seeds, rosemary to taste, pepper to taste, 2 tablespoons extra virgin olive oil, turkey breast 500 g, Juice of ½ lemon

DIRECTIONS

» For the turkey salad, let the turkey marinate for at least 1 hour the meat with the wine, a pinch of thyme, pepper, sunflower seeds, honey, oil and salt.
» After 1 hour, cut it into small pieces and cook in the oven (including the marinade) at 140° for 15 minutes.
» Filter the juices released during the Cooking Time and set them aside in a bowl; add the juice of ½ lemon and 1 tablespoon of oil, thus obtaining an emulsion.
» Clean the artichokes and slice them finely. Let them marinate with lemon, salt and pepper for at least 15 minutes.
» Complete the salad with the finely chopped turkey breast, the artichokes and dress with the previously obtained emulsion.

VEGETABLES AND EGGS

Servings: 1
Preparation Time: 10 min
Cooking Time: 25 min

INGREDIENTS

- 3 whole eggs, 10 cherry tomatoes, 2 courgettes, 2 carrots, 1 green pepper, ½ red onion, olive oil, salt to taste, fresh mushrooms 200 g

DIRECTIONS

» To prepare this recipe, start by washing the tomatoes, courgettes, carrots, bell pepper, onion and mushrooms. Cut the carrots and courgettes into thin slices, the tomatoes in half and mushrooms into pieces. Cut the pepper into 4 parts, remove the seeds and the central part and slice it into julienne strips.
» In a non-stick pan, fry the finely chopped onion in a drizzle of oil.
» Add the carrots and sauté for 5 minutes. Add zucchini and peppers and cook for another 5 minutes. If you see that it gets too dry in Cooking Time, add some water from the vegetable broth. When it is almost ready, finally add the tomatoes and mushrooms, letting them dry for another 10 minutes.
» When the vegetables are cooked add the eggs to the pan, season with salt and pepper and cover with a lid. Let it cook for 5 minutes and serve hot in a pan.

TURKEY BITES WITH RAISINS AND PINE NUTS

Servings: 4
Preparation Time: 10 min
Cooking Time: 25 min

INGREDIENTS

- 700 g of turkey breast, 250 g of courgettes, 60 g of raisins, 40 g of pine nuts, fresh thyme to taste, white wine to taste, 1 tablespoon olive oil, salt to taste, pepper to taste

DIRECTIONS

» Clean the courgettes and cut them into regular cubes. Cut the turkey breast into bite-sized pieces and marinate it with salt, oil and pepper for 10 minutes.
» Heat a little oil in a non-stick pan and brown the turkey; after a couple of minutes add the raisins, pine nuts, thyme and courgettes.
» Deglaze with a glass of white wine and season with salt and pepper; continue to cook for about 10 minutes.
» Serve with fresh thyme to taste.

CHICKEN WITH BALSAMIC VINEGAR AND CAULIFLOWER

Servings: 2
Preparation Time: 5 min
Cooking Time: 25 min

INGREDIENTS

- 500 g of chicken breast, 250 g of cabbage, 1 tablespoon of olive oil, 1 tablespoon of balsamic vinegar, 1 chopped red onion, 1 clove of garlic, Salt to taste

DIRECTIONS

» Heat some oil in a pan over medium heat, add the onion and garlic and let it go for 5 minutes.
» Add the chicken and immediately after all the other

Ingredients. Continue cooking for another 20 minutes over low heat. Serve hot.

TOMATO SOUP

Servings: 1
Preparation Time: 5 min
Cooking Time: 15 min

INGREDIENTS

- 1 clove of garlic, 1 chopped onion, 2 sliced carrots, 1 tablespoon of olive oil, 20 diced peeled tomatoes, 250 ml of water, 1 pinch of oregano, 1 basil leaf

DIRECTIONS

» Heat the oil in a pan and add the onion and garlic. Let it brown for 5 minutes.
» Add the rest of the Ingredients, cover and cook over low heat for another 10 minutes before serving.

CARROT SOUP

Servings: 1
Preparation Time: 5 min
Cooking Time: 25 min

INGREDIENTS

- 4 sliced carrots, 1 tablespoon of olive oil, 1 chopped onion, 250 ml of water, 2 eggs, Salt to taste, Pepper to taste, Oregano to taste

DIRECTIONS

» Heat the oil in a pan and add the onion. Let it brown for 5 minutes.
» Add the rest of the Ingredients, cover and cook over low heat for another 10 minutes before serving.

AVOCADO HUMUS

Servings: 1
Preparation Time: 10 min
Cooking Time: -

INGREDIENTS

- 1 large (or 2 small) avocado, 250 g of fresh peas, 1 lime, Cumin powder to taste, 2 tablespoons of extra virgin olive oil, Toasted pumpkin seeds to taste, Salt to taste,
- Pepper as needed

DIRECTIONS

» To make hummus, start by peeling the avocado, cutting it into small pieces and placing it in a bowl.
» Add the previously blanched peas; mix evenly.
» Add the lime juice taking care to remove the bones, cumin, salt and pepper. With an immersion blender, blend the Ingredients until you get a homogeneous mixture. Add the oil without turning off the blender and continue to work it until you get a cream; taste and adjust salt if necessary.
» Transfer to a bowl and add the toasted pumpkin seeds on top.

SHRIMP WITH CUCUMBERS, AVOCADO, TOMATOES AND APPLES

Servings: 1
Preparation Time: 10 min
Cooking Time: -

INGREDIENTS

- 2 cucumbers, 1 apple, 150 g of cherry tomatoes, 1 avocado, 150 g of prawns, 1 lime, olive oil to taste, salt to taste, pepper to taste

DIRECTIONS

» To make this recipe, start by cleaning the shrimp under running water for 1 minute. Shell them and transfer them to a pan with avocado and diced apples.
» Cut the datterini tomatoes into 4 parts and add them to the rest of the Ingredients. Cut the cucumbers into very thin slices and add them to the rest; season with lime juice.
» Taste and adjust with salt and pepper if necessary.

PAO DE VALENCIA

Servings: 1
Preparation Time: 15 min
Cooking Time: 20 min

INGREDIENTS

- Hazelnut flour 30 g, diced bacon 25 g, butter 20 g, grated pecorino cheese 30 g, cooking cream 25 g, olive oil 2 tablespoons

DIRECTIONS

» Weigh all the Ingredients and place them in the tray to process them. Start by mixing the hazelnut flour with the grated pecorino; mix them evenly and add the diced bacon. At this point you can start adding the fats: cream, oil and butter at room temperature; if the mixture is too dry you can add water to work it better. When the ingredients are well blended, start making small meatballs. Bake them in the oven at 170 degrees for 15-20 minutes.

SICILIAN COD WITH MARINATED COURGETTES

Servings: 1
Preparation Time: 10 min
Cooking Time: 10 min

INGREDIENTS

- Cod 130 g, Capers 10 g, Lard 10 g, Zucchini 80 g, Black

olives 30 g, Olive oil 1 tablespoon, Salt to taste, Mint, lemon and vinegar to taste

DIRECTIONS

» Start by heating the oil in a non-stick pan over low heat; after about 1 minute add the cod fillets, capers and black olives.
» Spread the lard over the fish, this will give it an unmistakable flavor and make it much more biting and less dry.
» Cover and cook on each side for about 5 minutes. Season with salt before serving.
» Wash, loose and finely slice the courgettes. Season them with a drizzle of oil, salt, mint, lemon or vinegar to taste. Serve them as a side dish for fish.

HAKE AND SOY SOUP WITH VEGETABLES

Servings: 2
Preparation Time: 15 min
Cooking Time: 80 min

INGREDIENTS

- 1 tablespoon of olive oil, ½ chopped onion, 1 clove of garlic, 1 carrot, 1 sprig of parsley, 200 g of hake, 250 g of soy

DIRECTIONS

» Put the soy in a container, add water to cover them and let them rest overnight, in order to rehydrate it. The next day pour into a pot full of water and cook for about 1 hour.
» In a pan, heat some oil and start cooking garlic, onion and carrot.
» Let it fry for a few minutes and then add the parsley. Pour the soy and hake, cook over low heat for about 20 minutes and the dish is finally ready.

SPELLED WITH BROCCOLI AND PEAS

Servings: 2
Preparation Time: 10 min
Cooking Time: 40 min

INGREDIENTS

- 100 g of spelled, 150 g of peas, 1 cabbage, 1 onion, 10 g of fresh ginger, 2 tablespoons of olive oil, Salt to taste, Pepper to taste

DIRECTIONS

» Boil the cabbage in salted water for about 10 minutes.
» Meanwhile, toast the spelled in a non-stick pan for 5 minutes, then drain the cabbage and use the same water to cook the spelled for about 20 minutes.
» In a separate pan, fry the onion and ginger in oil, add the cabbage, the peas and finally the spelled.
» Stir and cook over low heat for another 10 minutes. Serve still hot.

SPELLED BURGER

Servings: 2
Preparation Time: 15 min
Cooking Time: 40 min

INGREDIENTS

- 200 g of spelled, 100 g of lentils, 35 g of chopped pumpkin seeds, ½ chopped onion, 1 clove of garlic, 1 sprig of rosemary, 1 tablespoon of soy sauce, 1 tablespoon of wholemeal flour, ½ fresh chilli

DIRECTIONS

» Finely chop the garlic and onion and place them in a saucepan.
» Add the spices, spelled, lentils (the last two are obviously cooked previously) and add 600 ml of water.
» Turn on the heat or and cook until all the water has been absorbed. Remove the sprig of rosemary and transfer everything to a large enough salad bowl.
» Add the rest of the Ingredients and mix well until smooth.
» Shape the burgers with your hands, they don't have to be all the same, that's the beauty of cooking at home. Place them on a baking sheet and cook for 20 minutes at 180 °, taking care to turn them halfway through Cooking Time.

TURKEY SALAD, BEAN CREAM AND VINEGARED SHALLOTS

Servings: 2
Preparation Time: 60 min
Cooking Time: 60 min

INGREDIENTS

- Turkey breast 250 g, 150 g of dried beans, 150 g of shallots, 4 tablespoons olive oil, 20 ml of wine vinegar, Salt to taste, Pepper to taste

DIRECTIONS

» The first thing to do is to put the dried beans in water for 12 hours; after this time you can rinse them and cook them in salted water for about 45 minutes.
» Clean and slice the shallot, fry it in a non-stick pan with 1 tablespoon of oil and a pinch of salt; after about 5 minutes of Cooking Time add the vinegar and let it reduce for another 3 minutes, in this way they will remain fresh and crunchy.
» Grill the turkey in a pan with oil and salt for 2 minutes per side, once cooked, cut into cubes. Sauté the beans in a pan with oil for 10 minutes, at the end of which you can mash them with a fork to make them creamy.
» Combine the turkey, bean cream, and scallions in a salad bowl. Let it rest in the fridge for about 1 hour.

CHICKEN IN COCONUT MILK AND LIME JUICE

Servings: 4
Preparation Time: 60 min
Cooking Time: 60 min

INGREDIENTS

- 800 g of chicken legs, 250 g of sweet potatoes, 200 g of coconut milk, 150 g of broccoli, 150 g of carrots, 50 g of fresh ginger, 25 g of green pepper, 2 limes, 120 g of shallots, 2 cloves of garlic, 4 tbsp olive oil

DIRECTIONS

» For this oriental-flavored recipe, start by marinating the chicken with coconut milk, garlic, ginger, green pepper and 1 sliced lime; let it rest for about 1 hour, stirring it from time to time.
» Meanwhile, boil the sweet potato, it must cook for about 30 minutes; to be sure of the Cooking Time stick it with a fork, if it enters easily up to the center, it is ready.
» In a very large pan, heat the oil with the shallot and after two minutes start cooking the chicken with half of its marinade; cover for the first 15 minutes to keep liquids from evaporating too quickly.
» After 15 minutes, add the broccoli, carrots and sweet potato, sprinkle with the lime juice and season with salt.
» If it dries too much, add the marinade juice a little at a time to prevent burning. Cooking Time is very subjective, I personally like it well cooked and with crispy chicken skin, so it has to cook for at least 60 minutes.
» Serve hot with Cooking Time stock as a sauce.

SALMON MOUSSE

Servings: 1
Preparation Time: 75 min
Cooking Time: -

INGREDIENTS

- 100 g of smoked salmon, 200 g of robiola, 50 ml of cream, 15 g of capers, lemon peel to taste, salt to taste, pepper to taste

DIRECTIONS

» To prepare this fantastic salmon mousse, start by mixing the salmon with capers, cream and robiola; turn on the mixer and chop until you get a fairly homogeneous cream.
» Transfer the mixture obtained to a bowl and season it with salt and pepper; cover with plastic wrap and let it rest in the fridge for at least 1 hour.
» You can serve it in quenelles with grated lemon peel to add a touch of freshness.

SALMON WITH BUTTER SAUCE AND CAPERS

Servings: 4
Preparation Time: 15 min
Cooking Time: 15 min

INGREDIENTS

- 4 slices of fresh salmon of about 150 g each, 40 g of butter, 20 g of capers, olive oil to taste, salt to taste, pepper to taste

DIRECTIONS

» To prepare the salmon in a butter and caper sauce, start by peeling and drying the fish steaks; then heat some oil in a non-stick pan and start the Salmon Cooking Time.
» Cook over medium heat for about 6-7 minutes, when they are almost ready add salt and pepper.
» Meanwhile, let the butter melt in another pan over low heat; after about 1 minute add the capers and let it go off the heat.
» Season the salmon with the sauce and serve still hot.

FRESH ROBIOLA WITH COURGETTE SIDE DISH

Servings: 4
Preparation Time: 2 min
Cooking Time: 6 min

INGREDIENTS

- 60 g of robiola, 70 g of courgettes, 1 tablespoon olive oil, 2 chopped mint leaves, 1 tablespoon of olive oil

DIRECTIONS

» Heat the oil in a pan and start stewing the zucchini over low heat. Halfway through the Cooking Time (after about 3 minutes) add the mint and cover, in order to release the strong aroma.
» Cook for about 5-6 minutes, leave to cool and serve as a side dish for the robiola.

CHICKEN KABOBS

Preparation Time: 10 minutes
Cooking Time: 5 minutes
Servings: 4

INGREDIENTS:

- 1 pound skinless, boneless chicken breast halves, cut into 1-inch pieces
- 1/4 cup plain low-fat yogurt
- 1 tablespoon lemon juice
- 1 teaspoon dry mustard
- 1 teaspoon ground cinnamon
- 1 teaspoon curry powder
- 1/2 teaspoon salt
- 1/4 teaspoon red pepper, crushed
- 1 large red sweet pepper, diced
- 1 yellow squash, cut into 1/2-inch-thick slices

- Tomato Relish for garnish

DIRECTIONS:

- » Mix chicken with yogurt, mustard, cinnamon, salt, curry powder, red pepper, and lemon juice in a bowl.
- » Refrigerate for an hour.
- » Preheat the oven broiler.
- » Thread the marinated chicken sweet pepper and squash on the wooden skewers.
- » Grill all the skewers for 5 minutes per side on medium heat.
- » Serve warm with tomato relish.

Nutrition: Calories 345 Total Fat 16.4g 9.1 g Cholesterol 142mg Sodium 471 mg Carbs 8.7 g Protein 38.5 g

---

CURRIED CHICKEN PARCELS

Preparation Time: 15 minutes
Cooking Time: 20 minutes
Servings: 4

INGREDIENTS:

- 2 cups chopped cooked chicken
- 1/2 cup chopped celery
- 1/3 cup part-skim ricotta cheese
- 1/4 cup shredded carrot
- 1 tablespoon apricot preserves
- 1 teaspoon curry powder
- 1/4 teaspoon ground cinnamon
- Dash salt
- 1 10-oz. package refrigerated pizza dough

DIRECTIONS:

- » Mix chicken with ricotta, carrot, celery, preserves, cinnamon, salt and curry powder in a bowl.
- » Spread the pizza dough and slice it into 6 squares of equal size.
- » Divide the chicken carrot mixture over the squares.
- » Bring all the corners of each towards it center and seal the edges by pinching them together.
- » Place these bundles on a baking sheet.
- » Bake for 15 minutes at 375 degrees until golden brown. Allow them to cool.
- » Serve.

Nutrition: Calories 415 Total Fat 32.8g Saturated Fat 5.1 g Cholesterol 4.1 mg Sodium 278 mg Carbs 14.7 g Fiber 2.4 g Sugar 1.9 g Protein 31.2 g

---

TUNA SALAD-STUFFED TOMATOES WITH ARUGULA

Preparation Time: 5 minutes
Cooking Time: 15 minutes
Servings: 4

INGREDIENTS

- 1 teaspoon dried thyme
- 3 tablespoons sherry vinegar
- 3 tablespoons extra-virgin olive oil
- 1/3 cup chopped celery
- 1/4 teaspoon freshly ground pepper
- 4 large tomatoes
- 8 cups baby arugula
- 1/4 cup finely chopped red onion
- 1/4 teaspoon salt
- 1/4 cup chopped Kalamata olives
- 2 5-ounce cans chunk light tuna in olive oil, drained
- 1 15-ounce can great northern beans, rinsed

DIRECTIONS:

- » Whisk oil, salt, vinegar, and pepper in an average-sized bowl. Transfer 3 tablespoons of the dressing to a big bowl and set aside.
- » Slice enough off the top of each tomato to remove the core, chop enough of the tops to equal ½ cup and add to the average-sized bowl. Scoop out the tomato soft tissue using a teaspoon or melon baller and discard the pulp
- » Add tuna, onion, thyme, olives, and celery to the average-sized bowl; gently toss to mix. Fill the scooped tomatoes with the tuna mixture.
- » Add beans and arugula to the gauze in the large bowl and toss to mix. Divide the salad into four plates and top each with a satiated tomato.

Nutrition: 353 calories 17.6 g total fat 7 mg of cholesterol 501 mg sodium 878 mg potassium 29.9 g; carbohydrates 10.7 g fiber 9 g sugar 19.7 g protein

---

HERBED SEAFOOD CASSEROLE

Preparation Time: 40 minutes
Cooking Time: 50 minutes
Servings: 12

INGREDIENTS

- 1 ½ cups uncooked long grain rice
- 2 tablespoons butter
- ¼ teaspoon pepper
- 2 tablespoons minced fresh parsley
- 1 medium onion, finely chopped
- 3 garlic cloves, minced
- 1 medium carrot, shredded
- ½ teaspoon salt
- 3 celery ribs, thinly sliced
- 1 ½ teaspoon snipped fresh dill or ½ teaspoon dill weed
- SEAFOOD:
- 1-pound uncooked medium shrimp, peeled and deveined
- 1 can (16 ounces) crabmeat, drained, flaked and cartilage removed
- ¼ cup all-purpose flour
- 1-pound bay scallops
- ½ teaspoon salt
- 1 package (8 ounces) cream cheese, cubed
- 5 tablespoons butter, cubed
- 1 ½ cups half-and-half cream
- 1 ½ teaspoon snipped fresh dill or ½ teaspoon dill weed
- ¼ teaspoon dried thyme
- ¼ teaspoon pepper
- TOPPING:
- 2 tablespoons butter, melted
- 1 ½ cups soft bread crumbs

DIRECTIONS:

- Preheat oven to 325°F. Cook rice according to package directions. In the meantime, in a big skillet, heat butter over moderate heat. Add onion celery, and carrot; cook and stir until crisp-tender. Add garlic, pepper, and salt; cook 1 minute longer.
- Add to the cooked rice. Stir in parsley and dill. Transfer to a greased baking dish.
- Fill a large saucepan with 2/3 full with water and bring to a boil. Reduce heat to medium. Add shrimp; simmer, uncovered, for 30 seconds. Add scallops; simmer for 3 minutes or just until shrimp turn pink and scallops are firm and dense. Drain, reserving 1 cup cooking liquid. Place seafood in a large bowl; stir in crab.
- In a small saucepan, melt butter over medium heat. Stir in flour until mixed; slowly stir in cream and kept cooking liquid. Bring to a boil; cook and stir for 2 minutes or until condensed and foamy. Reduce heat. Stir in cream cheese, dill and season until smooth. Stir into the seafood blend.
- Pour over rice mixture. Toss bread crumbs with melted butter; sprinkle over top. Bake, uncovered, 50 minutes or until it turns golden brown. Stand 10 minutes before dishing.

Nutrition: 404 calories 20g fat 150mg cholesterol 616mg sodium 29g carbohydrate ;3g sugars 1g fiber 26g protein.

SHRIMP PASTA PRIMAVERA

Preparation Time: 5 minutes
Cooking Time: 15 minutes
Serving: 4

INGREDIENTS:

- 1-1/4 cup fresh asparagus, sliced into 1-inch lengths (about 1/2 pound)
- 1 tablespoon garlic, minced
- 12 ounces whole wheat penne pasta
- 1/2 cup green onion, sliced thinly
- 1 cup green peas, fresh or frozen
- 2 teaspoons olive oil
- 1/8 teaspoon red pepper, crushed
- 2 teaspoons fresh lemon juice
- 1 tablespoon fresh parsley, chopped
- 1/3 cup grated Parmesan cheese
- 1 lb. shrimp, peeled and deveined
- 1/2 teaspoons salt
- Fresh ground black pepper

DIRECTIONS:

- Boil water in a 6-quart pot and add asparagus and peas for 4 minutes.
- Drain and rinse then set them aside.
- Cook pasta as per the given instructions on the box.
- Drain and rinse the pasta.
- Heat oil in a skillet and add garlic and red pepper.
- Cook for 1 minute then adds shrimp.
- Sauté for 2 minutes per side.
- Stir in all the remaining ingredients.
- Cook for 4 to 5 minutes.
- Serve warm.

Nutrition: Calories 249 Total Carbs 1.8 g Total Fat 12 g Sodium 79 mg Fiber 1.1 g Sugar 0.3 g Protein 35 g

FAJITA CHICKEN WRAPS

Preparation Time: 10 minutes
Cooking Time: 10 minutes
Servings: 4

INGREDIENTS:

- 12 oz. skinless chicken breast strips
- 1/2 teaspoon chili powder
- 1/4 teaspoon garlic powder
- Nonstick cooking spray
- 1 red or green sweet pepper, seeded and cut into strips
- 2 tablespoons bottled reduced-calorie ranch salad dressing
- 2 10-inch whole wheat tortillas
- 1/2 cup Salsa
- 1/3 cup reduced-fat shredded cheddar cheese

DIRECTIONS:

- Mix chicken strips with garlic powder and chili powder.
- Heat a skillet greased with cooking spray on medium heat.
- Add chicken and sweet peppers. Cook for 6 minutes.
- Toss in salad dressing.
- Divide this mixture in warmed tortillas.
- Top each tortilla with cheese and salsa.
- Roll each tortilla and cut them in half.
- Serve.

Nutrition: Calories 245 Total Fat 16.4 g Saturated Fat 9.1g Cholesterol 143 mg Sodium 471 mg Total Carbs 8.7 g Fiber 0.7 g Sugar 0.3 g Protein 38.5 g

CURRIED PORK TENDERLOIN IN APPLE CIDER

Preparation Time: 10 minutes
Cooking Time: 26 minutes
Servings: 6

INGREDIENTS:

- 16 ounces pork tenderloin, cut into 6 pieces
- 1 ½ tablespoons curry powder
- 1 tablespoon extra-virgin olive oil
- 2 medium onions, chopped
- 2 cups apple cider, organic and unsweetened
- 1 tart apple, peeled and chopped into chunks

DIRECTIONS:

- In a bowl, season the pork with the curry powder and set aside.
- Heat oil in a pot over medium flame.
- Sauté the onions for one minute until fragrant.
- Stir in the seasoned pork tenderloin and cook for 5 minutes or until lightly golden.
- Add in the apple cider and apple chunks.
- Close the lid and bring to a boil.
- Allow to simmer for 20 minutes.

Nutrition: Calories: 244; Protein: 24g; Carbs: 18g; Fat: 8g; Saturated Fat: 2g; Sodium: 70mg

HONEY CRUSTED CHICKEN

Preparation Time: 10 minutes
Cooking Time: 25 minutes
Servings: 2

INGREDIENTS:

- 1 teaspoon paprika
- 8 saltine crackers, 2 inches square
- 2 chicken breasts, each 4 ounces
- 4 tsp honey

DIRECTIONS:

» Set the oven to heat at 375 degrees F. Grease a baking dish with cooking oil. Smash the crackers in a Ziplock bag and toss them with paprika in a bowl. Brush chicken with honey and add it to the crackers.
» Mix well and transfer the chicken to the baking dish. Bake the chicken for 25 minutes until golden brown. Serve.

Nutrition: Calories 219 Fat 17 g Sodium 456 mg Carbs 12.1 g Protein 31 g

Chapter 7
Side Dishes

TURMERIC ENDIVES

Preparation Time: 10 minutes
Cooking Time: 20 minutes
Servings: 4

INGREDIENTS:

- 2 endives, halved lengthwise
- 2 tablespoons olive oil
- 1 teaspoon rosemary, dried
- ½ teaspoon turmeric powder
- A pinch of black pepper

DIRECTIONS:

» Mix the endives with the oil and the other ingredients in a baking pan, toss gently, bake at 400 degrees F within 20 minutes. Serve as a side dish.

Nutrition: Calories 64; Protein 0.2g; Carbohydrates 0.8g; Fat: 7.1g; Fiber 0.6g; Sodium: 3mg; Potassium 50mg

PARMESAN ENDIVES

Preparation Time: 10 minutes
Cooking Time: 20 minutes
Servings: 4

INGREDIENTS:

- 4 endives, halved lengthwise
- 1 tablespoon lemon juice
- 1 tablespoon lemon zest, grated
- 2 tablespoons fat-free parmesan, grated
- 2 tablespoons olive oil
- A pinch of black pepper

DIRECTIONS:

» In a baking dish, combine the endives with the lemon juice and the other ingredients except for the parmesan and toss. Sprinkle the parmesan on top, bake the endives at 400 degrees F for 20 minutes, and serve.

Nutrition: Calories 71 Protein 0.9g Carbohydrates 2.2g; Fat: 7.1g Fiber 0.9g Sodium 71mg; Potassium 88mg

LEMON ASPARAGUS

Preparation Time: 10 minutes
Cooking Time: 20 minutes
Servings: 4

INGREDIENTS:

- 1-pound asparagus, trimmed
- 2 tablespoons basil pesto
- 1 tablespoon lemon juice
- A pinch of black pepper
- 3 tablespoons olive oil
- 2 tablespoons cilantro, chopped

DIRECTIONS:

» Arrange the asparagus n a lined baking sheet, add the pesto and the other ingredients, toss, bake at 400 degrees F within 20 minutes. Serve as a side dish.

Nutrition: Calories 114 Protein 2.6g; Carbohydrates 4.5g; Fat: 10.7g Fiber 2.4g; Sodium: 3mg; Potassium 240mg

LIME CARROTS

Preparation Time: 10 minutes
Cooking Time: 30 minutes
Servings: 4

INGREDIENTS:

- 1-pound baby carrots, trimmed
- 1 tablespoon sweet paprika
- 1 teaspoon lime juice
- 3 tablespoons olive oil
- A pinch of black pepper
- 1 teaspoon sesame seeds

DIRECTIONS:

» Arrange the carrots on a lined baking sheet, add the paprika and the other ingredients except for the sesame seeds, toss, bake at 400 degrees F within 30 minutes. Divide the carrots between plates, sprinkle sesame seeds on top and serve as a side dish.

Nutrition: Calories 139mProtein 1.1g; Carbohydrates 10.5g Fat 11.2g

4g fiber Sodium 89mg; Potassium 313mg

GARLIC POTATO PAN

Preparation Time: 10 minutes
Cooking Time: 1 hour
Servings: 8

INGREDIENTS:

- 1-pound gold potatoes, peeled and cut into wedges
- 2 tablespoons olive oil
- 1 red onion, chopped
- 2 garlic cloves, minced
- 2 cups coconut cream
- 1 tablespoon thyme, chopped
- ¼ teaspoon nutmeg, ground
- ½ cup low-fat parmesan, grated

DIRECTIONS:

» Warm-up a pan with the oil over medium heat, put the onion plus the garlic, and sauté for 5 minutes. Add the potatoes and brown them for 5 minutes more.
» Add the cream and the rest of the ingredients, toss gently, bring to a simmer and cook over medium heat within 40 minutes more. Divide the mix between plates and serve as a side dish.

Nutrition: Calories 230; Protein 3.6g; Carbohydrates 14.3g; Fat: 19.1g; Fiber 3.3g; Cholesterol 6mg; Sodium: 105mg; Potassium 426mg

BALSAMIC CABBAGE

Preparation Time: 10 minutes
Cooking Time: 20 minutes
Servings: 4

INGREDIENTS:

- 1-pound green cabbage, roughly shredded
- 2 tablespoons olive oil
- A pinch of black pepper
- 1 shallot, chopped
- 2 garlic cloves, minced
- 2 tablespoons balsamic vinegar
- 2 teaspoons hot paprika
- 1 teaspoon sesame seeds

DIRECTIONS:

» Heat-up a pan with the oil over medium heat, add the shallot and the garlic, and sauté for 5 minutes. Add the cabbage and the other ingredients, toss, cook over medium heat for 15 minutes, divide between plates and serve.

Nutrition: Calories 100; Protein 1.8g; Carbohydrates 8.2g; Fat: 7.5g; Fiber 3g; Sodium: 22mg; Potassium 225mg

CHILI BROCCOLI

Preparation Time: 10 minutes
Cooking Time: 30 minutes
Servings: 4

INGREDIENTS:

- 2 tablespoons olive oil
- 1-pound broccoli florets
- 2 garlic cloves, minced
- 2 tablespoons chili sauce
- 1 tablespoon lemon juice
- A pinch of black pepper
- 2 tablespoons cilantro, chopped

DIRECTIONS:

» In a baking pan, combine the broccoli with the oil, garlic, and the other, toss a bit, and bake at 400 degrees F for 30 minutes. Divide the mix between plates and serve as a side dish.

Nutrition: Calories 103 Protein 3.4g; Carbohydrates 8.3gz 7.4g fat 3g fiber; Sodium: 229mg Potassium 383mg

HOT BRUSSELS SPROUTS

Preparation Time: 10 minutes
Cooking Time: 25 minutes
Servings: 4

INGREDIENTS:

- 1 tablespoon olive oil
- 1-pound Brussels sprouts, trimmed and halved
- 2 garlic cloves, minced
- ½ cup low-fat mozzarella, shredded
- A pinch of pepper flakes, crushed

DIRECTIONS:

» In a baking dish, combine the sprouts with the oil and the other ingredients except for the cheese and toss. Sprinkle the cheese on top, introduce in the oven and bake at 400 degrees F for 25 minutes. Divide between plates and serve as a side dish.

Nutrition: Calories 111 Protein 10g Carbohydrates 11.6g; Fat: 3.9g Fiber 5g Cholesterol 4mg; Sodium: 209mg; Potassium 447mg

PAPRIKA BRUSSELS SPROUTS

Preparation Time: 10 minutes
Cooking Time: 25 minutes
Servings: 4

INGREDIENTS:

- 2 tablespoons olive oil
- 1-pound Brussels sprouts, trimmed and halved
- 3 green onions, chopped
- 2 garlic cloves, minced
- 1 tablespoon balsamic vinegar
- 1 tablespoon sweet paprika

- A pinch of black pepper

DIRECTIONS:

» In a baking pan, combine the Brussels sprouts with the oil and the other ingredients, toss and bake at 400 degrees F within 25 minutes. Divide the mix between plates and serve.

Nutrition: Calories 121 Protein 4.4g Carbohydrates 12.6g; Fat: 7.6g Fiber 5.2g Sodium 31mg Potassium 521mg

CREAMY CAULIFLOWER MASH

Preparation Time: 10 minutes
Cooking Time: 25 minutes
Servings: 4

INGREDIENTS:

- 2 pounds cauliflower florets
- ½ cup of coconut milk
- A pinch of black pepper
- ½ cup low-fat sour cream
- 1 tablespoon cilantro, chopped
- 1 tablespoon chives, chopped

DIRECTIONS:

» Put the cauliflower in a pot, add water to cover, bring to a boil over medium heat, cook for 25 minutes and drain. Mash the cauliflower, add the milk, black pepper, and the cream, whisk well, divide between plates, sprinkle the rest of the ingredients on top, and serve.

Nutrition: Calories 188 Protein 6.1g; Carbohydrates 15g; Fat: 13.4g Fiber 6.4g Cholesterol 13mg; Sodium: 88mg Potassium 811mg

AVOCADO, TOMATO, AND OLIVES SALAD

Preparation Time: 5 minutes
Cooking Time: 0 minutes
Servings: 4

INGREDIENTS:

- 2 tablespoons olive oil
- 2 avocados, cut into wedges
- 1 cup kalamata olives, pitted and halved
- 1 cup tomatoes, cubed
- 1 tablespoon ginger, grated
- A pinch of black pepper
- 2 cups baby arugula
- 1 tablespoon balsamic vinegar

DIRECTIONS:

» In a bowl, combine the avocados with the kalamata and the other ingredients, toss and serve as a side dish.

Nutrition: Calories 320 Protein 3g Carbohydrates 13.9g Fat 30.4g Fiber 8.7g Sodium 305mg Potassium 655mg

RADISH AND OLIVES SALAD

Preparation Time: 5 minutes
Cooking Time: 0 minutes
Servings: 4

INGREDIENTS:

- 2 green onions, sliced
- 1-pound radishes, cubed
- 2 tablespoons balsamic vinegar
- 2 tablespoon olive oil
- 1 teaspoon chili powder
- 1 cup black olives, pitted and halved
- A pinch of black pepper

DIRECTIONS:

» Mix radishes with the onions and the other ingredients in a large salad bowl, toss, and serve as a side dish.

Nutrition: Calories 123 Protein 1.3g; Carbohydrates 6.9g Fat 10.8g; Fiber 3.3g Sodium 345mg; Potassium 306mg

SPINACH AND ENDIVES SALAD

Preparation Time: 5 minutes
Cooking Time: 0 minutes
Servings: 4

INGREDIENTS:

- 2 endives, roughly shredded
- 1 tablespoon dill, chopped
- ¼ cup lemon juice
- ¼ cup olive oil
- 2 cups baby spinach
- 2 tomatoes, cubed
- 1 cucumber, sliced
- ½ cups walnuts, chopped

DIRECTIONS:

» In a large bowl, combine the endives with the spinach and the other ingredients, toss and serve as a side dish.

Nutrition: Calories 238; Protein 5.7g; Carbohydrates 8.4g; Fat: 22.3g; Fiber 3.1g; Sodium: 24mg; Potassium 506mg

BASIL OLIVES MIX

Preparation Time: 5 minutes
Cooking Time: 0 minutes
Servings: 4

INGREDIENTS:

- 2 tablespoons olive oil
- 1 tablespoon balsamic vinegar
- A pinch of black pepper
- 4 cups corn
- 2 cups black olives, pitted and halved
- 1 red onion, chopped
- ½ cup cherry tomatoes halved
- 1 tablespoon basil, chopped
- 1 tablespoon jalapeno, chopped

- 2 cups romaine lettuce, shredded

DIRECTIONS:
» Mix the corn with the olives, lettuce, and the other ingredients in a large bowl, toss well, divide between plates and serve as a side dish.

Nutrition: Calories 290; Protein 6.2g; Carbohydrates 37.6g; Fat: 16.1g; Fiber 7.4g; Sodium: 613mg; Potassium 562mg

ARUGULA SALAD

Preparation Time: 5 minutes
Cooking Time: 0 minutes
Servings: 4

INGREDIENTS:
- ¼ cup pomegranate seeds
- 5 cups baby arugula
- 6 tablespoons green onions, chopped
- 1 tablespoon balsamic vinegar
- 2 tablespoons olive oil
- 3 tablespoons pine nuts
- ½ shallot, chopped

DIRECTIONS:
» In a salad bowl, combine the arugula with the pomegranate and the other ingredients, toss and serve.

Nutrition: Calories 120; Protein 1.8g; Carbohydrates 4.2g; Fat: 11.6g; Fiber 0.9g; Sodium: 9mg; Potassium 163mg

SPANISH RICE

Preparation Time: 15 minutes
Cooking Time: 1 hour 35 minutes
Servings: 8

INGREDIENTS:
- Brown rice – 2 cups
- Extra virgin olive oil –.25 cup
- Garlic, minced – 2 cloves
- Onion, diced – 1
- Tomatoes, diced – 2
- Jalapeno, seeded and diced – 1
- Tomato paste – 1 tablespoon
- Cilantro, chopped -.5 cup
- Chicken broth, low-sodium – 2.5 cups

DIRECTIONS:
» Warm the oven to Fahrenheit 375 degrees. Puree the tomatoes, onion, plus garlic using a blender or food processor. Measure out two cups of this vegetable puree to use and discard the excess.
» Into a large oven-safe Dutch pan, heat the extra virgin olive oil over medium heat until hot and shimmering. Add in the jalapeno and rice to toast, cooking while occasionally stirring for two to three minutes.
» Slowly stir the chicken broth into the rice, followed by the vegetable puree and tomato paste. Stir until combine and increase the heat to medium-high until the broth reaches a boil.
» Cover the Dutch pan with an oven-safe lid, transfer the pot to the preheated oven, and bake within 1 hour and 15 minutes. Remove and stir the cilantro into the rice. Serve.

Nutrition: Calories: 265 Sodium: 32mg; Potassium: 322mg Carbs: 40g; Fat: 3g Protein: 5g

SWEET POTATOES AND APPLES

Preparation Time: 15 minutes
Cooking Time: 40 minutes
Servings: 4

INGREDIENTS:
- Sweet potatoes, sliced into 1" cubes – 2
- Apples, cut into 1" cubes – 2
- Extra virgin olive oil, divided – 3 tablespoons
- Black pepper, ground -.25 teaspoon
- Cinnamon, ground – 1 teaspoon
- Maple syrup – 2 tablespoons

DIRECTIONS:
» Warm the oven to Fahrenheit 425 degrees and grease a large baking sheet with non-stick cooking spray. Toss the cubed sweet potatoes with two tablespoons of the olive oil and black pepper until coated. Roast the potatoes within twenty minutes, stirring them once halfway through the process.
» Meanwhile, toss the apples with the remaining tablespoon of olive oil, cinnamon, and maple syrup until evenly coated. After the sweet potatoes have cooked for twenty minutes, add the apples to the baking sheet and toss the sweet potatoes and apples.
» Return to the oven, then roast it for twenty more minutes, once again giving it a good stir halfway through. Once the potatoes and apples are caramelized from the maple syrup, remove them from the oven and serve hot.

Nutrition: Calories: 100; Carbs: 22g; Fat: 0g; Protein: 2g; Sodium: 38mg; Potassium: 341mg

ROASTED TURNIPS

Preparation Time: 15 minutes
Cooking Time: 30 minutes
Servings: 4

INGREDIENTS:
- Turnips, peels, and cut into ½" cubes – 2 cups
- Black pepper, ground -.25 teaspoon
- Garlic powder -.5 teaspoon
- Onion powder -.5 teaspoon
- Extra virgin olive oil – 1 tablespoon

DIRECTIONS:
» Warm the oven to Fahrenheit 400 degrees and prepare a large baking sheet, setting it aside. Begin by trimming

the top and bottom edges off of the turnips and peeling them if you wish. Slice them into 1/2-inch cubes.
- Toss the turnips with the extra virgin olive oil and seasonings and then spread them out on the prepared baking sheet. Roast the turnips until tender, stirring them halfway through, about thirty minutes in total.

Nutrition: Calories: 50; Carbs: 5g; Fat: 4g; Protein: 1g; Sodium: 44mg; Potassium: 134mg

NO-MAYO POTATO SALAD

Preparation Time: 15 minutes
Cooking Time: 20 minutes
Servings: 8

INGREDIENTS:
- Red potatoes – 3 pounds
- Extra virgin olive oil - .5 cup
- White wine vinegar, divided – 5 tablespoons
- Dijon mustard – 2 teaspoons
- Red onion, sliced – 1 cup
- Black pepper, ground - .5 teaspoon
- Basil, fresh, chopped – 2 tablespoons
- Dill weed, fresh, chopped – 2 tablespoons
- Parsley, fresh, chopped – 2 tablespoons

DIRECTIONS:
- Add the red potatoes to a large pot and cover them with water until the water level is two inches above the potatoes. Put the pot on high heat, then boil potatoes until they are tender when poked with a fork, about fifteen to twenty minutes. Drain off the water.
- Let the potatoes to cool until they can easily be handled but are still warm, then cut it in half and put them in a large bowl. Stir in three tablespoons of the white wine vinegar, giving the potatoes a good stir so that they can evenly absorb the vinegar.
- Mix the rest of two tablespoons of vinegar, extra virgin olive oil, Dijon mustard, and black pepper in a small bowl. Add this mixture to the potatoes and give them a good toss to thoroughly coat the potatoes.
- Toss in the red onion and minced herbs. Serve at room temperature or chilled. Serve immediately or store in the fridge for up to four days.

Nutrition: Calories: 144; Carbs: 19g; Fat: 7g; Protein: 2g; Sodium: 46mg; Potassium: 814mg

ZUCCHINI TOMATO BAKE

Preparation Time: 15 minutes
Cooking Time: 30 minutes
Servings: 4

INGREDIENTS:
- Grape tomatoes, cut in half – 10 ounces
- Zucchini – 2
- Garlic, minced – 5 cloves
- Italian herb seasoning – 1 teaspoon
- Black pepper, ground - .25 teaspoon
- Parsley, fresh, chopped - .33 cup
- Parmesan cheese, low-sodium, grated - .5 cup

DIRECTIONS:
- Warm the oven to Fahrenheit 350 degrees and coat a large baking sheet with non-stick cooking spray. Mix the tomatoes, zucchini, garlic, Italian herb seasoning, Black pepper, and Parmesan cheese in a bowl.
- Put the mixture out on the baking sheet and roast until the zucchini for thirty minutes. Remove, and garnish with parsley over the top before serving.

Nutrition: Calories: 35; Carbs: 4g; Fat: 2g; Protein: 2g; Sodium: 30mg; Potassium: 649mg

CREAMY BROCCOLI CHEDDAR RICE

Preparation Time: 15 minutes
Cooking Time: 40 minutes
Servings: 6

INGREDIENTS:
- Brown rice – 1 cup
- Chicken broth, low-sodium – 2 cups
- Onion, minced – 1
- Extra virgin olive oil, divided – 3 tablespoons
- Garlic, minced – 2 cloves
- Skim milk - .5 cup
- Black pepper, ground - .25 teaspoon
- Broccoli, chopped – 1.5 cups
- Cheddar cheese, low-sodium, shredded – 1 cup

DIRECTIONS:
- Put one tablespoon of the extra virgin olive oil in a large pot and sauté the onion plus garlic over medium heat within two minutes.
- Put the chicken broth in a pot and wait for it to come to a boil before adding in the rice. Simmer the rice over low heat for twenty-five minutes.
- Stir the skim milk, black pepper, and remaining two tablespoons of olive oil into the rice. Simmer again within five more minutes. Stir in the broccoli and cook the rice for five more minutes, until the broccoli is tender. Stir in the rice and serve while warm.

Nutrition: Calories: 200 Carbs: 33g; Fat: 3g Protein: 10g; Sodium: 50mg Potassium: 344mg

SMASHED BRUSSELS SPROUTS

Preparation Time: 15 minutes
Cooking Time: 40 minutes
Servings: 6

INGREDIENTS:
- Brussels sprouts – 2 pounds
- Garlic, minced – 3 cloves
- Balsamic vinegar – 3 tablespoons
- Extra virgin olive oil - .5 cup
- Black pepper, ground - .5 teaspoon
- Leek washed and thinly sliced – 1
- Parmesan cheese, low-sodium, grated - .5 cup

DIRECTIONS:

» Warm the oven to Fahrenheit 450 degrees and prepare two large baking sheets. Trim the yellow leaves and stems off of the Brussels sprouts and then steam them until tender, about twenty to twenty-five minutes.

» Mix the garlic, black pepper, balsamic vinegar, and extra virgin olive oil in a large bowl. Add the steamed Brussels sprouts and leeks to the bowl and toss until evenly coated.

» Spread the Brussels sprouts and leaks divided onto the prepared baking sheets.

» Use a fork or a glass and press down on each of the Brussels sprouts to create flat patties. Put the Parmesan cheese on top and place the smashed sprouts in the oven for fifteen minutes until crispy. Enjoy hot and fresh from the oven.

Nutrition: Calories: 116; Carbs: 11g; Fat: 5g; Protein: 10g; Sodium: 49mg; Potassium: 642mg

CILANTRO LIME RICE

Preparation Time: 15 minutes
Cooking Time: 40 minutes
Servings: 6

INGREDIENTS:

- Brown rice – 1.5 cups
- Lime juice – 2 tablespoons
- Lemon juice – 1.5 teaspoons
- Lime zest -.5 teaspoon
- Cilantro, chopped -.25 cup
- Bay leaf – 1
- Extra virgin olive oil – 1 tablespoon
- Water

DIRECTIONS:

» Cook rice and bay leaf in a pot with boiling water. Mix the mixture and allow it to boil for thirty minutes, reducing the heat slightly if need be.

» Once the rice is tender, drain off the water and return the rice to the pot. Let it sit off of the heat within ten minutes. Remove the bay leaf and use a fork to fluff the rice. Stir the rest of the fixing into the rice and then serve immediately.

Nutrition: Calories: 94; Carbs: 15g; Fat: 3g; Protein: 2g; Sodium: 184mg; Potassium: 245mg

CORN SALAD WITH LIME VINAIGRETTE

Preparation Time: 15 minutes
Cooking Time: 7 minutes
Servings: 6

INGREDIENTS:

- Corn kernels, fresh – 4.5 cups
- Lemon juice – 1 tablespoon
- Red bell pepper, diced – 1
- Grape tomatoes halved – 1 cup
- Cilantro, chopped -.25 cup
- Green onion, chopped -.25 cup
- Jalapeno, diced – 1
- Red onion, thinly sliced -.25
- Feta cheese -.5 cup
- Truvia baking blend – 2 tablespoons
- Extra virgin olive oil – 2 tablespoons
- Honey -.5 tablespoon
- Lime juice – 3 tablespoons
- Black pepper, ground -.125 teaspoon
- Cayenne pepper, ground -.125 teaspoon
- Garlic powder -.125 teaspoon
- Onion powder -.125 teaspoon

DIRECTIONS:

» To create your lime vinaigrette, add the lime juice, onion powder, garlic powder, black pepper, cayenne pepper, and honey to a bowl. Mix, then slowly add in the extra virgin olive oil while whisking vigorously.

» Boil a pot of water and add in the lemon juice, Baking Truvia, and corn kernels. Allow the corn to boil for seven minutes until tender. Strain the boiling water and add the corn kernels to a bowl of ice water to stop the cooking process and cool the kernels. Drain off the ice water and reserve the corn.

» Add the tomatoes, red pepper, jalapeno, green onion, red onion, cilantro, and cooked corn to a large bowl and toss it until the vegetables are well distributed. Add the feta cheese and vinaigrette to the vegetables and then toss until well combined and evenly coated. Serve immediately.

Nutrition: Calories: 88; Carbs: 23g; Fat: 0g; Protein: 3g; Sodium: 124mg; Potassium: 508mg

MEDITERRANEAN CHICKPEA SALAD

Preparation Time: 15 minutes
Cooking Time: 0 minutes
Servings: 6

INGREDIENTS:

- Chickpeas, cooked – 4 cups
- Bell pepper, diced – 2 cups
- Cucumber, chopped – 1 cup
- Tomato, chopped – 1 cup
- Avocado, diced – 1
- Red wine vinegar – 2.5 tablespoons
- Lemon juice – 1 tablespoon
- Extra virgin olive oil – 3 tablespoons
- Parsley, fresh, chopped – 1 teaspoon
- Oregano, dried -.5 teaspoon
- Garlic, minced – 1 teaspoon
- Dill weed, dried -.25 teaspoon
- Black pepper, ground -.25 teaspoon

DIRECTIONS:

» Add the diced vegetables except for the avocado and the chickpeas to a large bowl and toss them. In a separate bowl, whisk the seasonings, lemon juice, red wine vinegar, and extra virgin olive oil to create a vinaigrette. Once combined, pour the mixture over the salad and toss to combine.

» Place the salad in the fridge and allow it to marinate

for at least a couple of hours before serving or up to two days. Immediately before serving the salad, dice the avocado and toss it in.

Nutrition: Calories: 120; Carbs: 14g; Fat: 5g; Protein: 4g; Sodium: 15mg; Potassium: 696mg

ITALIAN ROASTED CABBAGE

Preparation Time: 15 minutes
Cooking Time: 15 minutes
Servings: 8

INGREDIENTS:

- Cabbage, sliced into 8 wedges – 1
- Black pepper, ground – 1.5 teaspoons
- Extra virgin olive oil -.66 cup
- Italian herb seasoning – 2 teaspoons
- Parmesan cheese, low-sodium, grated -.66 cup

DIRECTIONS:

» Warm the oven to Fahrenheit 425 degrees. Prepare a large lined baking sheet with aluminum foil and then spray it with non-stick cooking spray.
» Slice your cabbage in half, remove the stem, and then cut each half into four wedges so that you are left with eight wedges in total.
» Arrange the cabbage wedges on the baking sheet and then drizzle half of the extra virgin olive oil over them. Sprinkle half of the seasonings and Parmesan cheese over the top.
» Place the baking sheet in the hot oven, allow the cabbage to roast for fifteen minutes, and then flip the wedges. Put the rest of the olive oil over the top and then sprinkle the remaining seasonings and cheese over the top as well.
» Return the cabbage to the oven and allow it to roast for fifteen more minutes, until tender.
» Serve fresh and hot.

Nutrition: Calories: 17; Carbs: 4g; Fat: 0g; Protein: 1g; Sodium: 27mg; Potassium: 213mg

TEX-MEX COLE SLAW

Preparation Time: 15 minutes
Cooking Time: 0 minutes
Servings: 12

INGREDIENTS:

- Black beans, cooked – 2 cups
- Grape tomatoes, sliced in half – 1.5 cups
- Grilled corn kernels – 1.5 cups
- Jalapeno, seeded and minced – 1
- Cilantro, chopped -.5 cup
- Bell pepper, diced – 1
- Coleslaw cabbage mix – 16 ounces
- Lime juice – 3 tablespoons
- Light sour cream -.66 cup
- Olive oil mayonnaise, reduced-fat – 1 cup
- Chili powder – 1 tablespoon
- Cumin, ground – 1 teaspoon
- Onion powder – 1 teaspoon
- Garlic powder – 1 teaspoon

DIRECTIONS:

» Mix the sour cream, mayonnaise, lime juice, garlic powder, onion powder, cumin, and chili powder in a bowl to create the dressing.
» In a large bowl, toss the vegetables and then add in the prepared dressing and toss again until evenly coated. Chill the mixture in the fridge for thirty minutes to twelve hours before serving.

Nutrition: Calories: 50 Carbs: 10g; Fat: 1g Protein: 3g; Sodium: 194mg Potassium: 345mg

ROASTED OKRA

Preparation Time: 15 minutes
Cooking Time: 20 minutes
Servings: 4

INGREDIENTS:

- Okra, fresh – 1 pound
- Extra virgin olive oil – 2 tablespoons
- Cayenne pepper, ground -.125 teaspoon
- Paprika – 1 teaspoon
- Garlic powder -.25 teaspoon

DIRECTIONS:

» Warm the oven to Fahrenheit 450 degrees and prepare a large baking sheet. Cut the okra into pieces appropriate 1/2-inch in size.
» Place the okra on the baking pan and top it with the olive oil and seasonings, giving it a good toss until evenly coated. Roast the okra in the heated oven until it is tender and lightly browned and seared. Serve immediately while hot.

Nutrition: Calories: 65; Carbs: 6g; Fat: 5g; Protein: 2g; Sodium: 9mg; Potassium: 356mg

BROWN SUGAR GLAZED CARROTS

Preparation Time: 15 minutes
Cooking Time: 25 minutes
Servings: 6

INGREDIENTS:

- Carrots, sliced into 1-inch pieces – 2 pounds
- Light olive oil -.33 cup
- Truvia Brown Sugar Blend -.25 cup
- Black pepper, ground -.25 teaspoon

DIRECTIONS:

» Warm the oven to Fahrenheit 400 degrees and prepare a large baking sheet. Toss the carrots with the oil, Truvia, and black pepper until evenly coated and then spread them out on the prepared baking sheet.
» Place the carrots in the oven and allow them to roast until tender, about twenty to twenty-five minutes. Halfway through the cooking time, give the carrots a good

serve. Remove the carrots from the oven and serve them alone or topped with fresh parsley.

Nutrition: Calories: 110; Carbs: 16g; Fat: 4g; Protein: 1g; Sodium: 105mg; Potassium: 486mg

OVEN-ROASTED BEETS WITH HONEY RICOTTA

Preparation Time: 15 minutes
Cooking Time: 40 minutes
Servings: 6

INGREDIENTS:

- Purple beets – 1 pound
- Golden beets – 1 pound
- Ricotta cheese, low-fat -.5 cup
- Extra virgin olive oil – 3 tablespoons
- Honey – 1 tablespoon
- Rosemary, fresh, chopped – 1 teaspoon
- Black pepper, ground -.25 teaspoon

DIRECTIONS:

» Warm the oven to Fahrenheit 375 degrees and prepare a large baking sheet by lining it with kitchen parchment. Slice the beets into 1/2-inch cubes before tossing them with the extra virgin olive oil and black pepper.
» Put the beets on the prepared baking sheet and allow them to roast until tender, about thirty-five to forty minutes. Halfway through the cooking process, flip the beets over.
» Meanwhile, in a small bowl, whisk the ricotta with the rosemary and honey. Fridge until ready to serve. Once the beets are done cooking, serve them topped with the ricotta mixture, and enjoy.

Nutrition: Calories: 195; Carbs: 24g; Fat: 8g; Protein: 8g; Sodium: 139mg; Potassium: 521mg

EASY CARROTS MIX

Preparation Time: 10 minutes
Cooking Time: 40 minutes
Servings: 6

INGREDIENTS:

- 15 carrots, halved lengthwise
- 2 tablespoons coconut sugar
- ¼ cup olive oil
- ½ teaspoon rosemary, dried
- ½ teaspoon garlic powder
- A pinch of black pepper

DIRECTIONS:

» In a bowl, combine the carrots with the sugar, oil, rosemary, garlic powder, and black pepper, toss well, spread on a lined baking sheet, introduce in the oven and bake at 400 degrees F for 40 minutes. Serve.

Nutrition: Calories: 60; Carbs: 9g; Fat: 0g; Protein: 2g; Sodium: 0 mg

TASTY GRILLED ASPARAGUS

Preparation Time: 10 minutes
Cooking Time: 6 minutes
Servings: 4

INGREDIENTS:

- 2 pounds asparagus, trimmed
- 2 tablespoons olive oil
- A pinch of salt and black pepper

DIRECTIONS:

» In a bowl, combine the asparagus with salt, pepper, and oil and toss well. Place the asparagus on a preheated grill over medium-high heat, cook for 3 minutes on each side, then serve.

Nutrition: Calories: 50; Carbs: 8g; Fat: 1g; Protein: 5g; Sodium: 420 mg

ROASTED CARROTS

Preparation Time: 10 minutes
Cooking Time: 30 minutes
Servings: 4

INGREDIENTS:

- 2 pounds carrots, quartered
- A pinch of black pepper
- 3 tablespoons olive oil
- 2 tablespoons parsley, chopped

DIRECTIONS:

» Arrange the carrots on a lined baking sheet, add black pepper and oil, toss, introduce in the oven, and cook within 30 minutes at 400 degrees F. Add parsley, toss, divide between plates and serve as a side dish.

Nutrition: Calories: 89; Carbs: 10g; Fat: 6g; Protein: 1g; Sodium: 0 mg

OVEN ROASTED ASPARAGUS

Preparation Time: 10 minutes
Cooking Time: 25 minutes
Servings: 4

INGREDIENTS:

- 2 pounds asparagus spears, trimmed
- 3 tablespoons olive oil
- A pinch of black pepper
- 2 teaspoons sweet paprika
- 1 teaspoon sesame seeds

DIRECTIONS:

» Arrange the asparagus on a lined baking sheet, add oil, black pepper, and paprika, toss, introduce in the oven and bake within 25 minutes at 400 degrees F. Divide the asparagus between plates, sprinkle sesame seeds on top, and serve as a side dish.

Nutrition: Calories: 45; Carbs: 5g; Fat: 2g; Protein: 2g; Sodium: 0 mg

BAKED POTATO WITH THYME

Preparation Time: 10 minutes
Cooking Time: 1 hour and 15 minutes
Servings: 8

INGREDIENTS:

- 6 potatoes, peeled and sliced
- 2 garlic cloves, minced
- 2 tablespoons olive oil
- 1 and ½ cups of coconut cream
- ¼ cup of coconut milk
- 1 tablespoon thyme, chopped
- ¼ teaspoon nutmeg, ground
- A pinch of red pepper flakes
- 1 and ½ cups low-fat cheddar, shredded
- ½ cup low-fat parmesan, grated

DIRECTIONS:

» Heat-up a pan with the oil over medium heat, add garlic, stir and cook for 1 minute. Add coconut cream, coconut milk, thyme, nutmeg, and pepper flakes, stir, bring to a simmer, adjust to low and cook within 10 minutes.
» Put one-third of the potatoes in a baking dish, add 1/3 of the cream, repeat the process with the remaining potatoes and the cream, sprinkle the cheddar on top, cover with tin foil, introduce in the oven and cook at 375 degrees F for 45 minutes. Uncover the dish, sprinkle the parmesan, bake everything for 20 minutes, divide between plates, and serve as a side dish.

Nutrition: Calories: 132; Carbs: 21g; Fat: 4g; Protein: 2g; Sodium: 56 mg

SPICY BRUSSELS SPROUTS

Preparation Time: 10 minutes
Cooking Time: 20 minutes
Servings: 6

INGREDIENTS:

- 2 pounds Brussels sprouts, halved
- 2 tablespoons olive oil
- A pinch of black pepper
- 1 tablespoon sesame oil
- 2 garlic cloves, minced
- ½ cup coconut aminos
- 2 teaspoons apple cider vinegar
- 1 tablespoon coconut sugar
- 2 teaspoons chili sauce
- A pinch of red pepper flakes
- Sesame seeds for serving

DIRECTIONS:

» Spread the sprouts on a lined baking dish, add the olive oil, the sesame oil, black pepper, garlic, aminos, vinegar, coconut sugar, chili sauce, and pepper flakes, toss well, introduce in the oven and bake within 20 minutes at 425 degrees F. Divide the sprouts between plates, sprinkle sesame seeds on top and serve as a side dish.

Nutrition: Calories: 64; Carbs: 13g; Fat: 0g; Protein: 4g; Sodium: 314 mg

BAKED CAULIFLOWER WITH CHILI

Preparation Time: 10 minutes
Cooking Time: 30 minutes
Servings: 4

INGREDIENTS:

- 3 tablespoons olive oil
- 2 tablespoons chili sauce
- Juice of 1 lime
- 3 garlic cloves, minced
- 1 cauliflower head, florets separated
- A pinch of black pepper
- 1 teaspoon cilantro, chopped

DIRECTIONS:

» In a bowl, combine the oil with the chili sauce, lime juice, garlic, and black pepper and whisk. Add cauliflower florets, toss, spread on a lined baking sheet, introduce in the oven and bake at 425 degrees F for 30 minutes.
» Divide the cauliflower between plates, sprinkle cilantro on top, and serve as a side dish.

Nutrition: Calories: 31; Carbs: 3g; Fat: 0g; Protein: 3g; Sodium: 4 mg

BAKED BROCCOLI

Preparation Time: 10 minutes
Cooking Time: 15 minutes
Servings: 4

INGREDIENTS:

- 1 tablespoon olive oil
- 1 broccoli head, florets separated
- 2 garlic cloves, minced
- ½ cup coconut cream
- ½ cup low-fat mozzarella, shredded
- ¼ cup low-fat parmesan, grated
- A pinch of pepper flakes, crushed

DIRECTIONS:

» In a baking dish, combine the broccoli with oil, garlic, cream, pepper flakes, mozzarella, and toss. Sprinkle the parmesan on top, introduce in the oven and bake at 375 degrees F for 15 minutes. Serve.

Nutrition: Calories: 90; Carbs: 6g; Fat: 7g; Protein: 3g; Sodium: 30 mg

SLOW COOKED POTATOES WITH CHEDDAR

Preparation Time: 10 minutes
Cooking Time: 6 hours
Servings: 6

INGREDIENTS:

- Cooking spray
- 2 pounds baby potatoes, quartered
- 3 cups low-fat cheddar cheese, shredded
- 2 garlic cloves, minced
- 8 bacon slices, cooked and chopped
- ¼ cup green onions, chopped
- 1 tablespoon sweet paprika
- A pinch of black pepper

DIRECTIONS:

» Spray a slow cooker with the cooking spray, add baby potatoes, cheddar, garlic, bacon, green onions, paprika, and black pepper, toss, cover, and cook on High for 6 hours. Serve.

Nutrition: Calories: 112; Carbs: 26g; Fat: 4g; Protein: 8g; Sodium: 234 mg

SQUASH SALAD WITH ORANGE

Preparation Time: 10 minutes
Cooking Time: 30 minutes
Servings: 6

INGREDIENTS:

- 1 cup of orange juice
- 3 tablespoons coconut sugar
- 1 and ½ tablespoons mustard
- 1 tablespoon ginger, grated
- 1 and ½ pounds butternut squash, peeled and roughly cubed
- Cooking spray
- A pinch of black pepper
- 1/3 cup olive oil
- 6 cups salad greens
- 1 radicchio, sliced
- ½ cup pistachios, roasted

DIRECTIONS:

» Mix the orange juice with the sugar, mustard, ginger, black pepper, squash in a bowl, toss well, spread on a lined baking sheet, spray everything with cooking oil, and bake for 30 minutes 400 degrees F.
» In a salad bowl, combine the squash with salad greens, radicchio, pistachios, and oil, toss well, then serve.

Nutrition: Calories: 17 Carbs: 2g; Fat: 0g; Protein: 0g; Sodium: 0 mg

COLORED ICEBERG SALAD

Preparation Time: 10 minutes
Cooking Time: 0 minutes
Servings: 4

INGREDIENTS:

- 1 iceberg lettuce head, leaves torn
- 6 bacon slices, cooked and halved
- 2 green onions, sliced
- 3 carrots, shredded
- 6 radishes, sliced
- ¼ cup red vinegar
- ¼ cup olive oil
- 3 garlic cloves, minced
- A pinch of black pepper

DIRECTIONS:

» Mix the lettuce leaves with the bacon, green onions, carrots, radishes, vinegar, oil, garlic, and black pepper in a large salad bowl, toss, divide between plates and serve as a side dish.

Nutrition: Calories: 15 Carbs: 3g; Fat: 0g; Protein: 1g; Sodium: 15 mg

FENNEL SALAD WITH ARUGULA

Preparation Time: 10 minutes
Cooking Time: 0 minutes
Servings: 4

INGREDIENTS:

- 2 fennel bulbs, trimmed and shaved
- 1 and ¼ cups zucchini, sliced
- 2/3 cup dill, chopped
- ¼ cup lemon juice
- ¼ cup olive oil
- 6 cups arugula
- ½ cups walnuts, chopped
- 1/3 cup low-fat feta cheese, crumbled

DIRECTIONS:

» Mix the fennel with the zucchini, dill, lemon juice, arugula, oil, walnuts, and cheese in a large bowl, toss, then serve.

Nutrition: Calories: 65 Carbs: 6g; Fat: 5g Protein: 1g Sodium: 140 mg

CORN MIX

Preparation Time: 10 minutes
Cooking Time: 0 minutes
Servings: 4

INGREDIENTS:

- ½ cup cider vinegar
- ¼ cup of coconut sugar
- A pinch of black pepper
- 4 cups corn

- ½ cup red onion, chopped
- ½ cup cucumber, sliced
- ½ cup red bell pepper, chopped
- ½ cup cherry tomatoes halved
- 3 tablespoons parsley, chopped
- 1 tablespoon basil, chopped
- 1 tablespoon jalapeno, chopped
- 2 cups baby arugula leaves

DIRECTIONS:

» Mix the corn with onion, cucumber, bell pepper, cherry tomatoes, parsley, basil, jalapeno, and arugula in a large bowl. Add vinegar, sugar, and black pepper, toss well, divide between plates and serve as a side dish.

Nutrition: Calories: 110; Carbs: 25g; Fat: 0g; Protein: 2g; Sodium: 120 mg

PERSIMMON SALAD

Preparation Time: 10 minutes
Cooking Time: 0 minutes
Servings: 4

INGREDIENTS:

- Seeds from 1 pomegranate
- 2 persimmons, cored and sliced
- 5 cups baby arugula
- 6 tablespoons green onions, chopped
- 4 navel oranges, cut into segments
- ¼ cup white vinegar
- 1/3 cup olive oil
- 3 tablespoons pine nuts
- 1 and ½ teaspoons orange zest, grated
- 2 tablespoons orange juice
- 1 tablespoon coconut sugar
- ½ shallot, chopped
- A pinch of cinnamon powder

DIRECTIONS:

» In a salad bowl, combine the pomegranate seeds with persimmons, arugula, green onions, and oranges and toss. In another bowl, combine the vinegar with the oil, pine nuts, orange zest, orange juice, sugar, shallot, and cinnamon, whisk well, add to the salad, toss and serve as a side dish.

Nutrition: Calories: 310; Carbs: 33g; Fat: 16g; Protein: 7g; Sodium: 320 mg

AVOCADO SIDE SALAD

Preparation Time: 10 minutes
Cooking Time: 0 minutes
Servings: 4

INGREDIENTS:

- 4 blood oranges, slice into segments
- 2 tablespoons olive oil
- A pinch of red pepper, crushed
- 2 avocados, peeled, cut into wedges
- 1 and ½ cups baby arugula
- ¼ cup almonds, toasted and chopped
- 1 tablespoon lemon juice

DIRECTIONS:

» Mix the oranges with the oil, red pepper, avocados, arugula, almonds, and lemon juice in a bowl, then serve.

Nutrition: Calories: 146; Carbs: 8g; Fat: 7g; Protein: 15g; Sodium: 320 mg

SPICED BROCCOLI FLORETS

Preparation Time: 10 minutes
Cooking Time: 3 hours
Servings: 10

INGREDIENTS:

- 6 cups broccoli florets
- 1 and ½ cups low-fat cheddar cheese, shredded
- ½ teaspoon cider vinegar
- ¼ cup yellow onion, chopped
- 10 ounces tomato sauce, sodium-free
- 2 tablespoons olive oil
- A pinch of black pepper

DIRECTIONS:

» Grease your slow cooker with the oil, add broccoli, tomato sauce, cider vinegar, onion, and black pepper, cook on High within 2 hours, and 30 minutes. Sprinkle the cheese all over, cover, cook on High for 30 minutes more, divide between plates, and serve as a side dish.

Nutrition: Calories 119; Fat: 8.7g; Sodium: 272mg; Carbohydrate 5.7g; Fiber 1.9g; Sugars 2.3g; Protein 6.2g

LIMA BEANS DISH

Preparation Time: 10 minutes
Cooking Time: 5 hours
Servings: 10

INGREDIENTS:

- 1 green bell pepper, chopped
- 1 sweet red pepper, chopped
- 1 and ½ cups tomato sauce, salt-free
- 1 yellow onion, chopped
- ½ cup of water
- 16 ounces canned kidney beans, no-salt-added, drained and rinsed
- 16 ounces canned black-eyed peas, no-salt-added, drained and rinsed
- 15 ounces corn
- 15 ounces canned lima beans, no-salt-added, drained and rinsed
- 15 oz canned black beans, no-salt-added, drained
- 2 celery ribs, chopped
- 2 bay leaves
- 1 teaspoon ground mustard
- 1 tablespoon cider vinegar

DIRECTIONS:

» In your slow cooker, mix the tomato sauce with the onion, celery, red pepper, green bell pepper, water, bay leaves, mustard, vinegar, kidney beans, black-eyed peas, corn, lima beans, and black beans, cook on Low within 5 hours. Discard bay leaves, divide the whole mix between plates, and serve.

Nutrition: Calories 602; Fat: 4.8g; Sodium: 255mg; Carbohydrate 117.7g; Fiber 24.6g; Sugars 13.4g; Protein 33g

---

SOY SAUCE GREEN BEANS

Preparation Time: 10 minutes
Cooking Time: 2 hours
Servings: 12

INGREDIENTS:

- 3 tablespoons olive oil
- 16 ounces green beans
- ½ teaspoon garlic powder
- ½ cup of coconut sugar
- 1 teaspoon low-sodium soy sauce

DIRECTIONS:

» In your slow cooker, mix the green beans with the oil, sugar, soy sauce, and garlic powder, cover, and cook on Low for 2 hours. Toss the beans, divide them between plates, and serve as a side dish.

Nutrition: Calories 46 Fat 3.6g; Sodium: 29mg Carbohydrate 3.6g; Fiber 1.3g; Sugars 0.6g; Protein 0.8g

---

BUTTER CORN

Preparation Time: 10 minutes
Cooking Time: 4 hours
Servings: 12

INGREDIENTS:

- 20 ounces fat-free cream cheese
- 10 cups corn
- ½ cup low-fat butter
- ½ cup fat-free milk
- A pinch of black pepper
- 2 tablespoons green onions, chopped

DIRECTIONS:

» In your slow cooker, mix the corn with cream cheese, milk, butter, black pepper, and onions, cook on Low within 4 hours. Toss one more time, divide between plates and serve as a side dish.

Nutrition: Calories 279 Fat 18g Cholesterol 52mg Sodium 165mg Carbohydrate 26g Fiber 3.5g; Sugars 4.8g Protein 8.1g

---

STEVIA PEAS WITH MARJORAM

Preparation Time: 10 minutes
Cooking Time: 5 hours
Servings: 12

INGREDIENTS:

- 1-pound carrots, sliced
- 1 yellow onion, chopped
- 16 ounces peas
- 2 tablespoons stevia
- 2 tablespoons olive oil
- 4 garlic cloves, minced
- ¼ cup of water
- 1 teaspoon marjoram, dried
- A pinch of white pepper

DIRECTIONS:

» In your slow cooker, mix the carrots with water, onion, oil, stevia, garlic, marjoram, white pepper, peas, toss, cover, and cook on High for 5 hours. Divide between plates and serve as a side dish.

Nutrition: Calories 71 Fat 2.5g Sodium 29mg; Carbohydrate 12.1g Fiber 3.1g Sugars 4.4g; Protein 2.5g Potassium 231mg

---

PILAF WITH BELLA MUSHROOMS

Preparation Time: 10 minutes
Cooking Time: 3 hours
Servings: 6

INGREDIENTS:

- 1 cup wild rice
- 6 green onions, chopped
- ½ pound baby Bella mushrooms
- 2 cups of water
- 2 tablespoons olive oil
- 2 garlic cloves, minced

DIRECTIONS:

» In your slow cooker, mix the rice with garlic, onions, oil, mushrooms, water, toss, cover, and cook on Low for 3 hours. Stir the pilaf one more time, divide between plates and serve.

Nutrition: Calories 151; Fat: 5.1g; Sodium: 9mg; Carbohydrate 23.3g; Fiber 2.6g; Sugars 1.7g; Protein 5.2g

---

PARSLEY FENNEL

Preparation Time: 10 minutes
Cooking Time: 2 hours and 30 minutes
Servings: 4

INGREDIENTS:

- 2 fennel bulbs, sliced
- Juice and zest of 1 lime
- 2 teaspoons avocado oil
- ½ teaspoon turmeric powder
- 1 tablespoon parsley, chopped

- ¼ cup veggie stock, low-sodium

DIRECTIONS:

» In a slow cooker, combine the fennel with the lime juice, zest, and the other ingredients, cook on Low within 2 hours and 30 minutes. Serve.

Nutrition: Calories 47 Fat 0.6g; Sodium: 71mg Carbohydrate 10.8g; Protein 1.7g

SWEET BUTTERNUT

Preparation Time: 10 minutes
Cooking Time: 4 hours
Servings: 8

INGREDIENTS:

- 1 cup carrots, chopped
- 1 tablespoon olive oil
- 1 yellow onion, chopped
- ½ teaspoon stevia
- 1 garlic clove, minced
- ½ teaspoon curry powder
- 1 butternut squash, cubed
- 2 and ½ cups low-sodium veggie stock
- ½ cup basmati rice
- ¾ cup of coconut milk
- ½ teaspoon cinnamon powder
- ¼ teaspoon ginger, grated

DIRECTIONS:

» Heat-up, a pan with the oil over medium-high heat, add the oil, onion, garlic, stevia, carrots, curry powder, cinnamon, ginger, stir, and cook 5 minutes and transfer to your slow cooker.
» Add squash, stock, and coconut milk, stir, cover, and cook on Low for 4 hours. Divide the butternut mix between plates and serve as a side dish.

Nutrition: Calories 134; Fat: 7.2g; Sodium: 59mg; Carbohydrate 16.5g; Fiber 1.7g; Sugars 2.7g; Protein 1.8g

MUSHROOM SAUSAGES

Preparation Time: 10 minutes
Cooking Time: 2 hours
Servings: 12

INGREDIENTS:

- 6 celery ribs, chopped
- 1 pound no-sugar, beef sausage, chopped
- 2 tablespoons olive oil
- ½ pound mushrooms, chopped
- ½ cup sunflower seeds, peeled
- 1 cup low-sodium veggie stock
- 1 cup cranberries, dried
- 2 yellow onions, chopped
- 2 garlic cloves, minced
- 1 tablespoon sage, dried
- 1 whole-wheat bread loaf, cubed

DIRECTIONS:

» Heat-up a pan with the oil over medium-high heat, add beef, stir and brown for a few minutes. Add mushrooms, onion, celery, garlic, and sage, stir, cook for a few more minutes and transfer to your slow cooker.
» Add stock, cranberries, sunflower seeds, and the bread cubes; cover and cook on High for 2 hours. Stir the whole mix, divide between plates and serve as a side dish.

Nutrition: Calories 188; Fat: 13.8g; Sodium: 489mg; Carbohydrate 8.2g; Fiber 1.9g; Protein 7.6g

PARSLEY RED POTATOES

Preparation Time: 10 minutes
Cooking Time: 6 hours
Servings: 8

INGREDIENTS:

- 16 baby red potatoes, halved
- 2 cups low-sodium chicken stock
- 1 carrot, sliced
- 1 celery rib, chopped
- ¼ cup yellow onion, chopped
- 1 tablespoon parsley, chopped
- 2 tablespoons olive oil
- A pinch of black pepper
- 1 garlic clove minced

DIRECTIONS:

» In your slow cooker, mix the potatoes with the carrot, celery, onion, stock, parsley, garlic, oil, and black pepper, toss, cover, and cook on Low for 6 hours.
» Serve.

Nutrition: Calories 257; Fat: 9.5g; Sodium: 845mg; Carbohydrate 43.4g; Protein 4.4g

JALAPENO BLACK-EYED PEAS MIX

Preparation Time: 10 minutes
Cooking Time: 5 hours
Servings: 12

INGREDIENTS:

- 17 ounces black-eyed peas
- 1 sweet red pepper, chopped
- ½ cup sausage, chopped
- 1 yellow onion, chopped
- 1 jalapeno, chopped
- 2 garlic cloves minced
- 6 cups of water
- ½ teaspoon cumin, ground
- A pinch of black pepper
- 2 tablespoons cilantro, chopped

DIRECTIONS:

» In your slow cooker, mix the peas with the sausage, onion, red pepper, jalapeno, garlic, cumin, black pepper, water, cilantro, cover, and cook low for 5 hours. Serve.

Nutrition: Calories 75; Fat: 3.5g; Sodium: 94mg; Carbohydrate 7.2g; Fiber 1.7g; Sugars 0.9g; Protein 4.3g

SOUR CREAM GREEN BEANS

Preparation Time: 10 minutes
Cooking Time: 4 hours
Servings: 8

INGREDIENTS:

- 15 ounces green beans
- 14 ounces corn
- 4 ounces mushrooms, sliced
- 11 ounces cream of mushroom soup, low-fat and sodium-free
- ½ cup low-fat sour cream
- ½ cup almonds, chopped
- ½ cup low-fat cheddar cheese, shredded

DIRECTIONS:

» In your slow cooker, mix the green beans with the corn, mushrooms soup, mushrooms, almonds, cheese, sour cream, toss, cover, and cook on Low for 4 hours. Stir one more time, divide between plates and serve as a side dish.

Nutrition: Calories360; Fat: 12.7g; Sodium: 220mg; Carbohydrate 58.3g; Fiber 10g; Sugars 10.3g; Protein 14g

CUMIN BRUSSELS SPROUTS

Preparation Time: 10 minutes
Cooking Time: 3 hours
Servings: 4

INGREDIENTS:

- 1 cup low-sodium veggie stock
- 1-pound Brussels sprouts, trimmed and halved
- 1 teaspoon rosemary, dried
- 1 teaspoon cumin, ground
- 1 tablespoon mint, chopped

DIRECTIONS:

» In your slow cooker, combine the sprouts with the stock and the other ingredients, cook on Low within 3 hours. Serve.

Nutrition: Calories 56; Fat: 0.6g; Sodium: 65mg; Carbohydrate 11.4g; Fiber 4.5g; Sugars 2.7g; Protein 4g

PEACH AND CARROTS

Preparation Time: 10 minutes
Cooking Time: 6 hours
Servings: 6

INGREDIENTS:

- 2 pounds small carrots, peeled
- ½ cup low-fat butter, melted
- ½ cup canned peach, unsweetened
- 2 tablespoons cornstarch
- 3 tablespoons stevia
- 2 tablespoons water
- ½ teaspoon cinnamon powder
- 1 teaspoon vanilla extract
- A pinch of nutmeg, ground

DIRECTIONS:

» In your slow cooker, mix the carrots with the butter, peach, stevia, cinnamon, vanilla, nutmeg, and cornstarch mixed with water, toss, cover, and cook on Low for 6 hours. Toss the carrots one more time, divide between plates and serve as a side dish.

Nutrition: Calories139; Fat: 10.7g; Sodium: 199mg; Carbohydrate 35.4g; Fiber 4.2g; Sugars 6.9g; Protein 3.8g

BABY SPINACH AND GRAINS MIX

Preparation Time: 10 minutes
Cooking Time: 4 hours
Servings: 12

INGREDIENTS:

- 1 butternut squash, peeled and cubed
- 1 cup whole-grain blend, uncooked
- 12 ounces low-sodium veggie stock
- 6 ounces baby spinach
- 1 yellow onion, chopped
- 3 garlic cloves, minced
- ½ cup of water
- 2 teaspoons thyme, chopped
- A pinch of black pepper

DIRECTIONS:

» In your slow cooker, mix the squash with whole grain, onion, garlic, water, thyme, black pepper, stock, spinach, cover, and cook on Low for 4 hours. Serve.

Nutrition: Calories78; Fat: 0.6g; Sodium: 259mg; Carbohydrate 16.4g; Fiber 1.8g; Sugars 2g; Protein 2.5g

QUINOA CURRY

Preparation Time: 15 minutes
Cooking Time: 4 hours
Servings: 8

INGREDIENTS:

- 1 chopped Sweet Potato
- 2 cups Green Beans
- ½ diced onion (white)
- 1 diced Carrot
- 15 oz Chick Peas (organic and drained)
- 28 oz. Tomatoes (diced)
- 29 oz Coconut Milk
- 2 minced cloves of garlic
- ¼ cup Quinoa
- 1 tbs. Turmeric (ground)
- 1 tbsp. Ginger (grated)
- 1 ½ cups Water
- 1 tsp. of Chili Flakes

- 2 tsp. of Tamari Sauce

DIRECTIONS:

» Put all the listed fixing in the slow cooker. Add 1 cup of water. Stir well. Cook on "high" for 4 hrs. Serve with rice.

Nutrition: Calories 297; Fat: 18 g; Sodium: 364 mg; Carbohydrates 9 mg; Protein 28 g

LEMON AND CILANTRO RICE

Preparation Time: 15 minutes
Cooking Time: 6 hours
Servings: 4

INGREDIENTS:

- 3 cups Vegetable Broth (low sodium)
- 1 ½ cups Brown Rice (uncooked)
- Juice of 2 lemons
- 2 tbsp. chopped cilantro

DIRECTIONS:

» In a slow cooker, place broth and rice. Cook on "low" for 5 hrs. Check the rice for doneness with a fork. Add the lemon juice and cilantro before serving.

Nutrition: Calories 56; Fats 0.3 g; Sodium: 174 mg; Carbohydrates 12 g; Protein 1 g

CHILI BEANS

Preparation Time: 15 minutes
Cooking Time: 4 hours
Servings: 5

INGREDIENTS:

- 1 ½ cup chopped Bell Pepper
- 1 ½ cup sliced Mushrooms (white)
- 1 cup chopped Onion
- 1 tbsp. Olive Oil
- 1 tbsp. Chili Powder
- 2 chopped cloves Garlic
- 1 tsp. chopped Chipotle Chili
- ½ tsp. Cumin
- 15.5 oz drained Black Beans
- 1 cup diced tomatoes (no salt)
- 2 tbsp. chopped cilantro

DIRECTIONS:

» Put all the fixing above in the slow cooker. Cook on "high" for 4 hrs. Serve

Nutrition: Calories 343 Fat 11 g; Sodium: 308 mg; Carbohydrates 9 mg; Protein 29 g

BEAN SPREAD

Preparation Time: 15 minutes
Cooking Time: 4 hours
Servings: 20

INGREDIENTS:

- 30 ounces Cannellini Beans
- ½ cup Broth (chicken or veg)
- 1 tbsp. Olive Oil
- 3 minced cloves Garlic
- ½ tsp. Marjoram
- ½ tsp. Rosemary
- 1/8 tsp. Pepper
- Pita Chips
- 1 tbsp Olive Oil

DIRECTIONS:

» Place olive oil, beans, broth, marjoram, garlic, rosemary, and pepper in the slow cooker. Cook on "low" for 4 hrs. Mash the mixture and transfer to a bowl. Serve with Pita.

Nutrition: Calories 298; Fat: 18 g; Sodium: 298 mg; Carbohydrates 30 mg; Protein 19 g

STIR-FRIED STEAK, SHIITAKE, AND ASPARAGUS

Preparation Time: 15 minutes
Cooking Time: 2 hours 20 minutes
Servings: 4

INGREDIENTS:

- 1 tbsp. Sherry (dry)
- 1 tbsp. Vinegar (rice)
- ½ tbsp. Soy Sauce (low sodium)
- ½ tbsp. Cornstarch
- 2 tsp. Canola Oil
- ¼ tsp. Black Pepper (ground)
- 1 minced clove Garlic
- ½ lb. sliced Sirloin Steak
- 3 oz. Shiitake Mushrooms
- ½ tbsp. minced Ginger
- 6 oz. sliced Asparagus
- 3 oz. Peas (sugar snap)
- 2 sliced scallions
- ¼ cup Water

DIRECTIONS:

» Combine cornstarch, soy sauce, sherry vinegar, broth, and pepper. Place the steaks in 1 tsp hot oil in the slow cooker for 2 mins. Transfer the steaks to a plate. Sauté ginger and garlic in the remaining oil. Add in the mushrooms, peas, and asparagus.
» Add water and cook on "low" for 1 hr. Add the scallions and cook again for 30 mins on low. Change the heat to "high" and add the vinegar. When the sauce has thickened, transfer the steaks to the slow cooker. Stir well and serve immediately.

Nutrition: Calories 182; Fats 7 g; Sodium: 157 mg; Carbohydrates 10 mg; Protein 20 g

CHICKPEAS AND CURRIED VEGGIES

Preparation Time: 15 minutes
Cooking Time: 4 hours
Servings: 2

INGREDIENTS:

- ½ tbsp. Canola Oil
- 2 sliced Celery Ribs
- 1/8 tsp. Cayenne Pepper
- ¼ cup Water
- 2 sliced Carrots
- 2 sliced red Potatoes (sliced)
- ½ tbsp. Curry Powder
- ½ cup of Coconut Milk (light)
- ¼ cup drained Chickpeas (low sodium)
- Chopped Cilantro
- ¼ cup Yogurt (low fat)

DIRECTIONS:

» Sauté potatoes for 5 mins in oil. Add the carrots, celery, and onion. Sauté for 5 more mins. Sprinkle on the curry powder and cayenne pepper. Stir well to combine.
» In a slow cooker, pour water and coconut milk. Add in the potatoes. Cook on "low" for 3 hrs. Add chickpeas and cook for 30 more mins.
» Serve in bowls along with the yogurt and cilantro garnish.

Nutrition: Calories 271; Fats 11 g; Sodium: 207 mg; Carbohydrates 39 g; Protein 7 g

BRUSSELS SPROUTS CASSEROLE

Preparation Time: 15 minutes
Cooking Time: 4 hours 15 minutes
Servings: 3

INGREDIENTS:

- ¾ lb. Brussels Sprouts
- 1 diced slice Pancetta
- 1 minced clove Garlic
- 1 tbsp. chopped Shallot
- ¼ cup pine nuts (toasted)
- ¼ tsp. Black Pepper (cracked)
- 4 tbsp. Water

DIRECTIONS:

» Slice sprouts and place them in the slow cooker along with the water. Cook on "high" for 1 hr. Drain well. Remove the fat from the pancetta. Sauté the pancetta for 4 mins. Add the shallots, garlic, and 1/8 cup of Pine Nuts to the sauté.
» Now, add the sprouts. Cook for 3 mins. Transfer the prepared mixture to the slow cooker. Add black pepper. 4 tbsp of water, and cook again on "low" for 2 hrs. Serve immediately.

Nutrition: Calories 128; Fats 9 g; Sodium: 56 mg; Carbohydrates 5 g; Protein 5 g

TASTY CAULIFLOWER

Preparation Time: 15 minutes
Cooking Time: 6 hours 15 minutes
Servings: 4

INGREDIENTS:

- 2 minced cloves Garlic
- 2 cups Cauliflower florets
- 2 tbsp. Olive Oil
- Pinch of Sea Salt
- ¼ tsp. Pepper Flakes (chili)
- Pinch of Black Pepper (cracked)
- 4 tbsp. Water
- Zest of ½ lemon

DIRECTIONS:

» In a slow cooker, place cauliflower and oil. Add vinegar. Toss well to coat thoroughly. Put in the rest of the ingredients and toss again. Cook on "low" for 2 hrs. Serve immediately.

Nutrition: Calories 150 Fats 14 g; Sodium: 69 mg Carbohydrates 6 g Protein 2.2 g

ARTICHOKE AND SPINACH DIP

Preparation Time: 15 minutes
Cooking Time: 2 hours 10 minutes
Servings: 2

INGREDIENTS:

- 1/8 tsp. Basil (dried)
- 14 oz. chopped Artichoke Hearts
- 1 ½ cups spinach
- ½ minced clove Garlic
- ¼ cup Sour Cream (low fat)
- ¼ cup shredded Cheese (Parmesan)
- ¼ cup Mozzarella Cheese (shredded)
- 1/8 tsp. Parsley (dried)
- ½ cup Yogurt (Greek)
- Pinch of Black Pepper
- Pinch of Kosher Salt

DIRECTIONS:

» Boil spinach in water for 1 min. Drain the water. Set the spinach aside to cool and then chop. Puree all the ingredients, including spinach, in a blender.
» Transfer the mixture to the slow cooker. Add cheeses and cook for 1 hour on "low." Serve with sliced vegetables.

Nutrition: Calories 263 Fats 14 g; Sodium: 537 mg; Carbohydrates 18 g; Protein 20 g

APPLE SALSA

Preparation Time: 15 minutes
Cooking Time: 2 hours
Servings: 3

INGREDIENTS:

- 7 ½ oz. drained Black Beans
- ¼ cubed Apples (Granny Smith)
- ¼ chopped Chili Pepper (Serrano)
- 1/8 cup chopped onion (red)
- 1 ½ tbsp. chopped cilantro
- ¼ Lemon
- ¼ Orange
- Pinch of Sea Salt
- Pinch of Black Pepper (cracked)

DIRECTIONS:

» Mix all the ingredients in the cooker (slow cooker). Cook on "low" for an hour. Transfer to a covered container and allow to cool for 1 hr. Serve.

Nutrition: Calories 100; Fats 0.4 g; Sodium: 50 mg; Carbohydrates 20 g; Protein 5 g

Chapter 8
Recipes For Dinner

BROCCOLI AU GRATIN

Servings: 1
Preparation Time: 5 min
Cooking Time: 10 min

INGREDIENTS

- Broccoli 100 g, 1 tablespoon of olive oil, 50 ml of whole milk, Cooking cream 50 g, Grated Parmesan 25 g

DIRECTIONS

» Wash the broccoli and cut them into coarse pieces.
» Prepare a simil-béchamel by dissolving the parmesan and cream in the milk.
» Place the broccoli in a baking dish and cover with the bechamel sauce.
» Bake them in the oven at 180 degrees for about 10 minutes or until they have obtained a succulent crust, it depends a lot on your personal tastes.
» Serve hot.

SUMMER TOMATO SALAD

Servings: 1
Preparation Time: 5 min
Cooking Time: -

INGREDIENTS

- 3 green salad tomatoes, 1 sprig of celery, 1 cucumber, 1 basil leaf, 1 tablespoon of olive oil

DIRECTIONS

» Cut all the Ingredients into thin slices and mix in a salad bowl. Season with salt if necessary.
» Preferably let it rest for a few minutes in the refrigerator before serving.

TYROLEAN SIDE DISH IN AVOCADO SAUCE

Servings: 1
Preparation Time: 10 min
Cooking Time: 10 min

INGREDIENTS

- Brussels sprouts 100 g, salad tomatoes 60 g, avocado 60 g, 1 tablespoon olive oil, salt to taste, pepper to taste

DIRECTIONS

» Heat a little oil in a pan and quickly roast the Brussels sprouts, previously blanched for about 5 minutes.
» Wash the salad tomatoes and cut them into thin slices.
» Prepare the avocado sauce by cutting it into chunks, adding the oil, salt and pepper; Blend it with the help of the hand blender until you get a homogeneous mixture. Mix all the ingredients well and leave to flavor for at least 10 minutes before serving.

CURRIED CHICKEN WINGS WITH CARROT CREAM AND YOGURT

Servings: 2
Preparation Time: 15 min
Cooking Time: 60 min

INGREDIENTS

- 8 chicken wings, 300 g of carrots, 120 g of Greek yogurt, 70 g of onion, 1 shallot, 20 g of butter, Thyme to taste, Curry to taste, Salt to taste, 100 ml of white cooking wine, Olive oil to taste

DIRECTIONS

» Heat about 2 tablespoons of olive oil in a pan, when ready, start cooking the chicken wings on a very low heat, adding the curry immediately; after about 10 minutes turn them, add the shallot and onion cut into slices and let them go for another 8 minutes.
» Raise the flame slightly and blend with the white wine; when the alcohol has evaporated, lower it again, cook with a lid and continue to cook for another 20 minutes; if it dries too much you can add a finger of water.
» Peel the carrots and cut them into thin slices. Heat the butter in a pan and when it is hot add them with some thyme to taste. Cook over low heat for at least 30 minutes.
» Add ½ liter of water and continue cooking for another 15 minutes. When the carrots are cooked, blend them with a hand blender and let them cool. Once cold, add the yogurt and use this fantastic sauce as an accompaniment to the curry chicken wings.

HASH BROWN

Servings: 1
Preparation Time: 5 min
Cooking Time: 35 min

INGREDIENTS

- 200 g of potatoes, 4 whole eggs, 1 chopped onion, 1 tablespoon of olive oil, 3 g of chili powder

DIRECTIONS

- » Chop the potatoes very finely, heat some oil in a pan and start cooking them over low heat.
- » Add the rest of the Ingredients except the eggs and cook for another 5 minutes.
- » In a separate pan, break the eggs and beat them (adding salt and pepper if you like), add it to the mixture and cover.
- » Continue to cook for another 25 minutes over low heat.

RISOTTO WITH MUSHROOMS

Servings: 2
Preparation Time: 5 min
Cooking Time: 30min

INGREDIENTS

- 1 chopped onion, 180 g of rice, 400 ml of vegetable broth, 1 tablespoon of oil, 10 g of butter, 40 g of mushrooms, preferably porcini

DIRECTIONS

- » Heat the oil in a saucepan and pour the chopped onion, letting it dry for 1 minute.
- » Add the rice and toast it for 3 minutes, taking care to turn it over to prevent it from burning.
- » At this point add the sliced mushrooms and the broth, a little at a time, repeat the operation every time the mixture dries until it is cooked, it will take about 20 minutes.
- » Turn off the heat and add the cold butter, stir to cream the risotto. Serve hot.

LEMON MARINATED CHICKEN

Servings: 1
Preparation Time: 120 min
Cooking Time: 20 min

INGREDIENTS

- 2 chicken drumsticks, 2 medium potatoes, 2 lemons, Rosemary to taste, Parsley to taste, Fresh chillies to taste, Vinegar 100 ml, Olive oil to taste

DIRECTIONS

- » Cut the chicken meat with fairly deep cuts and leave it to marinate with 3 tablespoons of oil, lemon juice and zest, pepper, salt, chilli and rosemary. Leave it to flavor for at least 2 hours.
- » In the meantime, wash the potatoes and cut them into slices about 1 cm thick; boil a pot of water in which you have added the vinegar and cook them for about 10 minutes. Once cooked, drain, remove excess liquid and season with a drizzle of olive oil.
- » Remove the chicken from the marinade and cook it on a hot grill along with the potatoes. Cook for about 8 minutes before turning it over to the other side and leaving it for the same amount of time.
- » Serve still hot with a sprinkling of finely chopped fresh parsley.

ROASTED TURKEY IN TUNA SAUCE

Servings: 5
Preparation Time: 15 min
Cooking Time: 20 min

INGREDIENTS

- 1 kg of turkey breast, 170 g of tuna in oil, 150 g of onion, 80 g of mayonnaise, 8 dried cherry tomatoes in oil, 3 anchovy fillets, 100 ml white wine for cooking, 10 g of capers

DIRECTIONS

- » The first thing to do is to prepare the tuna sauce. In a blender, place the drained tuna, mayonnaise, tomatoes, capers and anchovy fillets and blend until you get a pink and homogeneous paste; you can add a drizzle of oil if you see that it becomes too dry and blends with difficulty.
- » Finely slice the onions and turkey. Heat a drizzle of oil in a non-stick pan and start simmering the onions; after about 10 minutes add the turkey and the wine to blend it.
- » When the alcohol has evaporated, lower the heat and complete the Cooking Time.
- » Serve in a tray with the sauce on top and some capers for decoration.

CHICKEN WITH WALNUT PESTO AND SALAD

Servings: 5
Preparation Time: 15 min
Cooking Time: 20min

INGREDIENTS

- 150 g of chicken breast, 15 g of parsley, 20 g of walnuts, 15 g of Parmesan cheese, 1 tablespoon of olive oil, juice of ½ lemon, 50 ml of water, 20 g of chopped red onion, 50 g of salad green, 100 g of sliced cherry tomatoes, 1 tablespoon of balsamic vinegar

DIRECTIONS

- » To make the pesto, put the parsley, walnuts, parmesan, oil, lemon juice and water in a hand blender and blend until you get a smooth paste. Marinate the chicken breast in 1 tablespoon of pesto and a few drops of lemon juice, let it rest in the refrigerator for at least 30 minutes.
- » Heat 1 drizzle of oil in a non-stick pan and when hot, add the chicken breast, with the pesto in the pan and cook 4 minutes per side.
- » Once hot, serve on a plate with the rest of the sauce next to it.
- » For side dish, cut and mix the rest of the Ingredients in a salad bowl.

EGGS AND ZUCCHINI

Servings: 1
Preparation Time: 10 min
Cooking Time: 20 min

INGREDIENTS

- 3 whole eggs, courgettes 60 g, 1 tablespoon olive oil, salt to taste

DIRECTIONS

» Put an egg in cold water and boil it for 15 minutes, cut it in half and serve it on a plate. Slice the courgettes, grill them, season them with oil and salt and serve them as a side dish for the eggs.

RAW HAM WITH PUMPKIN PUREE FOR CHILDREN

Servings: 1
Preparation Time: 10 min
Cooking Time: 20 min

INGREDIENTS

- Raw ham 25 g, Pumpkin 80 g, 1 tablespoon of olive oil, Butter 10 g

DIRECTIONS

» Bake the pumpkin in the oven at 180 degrees for about 20 minutes.
» Clean it in a container, add salt, oil and with the help of an immersion blender transform it into a tasty puree. Add the butter and blend again to blend the mixture.
» Serve as a side dish for raw ham.

TUNA SALAD

Servings: 1
Preparation Time: 5 min
Cooking Time: 10 min

INGREDIENTS

- Fresh tuna steak 110 g, Lettuce 60 g, 1 salad tomato, 15 g black olives, 1 tablespoon olive oil, Sunflower seeds to taste, Salt to taste, Pepper to taste

DIRECTIONS

» Heat a drizzle of oil in a pan, once hot cook the fresh tuna steak for 3 minutes per side, leaving the center slightly cooked; season with salt and pepper and cut into thin strips.
» Wash the lettuce and the salad tomato, cut them into coarse chunks, add it to the tuna with olives. Drizzle with olive oil and sunflower seeds.

CREAM CHEESE WITH ZUCCHINI

Servings: 1
Preparation Time: 10 min
Cooking Time: 10 min

INGREDIENTS

- Wholemeal bread 40g, Quark cheese 60g, Zucchini 55g, Sale 11g, Mayonnaise 10g, Olive oil 10g

DIRECTIONS

» Weigh and grill or boil the courgettes. Season with oil, parmesan and salt to taste.
» Add the cream cheese to the center of the plate and decorate with the mayonnaise.
» Grease the slices with half a portion of butter.

MOUNTAIN DISH

Servings: 1
Preparation Time: 10 min
Cooking Time: -

INGREDIENTS

- Rosa Camuna cheese 24 g, Ox-eye tomato 45 g, Pitted black olives 22 g, Soya lecithin 6 g, Mayonnaise 147 g, Extra virgin olive oil 14 g, Mandarins 1 3 g

DIRECTIONS

» Weigh the cheese and cut it into thin slices on a wooden cutting board.
» Weigh and thinly slice the tomatoes and olives. Serve with a sauce made from oil, lecithin and mayonnaise. Garnish with fruit.

SIDE DISH IN AVOCADO SAUCE

Servings: 1
Preparation Time: 10 min
Cooking Time: 10 min

INGREDIENTS

- Brussels sprouts 100 g, salad tomatoes 60 g, avocado 60 g, 1 tablespoon olive oil, salt to taste, pepper to taste

DIRECTIONS

» Heat a little oil in a pan and quickly roast the Brussels sprouts, previously blanched for about 5 minutes.
» Wash the salad tomatoes and cut them into thin slices. Prepare the avocado sauce by cutting it into chunks, adding the oil, salt and pepper; Blend it with the help of the hand blender until you get a homogeneous mixture.
» Mix all the ingredients well and leave to flavor for at least 10 minutes before serving.

CURRIED CHICKEN WINGS WITH CREAM OF POTATOES AND YOGURT

Servings: 2
Preparation Time: 15 min
Cooking Time: 60 min

INGREDIENTS

- 8 chicken wings, 300 g of carrots, 120 g of Greek yogurt, 70 g of onion, 1 shallot, 20 g of butter, Thyme to taste, Curry to taste, Salt to taste, 100 ml of white cooking wine, Olive oil to taste

DIRECTIONS

» Heat about 2 tablespoons of olive oil in a pan, when ready, start cooking the chicken wings on a very low heat, adding the curry immediately; after about 10 minutes turn them, add the shallot and onion cut into slices and let them go for another 8 minutes. Raise the flame slightly and blend with the white wine; when the alcohol has evaporated, lower it again, cook with a lid and continue to cook for another 20 minutes; if it dries too much you can add a finger of water.
» Peel the carrots and cut them into thin slices. Heat the butter in a pan and when it is hot add them with some thyme to taste. Cook over low heat for at least 30 minutes.
» Add ½ liter of water and continue cooking for another 15 minutes. When the carrots are cooked, blend them with a hand blender and let them cool. Once cold, add the yogurt and use this fantastic sauce as an accompaniment to the curry chicken wings.

PORK SKEWER WITH GRILLED PEPPERS

Servings: 1
Preparation Time: 10 min
Cooking Time: 10 min

INGREDIENTS

- Pork fillet 60 g, Peppers 30 g, Lard 15 g, Salt to taste

DIRECTIONS

» Wash the peppers and cut them into small squares of about 2 cm each. Cut the fillet into cubes of about 2 cm each too.
» Repeat the same operation with the lard.
» Assemble the skewer alternating a piece of pork with a piece of lard and a square of pepper.
» You can cook them both on the grill and in a non-stick pan for 10 minutes. Serve hot.

SUMMER DISH

Servings: 1
Preparation Time: 10 min
Cooking Time: 10 min

INGREDIENTS

- Meat in jelly 53 g, Carrots 45 g, Slices of wholemeal bread 40 g, Extra virgin olive oil 12 g, Pitted black olives 10 g, Mayonnaise 30 g

DIRECTIONS

» Butter the slices of bread.
» Wash, weigh and grate the carrots and season them with olive oil and mayonnaise. Add the black olives and the jellied meat.

HASH BROWN POTATO CASSEROLE

Servings: 4
Preparation Time: 10 min
Cooking Time: 35 min

INGREDIENTS

- 450g hash brown potatoes, 4 beaten eggs, 1 chopped red onion, 1 red pepper, chopped, 1 tablespoon olive oil, Sliced sausage, 170g, ¼ teaspoon of red pepper, A pinch of black peppe r

DIRECTIONS

» Heat the oil in a pan over medium heat, add the onion and sausage, mix and sauté for 5 minutes.
» Add the hash browns and other Ingredients except the eggs and pepper, mix and cook for another 5 minutes. Pour the beaten eggs with black pepper over the sausage mix, place in the oven and bake at 170 degrees for 25 minutes. Spread the mix on plates and serve for breakfast.

RICE AND MUSHROOMS

Servings: 4
Preparation Time: 10 min
Cooking Time: 30 min

INGREDIENTS

- 1 chopped red onion, 1 cup rice, 2 garlic cloves, minced, 2 tablespoons olive oil, 2 cups chicken broth, 1 tablespoon chopped cilantro, ½ cup fat-free cheddar, grated, White mushrooms cut, 225 g

DIRECTIONS

» Heat the oil in a pan over medium heat, add the onion, garlic and mushrooms, mix and cook for 5-6 minutes.
» Add the rice and the rest of the Ingredients, bring to a boil and cook over medium heat for 25 minutes, stirring frequently.
» Divide the rice into plates and serve for breakfast.

CHICKEN WITH WALNUT PESTO AND RED SALAD

Servings: 4
Preparation Time: 10 min
Cooking Time: 30 min

INGREDIENTS

- 15g parsley, 15g walnuts, 15g parmesan, 1 tablespoon olive oil, 1/2 lemon juice, 50ml water, 150g skinless chicken breast, 20g red onions, thinly sliced, 1 tsp of red wine vinegar, 35g of rocket, 100g of cherry tomatoes, cut in half, 1 teaspoon of balsamic vinegar

DIRECTIONS

» To prepare the pesto, put the parsley, walnuts, parmesan, olive oil, half the lemon juice and a little water in a blender or food processor and blend until you get a paste. velvety. Gradually add more water until you get the desired consistency. Marinate the chicken breast in 1 tablespoon of pesto and the remaining lemon juice in the refrigerator for 30 minutes, more if possible. Heat the oven to 200 °.

» Heat a skillet over medium-high heat. Fry the chicken in its marinade sauce for 1 minute per side, then transfer to the oven and cook for 8 minutes or until Cooking Time. Marinate the onions in the red wine vinegar for 5-10 minutes. Drain the liquid. When the chicken is cooked, remove it from the oven, pour over another tablespoon of pesto and let the heat of the chicken melt it. Cover with aluminum foil and leave to rest for 5 minutes before serving. Mix the rocket, tomatoes and onions and season with balsamic vinegar. Serve with the chicken, pouring the remaining pesto over it.

PASTA WITH CABBAGE AND BLACK OLIVES

Servings: 1
Preparation Time: 10 min
Cooking Time: 15 min

INGREDIENTS

- 60 g of buckwheat pasta, 180 g of pasta, 6 washed kale leaves, 20 g of black olives, 2 tablespoons of oil, ½ chilli

DIRECTIONS

» Cut the kale leaves into strips about 4 cm wide; cook them in salted boiling water for 5 minutes. Add the pasta to the pot. While the pasta is cooking, pour the oil and olives into a non-stick pan. Drain the pasta and kale (keeping a little cooking time water aside) and add them to the olives. Mix well, adding a little Cooking Time water if necessary. Add the chilli.

RICE WITH CABBAGE AND RED WINE

Servings: 1
Preparation Time: 10 min
Cooking Time: 25 min

INGREDIENTS

- 80g of rice, 100g of kale, 100ml of vegetable broth, 50g of red onion, 50ml of red wine, 2 tablespoons of olive oil

DIRECTIONS

» Clean the kale by removing it from the central ribs, slice it coarsely, boil it for 5-6 minutes in boiling water, drain and cool it under cold water.
» Chop half an onion. Brown the onion in 2 tablespoons of oil for 1 minute, then add the rice, toast it for less than 1 minute, sprinkle with the red wine. Then start adding the vegetable broth and continue the Cooking Time, always stirring, for 7-8 minutes; add the kale and cook the rice adding the necessary broth.

SPICY CABBAGE CREAM

Servings: 1
Preparation Time: 10 min
Cooking Time: 15 min

INGREDIENTS

- 200g of cabbage, 100g of rocket, 200g of champignon mushrooms, 1/2 red onion, 1 teaspoon of ginger, 1 teaspoon of turmeric, 1 tablespoon of olive oil

DIRECTIONS

» Cut the onion into slices and sauté it with a teaspoon of mixed spices in a high-sided pan, stirring carefully so as not to burn the onion. Add the cabbage and rocket. Stir and add hot water to almost cover the surface. Add salt.Blend with an immersion blender until a homogeneous consistency is obtained. Cut the mushrooms into 4 parts and sauté them in a non-stick pan with a drizzle of extra virgin olive oil, a teaspoon of spices and a pinch of salt. Pour the cream into the bowls, place the spiced mushrooms on top and season with a drizzle of oil.

PORK RIBS WITH MUSHROOM SAUCE

Servings: 6
Preparation Time: 30 min
Cooking Time: 7 hours

INGREDIENTS

- 4 pork loin cutlets, cut about 1.9 cm thick, sliced fresh mushrooms (1 ½ cup), sliced fresh thyme (2 tsp) or dried thyme (¾ tsp), apple juice or cider (½ cup), Quick Cooking Time Tapioca (2 tablespoons), Onion (1 small), finely chopped, Oil (1 tablespoon),

Worcestershire sauce (1 1/2 teaspoons), Garlic powder (1 tablespoon)

DIRECTIONS

» Heat the oil to a low temperature in a large pan. Add the ribs; cook until golden brown, turning evenly. Drain the fat. Put the onion in a slow cooking time pot. Mash the tapioca using a blender or mortar. Combine the mushroom broth, tapioca, apple juice, garlic powder, Worcestershire sauce and dried thyme in a medium bowl; blend the champignons. In the slow cooking time pot, pour over the ribs.

BUCKWHEAT WITH ROCKET PESTO AND TOMATOES

Servings: 1
Preparation Time: 10 min
Cooking Time: 20 min

INGREDIENTS

- 80g of buckwheat, 100g of rocket, 150g of olive oil, 50g of hazelnuts, 50g of parmesan, 1 clove of garlic, 100g of tomatoes, pine nuts 10g

DIRECTIONS

» To prepare the rocket pesto, wash the rocket very well, dry it and put it in a glass of the mixer, add the pine nuts, the Grana Padano DOP and the garlic. At this point add a small part of the olive oil. Start blending everything at low speed and gradually add the remaining olive oil slowly, until you get a well blended and fluid cream. If you do not use the rocket pesto immediately, you can keep it in the refrigerator for a few days by placing it in a container with a lid, covered with a drizzle of olive oil. Cook the buckwheat according to the instructions on the package. Season with pesto and tomato slices.

SIRLOIN STEAK IN A BED OF ROCKET

Servings: 2
Preparation Time: 10 min
Cooking Time: 10 min

INGREDIENTS

- 500 g of sirloin, 100 g rocket, 100 g of tomatoes, 10 g of olive oil

DIRECTIONS

» Wash and dry the rocket well. Then wash and cut the tomatoes in half. Place the grill on the stove and let it heat well, over high heat. When the grill is hot, place the meat, then lower the heat to medium-high and cook for about 3 minutes on that side. Then you can turn the meat with the tongs and cook for another 3-4 minutes. Remove from the grill and leave a minute on the cutting board to let it rest so that the juices are preserved better (if you have to leave it longer you can cover it with aluminum foil). Then cut crosswise to obtain more slices with a well-sharpened smooth blade knife. Arrange a bed of rocket, the cut and some tomatoes on a serving plate.

CHICKEN IN GREEN SAUCE

Servings: 4
Preparation Time: 5 min
Cooking Time: 20 min

INGREDIENTS

- 500g chicken breast, 2 large parsley leaves, pagrattato, 1 clove of garlic, 1 teaspoon of capers, 2 unsalted anchovy fillets, 1 tablespoon of basamic vinegar, 1 tablespoon of olive oil

DIRECTIONS

» For the green sauce: dip the breadcrumbs in the vinegar, squeeze it and pass it through a sieve, collect the proceeds in a bowl, add all the other well-chopped ingredients, season with oil and vinegar according to your taste. Cook the chicken breast on a hot plate or pan. Cover the chicken with the green sauce.

LASAGNA

Servings: 1
Preparation Time: 15 min
Cooking Time: 45 min

INGREDIENTS

- 2 eggs, extra virgin olive oil 14 g, white flour 70 g„ peeled tomatoes 40 g, cheese 5 g, fresh pork sausage 8 g, cooking cream 40 g

DIRECTIONS

» For the pasta: add the eggs, 10 g of oil, flour and a pinch of salt.
» Knead and roll out the dough obtained with a rolling pin dividing it in half.
» For the filling: Put the first layer of pasta in the single-portion pan, fill with the previously sautéed sausage, the diced cheese
» Cover with the remaining dough and sprinkle with the cream and the remaining amount of oil. Bake it in the oven at 200 ° for 20 minutes.

PASTA WITH WALNUT PESTO

Servings: 1
Preparation Time: 5 min
Cooking Time: 15 min

INGREDIENTS

- 50g of buckwheat pasta, 15g of walnuts, 15g of parmesan, 1 tablespoon of olive oil, 1 sprig of parsley

DIRECTIONS

» Boil the pasta for 10 minutes. To make the pesto, put the parsley, walnuts, parmesan, olive oil, half the lemon juice and a little water in a blender or food processor and blend until you have a paste. velvety. Add more water gradually until you get the consistency you prefer.Season the pasta with the prepared pesto and serve hot.

SEA BREAM WITH RED WINE AND ONION

Servings: 4
Preparation Time: 10 min
Cooking Time: 30 min

INGREDIENTS

- 800g of sea bream, 750ml of red wine, 400g of red onion, 1 clove of garlic, 1 tablespoon of olive oil

DIRECTIONS

» Clean the sea bream. Open the belly of the sea bream with scissors (starting from the anal cavity up to the height of the gills) and remove the entrails (this operation will be done in case you have not asked to have the fish cleaned in the fish shop). Free from scales. Wash it under fresh running water, then dry it with paper towels or a tea towel. Season the inside with a pinch of salt, minced garlic and coarsely chopped pink pepper (I used the meat tenderizer). Cut the sea bream on the side by making a light zigzag cut, so as to allow a uniform diffusion of heat during the Cooking Time. Wrap some parchment paper around the end of the tail to prevent it from burning during the Cooking Time. Lightly grease a pan and place the fish, season with a drizzle of oil and bake for 5 minutes, until it browns, then add the onions and sprinkle them with a glass of wine, salt and pepper, then lower the oven to 180 ° and cook for another 25-30 minutes. Meanwhile, in a fairly large pot, boil the remaining wine until it reduces. Remove the fish from the oven and place it on a serving dish, then add the Cooking Time sauce, including the onions, to the sauce and pour it all over the sea bream before serving.

CHICKEN SALAD WITH SESAME

Servings: 1
Preparation Time: 5 min
Cooking Time: 15 min

INGREDIENTS

- 1 tablespoon of sesame seeds, 100g of cabbage, 50g of red onion, 20g of chopped parsley, 150g of chicken, 1 tablespoon of extra virgin olive oil, 1 teaspoon of sesame oil, Juice of 1 lemon, 1 teaspoon of honey, 2 teaspoons of soy sauce

DIRECTIONS

» Toast the sesame seeds for 3 minutes until lightly golden and fragrant. In another bowl, mix the olive oil, sesame oil, lemon juice, honey and soy sauce to make the dressing. Put the kale, red onion and parsley in a large bowl and mix. Add the dressing and mix again. Top with the shredded chicken, cooked in a pan for 15 minutes, and the sesame seeds just before serving.

CHUNKS OF SALMON AND BACON

Servings: 4
Preparation Time: 15 min
Cooking Time: 15 min

INGREDIENTS

- 700 g of salmon fillet, 150 g of sliced bacon, sage, butter for the pan, black pepper

DIRECTIONS

» To prepare the salmon and bacon morsels, wash and dry the salmon fillet by dabbing it with kitchen paper. Check that there are no residual thorns by running a finger on the surface of the meat to highlight them and, if necessary, remove them with the help of tweezers.
» Cut the salmon into cubes of about 2 cm per side, salt them, pepper them and wrap them in a slice of bacon each, with half a sage leaf. Secure each slice on the bite with a wooden toothpick and place them on a lightly greased baking sheet. Place in a preheated oven at 200 ° C and bake for 10-15 minutes, turning them occasionally. Transfer the salmon and bacon bites to a serving dish and serve hot.

EGGPLANT PARMIGIANA

Servings: 1
Preparation Time: 15 min
Cooking Time: 20 min

INGREDIENTS

- Aubergines 100 g, Defatted cooked ham 20 g, Peeled tomatoes 25 g, Black olives 30 g, Extra virgin olive oil 14 g, Basil to taste

DIRECTIONS

» Clean, wash and weigh the aubergines. Slice thinly and grill them.
» Put the aubergines in a single plate brushed with oil, alternating slices, peeled tomatoes and ham. Salt and add a little oil and garnish with finely chopped olives.
» Cook until Cooking Time.

SALMON ESCALOPE WITH PINK PEPPER

Servings: 1
Preparation Time: 15 min
Cooking Time: 5 min

INGREDIENTS

- Fresh salmon 57 g, Lettuce 50 g, Black olives 30 g, Extra virgin olive oil 15 g, 00 flour to taste

DIRECTIONS

» Chop the olives with the crescent, add the lecithin and pink pepper.
» Flour the fresh salmon escalope and cook it in a non-stick pan with some fresh sage leaves.
» Wash, peel and weigh the salad and dress it with an emulsion of oil and salt.

TAGLIATELLE WITH CREAM AND HAM

Servings: 1
Preparation Time: 15 min
Cooking Time: 5 min

INGREDIENTS

- Tagliatelle 150 g, cooked ham 40 g, cooking cream 40 g, parmesan 17 g, extra virgin olive oil 15 g

DIRECTIONS

» Cut the ham into cubes and heat it with the cooking cream, half the oil, salt and pepper. Drain the noodles and dress them with the sauce. Add the grated Parmesan.

BUCKWHEAT SPAGHETTI WITH PRAWNS

Servings: 1
Preparation Time: 5 min
Cooking Time: 20 min

INGREDIENTS

- 150ml vegetable broth, 80g prawns, 2 tablespoons extra virgin olive oil, 80g sraceno wheat spaghetti, 1 chopped chilli, 1 teaspoon chopped ginger, 2 garlic cloves, chopped, 20g red onions, chopped, 70g of green beans, 60g of cabbage, chopped

DIRECTIONS

» Heat a skillet over high heat, then cook the shrimp in 1 teaspoon of oil for 3 minutes. Transfer the shrimp to a plate. Cook the noodles in boiling water for 6.7 minutes or as directed on the package, then drain. Meanwhile, sauté the garlic, chilli, ginger, red onion, green beans and kale in the oil over medium-high heat for 3 minutes. Add the broth and bring to a boil, then simmer for a minute or two, until the vegetables are cooked but still crisp. Add the prawns, noodles, bring to the boil, remove from the heat and serve.

CHICKEN BREAST WITH RED ONION AND CABBAGE

Servings: 1
Preparation Time: 35 min
Cooking Time: 20 min

INGREDIENTS

- 60g of buckwheat, 140g of chicken breast, 2.5 teaspoons of turmeric powder, 60g of cabbage, chopped, 30g of red onion, chopped, 20g of celery, 1.5 teaspoons of fresh chopped ginger, Juice of 1 lemon, 1.5 tablespoons of olive oil, 150g tomato, 1 chilli, thinly sliced, 20g parsley, chopped

DIRECTIONS

» To make the sauce, remove the eye from the tomato and chop it very finely. Mix with the chilli, capers, parsley and lemon juice Marinate the chicken breast for 30 minutes in 1 teaspoon of turmeric, lemon juice, celery and ginger. Cook the marinated chicken in the oven for 10-12 minutes. Remove from the oven, cover with cling film and leave to rest for 5 minutes before serving. Meanwhile, cook the kale in a steamer for 5 minutes, then sauté the red onions and ginger in a little oil, until soft, then add the cooked kale and fry for another minute. Cook the buckwheat according to the instructions on the package. Serve with the chicken, vegetables and sauce.

SALMON WITH TURMERIC

Servings: 1
Preparation Time: 15 min
Cooking Time: 20 min

INGREDIENTS

- 180g salmon, 3 tablespoons of olive oil, 1 tablespoon of turmeric powder, Juice of 1/2 lemon, 50 g of red onion, finely chopped, 70g of green lentils, 1 clove of garlic, 150 g of celery, 100 ml of vegetable broth, 1 tablespoon of chopped parsley, 130 g of tomatoes

DIRECTIONS

» Heat a skillet on top, add the olive oil, then the onion, garlic, curry powder, ginger, chilli and celery. Fry for 6-7 minutes. Add the tomatoes, broth and lentils and cook for 15 minutes. Meanwhile, mix the turmeric, oil and lemon juice and rub into the salmon. Place on a baking sheet and cook for 8-10 minutes. Mix the parsley with the celery and serve with the salmon.

ROSBEEF COOKED AT A LOW TEMPERATURE

Servings: 1
Preparation Time: 15 min
Cooking Time: 60 min

INGREDIENTS

- 1 kg of rosbeef, pepper, fine salt, a tablespoon of brown sugar

DIRECTIONS

» For the rosbeef recipe with Low Temperature Cooking Time, start by finishing the meat in order to eliminate the fatty parts. On a cutting board, proceed with the so-called "dry iratura" technique, which consists in salting the meat before the Cooking Time: in a bowl add 4 parts of fine salt and a tablespoon of brown sugar to obtain a single mixture. The procedure is very simple: it is necessary to sprinkle the entire priest's hat with the mixture of salt and sugar, being careful to cover the entire portion of meat. At this point, let the meat rest in a closed container in the fridge for a time that can vary from 4 to 6 hours, depending on the desired result.
» This is an operation that we advise you to do the day before the actual Preparation Time: of the recipe in order to shorten the time. After the rest time in the fridge, prepare the necessary for cooking at a low temperature: in a large pot full of water, immerse the roner by setting the temperature to 62 ° C. At the same time, with the help of the machine for the vacuum extraction, pack the raw meat cut into an envelope. Let the air out of the enclosure, close it, fold the upper part of the enclosure on itself, insert it into the vacuum machine and operate it to extract the air and seal the enclosure.
» Once the set temperature of 62 ° C is reached, immerse the bag completely and cook the meat for 12 hours. When cooked, remove the bags from the pot. Keep it aside.
» At this point, remove the meat from the vacuum and place it in an oven pan. Bake at 220 ° for 10 minutes.
» Once this time has elapsed, remove it from the oven and leave it to rest for a few minutes before serving.

BEEF WITH RED ONIONS

Servings: 1
Preparation Time: 15 min
Cooking Time: 60 min

INGREDIENTS

- 1 tablespoon of olive oil, 100g of potatoes, 5g of chopped parsley, 50g of red onion, 50g of cabbage, sliced, 1 clove of garlic, 120g of beef fillet, 40ml of red wine, 150ml of broth

DIRECTIONS

» Place the potatoes in a pan with 1 teaspoon of oil and roast in the hot oven for 50 minutes. Turn the potatoes every 10 minutes to ensure uniform Cooking Time.
» When cooked, remove from the oven, sprinkle with chopped parsley and mix well. Fry the onion in a pan for 6-7 minutes, until soft and well caramelized. Steam the cabbage for 2-3 minutes, then drain. Gently fry the garlic; add the cabbage and fry for another 1-2 minutes. Stay warm. Heat an oven-proof skillet over high heat until smoking. Coat the meat in 1/2 teaspoon of oil and fry in the hot pan over medium-high heat. transfer the pan to an oven set at 220°C for about 4 minutes.
» Put the meat to rest on a cutting board, in the meantime put the pan back on the heat, over high heat, and add the wine. After a few minutes it will have become thick and will have absorbed all the remaining juices of the meat, thus creating a delicious sauce.

CHICKEN IN RED WINE

Servings: 4
Preparation Time: 15 min
Cooking Time: 50 min

INGREDIENTS

- 500g chicken, 500ml red wine, 1 clove of garlic, 1 tablespoon of olive oil, 10g rosemary

DIRECTIONS

» Heat the extra virgin olive oil over low heat in a saucepan with high sides together with the garlic clove left in a shirt and lightly crushed and a small sprig of rosemary. When the oil starts to sizzle, add the chopped chicken and let it brown evenly.
» Add plenty of wine to the well-roséed chicken until the chicken pieces are almost covered, cover the saucepan and cook over low heat for 50 minutes. If necessary, add some hot water while the chicken is cooking.
» When cooked, turn off the heat. and serve the chicken by adding the Cooking Time juices to the wine.

CHILLI WITH BEEF

Servings: 5
Preparation Time: 15 min
Cooking Time: 90 min

INGREDIENTS

- 800 g of beef pulp, 500 g of boiled red or black beans, 400 g of tomato pulp, 150 g of sweet peppers (red, yellow and green), 150 g of white onion, a clove of garlic, 30 g of cumin in the seeds, 20 g of sweet or spicy paprika to taste, 1 tablespoon of brown sugar, 1 pinch of oregano, 2 jalapeño peppers or 1 fresh red pepper, extra virgin olive oil

DIRECTIONS

» To make the chili con carne, start by cutting the meat into cubes. Coarsely chop the sweet peppers, onion and chillies as well. Put 2 or 3 tablespoons of oil and garlic in a large pot and when they start to fry add the chopped vegetables. Let it fry for about two minutes over high heat, then add half the spices, turning immediately to avoid burning. After a few moments, add the meat and the rest of the spices, a spoonful of salt and mix everything.
» Cover with a lid and lower the heat. After about 20 minutes of Cooking Time, add the tomato puree, brown sugar and a pinch of oregano. Stir and cook for about

70 minutes over low heat, stirring occasionally. After 70 minutes, add the beans, mix, season with salt if deemed necessary and cook over low heat for another 20 minutes. Turn off the heat, let it rest for a few minutes, then serve the chili con carne with white rice, tortillas or nachos.

SMOKED SALMON ROLL

Servings: 2
Preparation Time: 15 min
Cooking Time: -

INGREDIENTS

- 160 g of smoked salmon, 300 g of cream cheese, 1 lime, juice and zest, 1 avocado,
- Chives 15 g, Salt to taste, Pepper as needed

DIRECTIONS

» In a bowl, combine the cheese, finely chopped chives, salt, pepper, juice, and lime zest. Cut the avocado in half, remove the bone and cut it into slices of about 0.5 cm each. Carefully spread the smoked salmon slices without breaking them and spread the mixture previously obtained and the avocado slices over them. Create a "roll" by rolling the salmon slice on itself until you get a long sausage; cut it into pieces of about 5 cm and arrange them on a cutting board.
» Keep refrigerated until use.

PASTA ALLA CARRETTIERA

Servings: 5
Preparation Time: 10 min
Cooking Time: 15 min

INGREDIENTS

- 120 g of aged pecorino, 1 handful of parsley, 1 fresh chilli, 1 clove of garlic, 1 tablespoon of extra virgin olive oil, 360 g of spaghetti

DIRECTIONS

» Making pasta alla carrettiera is quick and easy. While the spaghetti is boiling, finely chop the garlic and chilli pepper, collect them in a bowl with plenty of oil. Drain the pasta al dente, transfer it to the bowl and dress it with the prepared emulsion, adjusting the consistency with a little cooking time pasta water. Add the grated pecorino and whisk. Add the chopped fresh parsley, transfer the pasta to the plates and serve immediately.

PENNE PASTA WITH ARRABBIATA SAUCE

Servings: 4
Preparation Time: 10 min
Cooking Time: 15 min

INGREDIENTS

- 320 g of penne, 1 red chilli pepper, 1 clove of garlic, extra virgin olive oil, chopped parsley, Pecorino cheese, salt, 5 ripe tomatoes

DIRECTIONS

» Prepare the penne all'arrabbiata sauce while the water is boiling and the pasta is cooking. Put 2-3 tablespoons of oil in a pan, the crushed garlic clove and the crushed red pepper, after removing all the seeds. The flame must be moderate, the oil must be flavored but not burned. Cut the tomatoes in half, remove the seeds and then cut them into cubes. Remove the garlic from the pan and pour in the tomato cubes.
» Let them heat for a few minutes until you get a light and still well colored sauce. Once the penne are cooked al dente, drain and pour them directly onto the sauce. Mix well so that the pasta is evenly seasoned, then add a dash of raw oil. Serve, complete with parsley, grated pecorino to taste.

BAKED CHILLIES WITH HERBS AND CAPERS

Servings: 2
Preparation Time: 10 min
Cooking Time: 20 min

INGREDIENTS

- 70 g grated bread, 2 tablespoons of salted capers, mix of aromatic herbs (thyme - basil - mint - marjoram - lemon - oregano), white wine, vinegar, extra virgin olive oil, 12 round chillies

DIRECTIONS

» Using gloves, we clean the peppers: we cut the hat and empty them from filaments and seeds, rinse them under water and then boil them for at least 5 minutes in water and vinegar in equal quantities (about 250 ml each). Drain the peppers when they are still firm and let them dry upside down. We rinse the capers several times under running water to remove the salt, add them to the chopped aromatic herbs and breadsticks and mince everything in the mixer. We will make the peppers with the mixture, place them in a lightly greased pan, sprinkle with oil and bake with the caps open at 180 ° C for about 10-15 minutes. We take everything out of the oven when the edges begin to toast.

SALMON SKEWERS IN SWEET AND SOUR SAUCE

Servings: 1
Preparation Time: 10 min
Cooking Time: 10 min

INGREDIENTS

- 2 small lemons, 1 onion, 5 g of fresh ginger, 1 handful of saffron pistils, 1 pinch of chilli powder, 1 teaspoon of acacia honey, extra virgin olive oil, 200 g of salmon fillet

DIRECTIONS

» Remove the salmon skin by sliding the knife blade parallel to the work surface and remove the bones with tweezers. Cut the pulp into cubes of about 2 centimeters and stick them on wooden or bamboo skewers. Squeeze the lemons, filter the juice and emulsify it in a bowl with 4 tablespoons of oil, a pinch of salt, saffron, chilli, peeled and grated ginger and honey. Brush the salmon with a drizzle of oil, season with a pinch of salt and cook under the grill of the preheated oven, turning the skewers on all sides for 3-4 minutes. Serve hot or lukewarm, to dip into the prepared citronette.

GRILLED SALMON FILLET WITH CHILI AND AVOCADO PUREE

Servings: 1
Preparation Time: 10 min
Cooking Time: 10 min

INGREDIENTS

- 2 ripe avocados, 2 tablespoons of lime juice, salt, pepper, 4 fresh salmon fillets of 200 g each, 2 chillies, 4 teaspoons of lime juice, 4 teaspoons of honey, 4 tablespoons of extra virgin olive oil, 1 shallot big, salt

DIRECTIONS

» Cut the two avocados in half and remove the pulp with a teaspoon. Transfer it to the mixer with the lime juice and reduce everything to a silky and homogeneous cream. Season with salt and pepper. Make the sauce by cutting the peppers into a round, removing the seeds. In a small bowl, mix them with the sliced shallot, lime juice, honey and oil. Season with salt and mix well.
» Cook the salmon fillets on a hot cast iron plate for about 4 minutes on the skin side. Turn them over, add a drizzle of oil and complete the Cooking Time according to the thickness. Season with salt and pepper, stuff the fillets with the chili sauce and serve immediately with the avocado puree.

FALAFEL WITH YOGURT SAUCE

Servings: 1
Preparation Time: 10 min
Cooking Time: 70 min

INGREDIENTS

- 400 g of chickpeas, 1 onion, 1/2 teaspoon of ground cumin, 1/2 teaspoon of ground coriander, 1/4 teaspoon of chili powder, 2 tablespoons of chopped parsley, flour, 3 eggs, oil, salt, pepper, 250 g of yogurt, 150 g of cucumbers, 1/2 teaspoon of kummel, 1/4 teaspoon of ground red pepper, 1 tablespoon of chopped parsley

DIRECTIONS

» Leave the chickpeas to soak overnight, then drain them, put them in a saucepan, cover them with water, bring to a boil and cook for about an hour. Drain the chickpeas and blend them with the chopped onion, eggs and spices.
» Add enough flour, parsley, salt and pepper to the smoothie.
» Taking a small mixture at a time, form small balls like a walnut, pass them in flour, fry them in hot oil and dry them on absorbent paper.
» For the sauce: pour the yogurt into a bowl, add the peeled and diced cucumbers, spices, parsley, salt and pepper, mix and refrigerate until ready to serve with the falafel.

SWEET AND SOUR ONIONS

Servings: 4
Preparation Time: 30 min
Cooking Time: 30 min

INGREDIENTS

- 1 shallot, 1 clove of garlic, 40 g of butter, 3 tablespoons of granulated sugar, 2 dl of white wine vinegar, salt, black pepper, 800 g of onions

DIRECTIONS

» To make the glazed onions, start peeling them and soak them in cold water for 30 minutes. Melt the butter in a large enough saucepan and add the sugar, diced shallot and minced garlic. After 2-3 minutes, when the sugar has completely dissolved, add the drained onions and mix well.
» Salt, pepper, turn up the heat and sprinkle with vinegar. Allow to evaporate partially then lower the heat, cover and simmer for 30 minutes. Check from time to time and sprinkle with a few tablespoons of hot water if necessary. At the end of the Cooking Time, rest the sweet and sour onions for about ten minutes, then transfer them to a serving dish and serve.

RISOTTO WITH BROCCOLI AND CHILLI

Servings: 6
Preparation Time: 10 min
Cooking Time: 30 min

INGREDIENTS

- 1 broccoli, 1 chilli, 1 shallot White wine, spicy oil, meat or vegetable broth, salt, pepper, butter, grated cheese, 350 g of carnaroli rice

DIRECTIONS

» Cut the broccoli into small pieces. Chop the shallot.
» In a saucepan heat the oil and brown the shallot, add the rice, toast for a few minutes, add salt and blend with the white wine.
» Start pouring in the broth and broccoli, continuing to mix.
» Add a chopped red pepper and cook. Mix with butter and grated cheese.
» Complete with chopped pepper and a drizzle of spicy oil.

MARINATED COD WITH GREEN BEANS AND SESAME

Servings: 2
Preparation Time: 45 min
Cooking Time: 20 min

INGREDIENTS

- 30g miso, 1 tbsp extra virgin olive oil, 250 g cod fillet, 20 g red onion, sliced, 30 g celery, sliced, 2 garlic cloves, finely chopped, 1 Thai chilli, finely chopped, 1 tsp finely chopped fresh ginger, 60 g green beans
- 60g cabbage, roughly chopped, 1 teaspoon sesame seeds, 60g buckwheat, 1 teaspoon ground turmeric

DIRECTIONS

» Mix the miso and oil, leave the cod to marinate for 40 minutes and then cook it in a pan for 15 minutes.
» Meanwhile, cook the onion for a few minutes, then add the celery, garlic, chilli, ginger, turmeric, green beans and cabbage. Add water if necessary.
» Cook the buckwheat in boiling water for about 10 minutes
» When all the ingredients are ready, assemble the dish and serve hot.

COD WITH CHERRY TOMATOES, OLIVES AND CAPERS

Servings: 3
Preparation Time: 10 min
Cooking Time: 20 min

INGREDIENTS

- extra virgin olive oil, salt, 50 g desalted capers, 50 g of pitted black olives, 300 g of cherry tomatoes, fresh parsley, 500 g of desalted cod fillet

DIRECTIONS

» To prepare the recipe for cod with cherry tomatoes, black olives and capers with Cooking Time at low temperature, start by dividing the desalted cod fillet into 4 pieces of about 100 g each. In the meantime, prepare the necessary for cooking at a low temperature: in a large pot full of water, immerse the roner by setting the temperature to 54 ° C. At the same time, with the help of the vacuum machine, prepare the pieces of cod in a bag. Pay attention to arrange the contents in the vacuum-sealed Cooking Time bag in an orderly manner so that the thickness is uniform.
» Once the set temperature of 54 ° C is reached, submerge the bag completely and cook the cod for 15 minutes. When cooked, remove the bag from the pot.
» Serve garnished with fresh cherry tomatoes, black olives and desaturated capers. Complete with a few sprigs of parsley, extra virgin olive oil and salt to taste.

BAKED SEA BREAM

Servings: 2
Preparation Time: 10 min
Cooking Time: 35 min

INGREDIENTS

- 3 tomatoes, 2 onions, 2 lemons, 1 glass of white wine, extra virgin olive oil, 1 sprig of celery, black pepper, 1 sea bream

DIRECTIONS

» To prepare the baked sea bream, start rinsing the fish very well. Dry it both inside and out with kitchen paper and put it in a pan on the bottom of which you will have placed a bed of sliced onions. Also cut the cherry tomatoes into slices, remove the seeds and arrange them around the fish and then cover it with the lemon slices. Season with salt and pepper, pour a tablespoon of oil and wine, then add a few bay leaves. Bake in a hot oven at 200 degrees for about 35 minutes. Remove from the oven, arrange the baked sea bream on a serving dish with its vegetables and lemon slices and then serve. If you like, you can sprinkle with chopped parsley and thyme.

ROASTED VEAL CURRY WITH SPRING ONIONS

Servings: 4
Preparation Time: 10 min
Cooking Time: 35 min

INGREDIENTS

- 1 veal about 800 g, 300 g of onions, 300 g of peeled peas, 2 carrots, 1 heaped tablespoon of curry powder, 2 tablespoons of flour, 2 dl of vegetable broth, 30 g of butter, salt

DIRECTIONS

» To make the curry roast with onions, salt the meat and roll it in flour mixed with the curry so that it adheres to the entire surface. Melt the butter in a saucepan and brown the roast for about ten minutes, turn it on all sides. When golden, add the onions, peeled and washed, and the peeled carrots cut into slices. Season with salt, pour in the hot broth and continue the Cooking Time, over low heat and in a partially covered pot, for about 30 minutes. Meanwhile, boil the peas in boiling salted water for 7-8 minutes, drain and add them to the meat, continuing the

Cooking Time for another 10 minutes. Turn off the heat, let it rest for about ten minutes, then serve the roasted veal curry with sliced onions.

FUSILLI WITH CHERRY TOMATOES, CAPERS AND CRISPY CRUMBS

Servings: 3
Preparation Time: 10 min
Cooking Time: 20 min

INGREDIENTS

- 40 g of wholemeal bread, salted capers, 1 clove of garlic, 1 chilli pepper, 100 g cherry tomatoes, extra virgin olive oil, salt, 240 g of fusilli

DIRECTIONS

» To prepare fusilli with cherry tomatoes, capers and crispy crumbs, start by putting a pan of lightly salted water on the stove to boil the pasta. So dedicate yourself to the dressing. Chop the bread and put it in a hot pan with the desalted capers, the clove of garlic and the chilli pepper. Toast, stirring often so that it is evenly colored without burning. Cut the cherry tomatoes in half and remove the seeds. Arrange in a colander, add a pinch of salt and let them lose excess vegetable water.

» Remove the garlic clove and transfer the toast with capers and chilli to the mixer. Cut into crumbs. Put everything back into a pan over high heat and give it one last toast to get a nice brown color, obviously without burning. Heat 3 or 4 tablespoons of oil in a pan and add the cherry tomatoes that fry for a few seconds over high heat. Drain the fusilli al dente, add them to the cherry tomatoes and sauté for a minute.

» Divide into individual plates, finish with a generous sprinkle of bread and a drizzle of oil to taste. Serve your fusilli with cherry tomatoes, capers and crispy crumbs immediately.

ONION PIE

Servings: 3
Preparation Time: 10 min
Cooking Time: 20 min

INGREDIENTS

- 1 kg of onions, 60 g of butter, 150 g of sultanas, 1/4 liter of dry white wine, sugar, salt, pepper, cooked beans 100 g, 200 g of shortcrust pastry

DIRECTIONS

» The first thing to do to prepare the onion cake is to steep the raisins in the wine. Then grease and flour a pan and line it up with the pastry rolled into a disc, making sure that it rises a little on the edge as well. Prick the bottom and edges with a fork.

» Fill with dried legumes and put in the oven at 160 ° C for 15 minutes. Meanwhile, cut the onions into thin slices and let them dry in a pan with the butter. As soon as they are golden, add the sultanas with the wine and a pinch of sugar.

» Mix, season with salt, pepper and let the wine evaporate. Remove the paper and legumes from the pan, pour the mixture. Distribute the filling well and then finish with a grid of thin strips made with the scraps of dough.

» Brush them with a little melted butter. Bake at 180 ° C for 15-30 minutes. Serve the onion pie hot, cut into wedges.

NEAPOLITAN COD

Servings: 4
Preparation Time: 10 min
Cooking Time: 35 min

INGREDIENTS

- 500 g of peeled tomatoes, 100 g of olives, 1 tablespoon of desalted capers, 1 clove of fresh garlic, parsley, dried oregano, flour, extra virgin olive oil, 1 fresh chilli, seed oil for frying, salt, pepper, 600 g of cod

DIRECTIONS

» Start making the Neapolitan cod recipe by slicing the peeled tomatoes, being careful to keep their sauce in a bowl. Pour 2-3 tablespoons of oil and peeled garlic into a saucepan. Brown, remove the garlic and add the chilli. Leave to flavor and add the tomatoes. Stir and add the sauce as well. Cook, stirring occasionally for a few minutes. Season with salt and pepper. Add the olives, desalted capers and oregano. Continue the Cooking Time for 15 minutes or until the sauce has reduced. In the meantime, dedicate to the cod: wash it, drain it and dry it with kitchen paper. Check for thorns.

» Cut it into slices of about 5 cm each, flour them and fry them in a pan with high sides with plenty of seed oil at 180 °. When they are golden, drain them with a slotted spoon and let them dry on a plate with kitchen paper to absorb the excess oil.

» Arrange the fried cod inside a pan, cover with the tomato sauce and bake in the preheated oven at 160 ° for 20 minutes. Remove from the oven and serve with fresh parsley to taste.

STEAMED SEA BASS

Servings: 4
Preparation Time: 10 min
Cooking Time: 25 min

INGREDIENTS

- 2 sea bass, 8 cherry tomatoes, 4 small potatoes, 2 untreated lemons, 1 ginger root, 1 clove of garlic, fresh thyme, fresh parsley, extra virgin olive oil, salt, pepper

DIRECTIONS

» To prepare the steamed sea bass, remove the entrails, and remove the gills with scissors. In a small bowl, collect the thyme, a little chopped parsley, the sliced garlic, the grated zest of 1/2 lemon and a freshly grated ginger. Cover everything with a layer of oil and mix. Salt the inside of the belly and then sprinkle it with oil using a brush. Put the sea bass in a pan with a sheet of parchment paper, wet and squeezed together with the tomatoes cut in half and cover with the chopped herbs.

» Cover the surface of each sea bass with one or two thin slices of lemon. Then fill the base of the pot with water, arrange the peeled potatoes. Cover and cook for about 20 minutes without ever opening. Put half a sea bass on each plate, sprinkle with a sprinkle of oil, pepper and serve.

SALMON AND BACON ROLLS

Servings: 3
Preparation Time: 15 min
Cooking Time: 20 min

INGREDIENTS

- 700 g of fresh salmon, 150 g o f bacon, Butter to taste, Salt to taste, Pepper to taste

DIRECTIONS

» To make the salmon and bacon rolls, we first start drying the salmon and making sure there are no residual thorns by passing a finger in the opposite direction to the ribs of the meat.
» Cut the salmon into cubes of about 2 cm per side, add salt and pepper and wrap them in a thin slice of bacon; to close them use a toothpick.
» Place them in a previously greased pan and bake them in the oven at 200 ° for 10-15 minutes, until they are soft on the inside and crunchy on the outside. Serve still hot.

SLICED BEEF WITH ARTICHOKES

Servings: 1
Preparation Time: 15 min
Cooking Time: 20 min

INGREDIENTS

- Sliced beef 150 g, 2 artichokes, Lard 10 g, Butter 10 g, Salt to taste

DIRECTIONS

» Wash the artichokes, clean them by removing the tips and all the outer leaves. Make a first Cooking Time steamed, in the oven or with a steamer to soften them; cook them for about 10 minutes and complete the Cooking Time on the grill or in a pan, covered and at low heat for about 10 minutes.
» You can also cook the tagliata on the grill or in a pan, in both cases lay the butter and lard on top, in order to make it softer and tastier.
» Let the meat rest for 2 minutes before cutting it and serving it with the artichokes as a side dish.

BAKED SQUID AND POTATOES

Servings: 5
Preparation Time: 10 min
Cooking Time: 40 min

INGREDIENTS

- 500 g of potatoes, 5 ripe tomatoes, 1 small onion, 1 clove of garlic, 3 tablespoons of chopped parsley, 2 cups of breadcrumbs, 60 g of grated pecorino, 1 egg, extra virgin olive oil, salt, pepper, 1 kg of squid cleaned

DIRECTIONS

» To prepare baked calamari and potatoes, start with the filling: in a bowl, combine the crumbled breadcrumbs, grated cheese, a tablespoon of chopped parsley and egg. Salt, pepper and mix very well with your hands or a spoon until the mixture is as homogeneous as possible. Clean the squid by separating the tentacles from the heads and fill them. Be careful not to overfill them to prevent the filling from coming out during the Cooking Time. Close them with a toothpick. Peel the potatoes, wash them, dry them and cut them into evenly sized pieces.
» Pour two tablespoons of oil into the bottom of a pan, spread the sliced onion, chopped garlic, half of the peeled and chopped tomatoes, a tablespoon of chopped parsley and a pinch of salt on top.
» Place the squid on top and then distribute the potato pieces. Sprinkle with the leftover parsley, distribute the remaining tomatoes, salt, pepper and fat with a little oil.
» Put in the oven, already hot at 200 °, and bake for about 40 minutes. Retire and let it sit for a few minutes. Serve baked squid and potatoes while they are still hot.

SALMON AND LEEK QUICHE

Servings: 5
Preparation Time: 10 min
Cooking Time: 40 min

INGREDIENTS

- 3 eggs, 2 dl of milk, 100 g of smoked salmon, nutmeg, extra virgin olive oil, salt, black pepper, a shortcrust pastry roll

DIRECTIONS

» To make the salmon and leek quiche, start cleaning the leek by cutting the thicker end and slicing the rest into thin slices. Heat a couple of tablespoons of oil in a pan and cook the leek slices for about ten minutes. Season with salt and pepper. Meanwhile, shell the eggs in a bowl and beat them with a fork together with the milk: add a pinch of grated nutmeg, a pinch of salt and a sprinkling of pepper.
» Line a circular mold of about 18 centimeters in diameter with the shortcrust pastry, letting the dough come out along the edges. Arrange the salmon cut into strips, the leeks and pour the egg mixture. Fold the excess dough inwards to form a frame and transfer it to the preheated oven at 180 °.Cook the quiche for about 25 minutes, then arrange it on a serving dish and serve in slices and accompanied by a fresh mixed salad.

HAKE FILLETS WITH QUINOA SALAD

Servings: 4
Preparation Time: 15 min
Cooking Time: 25 min

INGREDIENTS

- 4 hake fillets of about 150 g each, 150 g of quinoa, 40 g of pecans, 1 handful of dried raspberries, 200 g of valerian, extra virgin olive oil, apple vinegar to taste, salt to taste, pepper to taste

DIRECTIONS

» To prepare the hake fillet with quinoa salad, start by washing the latter several times before putting it in the pot. Add water until it is covered, you will need about 400 ml and bring to a boil by adding a handful of coarse salt. Cook for about 15 minutes, drain the quinoa and let it cool. Once cold, add the chopped valerian, pecans, dried raspberries, vinegar, salt, oil and pepper. Cook the hake in a very hot non-stick pan, in which you have previously poured a drizzle of oil. Cook on the skin side for about 3 minutes, flip the fish and continue the Cooking Time for another 2 minutes. Once cooked, transfer the fish to the plate and serve still hot with the quinoa salad.

TURKEY BITES WITH APPLE SAUCE

Servings: 4
Preparation Time: 15 min
Cooking Time: 25 min

INGREDIENTS

- 500 g of turkey breast, 80 g of chopped almonds, 100 ml of apple juice, Olive oil to taste, Salt to taste, Pepper to taste, 00 flour to taste

DIRECTIONS

» Cut the turkey breast into coarse chunks and breaded in a mix of flour and chopped almonds making sure there are no exposed pieces of meat. In a non-stick pan, heat some oil and cook the turkey morsels, being careful not to burn them. After about 5 minutes add the apple juice and continue mixing; the contact with the 00 flour will create a delicious sauce that will evenly envelop the turkey. When the sauce is thick enough, the dish is ready.

BAKED SEA BASS

Servings: 5
Preparation Time: 10 min
Cooking Time: 20 min

INGREDIENTS

- 2 sea bass of 500-600 g each, 2 spring onions, 1 lemon, 1-2 cloves of garlic, rosemary, parsley, dry white wine, extra virgin olive oil, salt, black pepper

DIRECTIONS

» To prepare the baked sea bass, place the cleaned, washed and stuffed fish on aluminum foil with a sprig of rosemary, a clove of garlic, salt and pepper. Spread some chopped parsley, lemon slices, chopped onions and garlic slices on the outside. Sprinkle with half a glass of white wine and close the sheet. Place the foil in a baking dish, and bake at 200 °.
» Cook for 15-20 minutes. Remove from the oven, open the sheet carefully, due to the steam that will come out and serve the sea bass hot, with a drizzle of oil to taste.

FISH BALLS

Servings: 5
Preparation Time: 10 min
Cooking Time: 20 min

INGREDIENTS

- 400 g of tomato sauce, 1 egg, 1 onion, breadcrumbs, flour, extra virgin olive oil, salt, peanut oil for frying, 500 g of sea bass

DIRECTIONS

» Boil the sea bass in salted or steamed water for 15-20 minutes. Drain it, gently chop the pulp, collect it in a bowl and mix it with the whole egg, a few tablespoons of very fine breadcrumbs and a pinch of salt. Stir with a wooden spoon until you get a mixture of the right consistency to form meatballs. With slightly damp hands, take one cube of mixture at a time and make small meatballs.
» Flour them lightly. Heat abundant oil in a pan with rather high sides and fry the meatballs. Drain when pale golden in color, pat dry on kitchen paper and set aside. In a saucepan large enough to hold all the meatballs without overlapping, heat two tablespoons of oil. Let the onion flavor finely chopped and when it has become transparent add the tomato puree. Stir, add salt, cover and cook in about 15 minutes over medium heat. After this time, place the meatballs in the sauce, turn them gently so that they remain covered, without breaking, and leave them to flavor for about ten minutes.
» Transfer the fish balls with their sauce to the serving dish and serve hot.

BAKED CHICKEN THIGHS

Servings: 2
Preparation Time: 2 hours
Cooking Time: 20 min

INGREDIENTS

- 2 tablespoons of desalted capers, aromatic herbs (thyme, rosemary, myrtle), extra virgin olive oil, 2 cloves of garlic, salt, black peppercorns, 8 chicken legs, 100 ml of dry white wine, 50 ml of Vermouth

DIRECTIONS

» To make chicken thighs in the oven, first remove the

- feathers with tweezers that are still being attached to the thighs.
» Put them in a bowl with the wine, vermouth, peeled garlic cloves, herbs, salt and freshly crushed pepper. Cover with plastic wrap, refrigerate and marinate for 2 hours. At this point, transfer the thighs to a pan or oven dish along with 3 tablespoons of oil. Also add the herbs, garlic and about half of the marinade.
» Add the capers and cook in the preheated oven at 200 ° in the ventilated mode for 30 minutes, covering with aluminum foil. After this time continue to cook by removing the lid for another 30-40 minutes or until golden brown. Always check that the chicken is well cooked inside.

CHICKEN CACCIATORE

Servings: 2
Preparation Time: 10 min
Cooking Time: 45 min

INGREDIENTS

- 800 g of chopped tomatoes, 1 onion, 1 stick of celery, 1 carrot, 1 sprig of parsley, extra virgin olive oil, salt, black pepper, 1 chicken cut into pieces or 4 legs and 4 thighs, a knob of butter

DIRECTIONS

» To prepare the chicken cacciatore, rinse the pieces of meat and dry them well with kitchen paper. Put them in a saucepan with the butter, three tablespoons of oil and the sliced onion. Brown them well for about 15 minutes.
» Then add the chopped tomato pulp, carrot and celery. Mix well, sprinkle with hot water and bring to a boil, then lower the heat, cover and cook for another 40-45 minutes or until the meat is cooked through and the sauce reduced. If it gets too dry, you can add very little hot water to the kitchen. Finally add salt and chopped pepper.
» Leave the chicken cacciatore to rest for about ten minutes in the heat, then serve with a handful of chopped parsley.

MINI QUICHE WITH MOZZARELLA, SAUSAGES AND BROCCOLI

Servings: 2
Preparation Time: 10 min
Cooking Time: 25 min

INGREDIENTS

- 150 g of broccoli florets, 200 g of mozzarella, 150 g of sausage, 1 clove of garlic, extra virgin olive oil, salt, pepper, 1 roll of 230 g round puff pastry

DIRECTIONS

» To prepare mini quiches with mozzarella, sausage and broccoli, roll out the puff pastry with its paper directly on the work surface. With an 8 cm diameter pastry cutter, make 9 small discs that you will place inside all the buttered muffin molds. Have them attach to both the base and the edges.
» Prick the base of each with the protrusions of a fork, cover with a sheet of parchment paper and fill them with the appropriate ceramic weights (pulses can also be used). Bake in a preheated oven at 180 degrees for 15 minutes. Remove from the oven, allow to cool and discard the paper and meatballs / legumes. Meanwhile, prepare the filling: blanch the broccoli florets in salted water for 3-4 minutes.
» Drain and cool under cold running water. In a pan, sauté the garlic cut in half in the oil and brown the sausage without its wrapping.
» Shell with a spoon and add the broccoli florets. Salt, pepper and leave to flavor for a few minutes. Let it cool down. Cut the mozzarella into cubes and place it inside the puff pastry shells together with the broccoli and sausage.
» Bake in a preheated oven at 180 degrees for another 15-20 minutes. Remove from the oven, allow the mini quiches with mozzarella, sausage and broccoli to cool and serve immediately.

FRIED CHICKEN WITH SPICED BEANS

Servings: 4
Preparation Time: 60 min
Cooking Time: 60 min

INGREDIENTS

- 800 g of chicken nuggets, 500 g of beans, 2 tablespoons of sesame oil, sunflower oil for frying, 00 flour to taste, 15 g of fresh ginger, smoked parprika to taste, chilli to taste

DIRECTIONS

» Clean and cook the beans in salted water for about 30 minutes.
» Marinate the chicken for at least 1 hour with sesame oil, paprika, sliced ginger, salt and chilli.
» Drain it from the excess sesame oil and pass it in the flour, then fry it in hot seed oil until the breading becomes crunchy.
» Season the beans with salt and olive oil and serve as an accompaniment to the fried chicken.

SHRIMP AND CHICKEN SKEWERS WITH LEMON AND AVOCADO SAUCE

Servings: 4
Preparation Time: 20 min
Cooking Time: 15 min

INGREDIENTS

- 500 g of chicken breast, 500 g of avocado, 18 shrimp, 2 lemons, Tabasco to taste, Olive oil to taste, Salt to taste, Pepper to taste

DIRECTIONS

» Divide the chicken into 18 small pieces, season them with oil, salt, pepper, a tablespoon of lemon juice and let it marinate for 10 minutes.
» Remove the shells from the shrimp, set them aside in a bowl and let them marinate in the same way as the chicken.
» In another container put the avocado cut into small pieces, add a few drops of Tabasco (according to your taste), the juice of a lemon, a pinch of salt and a drizzle of oil; mix until you get a creamy sauce.
» After 10 minutes you will have to start forming the skewers: very simply alternate a piece of chicken with a shrimp until you have finished both of these Ingredients.

Cooking Time can be done both on the grill and in a nonstick pan with a drizzle of oil. Once cooked, season with salt and add a drizzle of oil to keep them from drying out.

» Serve just cooked, with the avocado and tabasco sauce on the side.

BEEF BURGER WITH LETTUCE AND CARROT SALAD

Servings: 1
Preparation Time: 10 min
Cooking Time: 10 min

INGREDIENTS

- 100 g of ground beef, 30 g of lettuce, 30 g of carrots, 10 g of lard, 15 g of black olives, Olive oil to taste, Salt to taste

DIRECTIONS

» Prepare the burger by forming a disc with the ground beef.
» Cook it on a very hot grill, about 4 minutes per side, adding salt according to your taste. Add the lard on top to make it tastier and softer.
» Wash and cut the lettuce and carrots; put them in a salad bowl with the pitted olives and season with oil and salt.
» Serve still hot with the salad as a side dish.

STUFFED EGGS

Servings: 2
Preparation Time: 15 min
Cooking Time: 25 min

INGREDIENTS

- 6 whole eggs, 200 g of cooked ham, 100 g of ricotta, parsley to taste, salt to taste, pepper to taste

DIRECTIONS

» The eggs in this recipe are hard-boiled, to prepare them put them in a pot full of cold water and bring it to a boil. Once boiling, cook for about 12 minutes; when they are cooked, add cold water and leave to rest, then shell them, divide them in half and separate the yolks from the whites.
» Put the egg yolks in a bowl with the finely chopped ham, ricotta, salt and pepper. Stir until you get a homogeneous mixture and generously fill the yolks of the previously separated eggs with it. Add chopped parsley on top for decoration.

POTATOS PIZZA

Servings: 2
Preparation Time: 10 min
Cooking Time: 25 min

INGREDIENTS

- 800 g of potatoes, 50 g of 00 flour, salt, pepper, 150 g of tomato sauce, 125 g of mozzarella fiordilatte, 60 g of sliced speck, grated parmesan, extra virgin olive oil, dried oregano, basil

DIRECTIONS

» To make potato pizza, start boiling the potatoes for 15 minutes in boiling salted water, then drain and peel them while still hot. Let them cool and grate them with a large hole grater, collecting the contents in a bowl.
» Add the flour, a pinch of salt and pepper. Mix and distribute this mixture on a baking sheet lined with parchment paper, giving it a thickness of about 5 mm. Bake in a preheated oven at 200 ° for 20 minutes. In a small bowl, season the tomato puree with oil, salt, pepper, Parmesan to taste and a little oregano.
» Mix well and spread over the potato base. Add the mozzarella, previously drained well and cut into cubes, and put it back in the oven at 200 ° until the mozzarella is melted and the potato base is golden. Remove the potato pizza from the oven, add the speck and basil and serve immediately.

CHICKEN BURGER WITH LIME MARINADE

Servings: 2
Preparation Time: 120 min
Cooking Time: 25 min

INGREDIENTS

- 300 g of chicken leg, 2 limes, extra virgin olive oil, green pepper, fresh chives, 1 clove of garlic, 1 tablespoon of cornstarch, salt, sour cream, 500 g of chicken breast

DIRECTIONS

» The first step in the Preparation Time: of this dish is to thoroughly clean the bone meat and residual waste. Then cut it with a knife point and transfer the mince to a large bowl.
» Peel the garlic and divide it in half, chop the chives and combine them both with the meat, along with the grated zest of 1 lime. Squeeze the juice of 1 1/2 lime and pour it over the meat, adding a tablespoon of oil, a pinch of salt and a sprinkle of freshly ground green pepper.
» Mix very well with a spoon or with your hands and

transfer the covered bowl to the refrigerator for 2 hours. After this time, remove from the refrigerator, remove the garlic and add the cornstarch. Mix well and shape the burgers.
- » Place a small mixture inside a circular pastry ring, 8 or 10 cm in diameter, placed on parchment paper. Fill up to the edge and with the back of a spoon give compactness to the mince, gently remove the ring and in the same way prepare all four.
- » Heat a plate or a non-stick pan and, when it is hot, place the burgers with the help of parchment paper. Cook over high heat for about ten minutes, being careful to turn them only once halfway through Cooking Time. Serve the chicken burgers with very hot lime marinade, accompanied by a salad of lettuce and cherry tomato and sour cream.

GRILLED SQUID STUFFED WITH BEANS AND PECORINO

Servings: 2
Preparation Time: 10 min
Cooking Time: 20 min

INGREDIENTS

- 300 g of boiled cannellini beans, 40 g of grated pecorino romano, 1 clove of garlic, 1 glass of white wine, 1 untreated lemon marjoram, extra virgin olive oil, salt, black pepper, 4 large fresh squid, whole and cleaned

DIRECTIONS

- » To prepare grilled squid stuffed with beans and pecorino, start by rinsing the squid under a stream of fresh running water, setting aside the tufts with the tentacles, which you will roughly cut with a knife.
- » Heat some oil in a large pan and brown the peeled and crushed clove of garlic with the palm of your hand. Add the chopped tufts and cook over high heat. Also add the beans and cook everything for a few minutes.
- » Glaze with 1/2 glass of white wine. When the tentacles are golden and cooked, turn off the heat. Remove the garlic and add the pecorino. Season with salt and mix. Fill each squid with the mixture of beans, tentacles and pecorino.
- » Close it at the base with a toothpick. Heat the bottom of the grill pan and place the squid without adding oil. Spread a few thin slices of lemon over each squid. Brown a couple of minutes. Pour with a drizzle of oil.
- » Flip the squid over, being careful to keep the lemon slices as a base.
- » Cook for about ten minutes until, piercing the squid with a toothpick, the fish is tender and will yield. Sprinkle with some pepper and serve one squid per dish. Remove the toothpick, sprinkle with a drizzle of oil.

FRIED EGGPLANT IN A PAN WITH OLIVES AND CAPERS

Servings: 2
Preparation Time: 10 min
Cooking Time: 10 min

INGREDIENTS

- 5 tomatoes, 2 onions, 2 cloves of garlic, 1 tablespoon of pitted Taggiasca olives, 1 tablespoon of salted capers, a sprig of parsley, extra virgin olive oil, 1 tablespoon of vinegar, 1 teaspoon of sugar, salt
- black pepper, 4 small eggplants

DIRECTIONS

- » To prepare the aubergines in a pan with olives and capers, start washing and drying the aubergines. Cut them into cubes after removing the central part, which is particularly rich in seeds. Leave them in salt for half an hour to lose some of their bitter water. After half an hour, rinse the eggplant cubes and dry them. In a saucepan, heat two tablespoons of oil, add the chopped onions and whole garlic cloves. When they are lightly browned, remove the garlic cloves and add the eggplant cubes, then add the fresh, seeded and diced tomatoes: salt and pepper.
- » Cook over medium heat for about a quarter of an hour, stirring frequently so that aubergines and tomatoes do not stick to the bottom of the pan. Now add the finely chopped parsley, olives, capers rinsed from salt and squeezed, vinegar and sugar. Let it flavor well and then taste the aubergines to check that they have a sweet and sour taste: if they were too acidic, add a pinch of sugar, if they were too sweet, add a dash of vinegar. After a few minutes, remove from the heat: it is possible to serve the aubergines in a pan with hot or warm olives and capers.

CHICKEN ESCALOPE IN WHITE WINE

Servings: 1
Preparation Time: 10 min
Cooking Time: 10 min

INGREDIENTS

- 150 g of chicken breast (sliced or bite-sized), 1 tablespoon of flour 00, 100 ml of white cooking wine, 15 g of butter, 1 tablespoon of olive oil, Salt to taste

DIRECTIONS

- » To prepare the chicken escalope, the first thing to do is to flour the meat. The amount of flour to use is minimal, it will not affect our diet, it will only be used to create a very pleasant sauce.
- » Once the chicken is floured, put the butter and oil in a non-stick pan and let it heat over low heat.
- » When the fats are hot we begin to cook the chicken, turning it from time to time to prevent it from sticking; after about 4 minutes of Cooking Time, add the wine and raise the flame slightly. Keep stirring and add a pinch of salt, as soon as the wine begins to reduce in

contact with the flour it will thicken, giving life to a very pleasant thick sauce.
» Serve hot.

ROAST PORK WITH BEER AND ONIONS

Servings: 4
Preparation Time: 10 min
Cooking Time: 150 min

INGREDIENTS
- 2 bay leaves, 3 sprigs of thyme, 300 ml of light beer, extra virgin olive oil, 30 g of butter, salt, black pepper, 1 kg of pork loin or shoulder, 800 g of blond onions

DIRECTIONS
» To make the beer roast pork with onions, start tying the piece of meat with several turns of kitchen rope. Massage it with a pinch of salt and ground pepper, then brown it in a saucepan with the butter and 4 tablespoons of oil. Turn it well on all sides so that browning takes place evenly. Take the roast out of the saucepan and keep it warm. Add the peeled and finely chopped onions, bay leaves and thyme sprigs to the Cooking Time juices. Mix well and leave to simmer gently for 5 minutes. Then transfer the onions to an ovenproof dish, add the meat and sprinkle it all with beer.
» Cover with a lid or aluminum foil and transfer the dish to the oven, preheated to 150 °, for 2 hours and 30 minutes. After the Cooking Time, remove the herbs and transfer the beer roast pork with onions to a serving dish. Serve it sliced with its Cooking Time sauce.

PEPPERONI PIZZA

Servings: 4
Preparation Time: 10 min
Cooking Time: 15 min

INGREDIENTS
- Onion (1/2), chopped, half chopped mozzarella, water (1/4 cup), tomato paste (1/3 cup), diced green, yellow and red pepper (1 1/2 cup), about 3 small peppers

DIRECTIONS
» Preheat the oven to 250 ° C.
» In a small bowl, combine the sauce, tomato paste and water; mix well. Ears over minced pie. Equally high with cheese. Sprinkle evenly with onion bell and pepper on the cheese.
» Bake for 10 - 12 minutes at 250 ° C, or until the cheese is melted.

PORK SAUSAGE WITH FENNEL SALAD GARNISH

Servings: 1
Preparation Time: 10 min
Cooking Time: 10 min

INGREDIENTS
- Pork sausage 120 g, ½ fresh fennel, 1 orange, olive oil to taste, salt to taste, pepper to taste

DIRECTIONS
» Let's start by preparing the fennel salad to use as a side dish. Wash the fennel and cut it very thinly, you can also use a mandolin to make your job easier; peel 1 orange and cut it into coarse pieces.
» In a salad bowl, mix the fennel, orange, oil, salt and pepper to taste; leave aside waiting for the sausage.
» The sausage can be cooked in different ways, personally if I can I cook it on the grill because it is tastier, but if I don't have much time available I cook it in a non-stick pan. Be careful not to use other fats, the sausage already contains a lot of its own and would be cloying; if you cook it in a pan I suggest you cut it in half lengthwise, to cook it more evenly.

TOMATO CREAM WITH CRISPY CAPERS

Servings: 4
Preparation Time: 10 min
Cooking Time: 15 min

INGREDIENTS
- 2 tablespoons of tomato paste, 1 clove of garlic, 1 onion dried oregano, lemon zest, salt, pepper, 4 tablespoons of salted capers, 4 tablespoons of extra virgin olive oil, 500 g of tomato pulp

DIRECTIONS
» In a saucepan, brown the onion and garlic in the olive oil, add the triple tomato concentrate and the pulp. Season with salt and cook until a thick cream is obtained. In a small pan, heat the oil, dip the desalted capers and leave them on the stove until they become crunchy.
» Collect them, dry them on kitchen paper. Transfer the tomato cream into four small cups, add the crispy capers, oregano and lemon zest to taste. Complete with a round of extra virgin olive oil and a fresh chopped pepper. Serve immediately.

CALAMARATA WITH SQUID, CAPERS AND LEMON

Servings: 4
Preparation Time: 10 min
Cooking Time: 15 min

INGREDIENTS
- 2 cleaned squid, 1 handful of salted capers, 1 shallot,

1 untreated lemon, a few sprigs of thyme, 1/2 glass of white wine, 300 g of squid

DIRECTIONS

» Clean the squid, removing the skin, eyes and mouth, then cut them into very thin rings. Cut the shallot into slices and brown it in a pan with a little oil. Then add the squid and cook over high heat, then mix with the wine and dry. Add the rinsed capers well and cook with a tablespoon of water. During the Calamarata Cooking Time, cut the lemon peel into julienne strips, taking care to remove the white part. Drain the pasta and fry over high heat for a few moments, then add the lemon and raw oil. Serve hot, flavoring with fresh thyme.

MACKEREL FILLETS WITH ROASTED PEPPERS

Servings: 1
Preparation Time: 15 min
Cooking Time: 25 min

INGREDIENTS

- Mackerel fillet in oil 37 g, yellow and red peeled peppers 72 g. Mayonnaise 25 g, Black olives 20 g, Extra virgin olive oil 14 g

DIRECTIONS

» Wash and peel the peppers, then roast them and remove the skin. Salt to taste. Serve the mackerel fillets with peppers seasoned with oil. Decorate with black olives.

SMOKED SALMON CROUTONS WITH GREEN BEANS

Servings: 1
Preparation Time: 5 min
Cooking Time: -

INGREDIENTS

- Smoked salmon 63 g, Lemon pulp 3 g, Croutons 4, Green beans 55 g, Parmesan 6 g, Oil 25 g

DIRECTIONS

» Butter the croutons and put the smoked salmon on top with the lemon pulp on top. Wash and weigh the green beans and steam them. Add them to the dish next to the croutons. Drizzle with oil and serve.

FRESH SALMON ESCALOPE WITH PINK PEPPER

Servings: 1
Preparation Time: 5 min
Cooking Time: 10 min

INGREDIENTS

- Fresh salmon 60 g, Lettuce 50 g, Black olives 30 g, Extra virgin olive oil 15 g

DIRECTIONS

» Chop the olives with the crescent, add the lecithin and pink pepper. Take the fresh salmon and cook it in a non-stick pan. Wash, peel and weigh the salad and dress it with an emulsion of oil and salt.

SALMON WITH RED WINE AND BROCCOLI

Servings: 1
Preparation Time: 10 min
Cooking Time: 15 min

INGREDIENTS

- 180g salmon, 50ml red wine, 200g broccoli, 2 tablespoons of olive oil, thyme

DIRECTIONS

» Remove the salmon fillets from the skin, wash the broccoli and divide them into florets. Bring the wine with the thyme to a boil in a large skillet over medium heat. Lower the heat, add the salmon slightly, salt and cover. Cook the fish for about 10 minutes and wet it from time to time with Cooking Time juices.
» Remove the salmon from the pan with a slotted spoon and keep it warm. Turn the heat up to high and quickly boil the wine sauce until it is reduced to about 1 dl. Remove the pan from the heat and gradually add the butter.
» The sauce should thicken slightly. Meanwhile, bring a large pot filled with water to a boil. Add the broccoli and cook for 3 minutes. Drain them and distribute them in the same way with the salmon on four serving plates.
» Pour the sauce over the salmon and serve hot.

PORK SAUSAGE WITH FENNEL

Servings: 1
Preparation Time: 5 min
Cooking Time: 10 min

INGREDIENTS

- Fresh pork sausage 40 g, Fennel 70 g, Olive oil 13 g

DIRECTIONS

» Wash, clean the fennel to eat raw, cut into thin slices

or steamed first and then finish the Cooking Time on the grill.
- Season with oil, salt and pepper. Roast the sausage on the griddle or in a non-stick pan.

HAM AND MELON

Servings: 1
Preparation Time: 5 min
Cooking Time: -

INGREDIENTS
- Lean and defatted raw ham 40 g, Melon 4 g

DIRECTIONS
- Arrange the thinly sliced raw ham and melon on the plate and keep in the refrigerator until a few minutes before consumption.

CHICKEN WITH CURRY

Servings: 1
Preparation Time: 15 min
Cooking Time: 15 min

INGREDIENTS
- 120g chicken breast, 100g pakchoi, 100g Beijing cabbage, 1 carrot, 1-2 cloves of garlic, ginger, 1-2 chillies, fresh coriander, 1 tablespoon of tandoori masala, 1-2 teaspoons turmeric, 1/2 teaspoon of salt, 1 teaspoon of cayenne pepper

DIRECTIONS
- Cut the chicken breast into small pieces and the vegetables into small pieces. Peel the garlic and ginger and cut them into thin slices.
- Preheat the pan well and grease it with oil. This gives a particularly nice touch to the dish. Brown the meat on all sides, add the vegetables, garlic, ginger and chilli and cook briefly.
- Lower the heat and add a little water. Add the spices and mix.
- Cook in a pan or wok over medium heat to evaporate the water. When a reduction of water and spices has formed, the chicken curry will be ready!

TURKEY SKEWER AND BEER SAUSAGES

Servings: 3
Preparation Time: 15 min
Cooking Time: 15 min

INGREDIENTS
- 300 g of turkey breast, 240 g of sausage, 100 ml of chicken broth, 12 Brussels sprouts, 120 ml of beer, Chives to taste, Salt to taste, Olive oil to taste

DIRECTIONS
- For the chicken and turkey skewer recipe, start by cleaning the brussel sprouts and cook them in boiling water for 3 minutes. Cut the turkey and sausage into small pieces, you should get 12, or a quantity equal to the sprouts. Start composing the skewer by alternating 1 piece of turkey, 1 piece of sausage and 1 brussels sprout. Heat some oil in a non-stick pan and start the Cooking Time of the skewer; when you have scalded it quickly on all sides add the beer and raise the heat. Let the alcohol evaporate and add the chicken broth, salt and pepper.
- When the broth has evaporated the dish is ready, serve it hot with some chopped chives.

OATS KICHDI

Servings: 5
Preparation Time: 30 min
Cooking Time: 35 min

INGREDIENTS
- Quick Cooking Oats (1/3 cup), 2 ½ cups Water, Salt to taste, Ginger (3/4 tsp), finely chopped, Carrot (1 small size), chopped, Small Onion (1), finely chopped, Powder turmeric (1/4 tsp), Moong dal (1/3 cup), chopped, Cumin seeds (1/2 tsp), Red chili powder (1/4 tsp), Tomato (1 medium size), chopped finely, green peas (45 grams), green chillies (1/2 teaspoon), chopped, extra virgin olive oil (1/2 tablespoon) Directions Heat the oil in a pressure cooker add butter, add cumin seeds to warm the butter, let them crackle. Cook with chopped onion until transparent, add ginger and green chillies, cook for a few seconds. Add turmeric powder and red chili powder and tomatoes following. Let them cook until tender. Remove all the vegetables and moong from the rinsed along with the oats. Give it a few seconds.. Remove spray and dust with oil. Cook on fire for 8 minutes.
- **Tortilla with poblano and black beans**

Servings: 2
Preparation Time: 15 min

- Cooking Time: 15 min

INGREDIENTS
- Low Fat Sour Cream (1/2 cup), Flour Tortillas (4), about 8 inches, Fresh Lime Juice (3 tablespoons), Finely Chopped Red Onion (1/4 cup), Ripe Diced Peeled Avocado (1 cup), 1 can (15 ounce) black beans, rinsed and drained, Ground Cumin (1/2 tsp), Poblano Pepper (1/2), finely chopped (about 1/3 cup), Chopped fresh coriander leaves (1/4 cup), Salt (1/4 tsp)

DIRECTIONS
- In a shallow cup, mix sour cream and cumin; and mix with a fork.
- Combine the beans in a cup and the next 6 Ingredients. Tablespoon equivalent amount of mixed black beans in the center of each tortilla. Roll up, cut in half and, where possible, protect with wooden picks. Serve in combination with ice cream.

TOASTED VEGETABLES

Servings: 4
Preparation Time: 10 min
Cooking Time: 20 min

INGREDIENTS

- Red pepper (1 large), chopped, Small zucchini (2), sliced, Sliced mushrooms (2 cups)

DIRECTIONS

» Place a large non-stick skillet over medium-high heat, sprayed with cooking spray until heated. Place zucchini, mushrooms and bell pepper in a saucepan. Pour for 3 - 5 minutes or before the vegetable mind. On each tostada, pour about 3/4 cup of the vegetable blend over the black bean blend. Top with salsa, lettuce, and cheese.

SPICY ASPARAGUS

Servings: 4
Preparation Time: 10 min
Cooking Time: 15 min

INGREDIENTS

- Asparagus (600g), Instant hot cooked brown rice (3 cups), Crushed red pepper (1/2 tsp), Five Grain Tempeh (1 package), Corn starch (2 tsp), Vegetable broth (3/4 cup), Low Sodium Soy Sauce (1/4 cup), Sesame Oil (2 Tbsp), split, Garlic (4 wedges), chopped, Sliced Shiitake Mushrooms (1 pack)

DIRECTIONS

» Peel off the hard ends of the asparagus. Cut the spears diagonally into 2-inch pieces. set aside
» In a shallow pot, mix the soy sauce, vegetable broth and corn starch; mix until it becomes creamy with a fork.

OMELETTE

Servings: 1
Preparation Time: 10 min
Cooking Time: 10 min

INGREDIENTS

- 3 whole eggs, 40 g datterini tomatoes, 10 g parmesan, 2 tablespoons olive oil, salt to taste

DIRECTIONS

» Break the eggs and beat them with salt. In a pan, heat 1 tablespoon of oil, when it is hot add the mixture and let it cook for 2 minutes on each side.
» In a second pan, heat some oil and cook the halved datterini tomatoes for about 3 minutes.
» Assemble the dish by placing the omelette on the bottom with the tomatoes on top and a grating of parmesan, as if it were a pizza.

SAUSAGE AND TURKEY SKEWERS IN BEER

Servings: 4
Preparation Time: 10 min
Cooking Time: 35 min

INGREDIENTS

- 300 g of turkey breast, 240 g of sausage, 200 g of chicken broth, 12 Brussels sprouts, 100 g of beer, flour, chives, extra virgin olive oil, salt, pepper

DIRECTIONS

» For the recipe of the turkey and beer sausage skewers, clean the Brussels sprouts and blanch them in boiling salted water for 3 '.
» Drain and dry them.
» Cut the turkey and sausage to get 12 pieces each. Assemble the skewers by alternating 3 bites of sausage, 3 of turkey and 3 sprouts for each.
» Flour and brown them in a pan with a drizzle of oil; turn them on all sides until well roasted, then sprinkle them with beer.
» Let it evaporate then add the chicken broth. Salt and pepper. Cook with the lid on for 5-6 ', then remove it and cook for another 5-6'. Complete with some chives. Serve the skewers with their sauce.

ASIAN BEEF AND NOODLES

Preparation Time: 10 minutes
Cooking Time: 16 minutes
Serving: 2

INGREDIENTS

- 2 cups water
- 1/2-pound lean ground beef
- 2 packages ramen-style noodles, broken into small pieces
- 1 seasoning packet ramen-style noodles
- 16 ounces frozen vegetables
- 2 green onions, thinly sliced
- 1/4 teaspoon ground ginger
- 2 cloves garlic, minced

DIRECTIONS:

» Heat a non-stick frying pan over medium heat and sauté beef until brown.
» Stir in 2 cups water and seasoning packet.
» Add all the vegetables and bring the mixture to a boil.
» Stir in ramen noodles and cook for 5 minutes.
» Serve warm.

Nutrition: Calories 411 Total Fat 10.5 g Saturated Fat 2.4 g Cholesterol 19 mg Sodium 358 mg Total Carbs 14.4 g Fiber 0.4 g Sugar 0.1 g Protein 13.4 g

BEEF KABOBS WITH GRILLED PINEAPPLE SALSA

Preparation Time: 10 minutes
Cooking Time: 15 minutes
Serving: 4

INGREDIENTS:

- 1-1/2 pounds beef shoulder center (Ranch) steaks, cut into cubes
- Salt and pepper, to taste
- Pineapple Salsa:
- 1 bell pepper, cut into 1-inch pieces
- 1 red onion, cut into 12 wedges
- 1/2 pineapple, peeled, cored, cut into 1-1/2-inch chunks
- 2 teaspoons grated lime peel
- 1/2 teaspoon salt
- Marinade:
- 2 tablespoons fresh lime juice
- 2 tablespoons olive oil
- 2 large cloves garlic, minced
- 1 medium jalapeno pepper, minced
- 1/2 teaspoon ground cumin

DIRECTIONS:

- Slice the beef steaks in small pieces.
- Season the beef with all the ingredients of the marinade in a bowl.
- Cover the beef and refrigerate for 30 minutes.
- Remove the beef from the marinade.
- Thread the beef on the skewers alternately with vegetables and fruits.
- Grill the skewers for 15 minutes on a preheated grill.
- Mix all the ingredients for pineapple salsa.
- Serve skewers with the salsa

Nutrition: Calories 434 Total Fat 15.6 g Saturated Fat 1.1 g Cholesterol 11 mg Sodium 814 mg Total Carbs 23.4g Fiber 0.4 g Sugar 5.3 g Protein 14.6 g

PORK MEDALLIONS WITH PEAR-MAPLE SAUCE

Preparation Time: 5 minutes
Cooking Time: 5 minutes
Serving: 2

INGREDIENTS:

- 1 12- to 16-ounce pork tenderloin
- 2 teaspoons snipped fresh rosemary
- 1 teaspoon snipped fresh thyme
- 1/4 teaspoon black pepper
- 1 tablespoon olive oil or cooking oil
- 2 medium pears, peeled and coarsely chopped
- 1/4 cup pure maple syrup
- 2 tablespoons dried tart red cherries, halved
- 2 tablespoons dry white wine
- 1/4 teaspoon salt

DIRECTIONS:

- Slice the meat and mix with salt, pepper, thyme, and rosemary in a bowl.
- Heat cooking oil in a skillet and add meat to sear until brown.
- Stir in all the remaining ingredients and cook for 3 minutes.
- Serve warm.

Nutrition: Calories 318 Total Fat 3.8 g Saturated Fat 0.7 g Cholesterol 22 mg Sodium 620 mg Total Carbs 28.3 g Fiber 2.4 g Sugar 1.2 gProtein5.4g

MEXICAN CHICKEN

Preparation Time: 10 minutes
Cooking Time: 7 hours
Servings: 4

INGREDIENTS:

- 4 chicken breast, skinless and boneless
- 1/2 cup water
- 16 ounces chunky salsa
- 1 and 1/2 tablespoons parsley, chopped
- 1 teaspoon garlic powder
- 1/2 tablespoon cilantro, chopped
- 1 teaspoon onion powder
- 1/2 tablespoons oregano, dried
- 1/2 teaspoon sweet paprika
- 1 teaspoon chili powder
- 1/2 teaspoon cumin, ground
- Black pepper to taste

DIRECTIONS:

- Add water to your Slow Cooker
- Add chicken breast, parsley, salsa, garlic powder, onion powder, cilantro, oregano, chili powder, paprika, cumin and pepper
- Gently stir
- Place lid and cook LOW for 7 hours
- Divide the whole mix between serving platters and enjoy!

Nutrition: Calories: 200 Fat: 4g Carbohydrates: 12g Protein: 9g

SWEET POTATO TURKEY BREAST

Preparation Time: 10 minutes
Cooking Time: 8 hours
Servings: 4

INGREDIENTS:

- 3 pounds turkey breast, bone in
- 3 sweet potatoes, cut into wedges
- 1 cup dried cherries, pitted
- 2 white onion, cut into wedges
- 1/3 cup water
- 1 teaspoon onion powder
- 1 teaspoon garlic powder
- 1 teaspoon parsley flakes
- 1 teaspoon sage, dried

- 1 teaspoon thyme, dried
- 1 teaspoon paprika, dried
- Pepper to taste

DIRECTIONS:

» Add turkey breast to Slow Cooker
» Add sweet potatoes, cherries water, onion, parsley, garlic, onion powder, thyme, sage, paprika and pepper to your Slow Cooker as well
» Gently stir
» Place lid and cook on LOW for 8 hours
» Discard bones from turkey breast, carefully slice the meat
» Divide between plates and serve with vegetables and cherries
» Enjoy!

Nutrition: Calories: 220 Fat: 5g Carbohydrates: 8g Protein: 15g

---

PESTO TILAPIA

Preparation Time: 5 minutes
Cooking Time: 20 minutes
Serving: 2

INGREDIENTS:

- 1/4 cup dry white wine
- 1 teaspoon avocado oil
- 1 lemon, halved
- 2 tilapia fillets (5 to 7 ounces each)
- Freshly ground black pepper
- 2 tablespoons store-bought low-sodium pesto

DIRECTIONS:

» Preheat the oven to 350°F.
» In a 9-by-11-inch baking dish, whisk the wine, oil, and juice of half a lemon. Add the fish fillets and season lightly with pepper.
» Cover the baking dish with foil and bake for 15 minutes. Uncover the dish, top each fillet with 1 tablespoon pesto, and cook for 5 more minutes.
» Cut the remaining 1/2 lemon into wedges and serve each fillet with a lemon wedge

Nutrition: Per Serving Calories: 272; Total fat: 13g; Carbohydrates: 3g; Fiber: 0g; Protein: 30g; Calcium: 56mg; Sodium: 220mg; Potassium: 502mg; Vitamin D: 4mcg; Iron: 1mg; Zinc: 1mg

---

EGG-TOPPED RICE BOWL

Preparation Time: 5 minutes
Cooking Time: 10 minutes
Serving: 2

INGREDIENTS:

- 1 bunch spinach (about 5 ounces)
- 1/2 cup halved cherry tomatoes
- 1 teaspoon red wine vinegar
- 1 cup cooked brown rice, warm
- 1/3 cup sliced avocado
- 1 teaspoon olive oil
- 2 large eggs
- 1/8 teaspoon freshly ground black pepper
- 1/2 teaspoon hot sauce (optional)

DIRECTIONS:

» Heat a large nonstick skillet over medium heat. Add the spinach and cook for 2 minutes, or until the spinach wilts. Stir in the tomatoes and red wine vinegar, and remove the skillet from the heat.
» Divide the rice evenly between two bowls and top evenly with the spinach mixture. Arrange the avocado slices alongside the spinach mixture.
» Wipe the skillet dry with a paper towel, and return it to medium heat. Add the olive oil to the skillet and swirl to coat. Crack the eggs, one at a time, into the skillet. Cook the eggs for 2 minutes, and then cover and cook for 1 minute, or until the whites are set.
» Top each bowl of rice with the cooked egg. Sprinkle evenly with the black pepper and hot sauce (if using). Serve immediately.

Nutrition: Calories: 312; Total Fat: 15g; Saturated Fat: 3g; Cholesterol: 186mg; Sodium: 213mg; Potassium: 1,372mg; Magnesium: 192mg; Total Carbohydrates: 35g; Fiber: 9g; Sugars: 1g; Protein: 15g

---

CHICKPEA BURGERS

Preparation Time: 5 minutes
Cooking Time: 30 minutes
Serving: 4

INGREDIENTS:

- 2 teaspoons olive oil
- 1 small yellow onion, diced
- 2 cups rolled oats (not instant)
- ½ cup ground walnuts
- 1 (15-ounce) can chickpeas, drained and rinsed
- 3/4 cup nonfat or low-fat milk
- 1/2 teaspoon garlic powder
- 1/2 teaspoon onion powder
- 1/2 teaspoon dried sage

DIRECTIONS:

» In a large skillet, heat the olive oil. Add the onions and cook for about 10 minutes, until very tender and golden brown. Set aside.
» In a large bowl, toss together the oats and ground walnuts. Set aside.
» In a blender, combine the chickpeas, milk, garlic powder, onion powder, and dried sage, and process until smooth and creamy.
» Pour the chickpea mixture into the bowl with the oats and walnuts. Add the browned onions and mix well.
» Allow the mixture to rest for 5 to 10 minutes, so the oats can absorb the liquid.
» Form the mixture into eight thin, flat patties. Using the same skillet, brown the burgers over medium-low heat for 5 to 7 minutes on each side.
» Serve with your favorite toppings.

Nutrition: Calories: 375; Total Fat: 16g; Saturated Fat: 1g; Cholesterol: 1mg; Sodium: 112mg; Potassium: 172mg; Magnesium: 40mg; Total Carbohydrates: 48g; Fiber: 11g; Sugars: 4g; Protein: 14g

BEEF STROGANOFF

Preparation Time: 10 minutes
Cooking Time: 25 minutes
Servings: 4

INGREDIENTS:

- ½ cup chopped onion
- ½ pound boneless beef round steak, cut into ¾ inch thick
- 4 cups pasta noodles
- ½ cup fat-free cream of mushroom soup
- ½ cup water
- ½ teaspoon paprika
- ½ cup fat-free sour cream

DIRECTIONS:

» In a non-stick frying pan, sauté the onions over low to medium heat without oil while stirring constantly for about 5 minutes.
» Stir in the beef and cook for another 5 minutes until the beef is tender and turn brown on all sides. Set aside.
» In a large pot, fill it with water until ¾ full and bring to a boil. Cook the noodles until done according to package instructions. Drain the noodles and set aside.
» In a saucepan, whisk the mushroom soup and water. Bring to a boil over medium heat and stir constantly until the sauce has reduced.
» Add in paprika and sour cream.
» Assemble the stroganoff by placing the pasta in a bowl and pouring over the sauce. Top with the meat.
» Serve warm.

Nutrition: Calories: 273; Protein: 20g; Carbs: 37g; Fat: 5g; Saturated Fat: 2g; Sodium: 193mg

Chapter 9
Snacks and Desserts

HEARTY CHIA AND BLACKBERRY PUDDING

Preparation Time: 45 mins | Servings: 2

INGREDIENTS:

- ¼ cup chia seeds
- ½ cup blackberries, fresh
- 1 tsp liquid sweetener
- 1 cup coconut almond milk, full fat and unsweetened
- 1 tsp vanilla extract

DIRECTIONS::S

» Take the vanilla, liquid sweetener and coconut almond milk and add to blender
» Process until thick
» Add in blackberries and process until smooth
» Divide the mixture between cups and chill for 30 mins

Nutrition: Calories 314.8, Fat 25.0 g, Carbs 22.1 g, Protein 4.5 g

SPECIAL COCOA BROWNIES

Preparation Time: 15 mins | Servings: 12
Cooking Time: 25 mins

INGREDIENTS:

- 2 tbsps grass-fed almond butter
- 1 whole egg
- 2 tsps vanilla extract
- ¼ tsp baking powder
- 1/3 cup heavy cream
- 3/4 cup almond butter
- ¼ cocoa powder
- A pinch of sunflower seeds

DIRECTIONS:

» Break the eggs and whisk until smooth
» Add in all the wet Ingredients: and mix well
» Make the batter by mixing all the dry Ingredients: and sifting them into the wet Ingredients:
» Pour into a greased baking pan Bake for 25 mins at 350 degrees F or until a toothpick inserted in the middle comes out clean

Nutrition: Calories 355.8, Fat 25.0 g, Carbs 22.1 g, Protein 4.5 g

- **Gentle Blackberry Crumble**

Preparation Time: 10 mins | Servings: 4
Cooking Time: 45 mins

INGREDIENTS:

- ½ a cup of coconut flour
- ½ a cup of banana, peeled and mashed
- 6 tbsp of water
- 3 cups of fresh blackberries
- ½ a cup of arrowroot flour
- 1 and a ½ tsp of baking soda
- 4 tbsp of almond butter, melted
- 1 tbsp of fresh lemon juice

DIRECTIONS:

» Pre-heat your oven to 300 degrees F
» Take a baking dish and grease it lightly
» Take a bowl and mix all of the Ingredients: except blackberries, mix well
» Place blackberries in the bottom of your baking dish and top with flour
» Bake for 40 mins

Nutrition: Calories 325.8, Fat 20.0 g, Carbs 22.1 g, Protein 5.5 g

NUTMEG NOUGATS

Preparation Time: 10 mins | Servings: 12
Cooking Time: 5 mins +30mins

» Freeze Time: 30 mins

INGREDIENTS:

- 1 cup coconut, shredded
- 1 cup low-fat cream
- 1 cup cashew almond butter
- ½ tsp ground nutmeg

DIRECTIONS:

» Melt the cashew almond butter over a double boiler
» Stir in nutmeg and dairy cream
» Remove from the heat
» Allow to cool down a little
» Keep in the refrigerator for at least 30 mins
» Take out from the fridge and make small balls
» Coat with shredded coconut
» Let it cool for 2 hours and then serve

Nutrition: Calories 334, Fat 28.0 g, Carbs 20.1 g, Protein 4.5 g

APPLE AND ALMOND MUFFINS

Preparation Time: 10 mins | **Servings:** 6
Cooking Time: 20 mins

INGREDIENTS:

- 6 oz ground almonds
- 1 tsp cinnamon
- ½ tsp baking powder
- 1 pinch sunflower seeds
- 1 whole egg
- 1 tsp apple cider vinegar
- 2 tbsps Erythritol
- 1/3 cup apple sauce

DIRECTIONS:

» Pre-heat your oven to 350° F
» Line muffin tin with paper muffin cups, keep them on the side Mix in almonds, cinnamon, baking powder, sunflower seeds and keep it on the side
» Take another bowl and beat in eggs, apple cider vinegar, apple sauce, Erythritol
» Add the mix to dry Ingredients: and mix well until you have a smooth batter
» Pour batter into tin and bake for 20 mins
» Once done, let them cool

Nutrition: Calories 314, Fat 21.0 g, Carbs 18.1 g, Protein 6.5 g

SWEET POTATOES AND APPLES MIX

Preparation Time: 10 mins
Servings: 1

INGREDIENTS:

- 1 tbsp low-fat butter
- ½ lb. cored and chopped apples
- 2 tbsp water
- 2 lbs. sweet potatoes

DIRECTIONS:

» Arrange the potatoes around the lined baking sheet, bake inside oven at 400 0 F for an hour, peel them and mash them in the meat processor.
» Put apples in the very pot, add the river, bring using a boil over medium heat, reduce temperature, and cook for ten mins. Transfer to your bowl, add mashed potatoes, stir well and serve every day.
» Enjoy!

Nutrition: Calories 140, Fat 1 g, Carbs 8 g, Protein 6 g

SAUTÉED BANANAS WITH ORANGE SAUCE

Preparation Time: 5 mins
Servings: 4

INGREDIENTS:

- ¼ cup frozen pure orange juice concentrate
- 2 tbsp margarine
- ¼ cup sliced almonds
- 1 tsp. orange zest
- 1 tsp. fresh grated ginger
- 4 firm, sliced ripe bananas
- 1 tsp. cinnamon

DIRECTIONS:

» Melt the margarine over medium heat in a large skillet, until it bubbles but before it begins to brown.
» Add the cinnamon, ginger, and orange zest. Cook, while stirring, for 1 minute before adding the orange juice concentrate. Cook, while stirring until an even sauce has formed.
» Add the bananas and cook, stirring carefully for 1-2 mins, or until warmed and evenly coated with the sauce.
» Serve warm with sliced almonds.

Nutrition: Calories 164.3, Fat 9.0 g, Carbs 21.4 g, Protein 2.3 g

CARAMELIZED APRICOT

Preparation Time: 10 mins
Servings: 6

INGREDIENTS:

- ¼ cup white sugar
- 2 tsps. lemon juice
- ½ tsp. thyme
- 3 cup sliced apricots
- 1 tbsp brown sugar
- 1 cup part skim ricotta cheese
- 1 tsp. lemon zest

DIRECTIONS:

» Preheat the broiler of your oven.
» Place the apricots in a bowl and toss with the lemon juice.
» In another bowl, combine the ricotta cheese, thyme, and lemon zest. Mix well.
» Spread a layer of the ricotta mixture into the bottoms of 6 large baking ramekins.
» Spoon the apricots over the top of the ricotta cheese in each.
» Combine the white sugar and brown sugar. Sprinkle evenly over the apricots, avoiding large clumps of sugar as much as possible.
» Place the ramekins under the broiler for approximately 5 mins, or until caramelized.
» Serve warm.

Nutrition: Calories 133.6, Fat 3.6 g, Carbs 21.6 g, Protein 5.8 g

RHUBARB PIE

Preparation Time: 10 mins
Servings: 12

INGREDIENTS:

- 4 cup chopped rhubarb
- 8 oz. low-fat cream cheese
- 1 cup melted low-fat butter
- 1 ¼ cup coconut sugar
- 2 cup whole wheat flour
- 1 cup chopped pecans
- 1 cup sliced strawberries

DIRECTIONS:

» In a bowl, combine the flour while using the butter, pecans and ¼ cup sugar and stir well.
» Transfer this for some pie pan, press well in for the pan, introduce inside the oven and bake at 350 0 F for 20 mins.
» In a pan, combine the strawberries with all the current rhubarb, cream cheese and 1 cup sugar, stir well and cook over medium heat for 4 mins.
» Spread this inside the pie crust whilst inside fridge for the couple hours before slicing and serving.

Nutrition: Calories 162, Fat 5 g, Carbs 15 g, Protein 6 g

BERRY BARS

Preparation Time: 10 mins
Servings: 18

INGREDIENTS:

- 1 cup natural peanut butter
- ¼ cup chopped dried blueberries
- 3 cup oatmeal
- ¼ cup chopped dried cranberries
- 3 tbsp honey

DIRECTIONS:

» Line a baking pan with wax paper or parchment paper.
» Microwave the peanut butter for 10-15 seconds, just until it softens and begins to liquefy.
» Combine the oatmeal, peanut butter, honey, cranberries, and blueberries together in a bowl and mix until blended.
» Spread the mixture out evenly into the pan.
» Place in the refrigerator and let set for 2 hours before cutting into squares.

Nutrition: Calories 145.0, Fat 6.4 g, Carbs 17.9 g, Protein 4.4 g

CHOCOLATE AVOCADO PUDDING

Preparation Time: 30 mins | **Servings:** 2

INGREDIENTS:

- 1 avocado, chunked
- 1 tbsp natural sweetener such as stevia
- 2 oz cream cheese, at room temp
- ¼ tsp vanilla extract
- 4 tbsps cocoa powder, unsweetened

DIRECTIONS:

» Blend listed Ingredients: in blender until smooth
» Divide the mix between dessert bowls, chill for 30 mins

Nutrition: Calories 284, Fat 18.0 g, Carbs 20.1 g, Protein 5.5 g

POMEGRANATE MIX

Preparation Time: 10 mins
Servings: 2

INGREDIENTS:

- Single pomegranate seeds
- 2 cup pomegranate juice
- 1 cup steel cut oats

DIRECTIONS:

» In a bit pot, combine the pomegranate juice with pomegranate seeds and oats, toss, cook over medium heat for 5 mins, divide into bowls and serve cold.

Nutrition: Calories 172, Fat 4 g, Carbs 10 g, Protein 5 g

BLUEBERRY CREAM

Preparation Time: 5 mins
Servings: 1

INGREDIENTS:

- 1 tbsp low-fat peanut butter
- 2 dates
- ¾ cup blueberries
- 1 peeled banana
- ¾ cup almond milk

DIRECTIONS:

» In a blender, combine the blueberries with peanut butter, milk, banana and dates, pulse well, divide into small cups and serve cold.

Nutrition: Calories 120, Fat 3 g, Carbs 6 g, Protein 7 g

MOCHA RICOTTA CREAM

Preparation Time: 10 mins
Servings: 4

INGREDIENTS:

- 2 cup part skin ricotta cheese
- 1 tbsp espresso powder
- Almond cookie crumbs
- ½ cup powdered sugar
- 1 tbsp dark cocoa powder
- 1 tsp. pure vanilla extract

DIRECTIONS:

- Combine the ricotta cheese, powdered sugar, espresso powder, cocoa powder, and vanilla extract in a bowl. Using an electric mixer, blend until creamy.
- Cover and refrigerate for at least 4 hours.
- Serve in individual dishes, garnished with cookie crumbs, if desired.

Nutrition: Calories 230.6, Fat 9.9g, Carbs 22.0g, Protein 14.3g

---

MANGO SWEET MIX

Preparation Time: 10 mins
Servings: 8

INGREDIENTS:

- 1 tsp. cinnamon powder
- 1 ½ lbs. peeled and cubed mango
- 3 tbsp coconut sugar
- ½ cup apple cider vinegar treatment
- 1 tsp. nigella seeds

DIRECTIONS:

- In a tiny pot, combine the mango while using nigella seeds, sugar, vinegar and cinnamon, toss, bring using a simmer over medium heat, cook for 10 mins, divide into bowls and serve.

Nutrition: Calories 160, Fat 3 g, Carbs 8 g, Protein 3 g

GINGER PEACH PIE

Preparation Time: 10 mins
Servings: 10

INGREDIENTS:

- 5 cup diced peaches
- ½ cup sugar
- 2 refrigerated whole wheat pie crust doughs
- 1 tsp. cinnamon
- ½ cup orange juice
- ¼ cup chopped candied ginger
- ½ cup cornstarch

DIRECTIONS:

- Preheat the oven to 425°F.
- Place one of the pie crusts in a standard size pie dish. Spread some coffee beans or dried beans in the bottom of the pie crust to use as a weight. Place the dish in the oven and bake for 10-15 mins, or until lightly golden. Remove from the oven and let cool.
- Combine the peaches, candied ginger, and cinnamon in a bowl. Toss to mix.
- Combine the sugar, cornstarch, and orange juice in a saucepan and heat over medium until syrup begins to thicken.
- Pour the syrup over the peaches and toss to coat.
- Spread the peaches in the pie crust and top with the remaining crust. Crimp along the edges and cut several small slits in the top.
- Place in the oven and bake for 25-30 mins, or until golden brown.
- Let set before slicing.

Nutrition: Calories 289.0, Fat 13.1 g, Carbs 41.6 g, Protein 3.9 g

---

BERRIES MIX

Preparation Time: 10 mins
Servings: 6

INGREDIENTS:

- 4 tbsp coconut sugar
- 2 tsps. freshly squeezed fresh lemon juice
- 1 lb. strawberries
- 1 lb. blackberries

DIRECTIONS:

- In a pan, combine the strawberries with blackberries and sugar, stir, provide your simmer over medium heat and cook for ten mins.
- Divide into cups and serve cold.

Nutrition: Calories 120, Fat 2 g, Carbs 4 g, Protein 4 g

COCONUT CREAM

Preparation Time: 1 hour
Servings: 4

INGREDIENTS:

- 1 tsp. cinnamon powder
- 5 tbsp coconut sugar
- 2 cup coconut cream
- Zest of one grated lemon
- 3 whisked eggs

DIRECTIONS:

- In just a little pan, combine the cream with cinnamon, eggs, sugar and lemon zest. Whisk well
- Simmer over medium heat for 10 mins.
- Divide into ramekins and inside fridge for an hour before serving

Nutrition: Calories 130, Fat 5 g, Carbs 8 g, Protein 6 g

COCONUT FIGS

Preparation Time: 6 mins
Servings: 4

INGREDIENTS:

- 12 halved figs
- 1 cup toasted and chopped almonds
- 2 tbsp coconut butter
- ¼ cup coconut sugar

DIRECTIONS:

- Put butter inside the pot, get hot over medium heat, add sugar, whisk well, include almonds and figs, toss, cook for 5 mins, divide into small cups and serve cold.

Nutrition: Calories 150, Fat 4 g, Carbs 7 g, Protein 4 g

CINNAMON APPLES

Preparation Time: 10 mins
Servings: 4

INGREDIENTS:

- 1 tbsp cinnamon powder
- 4 tbsp raisins
- 4 cored big apples

DIRECTIONS:

- Stuff the apples while using the raisins, sprinkle the cinnamon, stick them inside a baking dish, introduce inside oven at 375 0 F, bake for 20 mins and serve cold.

Nutrition: Calories: 205, Fat: 1 g, Carbs:8 g, Protein:4 g

GREEN APPLE BOWLS

Preparation Time: 10 mins
Servings: 3

INGREDIENTS:

- 1 tbsp coconut sugar
- ½ tsp. vanilla flavoring
- 1 cup halved strawberries
- 3 cored and cubed big green apples
- ½ tsp. cinnamon powder

DIRECTIONS:

- In a bowl, combine the apples with strawberries, sugar, cinnamon and vanilla, toss and serve.

Nutrition: Calories 205, Fat 1 g, Carbs 8 g, Protein 4 g

PECAN GRANOLA

Preparation Time: 5 mins
Servings: 10

INGREDIENTS:

- 50 g maple syrup
- ½ g nutmeg
- 1400 g raw pecans
- 2 ½ g cayenne pepper
- 5 g ground cinnamon

DIRECTIONS:

- Preheat oven to about 400 0 F.
- In a large bowl, mix the pecans maple syrup, and spices, and toss till perfectly coated.
- Spread out nuts on a baking sheet and roast for about 10 mins.
- Cool for another 10 mins, then store or serve.

Nutrition: Calories 174, Fat 100.8 g, Carbs 23 g, Protein 13 g

BANANA SASHIMI

Preparation Time: 5 mins| **Servings:** 1

INGREDIENTS:

- ¼ tsp. chia seeds
- 15 g almond butter
- 1 medium banana

DIRECTIONS:

- Peel banana and cover one side in the nut butter, while placing it face up.
- Slice banana evenly into even 1-centimeter thick pieces.
- Sprinkle on toppings and serve!

Nutrition: Calories 194, Fat 8 g, Carbs 30 g, Protein 5 g

CREAMY PEANUTS WITH APPLES

Preparation Time: 10 mins
Servings: 2

INGREDIENTS:

- 4 oz. fat-free cream cheese
- 1 tbsp diced peanuts
- ¼ cup orange juice
- 2 cored and sliced medium apples
- 1 tbsp brown sugar
- ¾ tsp. vanilla

DIRECTIONS:

- Set your cream cheese on the counter for about five mins to soften it.
- Make the dip by mixing the cream cheese, vanilla, and brown sugar in a bowl. Add peanuts and mix until combined.
- Add the sliced apples in a separate bowl and drizzle with orange juice to stop the apples from turning brown.
- Serve the apples with the dip and enjoy!

Nutrition: Calories 110, Fat 2 g, Carbs 18 g, Protein 5 g

MAPLE MALT

Preparation Time: 10 mins
Servings: 2

INGREDIENTS:

- 2 ½ g vanilla essence
- 45 g maple syrup
- 5 g cinnamon
- 30 g chocolate
- 45 g cocoa powder
- 340 g almond milk

DIRECTIONS:

» Literally just pour it all into a saucepan and boil till it thickens.

Nutrition: Calories 1180, Fat 85.8 g, Carbs 80 g, Protein 40 g

WALNUT GREEN BEANS

Preparation Time: 15-20 mins
Servings: 2-3

INGREDIENTS:

- 2 cup roughly cut green beans
- 1 tbsp olive oil
- 3 minced garlic cloves
- ½ cup chopped walnuts

DIRECTIONS:

» In a cooking pot, add and boil the beans in salted water until tender.
» In a saucepan, add the beans, garlic, oil, and walnuts; cook for about 5-7 mins stirring constantly.
» Serve warm.

Nutrition: Calories 130, Fat 7 g, Carbs 15 g, Protein 5 g

CHEESE STUFFED APPLES

Preparation Time: 20-25 min.
Servings: 4

INGREDIENTS:

- 1 tbsp raisins
- 1 whisked egg
- 8 oz. cottage cheese
- 1 tsp. confectioners' sugar
- 2 tbsp honey
- 4 cored apples

DIRECTIONS:

» Preheat the oven to 400 0 F.
» In a mixing bowl, thoroughly mix the egg, cheese, honey, and raisins.
» Spoon some flesh from the core part of the apples and fill with the cheese mix.
» Bake for 18-20 mins; top with confectioner's sugar and serve.

Nutrition: Calories 194, Fat 5.2 g, Carbs 23.8 g, Protein 3.6 g

GREEN TEA CREAM

Preparation Time: 1 hour |**Servings:** 6

INGREDIENTS:

- 2 tbsp green tea extract powder
- 3 tbsp coconut sugar
- 14 oz. coconut milk
- 14 oz. coconut cream

DIRECTIONS:

» Put the milk in the very pan, add sugar and green tea herb powder, stir, give your simmer, cook for two mins, remove heat, cool down, add coconut cream, whisk well, divide into small bowls whilst from the fridge for just two hours before serving.

Nutrition: Calories 160, Fat 3 g, Carbs 7 g, Protein 6 g

FRESH FIGS WITH WALNUTS AND RICOTTA

Preparation Time: 5 mins |**Servings:** 4
Cooking Time: 2-3 mins

INGREDIENTS:

- 8 dried figs, halved
- ¼ cup ricotta cheese
- 16 walnuts, halved - 1 tbsp honey

DIRECTIONS:

» Take a skillet and place it over medium heat, add walnuts and toast for 2 mins Top figs with cheese and walnuts Drizzle honey on top

Nutrition: Calories 204, Fat 10.0 g, Carbs 12.1 g, Protein 4.5 g

COCONUT MOUSSE

Preparation Time: 10 mins
Servings: 12

INGREDIENTS:

- 1 tsp. vanilla flavoring
- 1 tsp. coconut extract
- 1 cup toasted coconut
- 2 ¾ cup coconut milk
- 4 tsps. coconut sugar

DIRECTIONS:

» In a bowl, combine the coconut milk with the coconut extract, vanilla flavor, coconut and sugar, whisk well, divide into small cups and serve cold.

Nutrition: Calories 152, Fat 5 g, Carbs 11 g, Protein 3 g

RICE PUDDING WITH ORANGES

Preparation Time: 15 mins
Servings: 3-4

INGREDIENTS:

- 3 large navel oranges
- ¼ cup low-fat sweetened condensed milk
- 4 tbsp sugar
- ¾ cup Basmati rice white rice
- ½ halved vanilla bean
- 4 cup fat-free evaporated milk

DIRECTIONS:

» Take a 2 quart pan and boil 2 cups of water, add rice and cover it with lowering the heat.
» Cook it for 20 mins till it is soft and the water is taken up by the rice. Take a clean orange, extract 1 tsp of zest from it.
» Cut it in half and juice it, save it. Remove the rind from rest of the oranges, extract the white pith. Clear the bifurcations.
» When the rice is soft, add half cup of the orange juice, the zest, evaporated milk, condensed milk, vanilla bean and sugar. Cook the mix over medium flame for 20 to 25 mins, without the cover, stirring regularly till it creams up. Clear off the vanilla bean and pour the rice mixture among bowls to serve hot.

Nutrition: Calories 230.5, Fat 6.7 g, Carbs 39 g, Protein 4.2 g

CHICKPEAS AND PEPPER HUMMUS

Preparation Time: 10 mins
Servings: 4

INGREDIENTS:

- Juice of ½ lemon
- 4 chopped walnuts
- 1 tbsp sesame paste
- 14 oz. no-salt-added, drained and rinsed canned chickpeas
- 2 chopped roasted red peppers

DIRECTIONS:

» In your blender, combine the chickpeas with all the sesame paste, red peppers, lemon juice and walnuts, pulse well, divide into bowls and serve as being a snack. Enjoy!

Nutrition: Calories 231, Fat 12 g, Carbs 15 g, Protein 14 g

TORTILLA CHIPS

Preparation Time: 10 mins
Servings: 6

INGREDIENTS:

- ¼ tsp. cayenne
- 2 tbsp organic extra virgin olive oil
- 12 whole wheat grain tortillas
- 1 tbsp chili powder

DIRECTIONS:

» Spread the tortillas for the lined baking sheet, add the oil, chili powder and cayenne, toss, introduce inside oven and bake at 350 0 F for 25 mins.
» Divide into bowls and serve as a side dish.

Nutrition: Calories 199, Fat 3 g, Carbs 12 g, Protein 5 g

KALE POPCORN

Preparation Time: 10 mins
Servings: 4

INGREDIENTS:

- 2 tsps. grape seed oil
- 2 tsps. lemon zest
- 10 cup popped popcorn
- ½ bunch chopped kale

DIRECTIONS:

» Preheat the oven to 325°F.
» Pat the kale completely dry with kitchen paper and then coat with olive oil and salt.
» Place onto the baking sheet and bake for 11 mins until crispy.
» Stir once or twice halfway through cooking and be careful that the kale does not burn.
» Remove the kale and let cool.
» Place the cooled kale into a food processor together with the lemon zest and process into a fine powder.
» Add this seasoning to the prepared popcorn and serve.

Nutrition: Calories 131, Fat 4 g, Carbs 22 g, Protein 5 g

PEAS AND PARSLEY HUMMUS

Preparation Time: 10 mins
Servings: 4

INGREDIENTS:

- Juice of ½ lemon
- 2 cup drained chickpeas
- 2 tbsp oil
- 1 clove garlic
- 4 tbsp chopped parsley
- 12 black olives

DIRECTIONS:

» Pour the chickpeas and juice in a blender together with garlic and oil.
» Serve with olives and parsley.

Nutrition: Calories 107, Fat 9g, Carbs 15g, Protein 11g

WHITE BEANS HUMMUS

Preparation Time: 10 mins
Servings: 4

INGREDIENTS:

- Juice of ½ lemon
- 1 box of natural white beans
- 1 tbsp tahini
- 1 tsp garlic powder
- sesame seeds

DIRECTIONS:

» Pour the tbsp of tahini in a blender together with natural white beans (previously drained), and garlic powder.
» Pour the lemon juice and tase.

Nutrition: Calories 151, Fat 14 g, Carbs 12 g, Protein 11 g

PEANUTS SNACK BAR

Preparation Time: 15 mins
Servings: 10

INGREDIENTS:

- 420 g roasted peanuts
- 30 pitted dates

DIRECTIONS:

» Go ahead and throw your dates all into the food processor and add the salt and blend until it forms a smooth paste.
» Add in the roasted peanuts and pulse until the nuts are coarsely chopped and grab a spoon and make a big ball of date-nut dough.
» Roll your dough into a 1 inch thick mat and cut into sticks or bars and serve.

Nutrition: Calories 307, Fat 21g, Carbs 25g, Protein 11g

CHICKPEAS DIP

Preparation Time: 10 mins
Servings: 4

INGREDIENTS:

- ½ cup chopped coriander
- Zest one grated lemon
- 1 tbsp olive oil
- 4 tbsp pine nuts
- Juice of one lemon
- 14 oz. no-salt-added drained and rinsed canned chickpeas

DIRECTIONS:

» In a blender, combine the chickpeas with lemon zest, freshly squeezed lemon juice, coriander and oil, pulse well, divide into small bowls, sprinkle pine nuts at the pinnacle and serve as a conference dip.

Nutrition: Calories 200, Fat 12 g, Carbs 9 g, Protein 7 g

SPECIAL RASPBERRY CHOCOLATE BOMBS

Preparation Time: 10 mins | **Servings:** 6 | **Freeze time:** 1 hours

INGREDIENTS:

- ½ cacao almond butter
- ½ coconut manna
- 4 tbsps powdered coconut almond milk
- 3 tbsps granulated stevia
- ¼ cup dried and crushed raspberries, frozen

DIRECTIONS:

» Prepare your double boiler to medium heat and melt cacao almond butter and coconut manna
» Stir in vanilla extract
» Take another dish and add coconut powder and sugar substitute
» Stir the coconut mix into the cacao almond butter, 1 tbsp at a time, making sure to keep mixing after each addition
» Add the crushed dried raspberries
» Mix well and portion it out into muffin tins
» Chill for 60 mins and enjoy!

Nutrition: Calories 264, Fat 25.0 g, Carbs 20.1 g, Protein 6.5 g

CRANBERRY MUFFINS

Preparation Time: 10 mins | **Servings:** 24
Cooking Time: 20mins

INGREDIENTS:

- 2 cups almond flour
- 2 tsps baking soda
- ¼ cup avocado oil
- 1 whole egg
- ¾ cup almond milk
- ½ cup Erythritol
- ½ cup apple sauce
- Zest of 1 orange
- 2 tsps ground cinnamon
- 2 cup fresh cranberries

DIRECTIONS:

» Pre-heat your oven to 350 °F
» Line muffin tin with paper muffin cups and keep them on the side
» Add flour, baking soda and keep it on the side
» Take another bowl and whisk in remaining Ingredients: and add flour, mix well
» Pour batter into prepared muffin tin and bake for 20 mins
» Once done, let it cool for 10 mins

Nutrition: Calories 232, Fat 25.0 g, Carbs 24.1 g, Protein 4.5 g

BROAD BEAN HUMMUS

Preparation Time: 5 mins | **Servings:** 4

INGREDIENTS:

- 2 cup cooked chickpeas
- 1 cup fresh beans
- 2 tbsp olive oil
- 1 lime
- 2 tsp of tahini
- 1 tsp of oregano
- 1 tsp ground cumin
- 1 tsp garlic

DIRECTIONS:

» Shovel the beans and cook for 8 minutes in boiling water. Rinse the chickpeas and drain. In the blender mix all the ingredients blend until smooth and serve

Nutrition: Calories 151, Fat 14 g, Carbs 12 g, Protein 11 g

CARROT CAKE

Preparation Time: 5 mins | **Servings:** 10
Cooking Time: 35 mins

INGREDIENTS:

- 2 cups of flour
- 1 cup grated carrots on a fine grater
- 4 eggs
- 1 cup of sugar
- cup of vegetable oil
- 0.5 cup of chopped walnuts and raisins
- 2 tsp baking powder
- tsp ground cinnamon
- 1 tsp vanilla sugar

DIRECTIONS:

» Beat eggs with regular and vanilla sugar in a blender.
» Add vegetable oil, carrots, sifted flour with baking powder, cinnamon, and a pinch of salt.
» Stir until a thick dough.
» Add raisins and walnuts to the dough.
» Pour the dough into a heat-resistant round mold with a diameter of 22-24 cm, greased with oil and covered with parchment, and bake at 350°F for 35 minutes.
» Before serving, sprinkle with powdered sugar.

Nutrition: Calories 188, Total Fat 5 g, Carbs 24.1 g, Protein 4.5 g

HEARTY ALMOND BREAD

Preparation Time: 15 mins | **Servings:** 8
Cooking Time: 60 mins

INGREDIENTS:

- 3 cups almond flour
- 1 tsp baking soda
- 2 tsps baking powder
- ¼ tsp sunflower seeds
- ¼ cup almond milk
- ½ cup + 2 tbsps olive oil
- 3 whole eggs

DIRECTIONS:

» Pre-heat your oven to 300° F
» Take an 9x5 inch loaf pan and grease, keep it on the side Add listed Ingredients: to a bowl and pour the batter into the loaf pan
» Bake for 60 mins
» Once baked, remove from oven and let it cool

Nutrition: Calories 256, Fat 20.0 g, Carbs 28.1 g, Protein 4.5 g

APPLE COFFEE CAKE

Preparation Time: 5 mins | **Servings:** 20
Cooking Time: 40 mins

INGREDIENTS:

- 5 cups tart apples, cored, peeled, chopped
- 1 cup sugar
- 1 cup dark raisins
- 1/2 cup pecans, chopped
- 1/4 cup vegetable oil
- 2 tsps vanilla
- 1 egg, beaten
- 2-1/2 cups sifted all-purpose flour
- 1-1/2 tsps baking soda
- 2 tsps ground cinnamon

DIRECTIONS:

» Preheat oven to 350°F.
» Lightly oil a 13x9x2-inch pan.
» In a large mixing bowl, combine apples with sugar, raisins, and pecans; mix well. Let stand 30 mins.
» Stir in oil, vanilla, and egg. Sift together flour, soda, and cinnamon; stir into apple mixture about 1/3 at a time just enough to moisten dry Ingredients:.
» Turn batter into pan. Bake 35 to 40 mins. Cool cake slightly before serving.

Nutrition: Calories 188, Total Fat 5 g, Carbs 24.1 g, Protein 4.5 g

BAKED APPLE SLICES

Preparation Time: 5 mins | **Servings:** 4
Cooking Time: 30 mins

INGREDIENTS:

- 2 oranges
- 2 tbsps honey
- 1/4 tsp ground cinnamon
- 1/4 tsp ground cloves
- 3 Granny Smith apples, peeled, cored, and cut into 1/2-inch slices
- 5 tbsps raisins
- 1/4 cup chopped walnuts, divided
- 1/4 cup vanilla yogurt, low-fat

DIRECTIONS:

» Preheat the oven to 500°F.
» Grate the zest of one of the oranges and set aside.
» Squeeze the juice from both oranges into a small bowl. Stir the honey, cinnamon, cloves, and half the zest into the juice.
» Lay half the apple slices in a glass baking dish. Scatter the raisins and 2 tbsps of the walnuts on top. Pour on half the juice mixture and top with the remaining apples and juice. Combine the remaining 2 tbsps of walnuts with the orange zest and scatter over the top.
» Cover lightly with foil, and bake 30 mins or until the apples are soft and the juices, bubbly. Serve warm or cold with a dollop of low-fat vanilla yogurt.

Nutrition: Calories 206, Fat 6 g, Carbs 41 g, Protein 5.8 g

FROSTED CAKE

Preparation Time: 5 mins |**Servings:** 10
Cooking Time: 50 mins

INGREDIENTS:

- Cake
- 2-1/4 cups cake flour
- 2-1/4 tsp baking powder
- 4 tbsps margarine
- 1-1/4 cups sugar
- 4 eggs
- 1 tsp vanilla
- 1 tbsp orange peel
- 3/4 cup skim milk
- Icing
- 3 oz low fat cream cheese
- 2 tbsps skim milk
- 6 tbsps cocoa
- 2 cups sifted confectioners sugar
- 1/2 tsp vanilla extract

DIRECTIONS:

» Preheat the oven to 325° F.
» Grease with small amount of cooking oil or use nonstick cooking oil spray on a 10-inch round pan (at least 2-1/2 inches high). Powder pan with flour. Tap out excess flour.
» Sift together flour and baking powder.
» In a separate bowl, beat together margarine and sugar until soft and creamy.
» Beat in eggs, vanilla, and orange peel.
» Gradually add the flour mixture alternating with the milk, beginning and ending with flour.
» Pour the mixture into the pan. Bake for 40 to 45 mins or until done. Let cake cool for 5 to 10 mins before removing from the pan. Let cool completely before icing.
» Icing
» Cream together cream cheese and milk until smooth. Add cocoa. Blend well.
» Slowly add sugar until icing is smooth. Mix in vanilla.
» Smooth icing over top and sides of cooled cake.

Nutrition: Calories 241, Fat 5 g, Carbs 48 g, Protein 4.8 g

FRUIT SKEWERS WITH YOGURT DIP

Preparation Time: 5 mins |**Servings:** 4
Cooking Time: 10 mins

INGREDIENTS:

- 1 cup strawberries, rinsed, stems removed, and cut in half
- 1 cup fresh pineapple, diced (or canned pineapple chunks in juice, drained)
- 1/2 cup blackberries
- 1 tangerine or Clementine, peeled and cut into 8 segments
- 8 6-inch wooden skewers
- For dip
- 1 cup strawberries, rinsed, stems removed, and cut in half
- 1/4 cup fat-free plain yogurt
- 1/8 tsp vanilla extract
- 1 tbsp honey

DIRECTIONS:

» Thread two strawberry halves, two pineapple chunks, two blackberries, and one tangerine segment on each skewer.
» To prepare the dip, puree strawberries in a blender or food processor. Add yogurt, vanilla, and honey, and mix well.
» Serve two skewers with yogurt dip on the side.

Nutrition: Calories 71, Fat 0 g, Protein 1 g, Carbs 18 g

FUDGY FRUIT

Preparation Time: 5 mins |**Servings:** 4
Cooking Time: 10 mins

INGREDIENTS:

- 2 tbsps semi-sweet chocolate chips
- 2 large bananas, peeled and cut into quarters
- 8 large strawberries
- 1/4 cup chopped unsalted peanuts

DIRECTIONS:

» Place chocolate chips in a small microwave safe bowl. Heat on high for 10 seconds and stir. Repeat until chocolate is melted, about 30 seconds.
» Place fruit on a small tray covered with a piece of waxed paper. Use a spoon to drizzle the melted chocolate on top of the fruit.
» Sprinkle the fruit with chopped nuts.
» Cover the fruit and place in the refrigerator for 10 mins or until the chocolate hardens. Serve chilled.

Nutrition: Calories 151, Carbs 24 g, Protein 3 g, Fat 6 g

MOUSSE VANILLA BANANA

Preparation Time: 5 mins |**Servings:** 4

INGREDIENTS:

- 2 tbsps low fat (1%) milk
- 4 tsps sugar
- 1 tsp vanilla
- 1 medium banana, cut in quarters
- 1 cup plain low fat yogurt
- 8 1/4-inch banana slices

DIRECTIONS:

» Place milk, sugar, vanilla, and banana in blender. Process 15 seconds at high speed until smooth.
» Pour mixture into a small bowl; fold in yogurt. Chill. Spoon into 4 dessert dishes; garnish each with 2 banana slices just before serving.

Nutrition: Information

» Calories 94, Fat 1 g, Carbs 24 g, Protein 3 g

OATMEAL COOKIES

Preparation Time: 5 mins |**Servings:** 8
Cooking Time: 18 mins

INGREDIENTS:

- 3/4 cup sugar
- 2 tbsps margarine
- 1 egg
- 1/4 cup canned applesauce
- 2 tbsps milk, low-fat
- 1 cup flour
- 1/4 tsp baking soda
- 1/2 tsp ground cinnamon
- 1 cup + 2 tbsps quick rolled oats

DIRECTIONS:

» Preheat oven to 350° F and lightly grease cookie sheets.
» In a large bowl, use an electric mixer on medium speed to mix sugar and margarine. Mix until well blended, about 3 mins.
» Slowly add egg; mix on medium speed 1 minute. Gradually add applesauce and milk; mix on medium speed 1 minute. Scrape sides of bowl.
» In another bowl, combine flour, baking soda, and cinnamon. Slowly add to applesauce mixture; mix on low speed until blended, about 2 mins. Add oats and blend 30 seconds on low speed. Scrape sides of bowl.
» Drop by tspfuls onto cookie sheet, about 2 inches apart.
» Bake until lightly browned, about 13-15 mins. Remove from baking sheet while still warm. Cool on wire rack.

Nutrition: Calories 215, Fat 4 g, Carbs 24 g, Protein 3 g

OVEN FRIED PLANTAINS

Preparation Time: 5 mins |**Servings:** 8
Cooking Time: 45 mins

INGREDIENTS:

- nonstick cooking spray
- 4 very ripe medium plantains
- 1/8 tsp ground nutmeg
- 4 tbsps brown sugar

DIRECTIONS:

» Placean oven rack in the middle of the oven. Preheat oven to 425°F.
» Spray cookie sheet well with nonstick cooking spray.
» Peel and slice each plantain into 16 thin diagonal slices.
» Sprinkle plantains with nutmeg and brown sugar.
» Bake until crisp, about 45 mins. Serve while warm.

Nutrition: Calories 158, Carbs 42 g, Protein 1 g, Fat 0 g

MIXED FRUITS FREEZE

Preparation Time: 5 mins |**Servings:** 4

INGREDIENTS:

- 1 large banana
- 2 cups strawberries
- 2 ripe mangos, chopped
- 1/2 cup of ice cubes

DIRECTIONS:

» Combine all Ingredients: in a blender or food processor container. Blend until mixture is smooth.
» Pour into glasses and serve.

Nutrition: Calories 121, Carbs 31 g, Fiber 4 g, Protein 1 g, Fat 1 g

PEACH APPLE CRISP

Preparation Time: 5 mins |**Servings:** 8
Cooking Time: 20 mins

INGREDIENTS:

- 20 oz canned peaches, light-syrup pack, drained
- 2 medium apples, tart, peeled and sliced
- 1/2 tsp vanilla
- 1/4 tsp ground cinnamon
- 3/4 cup + 3 tbsps flour
- 1/4 cup brown sugar, packed
- 3 tbsps soft (tub) margarine

DIRECTIONS:

» Preheat oven to 350° F. Lightly grease 9- by 9- by 2-inch casserole dish.
» Combine peaches, apples, vanilla, and cinnamon in a bowl. Toss well and spread evenly in greased casserole dish.
» Combine flour and sugar in small bowl. Cut in mar-

garine with two knives until the mixture resembles coarse meal.
- Sprinkle flour mixture evenly over fruit.
- Bake until lightly browned and bubbly, about 20 mins.

Nutrition: Calories 175, Fat 5 g, Carbs 24 g, Protein 3 g

PEACH CRUMBLE

Preparation Time: 5 mins | **Servings:** 12
Cooking Time: 25 mins

INGREDIENTS:
- nonstick cooking spray
- 4 (15-ounce) cans juice packed peach slices, drained*
- 2 tbsps cornstarch
- 1 tsp vanilla
- 1-1/4 tsp ground cinnamon
- 2/3 cup old fashioned oats
- 1/4 cup brown sugar
- 1/3 cup flour
- 2-1/2 tbsps butter

DIRECTIONS:
- Preheat oven to 400°F.
- Spray a 9-inch deep dish pie pan with nonstick cooking spray and pour peaches in the pan.
- In a small bowl, stir in cornstarch, vanilla, and 1 tsp cinnamon; pour the mixture over peaches.
- In a large bowl, mix the remaining cinnamon, oats, brown sugar, flour, and butter with a fork until crumbly; sprinkle over peaches.
- Bake for 20 to 25 mins or until juices are thickened and bubbly, and topping is lightly browned. Serve while hot.

Nutrition: Calories 139, Carbs 28 g, Protein 2 g, Fat 3 g

PEACHY PITA

Preparation Time: 5 mins
Servings: 4
Cooking Time: 1 mins

INGREDIENTS:
- 2 medium whole wheat pita pockets
- 1/4 cup reduced fat chunky peanut butter
- 1/2 apple, cored and thinly sliced
- 1/2 banana, thinly sliced
- 1/2 fresh peach, thinly sliced

DIRECTIONS:
- Cut pitas in half to make 4 pockets and warm in the microwave for about 10 seconds to make them more flexible.
- Carefully open each pocket and spread a thin layer of peanut butter on the inside walls.
- Fill with a combination of apple, banana, and peach slices. Serve at room temperature.

Nutrition: Calories 180, Carbs 26 g, Protein 7 g, Fat 3 g

PEANUT BUTTER HUMMUS

Preparation Time: 5 mins | **Servings:** 8
Cooking Time: 10 mins

INGREDIENTS:
- For dip
- 2 cups low-sodium garbanzo beans (chick peas), rinsed
- 1/4 cup low-sodium chicken broth
- 1/4 cup lemon juice
- 2–3 tbsps garlic, diced (about 4–6 garlic cloves, depending on taste)
- 1/4 cup creamy peanut butter (or substitute other nut or seed butter)
- 1/4 tsp cayenne pepper (or substitute paprika for less spice)
- 1 tbsp olive oil
- For pita chips
- 4 (6-1/2-inch) whole-wheat pitas, each cut into 10 triangles
- 1 tbsp olive oil
- 1 tsp garlic, minced (about 1 clove) (or 1/2 tsp garlic powder)
- 1/4 tsp ground black pepper

DIRECTIONS:
- Preheat oven to 400°F.
- To prepare the hummus, combine all Ingredients: for the dip and mix them in a food processor or blender. Puree until smooth.
- Prepare the chips, toss the pita triangles with the olive oil, garlic, and pepper.
- Bake chips on a baking sheet in a 400°F oven for 10 mins, or until crispy.
- Arrange pita chips on a platter, and serve with the hummus.

Nutrition: Calories 235, Fat 9 g, Protein 9 g, Carbs 32 g

RAINBOW SALAD

Preparation Time: 5 mins | **Servings:** 8

INGREDIENTS:
- Fruit salad
- 1 large mango, peeled and diced
- 2 cups fresh blueberries
- 2 bananas, sliced
- 2 cups fresh strawberries, halved
- 2 cups seedless grapes
- 2 nectarines, unpeeled and sliced
- 1 kiwi fruit, peeled and sliced
- Honey orange sauce
- 1/3 cups unsweetened orange juice
- 2 tbsps lemon juice
- 1-1/2 tbsps honey
- 1/4 tsp ground ginger
- dash nutmeg

DIRECTIONS:
- Prepare the fruit.
- Combine all the Ingredients: for the sauce and mix.
- Just before serving, pour honey orange sauce over the fruit.

Nutrition: Calories 96, Fat 1 g, Carbs 32 g

SAVORY GRILLED FRUIT

Preparation Time: 5 mins |Servings: 8

INGREDIENTS:
- 4 peaches, plums, or nectarines, halved and pitted

DIRECTIONS:
- Cook 4 halved peaches, plums, and/or nectarines over medium, indirect heat for 8 mins in a covered barbecue grill. Turn after 4 mins. Serve while hot.

Nutrition: Calories 19, Carbs 5 g, Protein 0 g, Total Fat 0 g

SOUTHERN BANANA PUDDING

Preparation Time: 5 mins |Servings: 10

INGREDIENTS:
- 3-3/4 cups cold, fat-free milk
- 2 small packages (4 serving size) of fat-free, sugar-free instant vanilla pudding and pie-filling mix
- 32 reduced-fat vanilla wafers
- 2 medium bananas, sliced
- 2 cups fat-free, frozen whipped topping, thawed

DIRECTIONS:
- Mix 3-1/2 cups of the milk with the pudding mixes. Beat the pudding mixture with a wire whisk for 2 mins until it is well blended. Let stand for 5 mins.
- Fold 1 cup of the whipped topping into the pudding mix.
- Arrange a layer of wafers on the bottom and sides of a 2-quart serving bowl. Drizzle 2 tbsps of the remaining milk over the wafers. Add a layer of banana slices and top with one-third of the pudding.
- Repeat layers, drizzling wafer layer with remaining milk and ending with pudding. Spread the remaining whipped topping over the pudding.
- Refrigerate for at least 3 hours before serving.

Nutrition: Calories 143, Fat 2 g, Protein 4 g, Carbs 29 g

TROPICAL FRUIT AND NUT SNACK MIX

Preparation Time: 5 mins |Servings: 10

INGREDIENTS:
- 1 tbsp butter
- 1/4 cup honey*
- 1 tsp almond or coconut extract
- 1 tsp ground cinnamon
- 2 cups old fashioned oats
- nonstick cooking spray
- 1/2 cup sliced almonds
- 3/4 cup dried tropical fruit bits
- 1/2 cup banana chips
- 1/4 cup raisins

DIRECTIONS:
- Preheat oven to 350°F.
- Melt butter in a medium saucepan. Add honey, almond or coconut extract, and cinnamon; mix well.
- Stir in oats and transfer to a baking sheet coated with nonstick cooking spray. Spread into a 1-inch thick layer.
- Bake for 10 mins, stirring once. Stir in almonds and bake for 5 to 10 mins more.
- Remove from oven and toss with dried fruit. Let cool completely and serve.

Nutrition: Calories 384, Carbs 62 g, Protein 9 g, Fat 13 g

FRUIT COMPOTE

Preparation Time: 5 mins |Servings: 8

INGREDIENTS:
- 3/4 cup water
- 1/2 cup sugar
- 2 tsps fresh lemon juice
- 1 piece lemon peel
- 1/2 tsp rum or vanilla extract (optional)
- 1 pineapple cored and peeled, cut into 8 slices
- 2 mangos peeled and pitted, cut into 8 pieces
- 3 bananas peeled, cut into 8 diagonal pieces

DIRECTIONS:
- In a saucepan combine 3/4 cup of water with the sugar, lemon juice, and lemon peel (and rum or vanilla extract if desired). Bring to a boil, then reduce the heat and add the fruit. Cook at a very low heat for 5 mins.
- Pour the syrup in a cup. Remove the lemon rind and cool the cooked fruit for 2 hours.
- To serve the compote, arrange the fruit in a serving dish and pour a few tsps of syrup over the fruit. Garnish with mint leaves.
- Serve with Homemade Sour Cream

Nutrition: Calories 148, Fat 1 g, Protein 4 g, Carbs 29 g

WINTER/SUMMER CRISP

Preparation Time: 5 mins |Servings: 6

INGREDIENTS:
- Filling
- 1/2 cup sugar
- 3 tbsps all-purpose flour
- 1 tsp lemon peel, grated
- 3/4 tsps lemon juice
- 5 cups apples, unpeeled, sliced

- 1 cup cranberries
- Topping
- 2/3 cups rolled oats
- 1/3 cups brown sugar, packed
- 1/4 cup whole wheat flour
- 2 tsps ground cinnamon
- 1 tbsp soft margarine, melted

DIRECTIONS:

» To prepare filling, in a medium bowl combine sugar, flour, and lemon peel; mix well. Add lemon juice, apples, and cranberries; stir to mix. Spoon into a 6-cup baking dish.
» To prepare topping, in a small bowl, combine oats, brown sugar, flour, and cinnamon. Add melted margarine; stir to mix.
» Sprinkle topping over filling. Bake in a 375°F oven for approximately 40-50 mins or until filling is bubbly and top is brown. Serve warm or at room temperature.
» Variation
» Summer Crisp: Prepare as directed, substituting 4 cups fresh or unsweetened frozen (thawed) peaches and 3 cups fresh or unsweetened frozen (unthawed) blueberries for apples and cranberries. If frozen, thaw peaches completely (do not drain). Do not thaw blueberries before mixing or they will be crushed.

Nutrition: Calories 28, Fat 2 g, Protein 4 g, Carbs 29 g

HEARTY CASHEW AND ALMOND BUTTER

Preparation Time: 5 minutes
Cooking Time: 0 minutes
Servings: 1 and 1/2 cups

INGREDIENTS:

- 1 cup almonds, blanched
- 1/3 cup cashew nuts
- 2 tablespoons coconut oil
- Sunflower seeds as needed
- 1/2 teaspoon cinnamon

DIRECTIONS:

» Pre-heat your oven to 350 degrees F.
» Bake almonds and cashews for 12 minutes.
» Let them cool.
» Transfer to food processor and add remaining ingredients.
» Add oil and keep blending until smooth.
» Serve and enjoy!

Nutrition: Calories: 205 Carbohydrates: 3 g Fat: 19g Protein: 2.8g

STYLISH CHOCOLATE PARFAIT

Preparation Time: 2 hours
Cooking Time: 0 minute
Servings: 4

INGREDIENTS:

- 2 tablespoons cocoa powder
- 1 cup almond milk
- 1 tablespoon chia seeds
- Pinch of sunflower seeds
- 1/2 teaspoon vanilla extract

DIRECTIONS:

» Take a bowl and add cocoa powder, almond milk, chia seeds, vanilla extract and stir.
» Transfer to dessert glass and place in your fridge for 2 hours.
» Serve and enjoy!

Nutrition: Calories: 130 Carbohydrates: 7g Fat: 5g Protein: 16g

SUPREME MATCHA BOMB

Preparation Time: 100 minutes
Cooking Time: 0 minutes
Servings: 10

INGREDIENTS:

- 3/4 cup hemp seeds
- 1/2 cup coconut oil
- 2 tablespoons coconut almond butter
- 1 teaspoon Matcha powder
- 2 tablespoons vanilla bean extract
- 1/2 teaspoon mint extract
- Liquid stevia

DIRECTIONS:

» Take your blender/food processor and add hemp seeds, coconut oil, Matcha, vanilla extract and stevia.
» Blend until you have a nice batter and divide into silicon molds.
» Melt coconut almond butter and drizzle on top.
» Let the cups chill and enjoy!

Nutrition: Calories: 200 Carbohydrates: 3g Fat: 20g Protein: 5g

PURE AVOCADO PUDDING

Preparation Time: 3 hours
Cooking Time: 0 minutes
Servings: 4

INGREDIENTS:

- 1 cup almond milk
- 2 avocados, peeled and pitted
- ¾ cup cocoa powder
- 1 teaspoon vanilla extract
- 2 tablespoons stevia
- ¼ teaspoon cinnamon

- Walnuts, chopped for serving

DIRECTIONS:

» Add avocados to a blender and pulse well.
» Add cocoa powder, almond milk, stevia, vanilla bean extract and pulse the mixture well.
» Pour into serving bowls and top with walnuts.
» Chill for 2-3 hours and serve!
» 5.

Nutrition: Carbohydrates: 7g Fat: 8g Protein: 3g

SWEET ALMOND AND COCONUT FAT BOMBS

Preparation Time: 10 minutes
Cooking Time: 0 minutes
Servings: 6

INGREDIENTS:

- ¼ cup melted coconut oil
- 9 ½ tablespoons almond butter
- 90 drops liquid stevia
- 3 tablespoons cocoa
- 9 tablespoons melted almond butter, sunflower seeds

DIRECTIONS:

» Take a bowl and add all of the listed ingredients. Mix them well. Pour 2 tablespoons of the mixture into as many muffin molds as you like. Chill for 20 minutes and pop them out.
» Serve and enjoy!

Nutrition: Calories: 136 Total Carbs: 2g Protein: 2.53g Fiber: 0g Fat: 14g

SIMPLE BROWNIES

Preparation Time: 10 minutes
Cooking Time: 30 minutes **Servings:** 8

INGREDIENTS:

- 6 ounces dark chocolate, chopped
- 4 egg whites
- ½ cup hot water
- 1 teaspoon vanilla extract
- 2/3 cup coconut sugar
- 1 and 1/2 cups whole flour
- 1/2 cup walnuts, chopped
- Cooking spray
- 1 teaspoon baking powder

DIRECTIONS:

» In a bowl, combine the chocolate and the hot water and whisk really well.
» Add vanilla extract and egg whites and whisk well again. In another bowl, combine the sugar with flour, baking powder and walnuts and stir. Combine the 2 mixtures, stir well, pour this into a cake pan greased with cooking spray, spread well, bake in the oven for 30 minutes, cool down, slice and serve. Enjoy!

Nutrition: calories 144, fat 4, fiber 4, carbs 9, protein 8

GRAPEFRUIT GRANITA

Preparation Time: 20 minutes
Cooking Time: 5 minutes
Servings: 3

INGREDIENTS:

- 1 c. water
- 1 c. coconut sugar
- ½ c. chopped mint
- 64 oz. red grapefruit juice

DIRECTIONS:

» Put the water in a pan, bring to a boil over medium heat, add sugar, stir until it dissolves, take off heat, add mint, stir, cover and leave aside for 5 minutes
» Strain into a container, add grapefruit juice, stir, cover and freeze for 4 hours before serving. Enjoy!

Nutrition: Calories: 80, Fat 0g, Carbs 14g, Protein 3g.

BANANA DELIGHT

Preparation Time: 15 minutes
Cooking Time: 12 minutes
Servings: 4

INGREDIENTS:

- 1 tbsp sodium-free baking powder
- 1 tbsp sugar
- 1 cup flour
- 1 tbsp oil
- ¼ cup egg substitute
- ½ tsp nutmeg
- 1 cup banana (chopped)
- 1 tbsp oil
- ½ cup skim milk

DIRECTIONS:

» In a bowl, mix and stir baking powder, sugar, and flour. Mix oil, egg, and milk, then add nutmeg and banana in a separate bowl. Add the mixture into the bowl of dry ingredients.
» In a hot frying pan, drop just by tablespoonfuls and fry for about 2 to 3 minutes. Wait until it is golden brown, then drain and serve.

Nutrition: Calories: 210.1 Protein: 5.7g Carbs: 37.6g Fat: 4.1g Sodium: 141mg

Chapter 10
Broths, Condiments, and Sauces

POTATO VEGETABLE BROTH

Preparation Time: 15 minutes
Cook time: 30 minutes
Makes: 10 cups

INGREDIENTS:

- 2 pounds (907 g) potatoes, scrubbed, peeled, and cut into 1-inch pieces
- 4 large leeks, white parts only, split, well-rinsed, and sliced
- 2 medium carrots, scrubbed and cut into 1-inch pieces
- ½ teaspoon freshly ground black pepper
- 1 bay leaf
- 1 teaspoon dried thyme

DIRECTIONS:

» In a heavy-bottomed stockpot, combine all of the ingredients. Add about 8 cups of water or more as needed to completely cover the vegetables.
» Bring to a boil, reduce heat, cover, and simmer for 30 minutes.
» Pass the broth through a large sieve or colander, pressing on the vegetables to extract as much juice as possible. Discard the vegetable pulp.
» Store in the refrigerator in an airtight container for four to five days. Use it generously as needed in your favorite recipes.

Per Serving (1 cup): calories: 10 | fat: 0g | protein: 1g | carbs: 2g | sugars: 0g | fiber: 0g | sodium: 29mg | cholesterol: 0mg

HOMEMADE CHICKEN BROTH

Preparation Time: 15 minutes
Cook time: 2 hours
Makes: 8 cups

INGREDIENTS:

- 4 quarts cold water
- 1 (3-pound / 1.4-kg) whole chicken (or chicken parts, such as wings and breasts)
- 4 celery stalks with leaves, trimmed and cut into 2-inch pieces
- 4 medium carrots, peeled and cut into 2-inch pieces
- 1 medium onion, peeled and quartered
- 1 medium potato, peeled and quartered
- 6 garlic cloves
- 1 small bunch parsley
- 1 teaspoon dried thyme
- 2 bay leaves

DIRECTIONS:

» In a large stockpot, combine all of the ingredients, and bring to a boil over medium-high heat. Reduce the heat to medium-low and simmer, partially covered, until the chicken is falling apart, about 2 hours.
» Strain the broth through a large sieve or colander into a large bowl. Use a wooden spoon to press on the solids to extract as much of the broth as possible. Save the chicken meat if desired or discard along with the vegetable pulp and bones.
» Allow the broth to cool in the bowl or divide the broth among several shallow containers to cool it quickly.
» Cover loosely and refrigerate overnight. Use a spoon to remove the fat that congeals on the surface before using.

Per Serving (1 cup): calories: 86 | fat: 3g | protein: 6g | carbs: 9g | sugars: 1g | fiber: 0g | sodium: 50mg | cholesterol: 7mg

RED PEPPER PESTO

Preparation Time: 20 minutes
Cook time: 10 minutes
Makes: 3 cups

INGREDIENTS:

- 4 red bell peppers, tops sliced off and deseeded
- 3 cups fresh basil leaves
- 3 tablespoons cashews
- 3 tablespoons grated Parmesan cheese
- 1 tablespoon olive oil
- 3 garlic cloves
- ¼ teaspoon salt

DIRECTIONS:

» Place peppers in the oven on a sheet pan and turn broiler to high. Broil until peppers have blackened on all sides, turning a few times, for about 10 minutes total.
» Remove peppers from heat and place in a bowl. Cover with plastic wrap and set aside to cool.
» Peel the cooled peppers. In a food processor, combine peeled peppers with the remaining ingredients. Process until mixture is smooth and resembles a pesto.

Per Serving (¼ cup): calories: 50 | fat: 3g | protein: 2g | carbs: 5g | sugars: 0g | fiber: 1g | sodium: 74mg | cholesterol: 0mg

BASIL PESTO

Preparation Time: 15 minutes
Cook time: 5 minutes
Makes: 3½ cups

INGREDIENTS:

- 1 cup fresh basil leaves
- 1 cup fresh baby spinach leaves
- ½ cup freshly grated Parmesan cheese
- ½ cup olive oil
- ¼ cup pine nuts
- 4 garlic cloves, peeled
- ¼ teaspoon kosher or sea salt
- ¼ teaspoon ground black pepper

DIRECTIONS:

» Place all the ingredients in the bowl of a food processor and process until a paste forms, scraping down the sides of the bowl with a spatula as needed. Taste and adjust the seasoning, if necessary.
» Place leftovers in airtight containers and refrigerate for up to 5 days, or freeze pesto in an airtight container for up to 2 months and thaw as needed. Or divide pesto into cube trays, seal in a plastic bag, and freeze for up to 2 months. Pop pesto cubes out of the ice cube tray as needed.

Per Serving (½ cup): calories: 209 | fat: 20g | protein: 4g | carbs: 2g | sugars: 0g | fiber: 1g | sodium: 231mg | cholesterol: 0mg

GREEK YOGURT MAYONNAISE

Preparation Time: 2 minutes
Cook time: 0 minutes
Serves: 12

INGREDIENTS:

- 6 ounces (170 g) nonfat or low-fat plain Greek yogurt
- 1 teaspoon apple cider vinegar
- ¼ teaspoon yellow mustard
- ¼ teaspoon hot sauce
- ¼ teaspoon freshly ground black pepper
- ¼ teaspoon paprika
- ¼ teaspoon salt

DIRECTIONS:

» Mix all the ingredients together and blend well. Adjust seasonings to suit taste.

Per Serving (2 tablespoons): calories: 8 | fat: 0g | protein: 1g | carbs: 1g | sugars: 1g | fiber: 0g | sodium: 65mg | cholesterol: 0mg

FRESH VEGETABLE SALSA

Preparation Time: 10 minutes
Cook time: 0 minutes
Makes: 6 cups

INGREDIENTS:

- 2 cups cored and diced bell peppers
- 2 cups diced tomatoes
- 1 cup diced zucchini
- ½ cup chopped red onion
- ¼ cup freshly squeezed lime juice
- 2 garlic cloves, minced
- 1 teaspoon freshly ground black pepper
- ¼ teaspoon salt

DIRECTIONS:

» Wash the vegetables and prepare as directed.
» In a large bowl, combine all the ingredients. Toss gently to mix.
» Cover and refrigerate for at least 30 minutes to allow the flavors to blend.

Per Serving (¼ cup): calories: 10 | fat: 0g | protein: 0g | carbs: 2g | sugars: 1g | fiber: 1g | sodium: 26mg | cholesterol: 0mg

CHILI LIME MARINADE

Preparation Time: 10 minutes
Cook time: 0 minutes
Serves: 2

INGREDIENTS:

- ¼ cup canola oil
- Zest and juice of 1 lime
- 2 tablespoons apple cider vinegar
- 1 tablespoon chili powder
- 1 teaspoon garlic powder
- 1 teaspoon onion powder
- ¼ teaspoon kosher or sea salt
- ¼ teaspoon ground black pepper

DIRECTIONS:

» Whisk all the ingredients together, and store in an airtight container in the refrigerator for up to 5 days or freeze it for up to 2 months.
» Per Serving
» calories: 266 | fat: 27g | protein: 1g | carbs: 4g | sugars: 1g | fiber: 1g | sodium: 291mg | cholesterol: 0mg

CREAMY AVOCADO "ALFREDO" SAUCE

Preparation Time: 10 minutes
Cook time: 0 minutes
Serves: 4

INGREDIENTS:

- 1 ripe avocado, peeled and pitted
- 1 tablespoon dried basil
- 1 clove garlic

- 1 tablespoon lemon juice
- 1 tablespoon olive oil
- ⅛ teaspoon salt

DIRECTIONS:

» Add the avocado, basil, garlic clove, lemon juice, olive oil, and salt to a food processor. Blend until a smooth, creamy sauce forms.
» Pour the sauce over hot pasta or vegetable noodles.
» Per Serving
» calories: 104 | fat: 10g | protein: 1g | carbs: 4g | sugars: 0g | fiber: 3g | sodium: 43mg | cholesterol: 0mg

SIMPLE TOMATO SAUCE

Preparation Time: 5 minutes
Cook time: 1 hour
Makes: 4 cups

INGREDIENTS:

- 1 tablespoon olive oil
- 1 cup minced yellow onion
- 4 garlic cloves, minced
- 1 (28-ounce / 794-g) can no-salt crushed tomatoes
- ¼ cup water
- 2 tablespoons no-salt added tomato paste
- 2 tablespoons honey
- 2 tablespoons oregano
- 1 tablespoon basil
- ½ teaspoon crushed red pepper flakes

DIRECTIONS:

» In a large pot over medium heat, heat the olive oil. Add the onion and garlic and cook for 3 to 5 minutes, or until tender. Reduce the heat to low.
» Add the remaining ingredients, and cover. Cook over low heat for 50 to 60 minutes.
» Taste to adjust seasonings.
» Serve hot as you would store-bought tomato sauce. Store any leftovers in an airtight container in the refrigerator for up to one week.

Per Serving (½ cup): calories: 71 | fat: 2g | protein: 2g | carbs: 13g | sugars: 5g | fiber: 2g | sodium: 16mg | cholesterol: 0mg

TZATZIKI SAUCE

Preparation Time: 5 minutes
Cook time: 0 minutes
Makes: 2 cups

INGREDIENTS:

- 1 medium English cucumber, seeded
- 1½ cups plain low-fat Greek yogurt
- 2 small garlic cloves, minced
- 1 teaspoon freshly squeezed lemon juice
- Dash freshly ground black pepper
- 2 tablespoons finely chopped fresh mint or dill

DIRECTIONS:

» Coarsely grate the cucumber into a medium bowl, and drain off the excess liquid.
» Add the yogurt, garlic, lemon juice, black pepper, and mint or dill. Mix well.
» Refrigerate to chill for about an hour before serving.

Per Serving (1 tablespoon): calories: 10 | fat: 0g | protein: 1g | carbs: 1g | sugars: 1g | fiber: 0g | sodium: 4mg | cholesterol: 1mg

HONEY CHIPOTLE SAUCE

Preparation Time: 10 minutes
Cook time: 15 minutes
Makes: about ½ cup

INGREDIENTS:

- 1 tablespoon chopped chipotle chiles in adobo sauce
- 3 tablespoons honey
- 3 tablespoons no-salt-added tomato paste
- 3 tablespoons unsalted vegetable or chicken stock
- 2½ tablespoons white wine vinegar

DIRECTIONS:

» Pour all the ingredients into a small saucepan and bring to a simmer for about 15 minutes, until slightly thickened.
» Store in an airtight container in the refrigerator for up to 7 days.

Per Serving (¼ cup): calories: 136 | fat: 0g | protein: 1g | carbs: 32g | sugars: 30g | fiber: 2g | sodium: 124mg | cholesterol: 0mg

CREAMY SPINACH-ARTICHOKE SAUCE

Preparation Time: 5 minutes
Cook time: 15 minutes
Makes: 3 cups

INGREDIENTS:

- 2 teaspoons extra-virgin olive oil
- 4 cloves garlic, minced
- ½ cup diced onion
- 1 tablespoon whole-wheat flour
- 1 cup fat-free milk
- ½ cup shredded part-skim Mozzarella cheese (2 ounces / 57 g)
- ½ cup nonfat (0%) plain Greek yogurt
- 2 ounces (57 g) ⅓-less-fat cream cheese
- 10 ounces (283 g) frozen chopped spinach, thawed and squeezed of excess water
- 1 (14-ounce / 397-g) can water-packed artichoke hearts, rinsed, drained, and chopped
- ¼ cup grated Parmesan cheese
- ¼ teaspoon salt
- ½ teaspoon freshly ground black pepper
- ½ teaspoon red pepper flakes
- ¼ teaspoon grated lemon zest

DIRECTIONS:

- In a large skillet, heat the olive oil over medium heat. Add the garlic and onion and cook until softened, 3 to 4 minutes. Add the flour and stir until the flour begins to brown. Stir in the milk and bring to a boil, then immediately reduce the heat to low and simmer for 3 to 4 minutes, until it starts to thicken.
- Add the Mozzarella, Greek yogurt, and cream cheese and stir until melted, 2 to 3 minutes. Add the spinach and artichoke hearts and cook stirring constantly for 3 to 4 minutes to warm through.
- Add the Parmesan, salt, black pepper, pepper flakes, and lemon zest and cook until the cheese has melted and the ingredients are thoroughly combined, an additional 2 to 3 minutes.
- Serve immediately or refrigerate in a covered container for 3 to 4 days.

Per Serving (⅓ cup): calories: 104 | fat: 4g | protein: 8g | carbs: 11g | sugars: 3g | fiber: 5g | sodium: 244mg | cholesterol: 9mg

Chapter 11
Nourishing DASH Bowls

MEDITERRANEAN CHICKPEA QUINOA BOWL

Servings: 2
Preparation Time: 25 minutes

INGREDIENTS:

- 1 cup cooked quinoa
- 1 cup canned chickpeas, drained and rinsed
- 1 cucumber, diced
- 1 tomato, diced
- ¼ cup feta cheese, crumbled
- ¼ cup kalamata olives
- 2 tbsp hummus
- 1 tbsp olive oil
- 1 tbsp lemon juice
- Fresh parsley, chopped
- Salt and pepper to taste

DIRECTIONS:

» In two serving bowls, evenly divide quinoa, chickpeas, cucumber, tomato, feta, and olives.
» Whisk together olive oil, lemon juice, salt, and pepper. Drizzle over bowls.
» Top each bowl with a dollop of hummus and sprinkle with parsley.

Nutrition (per serving): Calories: 430 | Protein: 16g | Carbs: 51g | Fat: 18g | Fiber: 9g

GRILLED CHICKEN AVOCADO BROWN RICE BOWL

Servings: 2
Preparation Time: 30 minutes

INGREDIENTS:

- 1 cup cooked brown rice
- 2 chicken breasts, grilled and sliced
- 1 avocado, sliced
- 1 cup cherry tomatoes, halved
- ½ cup black beans
- 1 lime, sliced
- 2 tbsp cilantro, chopped
- Salt, pepper, and chili powder to taste

DIRECTIONS:

» Season chicken with salt, pepper, and chili powder. Grill and slice.
» Arrange rice, chicken, avocado, tomatoes, and black beans evenly in two bowls.
» Garnish with lime wedges and sprinkle with cilantro.

Nutrition (per serving): Calories: 520 | Protein: 36g | Carbs: 48g | Fat: 22g | Fiber: 10g

VEGAN BUDDHA BOWL WITH ROASTED VEGGIES

Servings: 2
Preparation Time: 35 minutes

INGREDIENTS:

- 1 cup cooked quinoa
- 1 cup roasted sweet potato cubes
- ½ cup roasted broccoli florets
- ½ cup roasted Brussels sprouts
- ½ avocado, sliced
- ¼ cup chickpeas, roasted
- 2 tbsp tahini dressing
- Salt and pepper to taste

DIRECTIONS:

» Arrange quinoa, roasted vegetables, avocado slices, and roasted chickpeas into two bowls.
» Drizzle generously with tahini dressing. Season with salt and pepper.

Nutrition (per serving): Calories: 480 | Protein: 13g | Carbs: 56g | Fat: 22g | Fiber: 12g

DASH SALMON SWEET POTATO BOWL

Servings: 2
Preparation Time: 30 minutes

INGREDIENTS:

- 2 salmon fillets
- 1 cup roasted sweet potato cubes
- 1 cup steamed broccoli
- ½ cup cooked quinoa
- 1 tbsp olive oil
- 1 tbsp lemon juice
- Salt, pepper, garlic powder to taste

DIRECTIONS:

» Season salmon with salt, pepper, garlic powder, and grill or bake until cooked through.
» Divide quinoa, sweet potatoes, broccoli, and salmon between two bowls.
» Whisk olive oil and lemon juice; drizzle over bowls.

Nutrition (per serving): Calories: 510 | Protein: 35g | Carbs: 40g | Fat: 23g | Fiber: 8g

SPICY BLACK BEAN CORN POWER BOWL

Servings: 2
Preparation Time: 25 minutes

INGREDIENTS:

- 1 cup cooked brown rice
- 1 cup canned black beans, rinsed
- ½ cup corn kernels
- ½ avocado, diced
- 1 red bell pepper, diced
- 2 tbsp salsa
- 1 tsp cumin
- Salt, pepper, and chili flakes to taste
- Fresh cilantro for garnish

DIRECTIONS:

- » Combine black beans, corn, and bell pepper in a pan; season with cumin, salt, pepper, and chili flakes. Cook briefly until warmed through.
- » Divide rice into bowls and top with bean mixture, avocado, and salsa.
- » Garnish with fresh cilantro.

Nutrition (per serving): Calories: 430 | Protein: 15g | Carbs: 62g | Fat: 12g | Fiber: 14g

TOFU TERIYAKI EDAMAME BOWL

Servings: 2
Preparation Time: 30 minutes

INGREDIENTS:

- 1 cup cooked brown rice
- 1 block firm tofu, cubed
- ½ cup edamame, shelled
- ½ cup shredded carrots
- ¼ cup teriyaki sauce
- 2 tbsp green onions, sliced
- 1 tsp sesame seeds

DIRECTIONS:

- » Pan-fry tofu cubes until crispy. Add teriyaki sauce, cook until coated.
- » Divide rice into two bowls; add tofu, edamame, and shredded carrots.
- » Sprinkle with green onions and sesame seeds.

Nutrition (per serving): Calories: 460 | Protein: 22g | Carbs: 56g | Fat: 16g | Fiber: 7g

CAULIFLOWER SHAWARMA BOWL

Servings: 2
Preparation Time: 35 minutes

INGREDIENTS:

- 1 cup cooked couscous
- 2 cups cauliflower florets, roasted with shawarma spices
- ½ cucumber, diced
- ½ cup cherry tomatoes, halved
- ¼ cup tahini sauce
- 2 tbsp fresh parsley, chopped
- Salt and pepper to taste

DIRECTIONS:

- » Roast cauliflower with shawarma spices until tender.
- » Arrange couscous, cauliflower, cucumber, and tomatoes into bowls.
- » Drizzle with tahini sauce and sprinkle with parsley.

Nutrition (per serving): Calories: 410 | Protein: 14g | Carbs: 52g | Fat: 17g | Fiber: 8g

TUNA NICOISE GRAIN BOWL

Servings: 2
Preparation Time: 25 minutes

INGREDIENTS:

- 1 cup cooked farro
- 1 can tuna, drained
- 1 hard-boiled egg, quartered
- ½ cup steamed green beans
- ½ cup cherry tomatoes, halved
- ¼ cup kalamata olives
- 2 tbsp vinaigrette dressing

DIRECTIONS:

- » Divide farro between two bowls; add tuna, egg, green beans, tomatoes, and olives.
- » Drizzle with vinaigrette dressing.

Nutrition (per serving): Calories: 430 | Protein: 25g | Carbs: 45g | Fat: 16g | Fiber: 7g

LENTIL KALE ANTI-INFLAMMATORY BOWL

Servings: 2
Preparation Time: 30 minutes

INGREDIENTS:

- 1 cup cooked lentils
- 1 cup sautéed kale
- ½ cup roasted sweet potato
- ½ avocado, sliced
- 2 tbsp turmeric dressing
- Salt and pepper to taste

DIRECTIONS:

» Assemble lentils, kale, sweet potato, and avocado in bowls.
» Drizzle generously with turmeric dressing.

Nutrition (per serving): Calories: 440 | Protein: 18g | Carbs: 50g | Fat: 19g | Fiber: 14g

TURKEY CRANBERRY BARLEY BOWL

Servings: 2
Preparation Time: 35 minutes

INGREDIENTS:

- 1 cup cooked barley
- 8 oz cooked turkey breast, sliced
- ¼ cup dried cranberries
- ½ cup steamed broccoli
- 2 tbsp balsamic vinaigrette
- Salt and pepper to taste

DIRECTIONS:

» Arrange barley, turkey, cranberries, and broccoli into two bowls.
» Drizzle with balsamic vinaigrette.

Nutrition (per serving): Calories: 470 | Protein: 32g | Carbs: 58g | Fat: 10g | Fiber: 10g

GREEK LENTIL FETA BOWL

Servings: 2
Preparation Time: 25 minutes

INGREDIENTS:

- 1 cup cooked lentils
- ½ cup cherry tomatoes, halved
- ½ cucumber, diced
- ¼ cup feta cheese, crumbled
- ¼ cup kalamata olives
- 2 tbsp Greek vinaigrette
- Fresh parsley for garnish

DIRECTIONS:

» Divide lentils, tomatoes, cucumber, feta, and olives into bowls.
» Drizzle with Greek vinaigrette and garnish with parsley.

Nutrition (per serving): Calories: 380 | Protein: 17g | Carbs: 41g | Fat: 16g | Fiber: 12g

SPICED QUINOA ROASTED SQUASH BOWL

Servings: 2
Preparation Time: 35 minutes

INGREDIENTS:

- 1 cup cooked quinoa
- 1 cup roasted butternut squash
- ½ cup spinach leaves
- ¼ cup dried cranberries
- 2 tbsp pumpkin seeds
- 2 tbsp balsamic glaze

DIRECTIONS:

» Arrange quinoa, squash, spinach, cranberries, and pumpkin seeds into bowls.
» Drizzle with balsamic glaze.

Nutrition (per serving): Calories: 410 | Protein: 12g | Carbs: 58g | Fat: 14g | Fiber: 8g

DASH CHICKEN GYRO BOWL

Servings: 2
Preparation Time: 30 minutes

INGREDIENTS:

- 1 cup cooked brown rice
- 8 oz grilled chicken breast, sliced
- ½ cucumber, diced
- ½ cup cherry tomatoes, halved
- ¼ cup red onion, thinly sliced
- 2 tbsp tzatziki sauce
- Fresh dill for garnish

DIRECTIONS:

» Divide rice, chicken, cucumber, tomatoes, and red onion into bowls.
» Top with tzatziki sauce and garnish with fresh dill.

Nutrition (per serving): Calories: 450 | Protein: 33g | Carbs: 43g | Fat: 15g | Fiber: 5g

MISO MUSHROOM BROWN RICE BOWL

Servings: 2
Preparation Time: 30 minutes

INGREDIENTS:

- 1 cup cooked brown rice
- 1½ cups sautéed mushrooms
- 1 tbsp miso paste
- ½ avocado, sliced
- 2 tbsp green onions, chopped
- Sesame seeds for garnish

DIRECTIONS:

- Stir miso paste into sautéed mushrooms until evenly coated.
- Divide rice, mushrooms, and avocado slices into bowls.
- Sprinkle with green onions and sesame seeds.

Nutrition (per serving): Calories: 390 | Protein: 12g | Carbs: 47g | Fat: 18g | Fiber: 7g

---

RAINBOW SLAW TOFU BOWL

Servings: 2
Preparation Time: 25 minutes

INGREDIENTS:

- 1 cup cooked quinoa
- 1 block firm tofu, pan-fried and cubed
- 1 cup rainbow slaw (cabbage, carrot, bell peppers)
- ¼ cup peanut sauce
- 2 tbsp peanuts, crushed
- Cilantro for garnish

DIRECTIONS:

- Assemble quinoa, tofu, and rainbow slaw into bowls.
- Drizzle generously with peanut sauce.
- Sprinkle with crushed peanuts and garnish with cilantro.

Nutrition (per serving): Calories: 460 | Protein: 20g | Carbs: 48g | Fat: 22g | Fiber: 7g

---

HARISSA CHICKPEA CAULIFLOWER BOWL

Servings: 2
Preparation Time: 30 minutes

INGREDIENTS:

- 1 cup cooked couscous
- 1 cup roasted cauliflower florets
- ½ cup chickpeas, roasted with harissa
- ¼ cup hummus
- 2 tbsp fresh cilantro, chopped
- Salt and pepper to taste

DIRECTIONS:

- Divide couscous, roasted cauliflower, and chickpeas between two bowls.
- Top each bowl with a generous dollop of hummus.
- Garnish with fresh cilantro.

Nutrition (per serving): Calories: 420 | Protein: 14g | Carbs: 56g | Fat: 15g | Fiber: 9g

---

BBQ TEMPEH SWEET POTATO BOWL

Servings: 2
Preparation Time: 35 minutes

INGREDIENTS:

- 1 cup cooked brown rice
- 8 oz tempeh, cubed and baked with BBQ sauce
- 1 cup roasted sweet potato cubes
- ½ cup steamed broccoli
- 2 tbsp BBQ sauce (extra)
- Green onions for garnish

DIRECTIONS:

- Arrange rice, tempeh, sweet potato, and broccoli into bowls.
- Drizzle with additional BBQ sauce.
- Sprinkle with green onions.

Nutrition (per serving): Calories: 470 | Protein: 20g | Carbs: 64g | Fat: 14g | Fiber: 10g

---

DASH FALAFEL COUSCOUS BOWL

Servings: 2
Preparation Time: 30 minutes

INGREDIENTS:

- 1 cup cooked couscous
- 6 falafel balls, baked
- ½ cucumber, diced
- ½ cup cherry tomatoes, halved
- ¼ cup tahini sauce
- Fresh parsley for garnish

DIRECTIONS:

- Divide couscous, falafel, cucumber, and tomatoes into bowls.
- Drizzle with tahini sauce.
- Garnish with fresh parsley.

Nutrition (per serving): Calories: 460 | Protein: 15g | Carbs: 58g | Fat: 19g | Fiber: 8g

---

GRILLED SHRIMP AVOCADO BOWL

Servings: 2
Preparation Time: 25 minutes

INGREDIENTS:

- 1 cup cooked quinoa
- 10 grilled shrimp
- 1 avocado, sliced
- ½ cup corn kernels
- ½ cup cherry tomatoes, halved
- 2 tbsp lime vinaigrette
- Cilantro for garnish

DIRECTIONS:

- » Arrange quinoa, grilled shrimp, avocado, corn, and tomatoes into bowls.
- » Drizzle with lime vinaigrette.
- » Garnish with cilantro.

Nutrition (per serving): Calories: 450 | Protein: 28g | Carbs: 45g | Fat: 19g | Fiber: 9g

DASH CHICKEN CAESAR GRAIN BOWL

Servings: 2
Preparation Time: 30 minutes

INGREDIENTS:

- 1 cup cooked farro
- 8 oz grilled chicken breast, sliced
- 2 cups chopped romaine lettuce
- ¼ cup Caesar dressing
- 2 tbsp Parmesan cheese, grated
- Whole grain croutons (optional)

DIRECTIONS:

- » Divide farro, grilled chicken, and lettuce between two bowls.
- » Drizzle with Caesar dressing and sprinkle with Parmesan cheese.
- » Add croutons if desired.

Nutrition (per serving): Calories: 470 | Protein: 34g | Carbs: 38g | Fat: 18g | Fiber: 7g

ROASTED PEPPER HUMMUS BOWL

Servings: 2
Preparation Time: 30 minutes

INGREDIENTS:

- 1 cup cooked quinoa
- 1 cup roasted bell peppers
- ½ cup roasted chickpeas
- ¼ cup hummus
- 2 tbsp fresh parsley, chopped
- Salt and pepper to taste

DIRECTIONS:

- » Divide quinoa, roasted peppers, and chickpeas between two bowls.
- » Top each bowl with hummus.
- » Garnish with fresh parsley.

Nutrition (per serving): Calories: 410 | Protein: 13g | Carbs: 53g | Fat: 15g | Fiber: 9g

DASH VEGGIE CHILI RICE BOWL

Servings: 2
Preparation Time: 35 minutes

INGREDIENTS:

- 1 cup cooked brown rice
- 1½ cups veggie chili
- ½ avocado, diced
- 2 tbsp cheddar cheese, shredded
- Fresh cilantro for garnish

DIRECTIONS:

- » Divide rice and veggie chili between two bowls.
- » Top with diced avocado and shredded cheddar.
- » Garnish with cilantro.

Nutrition (per serving): Calories: 450 | Protein: 16g | Carbs: 60g | Fat: 16g | Fiber: 10g

ASIAN NOODLE EDAMAME BOWL

Servings: 2
Preparation Time: 25 minutes

INGREDIENTS:

- 2 cups cooked soba noodles
- 1 cup shelled edamame
- ½ cup shredded carrots
- ¼ cup sliced red bell pepper
- 2 tbsp soy ginger dressing
- Sesame seeds for garnish

DIRECTIONS:

- » Divide noodles, edamame, carrots, and bell pepper into two bowls.
- » Drizzle with soy ginger dressing.
- » Sprinkle with sesame seeds.

Nutrition (per serving): Calories: 420 | Protein: 19g | Carbs: 62g | Fat: 10g | Fiber: 8g

DASH KIMCHI EGG GRAIN BOWL

Servings: 2
Preparation Time: 25 minutes

INGREDIENTS:

- 1 cup cooked barley
- 2 soft-boiled eggs, halved
- ½ cup kimchi
- ½ avocado, sliced
- 2 tbsp green onions, chopped
- Sesame seeds for garnish

DIRECTIONS:

- » Divide barley, kimchi, and avocado slices between two bowls.
- » Top with egg halves.
- » Garnish with green onions and sesame seeds.

Nutrition (per serving): Calories: 430 | Protein: 16g | Carbs: 50g | Fat: 18g | Fiber: 9g

---

DASH CAPRESE BARLEY BOWL

Servings: 2
Preparation Time: 25 minutes

INGREDIENTS:

- 1 cup cooked barley
- 1 cup cherry tomatoes, halved
- 4 oz fresh mozzarella, sliced
- Fresh basil leaves
- 2 tbsp balsamic glaze
- Salt and pepper to taste

DIRECTIONS:

» Divide barley, tomatoes, and mozzarella slices between two bowls.
» Top with fresh basil leaves and drizzle with balsamic glaze.
» Season with salt and pepper.

Nutrition (per serving): Calories: 420 | Protein: 17g | Carbs: 51g | Fat: 15g | Fiber: 8g

---

DASH ZOODLE ROASTED TOMATO BOWL

Servings: 2
Preparation Time: 20 minutes

INGREDIENTS:

- 2 cups zucchini noodles (zoodles)
- 1 cup roasted cherry tomatoes
- ½ cup chickpeas, roasted
- ¼ cup pesto
- 2 tbsp Parmesan cheese, grated

DIRECTIONS:

» Divide zoodles, roasted tomatoes, and chickpeas between two bowls.
» Top each bowl with pesto and sprinkle with Parmesan cheese.

Nutrition (per serving): Calories: 380 | Protein: 12g | Carbs: 32g | Fat: 23g | Fiber: 7g

---

ROASTED BUTTERNUT FARRO BOWL

Servings: 2
Preparation Time: 35 minutes

INGREDIENTS:

- 1 cup cooked farro
- 1½ cups roasted butternut squash cubes
- ½ cup baby spinach
- ¼ cup dried cranberries
- 2 tbsp toasted walnuts
- 2 tbsp maple vinaigrette

DIRECTIONS:

» Divide farro, squash, spinach, cranberries, and walnuts between two bowls.
» Drizzle each bowl with maple vinaigrette.

Nutrition (per serving): Calories: 440 | Protein: 11g | Carbs: 64g | Fat: 16g | Fiber: 9g

---

DASH PESTO QUINOA BOWL

Servings: 2
Preparation Time: 25 minutes

INGREDIENTS:

- 1 cup cooked quinoa
- ½ cup cherry tomatoes, halved
- ½ cup cucumber, diced
- ¼ cup pesto sauce
- ¼ cup feta cheese, crumbled
- Fresh basil leaves for garnish

DIRECTIONS:

» Divide quinoa, tomatoes, cucumber, pesto, and feta cheese between two bowls.
» Garnish with fresh basil leaves.

Nutrition (per serving): Calories: 400 | Protein: 12g | Carbs: 42g | Fat: 20g | Fiber: 5g

---

GRILLED VEGGIE HALLOUMI BOWL

Servings: 2
Preparation Time: 30 minutes

INGREDIENTS:

- 1 cup cooked couscous
- 4 oz grilled halloumi cheese, sliced
- 1 cup grilled vegetables (zucchini, bell peppers, eggplant)
- ¼ cup hummus
- Fresh parsley for garnish

DIRECTIONS:

» Divide couscous, grilled halloumi, and vegetables between two bowls.
» Top with hummus.
» Garnish with fresh parsley.

Nutrition (per serving): Calories: 470 | Protein: 20g | Carbs: 40g | Fat: 24g | Fiber: 6g

DASH SOUTHWESTERN BEAN CORN BOWL

Servings: 2
Preparation Time: 25 minutes

INGREDIENTS:

- 1 cup cooked quinoa
- ½ cup black beans
- ½ cup corn kernels
- ½ avocado, diced
- ¼ cup salsa
- 2 tbsp cheddar cheese, shredded
- Fresh cilantro for garnish

DIRECTIONS:

- » Divide quinoa, beans, corn, avocado, and salsa between two bowls.
- » Sprinkle with shredded cheddar and garnish with cilantro.

Nutrition (per serving): Calories: 430 | Protein: 15g | Carbs: 55g | Fat: 16g | Fiber: 11g

DASH AVOCADO LENTIL BOWL

Servings: 2
Preparation Time: 30 minutes

INGREDIENTS:

- 1 cup cooked lentils
- ½ avocado, sliced
- ½ cup roasted cherry tomatoes
- ¼ cup red onion, diced
- 2 tbsp lemon vinaigrette
- Fresh parsley for garnish

DIRECTIONS:

- » Divide lentils, avocado, tomatoes, and onion into bowls.
- » Drizzle with lemon vinaigrette.
- » Garnish with fresh parsley.

Nutrition (per serving): Calories: 410 | Protein: 17g | Carbs: 48g | Fat: 17g | Fiber: 13g

DASH ITALIAN CHICKPEA BOWL

Servings: 2
Preparation Time: 25 minutes

INGREDIENTS:

- 1 cup cooked quinoa
- ½ cup chickpeas, roasted with Italian spices
- ½ cup cherry tomatoes, halved
- ½ cucumber, diced
- ¼ cup Italian dressing
- Fresh basil leaves for garnish

DIRECTIONS:

- » Divide quinoa, chickpeas, tomatoes, and cucumber between two bowls.
- » Drizzle with Italian dressing.
- » Garnish with basil.

Nutrition (per serving): Calories: 400 | Protein: 14g | Carbs: 50g | Fat: 15g | Fiber: 8g

DASH TOFU AVOCADO LIME BOWL

Servings: 2
Preparation Time: 30 minutes

INGREDIENTS:

- 1 cup cooked brown rice
- 8 oz firm tofu, pan-fried and cubed
- ½ avocado, sliced
- ½ cup cherry tomatoes, halved
- 2 tbsp lime dressing
- Fresh cilantro for garnish

DIRECTIONS:

- » Divide rice, tofu, avocado, and tomatoes into two bowls.
- » Drizzle with lime dressing.
- » Garnish with cilantro.

Nutrition (per serving): Calories: 420 | Protein: 19g | Carbs: 50g | Fat: 16g | Fiber: 8g

DASH SWEET CORN TOMATO BOWL

Servings: 2
Preparation Time: 20 minutes

INGREDIENTS:

- 1 cup cooked quinoa
- 1 cup corn kernels
- ½ cup cherry tomatoes, halved
- ¼ cup feta cheese, crumbled
- 2 tbsp basil vinaigrette
- Fresh basil leaves for garnish

DIRECTIONS:

- » Divide quinoa, corn, and tomatoes into two bowls.
- » Sprinkle with feta cheese and drizzle with basil vinaigrette.
- » Garnish with basil leaves.

Nutrition (per serving): Calories: 400 | Protein: 12g | Carbs: 50g | Fat: 15g | Fiber: 7g

DASH SPICY TURKEY WILD RICE BOWL

Servings: 2
Preparation Time: 35 minutes

INGREDIENTS:

- 1 cup cooked wild rice
- 8 oz spicy cooked turkey breast, sliced
- ½ cup roasted bell peppers
- ¼ cup avocado, sliced
- 2 tbsp salsa
- Fresh cilantro for garnish

DIRECTIONS:

» Divide rice, turkey, peppers, and avocado slices into two bowls.
» Top with salsa and garnish with cilantro.

Nutrition (per serving): Calories: 470 | Protein: 30g | Carbs: 45g | Fat: 16g | Fiber: 6g

DASH MANGO BLACK BEAN BOWL

Servings: 2
Preparation Time: 25 minutes

INGREDIENTS:

- 1 cup cooked brown rice
- ½ cup black beans
- ½ cup diced mango
- ½ avocado, sliced
- 2 tbsp lime dressing
- Fresh cilantro for garnish

DIRECTIONS:

» Divide rice, beans, mango, and avocado between two bowls.
» Drizzle with lime dressing.
» Garnish with cilantro.

Nutrition (per serving): Calories: 430 | Protein: 12g | Carbs: 62g | Fat: 15g | Fiber: 10g

DASH CURRY VEGGIE BOWL

Servings: 2
Preparation Time: 30 minutes

INGREDIENTS:

- 1 cup cooked quinoa
- 1 cup roasted mixed vegetables (cauliflower, carrots, zucchini)
- ¼ cup chickpeas
- ¼ cup curry sauce
- Fresh cilantro for garnish

DIRECTIONS:

» Divide quinoa, vegetables, and chickpeas into two bowls.
» Drizzle generously with curry sauce.
» Garnish with cilantro.

Nutrition (per serving): Calories: 420 | Protein: 14g | Carbs: 60g | Fat: 12g | Fiber: 10g

DASH ROASTED EGGPLANT TAHINI BOWL

Servings: 2
Preparation Time: 35 minutes

INGREDIENTS:

- 1 cup cooked farro
- 1 cup roasted eggplant cubes
- ½ cup cherry tomatoes, halved
- ¼ cup tahini sauce
- Fresh parsley for garnish

DIRECTIONS:

» Divide farro, eggplant, and tomatoes into bowls.
» Drizzle with tahini sauce.
» Garnish with parsley.

Nutrition (per serving): Calories: 440 | Protein: 12g | Carbs: 54g | Fat: 18g | Fiber: 9g

DASH SAUTEED GREENS POTATO BOWL

Servings: 2
Preparation Time: 30 minutes

INGREDIENTS:

- 1 cup roasted potato cubes
- 1 cup sautéed greens (spinach, kale)
- ½ cup cherry tomatoes, halved
- ¼ cup feta cheese, crumbled
- 2 tbsp balsamic vinaigrette

DIRECTIONS:

» Divide potatoes, sautéed greens, and tomatoes into bowls.
» Sprinkle with feta and drizzle with balsamic vinaigrette.

Nutrition (per serving): Calories: 400 | Protein: 11g | Carbs: 48g | Fat: 18g | Fiber: 7g

DASH PEANUT NOODLE BOWL

Servings: 2
Preparation Time: 25 minutes

INGREDIENTS:

- 2 cups cooked soba noodles

- ½ cup shredded carrots
- ½ cup sliced bell peppers
- ¼ cup peanut sauce
- 2 tbsp peanuts, crushed
- Cilantro for garnish

DIRECTIONS:

» Divide noodles, carrots, and peppers into bowls.
» Drizzle with peanut sauce.
» Sprinkle with peanuts and garnish with cilantro.

Nutrition (per serving): Calories: 460 | Protein: 16g | Carbs: 60g | Fat: 18g | Fiber: 7g

DASH SWEET POTATO KALE BOWL

Servings: 2
Preparation Time: 35 minutes

INGREDIENTS:

- 1 cup cooked quinoa
- 1 cup roasted sweet potato cubes
- 1 cup sautéed kale
- ¼ cup dried cranberries
- 2 tbsp balsamic vinaigrette

DIRECTIONS:

» Divide quinoa, sweet potato, kale, and cranberries between bowls.
» Drizzle with balsamic vinaigrette.

Nutrition (per serving): Calories: 420 | Protein: 11g | Carbs: 65g | Fat: 12g | Fiber: 10g

DASH CARROT GINGER WILD RICE BOWL

Servings: 2
Preparation Time: 35 minutes

INGREDIENTS:

- 1 cup cooked wild rice
- 1 cup roasted carrots
- ½ cup chickpeas
- 2 tbsp ginger dressing
- Fresh parsley for garnish

DIRECTIONS:

» Divide rice, carrots, and chickpeas between two bowls.
» Drizzle with ginger dressing and garnish with parsley.

Nutrition (per serving): Calories: 400 | Protein: 12g | Carbs: 58g | Fat: 12g | Fiber: 9g

DASH TOMATO CUCUMBER BULGAR BOWL

Servings: 2
Preparation Time: 25 minutes

INGREDIENTS:

- 1 cup cooked bulgur wheat
- 1 cup cherry tomatoes, halved
- ½ cucumber, diced
- ¼ cup feta cheese
- 2 tbsp lemon vinaigrette
- Fresh mint for garnish

DIRECTIONS:

» Divide bulgur, tomatoes, cucumber, and feta between bowls.
» Drizzle with lemon vinaigrette.
» Garnish with mint.

Nutrition (per serving): Calories: 380 | Protein: 13g | Carbs: 52g | Fat: 13g | Fiber: 8g

DASH BAKED FALAFEL GRAIN BOWL

Servings: 2
Preparation Time: 30 minutes

INGREDIENTS:

- 1 cup cooked quinoa
- 6 baked falafel balls
- ½ cup cherry tomatoes, halved
- ¼ cup tahini sauce
- Fresh parsley for garnish

DIRECTIONS:

» Divide quinoa, falafel, and tomatoes into bowls.
» Drizzle with tahini sauce.
» Garnish with parsley.

Nutrition (per serving): Calories: 440 | Protein: 16g | Carbs: 56g | Fat: 17g | Fiber: 9g

DASH GARLIC MUSHROOM SPINACH BOWL

Servings: 2
Preparation Time: 30 minutes

INGREDIENTS:

- 1 cup cooked farro
- 1 cup sautéed garlic mushrooms
- 1 cup sautéed spinach
- ¼ cup Parmesan cheese, grated
- Fresh parsley for garnish

DIRECTIONS:

» Divide farro, mushrooms, and spinach into bowls.
» Sprinkle with Parmesan cheese.
» Garnish with parsley.

Nutrition (per serving): Calories: 410 | Protein: 16g | Carbs: 54g | Fat: 13g | Fiber: 8g

SPICY TOFU SWEET POTATO SKILLET

Servings: 2
Preparation Time: 30 minutes

INGREDIENTS:

- 8 oz firm tofu, cubed
- 1 large sweet potato, diced
- 1 bell pepper, sliced
- 2 tbsp olive oil
- 1 tsp chili powder
- Salt and pepper

DIRECTIONS:

» Heat olive oil in skillet over medium-high heat.
» Cook tofu, sweet potato, and pepper for 20 minutes, stirring occasionally.
» Season with chili powder, salt, and pepper.

Nutrition (per serving): Calories: 380 | Protein: 16g | Carbs: 45g | Fat: 16g | Fiber: 7g

SHEET PAN TURKEY SAUSAGE PEPPERS

Servings: 2
Preparation Time: 30 minutes

INGREDIENTS:

- 4 turkey sausage links
- 2 bell peppers, sliced
- 1 onion, sliced
- 2 tbsp olive oil
- Salt and pepper

DIRECTIONS:

» Preheat oven to 400°F (200°C).
» Place sausage, peppers, and onion on baking sheet.
» Drizzle with olive oil, salt, and pepper.
» Bake for 25 minutes.

Nutrition (per serving): Calories: 360 | Protein: 24g | Carbs: 15g | Fat: 23g | Fiber: 3g

BAKED EGGPLANT TOMATO PARMESAN

Servings: 2
Preparation Time: 35 minutes

INGREDIENTS:

- 1 eggplant, sliced
- 1 cup cherry tomatoes
- ¼ cup Parmesan cheese
- 2 tbsp olive oil
- Salt, pepper, and basil

DIRECTIONS:

» Preheat oven to 375°F (190°C).
» Arrange eggplant slices and tomatoes on tray.
» Drizzle with olive oil, sprinkle Parmesan, salt, pepper, and basil.
» Bake for 30 minutes.

Nutrition (per serving): Calories: 290 | Protein: 9g | Carbs: 20g | Fat: 20g | Fiber: 6g

DASH PESTO CHICKEN THIGHS CARROTS

Servings: 2
Preparation Time: 35 minutes

INGREDIENTS:

- 4 chicken thighs
- 2 cups baby carrots
- 2 tbsp pesto
- Salt and pepper

DIRECTIONS:

» Preheat oven to 400°F (200°C).
» Spread pesto on chicken thighs, arrange with carrots on tray.
» Season with salt and pepper.
» Roast for 30 minutes.

Nutrition (per serving): Calories: 420 | Protein: 29g | Carbs: 15g | Fat: 26g | Fiber: 4g

CINNAMON-SPICED ROASTED ROOT VEGGIES

Servings: 2
Preparation Time: 35 minutes

INGREDIENTS:

- 2 cups mixed root vegetables (sweet potato, carrots, parsnips)
- 2 tbsp olive oil
- 1 tsp cinnamon
- Salt and pepper

DIRECTIONS:

- » Preheat oven to 400°F (200°C).
- » Toss vegetables with olive oil, cinnamon, salt, and pepper.
- » Roast for 30 minutes.

Nutrition (per serving): Calories: 300 | Protein: 4g | Carbs: 45g | Fat: 12g | Fiber: 8g

DASH HONEY MUSTARD CHICKEN TRAY BAKE

Servings: 2
Preparation Time: 35 minutes

INGREDIENTS:

- 2 chicken breasts
- 1 cup green beans
- 2 tbsp honey mustard sauce
- Salt and pepper

DIRECTIONS:

- » Preheat oven to 400°F (200°C).
- » Arrange chicken and green beans on baking sheet.
- » Brush with honey mustard, season with salt and pepper.
- » Bake for 30 minutes.

Nutrition (per serving): Calories: 370 | Protein: 33g | Carbs: 14g | Fat: 18g | Fiber: 3g

GARLIC SHRIMP ASPARAGUS SHEET PAN

Servings: 2
Preparation Time: 25 minutes

INGREDIENTS:

- 10 shrimp, peeled and deveined
- 2 cups asparagus spears
- 2 tbsp olive oil
- 2 cloves garlic, minced
- Salt and pepper

DIRECTIONS:

- » Preheat oven to 400°F (200°C).
- » Arrange shrimp and asparagus on baking sheet.
- » Drizzle with olive oil and garlic, season with salt and pepper.
- » Bake for 15 minutes.

Nutrition (per serving): Calories: 280 | Protein: 23g | Carbs: 7g | Fat: 17g | Fiber: 3g

ROASTED CAULIFLOWER CHICKPEAS

Servings: 2
Preparation Time: 30 minutes

INGREDIENTS:

- 2 cups cauliflower florets
- 1 cup chickpeas, drained
- 2 tbsp olive oil
- 1 tsp cumin
- Salt and pepper

DIRECTIONS:

- » Preheat oven to 400°F (200°C).
- » Toss cauliflower and chickpeas with oil, cumin, salt, and pepper.
- » Roast for 25 minutes.

Nutrition (per serving): Calories: 320 | Protein: 10g | Carbs: 35g | Fat: 16g | Fiber: 9g

ONE-PAN SPINACH FETA TURKEY BURGERS

Servings: 2
Preparation Time: 30 minutes

INGREDIENTS:

- 8 oz ground turkey
- ½ cup chopped spinach
- ¼ cup feta cheese, crumbled
- Salt and pepper

DIRECTIONS:

- » Mix turkey, spinach, feta, salt, and pepper; form into burgers.
- » Cook in skillet over medium heat, 5 minutes per side.

Nutrition (per serving): Calories: 280 | Protein: 30g | Carbs: 2g | Fat: 16g | Fiber: 1g

DASH HERB-CRUSTED PORK WITH APPLES

Servings: 2
Preparation Time: 35 minutes

INGREDIENTS:

- 2 pork chops
- 1 apple, sliced
- 2 tbsp breadcrumbs
- 1 tbsp fresh herbs, chopped
- 1 tbsp olive oil
- Salt and pepper

DIRECTIONS:

- Preheat oven to 375°F (190°C).
- Coat pork chops with breadcrumbs, herbs, salt, and pepper.
- Arrange chops and apple slices on tray, drizzle with oil.
- Bake for 30 minutes.

Nutrition (per serving): Calories: 370 | Protein: 26g | Carbs: 20g | Fat: 18g | Fiber: 3g

SHEET PAN TEMPEH STIR-FRY

Servings: 2
Preparation Time: 30 minutes

INGREDIENTS:

- 8 oz tempeh, cubed
- 2 cups stir-fry vegetables
- 2 tbsp soy sauce
- 1 tbsp sesame oil

DIRECTIONS:

- Preheat oven to 400°F (200°C).
- Arrange tempeh and vegetables on baking sheet.
- Drizzle with soy sauce and sesame oil.
- Roast for 25 minutes.

Nutrition (per serving): Calories: 320 | Protein: 20g | Carbs: 20g | Fat: 18g | Fiber: 5g

MAPLE DIJON CHICKEN WITH GREEN BEANS

Servings: 2
Preparation Time: 35 minutes

INGREDIENTS:

- 2 chicken breasts
- 2 cups green beans
- 2 tbsp maple syrup
- 2 tbsp Dijon mustard
- Salt and pepper

DIRECTIONS:

- Preheat oven to 400°F (200°C).
- Arrange chicken and green beans on tray.
- Brush with maple syrup and Dijon mustard mixture.
- Bake for 30 minutes.

Nutrition (per serving): Calories: 360 | Protein: 33g | Carbs: 22g | Fat: 12g | Fiber: 4g

ROASTED BRUSSELS WITH BALSAMIC TOFU

Servings: 2
Preparation Time: 30 minutes

INGREDIENTS:

- 8 oz tofu, cubed
- 2 cups Brussels sprouts, halved
- 2 tbsp balsamic vinegar
- 2 tbsp olive oil
- Salt and pepper

DIRECTIONS:

- Preheat oven to 400°F (200°C).
- Arrange tofu and Brussels sprouts on baking sheet.
- Drizzle with balsamic vinegar, olive oil, salt, and pepper.
- Roast for 25 minutes.

Nutrition (per serving): Calories: 340 | Protein: 16g | Carbs: 20g | Fat: 22g | Fiber: 6g

DASH BBQ CHICKEN SWEET POTATO TRAY

Servings: 2
Preparation Time: 35 minutes

INGREDIENTS:

- 2 chicken breasts
- 1 large sweet potato, diced
- ¼ cup BBQ sauce
- 2 tbsp olive oil
- Salt and pepper

DIRECTIONS:

- Preheat oven to 400°F (200°C).
- Arrange chicken and sweet potatoes on tray.
- Brush with BBQ sauce, drizzle with oil, salt, and pepper.
- Bake for 30 minutes.

Nutrition (per serving): Calories: 400 | Protein: 30g | Carbs: 35g | Fat: 15g | Fiber: 5g

SHEET PAN SAUSAGE, SQUASH ONION

Servings: 2
Preparation Time: 30 minutes

INGREDIENTS:

- 4 chicken sausages, sliced
- 1 cup diced butternut squash
- 1 onion, sliced
- 2 tbsp olive oil
- Salt and pepper

DIRECTIONS:

- Preheat oven to 400°F (200°C).
- Arrange sausage, squash, and onion on baking sheet.
- Drizzle with olive oil, season with salt and pepper.
- Roast for 25 minutes.

Nutrition (per serving): Calories: 370 | Protein: 24g | Carbs: 22g | Fat: 22g | Fiber: 4g

DASH GINGER CHICKEN BROCCOLI

Servings: 2
Preparation Time: 30 minutes

INGREDIENTS:

- 2 chicken breasts
- 2 cups broccoli florets
- 2 tbsp ginger sauce
- 1 tbsp olive oil
- Salt and pepper

DIRECTIONS:

- Preheat oven to 400°F (200°C).
- Arrange chicken and broccoli on baking sheet.
- Drizzle with ginger sauce and olive oil.
- Roast for 25 minutes.

Nutrition (per serving): Calories: 340 | Protein: 33g | Carbs: 12g | Fat: 15g | Fiber: 4g

MEDITERRANEAN STUFFED PEPPERS BAKE

Servings: 2
Preparation Time: 35 minutes

INGREDIENTS:

- 2 bell peppers, halved
- 1 cup cooked quinoa
- ¼ cup feta cheese
- ½ cup diced tomatoes
- 1 tbsp olive oil
- Salt and pepper

DIRECTIONS:

- Preheat oven to 375°F (190°C).
- Mix quinoa, feta, and tomatoes; stuff peppers.
- Drizzle with olive oil, season with salt and pepper.
- Bake for 30 minutes.

Nutrition (per serving): Calories: 320 | Protein: 12g | Carbs: 36g | Fat: 14g | Fiber: 6g

DASH ZUCCHINI MUSHROOM BAKE

Servings: 2
Preparation Time: 30 minutes

INGREDIENTS:

- 2 zucchinis, sliced
- 1 cup mushrooms, sliced
- 2 tbsp olive oil
- ¼ cup Parmesan cheese, grated
- Salt, pepper, and Italian herbs

DIRECTIONS:

- Preheat oven to 375°F (190°C).
- Arrange zucchini and mushrooms on baking sheet.
- Drizzle with olive oil, sprinkle with cheese and herbs.
- Bake for 25 minutes.

Nutrition (per serving): Calories: 260 | Protein: 10g | Carbs: 12g | Fat: 20g | Fiber: 3g

TERIYAKI TOFU EDAMAME RICE TRAY

Servings: 2
Preparation Time: 30 minutes

INGREDIENTS:

- 8 oz firm tofu, cubed
- 1 cup shelled edamame
- 1 cup cooked brown rice
- 2 tbsp teriyaki sauce
- 1 tbsp sesame seeds

DIRECTIONS:

- Preheat oven to 400°F (200°C).
- Spread tofu, edamame, and rice evenly on baking sheet.
- Drizzle with teriyaki sauce and sprinkle with sesame seeds.
- Roast for 25 minutes.

Nutrition (per serving): Calories: 400 | Protein: 20g | Carbs: 45g | Fat: 12g | Fiber: 6g

DASH BAKED HADDOCK WITH LEEKS

Servings: 2
Preparation Time: 25 minutes

INGREDIENTS:

- 2 haddock fillets
- 1 cup sliced leeks
- 2 tbsp olive oil
- Salt, pepper, lemon juice

DIRECTIONS:

- Preheat oven to 375°F (190°C).
- Arrange haddock and leeks on baking tray.
- Drizzle with olive oil, lemon juice, salt, and pepper.
- Bake 20 minutes until fish is flaky.

Nutrition (per serving): Calories: 290 | Protein: 25g | Carbs: 8g | Fat: 16g | Fiber: 2g

DASH ROASTED VEGGIE FAJITAS

Servings: 2
Preparation Time: 30 minutes

INGREDIENTS:

- 2 cups mixed veggies (bell peppers, onions)
- 2 tbsp fajita seasoning
- 2 tbsp olive oil
- Whole grain tortillas

DIRECTIONS:

- Preheat oven to 400°F (200°C).
- Toss veggies with olive oil and fajita seasoning, roast 25 minutes.
- Serve in tortillas.

Nutrition (per serving, without tortillas): Calories: 220 | Protein: 4g | Carbs: 20g | Fat: 14g | Fiber: 5g

HONEY LIME CHICKEN CAULIFLOWER

Servings: 2
Preparation Time: 35 minutes

INGREDIENTS:

- 2 chicken breasts
- 2 cups cauliflower florets
- 2 tbsp honey
- Juice of 1 lime
- Salt and pepper

DIRECTIONS:

- Preheat oven to 400°F (200°C).
- Arrange chicken and cauliflower on tray.
- Drizzle with honey, lime juice, salt, and pepper.
- Roast 30 minutes.

Nutrition (per serving): Calories: 380 | Protein: 34g | Carbs: 26g | Fat: 14g | Fiber: 5g

DASH ONE-POT CABBAGE STIR-FRY

Servings: 2
Preparation Time: 25 minutes

INGREDIENTS:

- 4 cups shredded cabbage
- 1 cup sliced carrots
- 2 tbsp soy sauce
- 1 tbsp sesame oil

DIRECTIONS:

- Heat oil in skillet, stir-fry cabbage and carrots 15 minutes.
- Add soy sauce, cook 5 minutes.

Nutrition (per serving): Calories: 170 | Protein: 4g | Carbs: 16g | Fat: 10g | Fiber: 6g **hapter 9: One-Pan Sheet Pan Meals**581. Teriyaki Tofu Edamame Rice Tray

Servings: 2
Preparation Time: 30 minutes

INGREDIENTS:

- 8 oz firm tofu, cubed
- 1 cup shelled edamame
- 1 cup cooked brown rice
- 2 tbsp teriyaki sauce
- 1 tbsp sesame seeds

DIRECTIONS:

- Preheat oven to 400°F (200°C).
- Spread tofu, edamame, and rice evenly on baking sheet.
- Drizzle with teriyaki sauce and sprinkle with sesame seeds.
- Roast for 25 minutes.

Nutrition (per serving): Calories: 400 | Protein: 20g | Carbs: 45g | Fat: 12g | Fiber: 6g

DASH BAKED PORTOBELLO SPINACH

Servings: 2
Preparation Time: 30 minutes

INGREDIENTS:

- 2 Portobello mushrooms
- 2 cups spinach
- 2 tbsp olive oil
- ¼ cup mozzarella cheese
- Salt and pepper

DIRECTIONS:

- Preheat oven to 375°F (190°C).
- Stuff mushrooms with spinach, drizzle with olive oil, sprinkle cheese.
- Bake 25 minutes.

Nutrition (per serving): Calories: 260 | Protein: 10g | Carbs: 8g | Fat: 20g | Fiber: 3g

---

SHEET PAN CHICKPEA TIKKA MASALA

Servings: 2
Preparation Time: 35 minutes

INGREDIENTS:

- 1 can chickpeas, drained
- 1 cup cauliflower florets
- ½ cup tikka masala sauce
- 2 tbsp olive oil

DIRECTIONS:

» Preheat oven to 400°F (200°C).
» Toss chickpeas and cauliflower with sauce and oil.
» Roast 30 minutes.

Nutrition (per serving): Calories: 340 | Protein: 12g | Carbs: 40g | Fat: 15g | Fiber: 10g

---

DASH BUTTERNUT SQUASH RED ONION BAKE

Servings: 2
Preparation Time: 35 minutes

INGREDIENTS:

- 2 cups diced butternut squash
- 1 red onion, sliced
- 2 tbsp olive oil
- Salt, pepper, rosemary

DIRECTIONS:

» Preheat oven to 400°F (200°C).
» Toss squash and onion with oil and seasonings.
» Roast 30 minutes.

Nutrition (per serving): Calories: 280 | Protein: 4g | Carbs: 40g | Fat: 12g | Fiber: 6g

---

DASH GARLIC CHICKEN RAINBOW VEGGIES

Servings: 2
Preparation Time: 35 minutes

INGREDIENTS:

- 2 chicken breasts
- 2 cups mixed vegetables (peppers, carrots, broccoli)
- 2 tbsp olive oil
- 2 cloves garlic, minced
- Salt and pepper

DIRECTIONS:

» Preheat oven to 400°F (200°C).
» Arrange chicken and veggies on sheet, drizzle oil and garlic, season.
» Roast 30 minutes.

Nutrition (per serving): Calories: 380 | Protein: 33g | Carbs: 15g | Fat: 18g | Fiber: 5g

---

DASH SPICY SWEET POTATO HASH

Servings: 2
Preparation Time: 30 minutes

INGREDIENTS:

- 2 cups diced sweet potato
- ½ cup diced onions
- ½ cup diced bell pepper
- 2 tbsp olive oil
- 1 tsp chili powder

DIRECTIONS:

» Heat oil in skillet, cook vegetables and chili powder for 25 minutes, stirring.

Nutrition (per serving): Calories: 320 | Protein: 4g | Carbs: 42g | Fat: 16g | Fiber: 7g

---

SHEET PAN RATATOUILLE

Servings: 2
Preparation Time: 40 minutes

INGREDIENTS:

- 1 zucchini, sliced
- 1 eggplant, sliced
- 1 cup cherry tomatoes
- ½ onion, sliced
- 2 tbsp olive oil
- Salt, pepper, herbs de Provence

DIRECTIONS:

» Preheat oven to 400°F (200°C).
» Toss veggies with oil and herbs, spread on baking sheet.
» Roast for 35 minutes.

Nutrition (per serving): Calories: 220 | Protein: 6g | Carbs: 24g | Fat: 14g | Fiber: 8g

---

DASH ONE-PAN PASTA PRIMAVERA

Servings: 2
Preparation Time: 25 minutes

INGREDIENTS:

- 4 oz whole-grain pasta

- 2 cups mixed vegetables (zucchini, bell peppers, cherry tomatoes)
- 2 tbsp olive oil
- 2 cloves garlic, minced
- Salt, pepper, basil

DIRECTIONS:

» Cook pasta according to package instructions.
» In skillet, sauté vegetables and garlic in olive oil until tender.
» Toss pasta with veggies, season, and serve.

Nutrition (per serving): Calories: 320 | Protein: 10g | Carbs: 45g | Fat: 12g | Fiber: 7g

DASH BROCCOLI TOFU STIR-FRY TRAY

Servings: 2
Preparation Time: 30 minutes

INGREDIENTS:

- 8 oz firm tofu, cubed
- 2 cups broccoli florets
- 2 tbsp soy sauce
- 1 tbsp sesame oil
- 1 tsp sesame seeds

DIRECTIONS:

» Preheat oven to 400°F (200°C).
» Arrange tofu and broccoli on baking sheet.
» Drizzle with soy sauce and sesame oil, sprinkle sesame seeds.
» Roast 25 minutes.

Nutrition (per serving): Calories: 320 | Protein: 20g | Carbs: 15g | Fat: 18g | Fiber: 5g

BAKED LEMON CHICKEN BROWN RICE

Servings: 2
Preparation Time: 40 minutes

INGREDIENTS:

- 2 chicken breasts
- 1 cup cooked brown rice
- Juice of 1 lemon
- 2 tbsp olive oil
- Salt and pepper

DIRECTIONS:

» Preheat oven to 400°F (200°C).
» Place chicken breasts and rice on baking sheet.
» Drizzle with lemon juice, olive oil, salt, and pepper.
» Bake for 35 minutes.

Nutrition (per serving): Calories: 400 | Protein: 35g | Carbs: 25g | Fat: 16g | Fiber: 3g

DASH ROASTED KALE LENTIL MIX

Servings: 2
Preparation Time: 30 minutes

INGREDIENTS:

- 2 cups kale, chopped
- 1 cup cooked lentils
- 2 tbsp olive oil
- Salt, pepper, lemon zest

DIRECTIONS:

» Preheat oven to 400°F (200°C).
» Mix kale and lentils on baking sheet.
» Drizzle with olive oil, season with salt, pepper, and lemon zest.
» Roast 20 minutes.

Nutrition (per serving): Calories: 300 | Protein: 12g | Carbs: 30g | Fat: 14g | Fiber: 10g

DASH CAJUN TILAPIA VEGGIE SHEET

Servings: 2
Preparation Time: 30 minutes

INGREDIENTS:

- 2 tilapia fillets
- 1 cup mixed veggies (bell peppers, zucchini)
- 2 tbsp olive oil
- 1 tsp Cajun seasoning
- Salt and pepper

DIRECTIONS:

» Preheat oven to 400°F (200°C).
» Arrange fish and veggies on tray.
» Drizzle with olive oil, sprinkle seasoning, salt, and pepper.
» Bake 20 minutes.

Nutrition (per serving): Calories: 300 | Protein: 28g | Carbs: 10g | Fat: 16g | Fiber: 3g

ROASTED GARLIC SHRIMP WITH PEPPERS

Servings: 2
Preparation Time: 25 minutes

INGREDIENTS:

- 10 shrimp, peeled and deveined
- 2 bell peppers, sliced
- 2 cloves garlic, minced
- 2 tbsp olive oil
- Salt and pepper

DIRECTIONS:

- Preheat oven to 400°F (200°C).
- Arrange shrimp and peppers on baking sheet.
- Drizzle with olive oil and garlic, season.
- Roast 15 minutes.

Nutrition (per serving): Calories: 260 | Protein: 22g | Carbs: 10g | Fat: 15g | Fiber: 3g

DASH PESTO SALMON WITH ZOODLES

Servings: 2
Preparation Time: 25 minutes

INGREDIENTS:

- 2 salmon fillets
- 2 cups zucchini noodles (zoodles)
- 2 tbsp pesto sauce
- Salt and pepper

DIRECTIONS:

- Preheat oven to 400°F (200°C).
- Arrange salmon and zoodles on baking sheet.
- Spread pesto on salmon, season with salt and pepper.
- Bake 20 minutes.

Nutrition (per serving): Calories: 350 | Protein: 28g | Carbs: 8g | Fat: 24g | Fiber: 2g

SHEET PAN VEGAN STIR-FRY WITH PEANUTS

Servings: 2
Preparation Time: 30 minutes

INGREDIENTS:

- 2 cups mixed stir-fry vegetables
- 1 cup chickpeas
- 2 tbsp peanut sauce
- 2 tbsp crushed peanuts

DIRECTIONS:

- Preheat oven to 400°F (200°C).
- Mix vegetables and chickpeas on tray, drizzle peanut sauce.
- Roast 25 minutes, garnish with peanuts.

Nutrition (per serving): Calories: 380 | Protein: 15g | Carbs: 35g | Fat: 20g | Fiber: 8g

DASH MUSHROOM GREEN BEAN BAKE

Servings: 2
Preparation Time: 30 minutes

INGREDIENTS:

- 2 cups green beans
- 1 cup mushrooms, sliced
- 2 tbsp olive oil
- Salt, pepper, garlic powder

DIRECTIONS:

- Preheat oven to 375°F (190°C).
- Arrange beans and mushrooms on sheet, drizzle oil, season.
- Roast 25 minutes.

Nutrition (per serving): Calories: 240 | Protein: 6g | Carbs: 12g | Fat: 18g | Fiber: 4g

DASH APPLE CHICKEN SKILLET

Servings: 2
Preparation Time: 35 minutes

INGREDIENTS:

- 2 chicken breasts
- 1 apple, sliced
- 2 tbsp olive oil
- 1 tsp cinnamon
- Salt and pepper

DIRECTIONS:

- Cook chicken and apple in skillet with olive oil, cinnamon, salt, pepper.
- Cook until chicken is done, about 25 minutes.

Nutrition (per serving): Calories: 360 | Protein: 32g | Carbs: 18g | Fat: 16g | Fiber: 3g

DASH SPICED SQUASH CHICKPEA BAKE

Servings: 2
Preparation Time: 35 minutes

INGREDIENTS:

- 2 cups diced squash
- 1 cup chickpeas
- 2 tbsp olive oil
- 1 tsp cumin
- Salt and pepper

DIRECTIONS:

- Preheat oven to 400°F (200°C).
- Toss squash and chickpeas with olive oil, cumin, salt, pepper.
- Roast 30 minutes.

Nutrition (per serving): Calories: 340 | Protein: 10g | Carbs: 40g | Fat: 15g | Fiber: 8g

SHEET PAN BRUSCHETTA CHICKEN

Servings: 2
Preparation Time: 35 minutes

INGREDIENTS:

- 2 chicken breasts
- 1 cup cherry tomatoes, halved
- ¼ cup basil, chopped
- 2 tbsp balsamic glaze
- 2 tbsp olive oil
- Salt and pepper

DIRECTIONS:

- » Preheat oven to 400°F (200°C).
- » Arrange chicken and tomatoes on baking sheet.
- » Drizzle with olive oil, balsamic glaze, basil, salt, and pepper.
- » Bake for 30 minutes.

Nutrition (per serving): Calories: 340 | Protein: 32g | Carbs: 12g | Fat: 18g | Fiber: 2g

DASH ROASTED BEETS CARROT CASSEROLE

Servings: 2
Preparation Time: 40 minutes

INGREDIENTS:

- 1 cup diced beets
- 1 cup diced carrots
- 2 tbsp olive oil
- Salt, pepper, thyme

DIRECTIONS:

- » Preheat oven to 400°F (200°C).
- » Mix beets and carrots with oil and seasonings.
- » Roast 35 minutes.

Nutrition (per serving): Calories: 280 | Protein: 4g | Carbs: 32g | Fat: 16g | Fiber: 7g

DASH SWEET CHILI TOFU SNAP PEAS

Servings: 2
Preparation Time: 30 minutes

INGREDIENTS:

- 8 oz firm tofu, cubed
- 1 cup snap peas
- 2 tbsp sweet chili sauce
- 1 tbsp sesame oil

DIRECTIONS:

- » Preheat oven to 400°F (200°C).
- » Arrange tofu and snap peas on baking sheet.
- » Drizzle with sweet chili sauce and sesame oil.
- » Roast 25 minutes.

Nutrition (per serving): Calories: 320 | Protein: 16g | Carbs: 20g | Fat: 18g | Fiber: 3g

DASH TRAY BAKE WITH BEANS TOMATO JAM

Servings: 2
Preparation Time: 30 minutes

INGREDIENTS:

- 1 cup white beans
- 1 cup cherry tomatoes
- 2 tbsp tomato jam
- 2 tbsp olive oil
- Salt, pepper, rosemary

DIRECTIONS:

- » Preheat oven to 400°F (200°C).
- » Mix beans and tomatoes on tray, drizzle with jam, olive oil, season.
- » Roast 25 minutes.

Nutrition (per serving): Calories: 340 | Protein: 12g | Carbs: 38g | Fat: 14g | Fiber: 9g

DASH MUSTARD CHICKEN VEGGIE ROAST

Servings: 2
Preparation Time: 35 minutes

INGREDIENTS:

- 2 chicken breasts
- 2 cups mixed veggies (potatoes, carrots, broccoli)
- 2 tbsp Dijon mustard
- 2 tbsp olive oil
- Salt and pepper

DIRECTIONS:

- » Preheat oven to 400°F (200°C).
- » Arrange chicken and veggies on tray, coat with mustard, olive oil, salt, pepper.
- » Roast 30 minutes.

Nutrition (per serving): Calories: 380 | Protein: 32g | Carbs: 22g | Fat: 18g | Fiber: 5g

DASH MAC CHEESE WITH BUTTERNUT SQUASH SAUCE

Servings: 2
Preparation Time: 35 minutes

INGREDIENTS:

- 4 oz whole-grain macaroni
- 1 cup roasted butternut squash, pureed
- ¼ cup cheddar cheese
- 2 tbsp milk
- Salt and pepper

DIRECTIONS:

» Cook macaroni according to package instructions.
» Combine squash puree, cheese, milk, salt, and pepper.
» Mix sauce into cooked macaroni.

Nutrition (per serving): Calories: 320 | Protein: 14g | Carbs: 50g | Fat: 8g | Fiber: 6g

LOW-SODIUM CHICKEN POT PIE

Servings: 2
Preparation Time: 40 minutes

INGREDIENTS:

- 1 cup cooked chicken, diced
- 1 cup mixed veggies (peas, carrots, corn)
- ½ cup low-sodium chicken broth
- ¼ cup whole-grain biscuit dough

DIRECTIONS:

» Preheat oven to 375°F (190°C).
» Combine chicken, veggies, broth in baking dish.
» Top with biscuit dough, bake 30 minutes.

Nutrition (per serving): Calories: 350 | Protein: 20g | Carbs: 35g | Fat: 12g | Fiber: 5g

BAKED TURKEY MEATLOAF WITH OAT CRUST

Servings: 2
Preparation Time: 45 minutes

INGREDIENTS:

- 8 oz ground turkey
- ½ cup oats
- ¼ cup tomato sauce
- 1 egg
- Salt and pepper

DIRECTIONS:

» Preheat oven to 375°F (190°C).
» Mix turkey, oats, tomato sauce, egg, salt, pepper.
» Shape into loaf, bake 35 minutes.

Nutrition (per serving): Calories: 300 | Protein: 25g | Carbs: 20g | Fat: 12g | Fiber: 3g

DASH CAULIFLOWER MASHED BOWL WITH GRAVY

Servings: 2
Preparation Time: 30 minutes

INGREDIENTS:

- 2 cups cauliflower florets, steamed and mashed
- ½ cup mushroom gravy
- Salt and pepper

DIRECTIONS:

» Prepare mashed cauliflower, season with salt, pepper.
» Serve topped with gravy.

Nutrition (per serving): Calories: 150 | Protein: 6g | Carbs: 12g | Fat: 8g | Fiber: 4g

LIGHTENED SHEPHERD'S PIE WITH LENTILS

Servings: 2
Preparation Time: 40 minutes

INGREDIENTS:

- 1 cup cooked lentils
- 1 cup mixed veggies (peas, carrots)
- 1 cup mashed cauliflower
- Salt, pepper, herbs

DIRECTIONS:

» Preheat oven to 375°F (190°C).
» Layer lentils and veggies in dish, top with cauliflower mash.
» Bake 30 minutes.

Nutrition (per serving): Calories: 250 | Protein: 12g | Carbs: 35g | Fat: 5g | Fiber: 10g

DASH TEX-MEX CASSEROLE

Servings: 2
Preparation Time: 35 minutes

INGREDIENTS:

- 1 cup cooked quinoa
- ½ cup black beans
- ½ cup corn
- ¼ cup salsa
- ¼ cup cheddar cheese

DIRECTIONS:

- Preheat oven to 375°F (190°C).
- Mix quinoa, beans, corn, salsa in baking dish, top with cheese.
- Bake 25 minutes.

Nutrition (per serving): Calories: 320 | Protein: 14g | Carbs: 45g | Fat: 10g | Fiber: 8g

SWEET POTATO LASAGNA

Servings: 2
Preparation Time: 40 minutes

INGREDIENTS:

- 1 large sweet potato, thinly sliced
- 1 cup marinara sauce
- ½ cup ricotta cheese
- ¼ cup mozzarella cheese

DIRECTIONS:

- Preheat oven to 375°F (190°C).
- Layer sweet potato slices, marinara, ricotta, and mozzarella in a baking dish.
- Bake for 30 minutes.

Nutrition (per serving): Calories: 360 | Protein: 14g | Carbs: 45g | Fat: 12g | Fiber: 6g

CRISPY BAKED ZUCCHINI FRIES

Servings: 2
Preparation Time: 30 minutes

INGREDIENTS:

- 2 zucchinis, sliced into fries
- ½ cup whole-grain breadcrumbs
- 2 tbsp grated Parmesan
- 1 egg, beaten
- Salt and pepper

DIRECTIONS:

- Preheat oven to 400°F (200°C).
- Dip zucchini fries in egg, coat with breadcrumbs and Parmesan.
- Bake for 25 minutes.

Nutrition (per serving): Calories: 180 | Protein: 10g | Carbs: 20g | Fat: 6g | Fiber: 3g

DASH ALFREDO PASTA WITH SPINACH

Servings: 2
Preparation Time: 25 minutes

INGREDIENTS:

- 4 oz whole-grain pasta
- ½ cup low-fat Alfredo sauce
- 2 cups fresh spinach

DIRECTIONS:

- Cook pasta according to package instructions.
- Mix cooked pasta with Alfredo sauce and spinach until spinach wilts.

Nutrition (per serving): Calories: 310 | Protein: 12g | Carbs: 40g | Fat: 12g | Fiber: 5g

DASH SLOPPY JOES WITH GROUND CHICKEN

Servings: 2
Preparation Time: 30 minutes

INGREDIENTS:

- 8 oz ground chicken
- ½ cup tomato sauce
- 1 tbsp Worcestershire sauce
- Whole-grain buns

DIRECTIONS:

- Cook chicken in skillet until browned.
- Add tomato and Worcestershire sauces; simmer 10 minutes.
- Serve on buns.

Nutrition (per serving, without bun): Calories: 220 | Protein: 20g | Carbs: 10g | Fat: 10g | Fiber: 2g

DASH CHICKEN ALFREDO CASSEROLE

Servings: 2
Preparation Time: 35 minutes

INGREDIENTS:

- 1 cup cooked chicken, diced
- 4 oz whole-grain pasta
- ½ cup low-fat Alfredo sauce
- ¼ cup mozzarella cheese

DIRECTIONS:

- Preheat oven to 375°F (190°C).
- Combine chicken, pasta, and Alfredo sauce in baking dish.
- Top with mozzarella, bake 25 minutes.

Nutrition (per serving): Calories: 380 | Protein: 28g | Carbs: 35g | Fat: 14g | Fiber: 4g

DASH TURKEY CHILI MAC

Servings: 2
Preparation Time: 35 minutes

INGREDIENTS:

- 4 oz whole-grain macaroni
- ½ cup cooked ground turkey
- ½ cup kidney beans
- ½ cup chili sauce
- ¼ cup cheddar cheese

DIRECTIONS:

» Cook macaroni according to package instructions.
» Mix with turkey, beans, chili sauce, and top with cheese.

Nutrition (per serving): Calories: 350 | Protein: 20g | Carbs: 40g | Fat: 12g | Fiber: 8g

LIGHT CHICKEN AND DUMPLINGS

Servings: 2
Preparation Time: 45 minutes

INGREDIENTS:

- 1 cup cooked chicken, diced
- 1 cup mixed vegetables (peas, carrots)
- 2 cups low-sodium chicken broth
- ¼ cup whole-grain biscuit dough

DIRECTIONS:

» Combine chicken, veggies, and broth in pot, simmer 30 minutes.
» Drop biscuit dough into pot, cook additional 10 minutes.

Nutrition (per serving): Calories: 320 | Protein: 22g | Carbs: 35g | Fat: 10g | Fiber: 5g

SWEET CORN BLACK BEAN ENCHILADA BAKE

Servings: 2
Preparation Time: 35 minutes

INGREDIENTS:

- 2 whole-grain tortillas
- ½ cup black beans
- ½ cup corn kernels
- ½ cup enchilada sauce
- ¼ cup cheddar cheese

DIRECTIONS:

» Preheat oven to 375°F (190°C).
» Fill tortillas with beans and corn, roll and place in dish.
» Top with enchilada sauce and cheese, bake 25 minutes.

Nutrition (per serving): Calories: 340 | Protein: 14g | Carbs: 45g | Fat: 10g | Fiber: 8g

DASH LOW-SODIUM MEATBALL STEW

Servings: 2
Preparation Time: 40 minutes

INGREDIENTS:

- 8 turkey meatballs
- 1 cup diced potatoes
- 1 cup mixed vegetables
- 2 cups low-sodium broth

DIRECTIONS:

» Combine meatballs, potatoes, veggies, and broth in pot.
» Simmer 30 minutes until vegetables are tender.

Nutrition (per serving): Calories: 320 | Protein: 20g | Carbs: 35g | Fat: 12g | Fiber: 5g

BUTTERNUT MAC AND CHEESE CUPS

Servings: 2
Preparation Time: 35 minutes

INGREDIENTS:

- 4 oz whole-grain macaroni
- 1 cup butternut squash puree
- ¼ cup cheddar cheese
- 2 tbsp whole-grain breadcrumbs

DIRECTIONS:

» Preheat oven to 375°F (190°C).
» Combine macaroni, squash puree, and cheese.
» Spoon into muffin cups, top with breadcrumbs.
» Bake 25 minutes.

Nutrition (per serving): Calories: 320 | Protein: 14g | Carbs: 48g | Fat: 8g | Fiber: 6g

DASH BAKED FISH AND CHIPS

Servings: 2
Preparation Time: 40 minutes

INGREDIENTS:

- 2 white fish fillets
- 1 large potato, sliced into wedges
- 2 tbsp olive oil
- ¼ cup whole-grain breadcrumbs
- Salt and pepper

DIRECTIONS:

» Preheat oven to 400°F (200°C).
» Coat fish in breadcrumbs, season with salt and pepper.
» Place fish and potato wedges on baking sheet, drizzle with olive oil.
» Bake for 30 minutes.

Nutrition (per serving): Calories: 340 | Protein: 24g | Carbs: 35g | Fat: 12g | Fiber: 4g

---

CREAMY MUSHROOM LENTIL POT PIE

Servings: 2
Preparation Time: 45 minutes

INGREDIENTS:

- 1 cup cooked lentils
- 1 cup mushrooms, sliced
- ½ cup cream of mushroom soup
- ¼ cup whole-grain biscuit dough

DIRECTIONS:

» Preheat oven to 375°F (190°C).
» Mix lentils, mushrooms, and soup in baking dish.
» Top with biscuit dough, bake 35 minutes.

Nutrition (per serving): Calories: 320 | Protein: 14g | Carbs: 40g | Fat: 10g | Fiber: 8g

---

DASH CHICKEN VEGGIE ENCHILADAS

Servings: 2
Preparation Time: 40 minutes

INGREDIENTS:

- 2 whole-grain tortillas
- 1 cup cooked chicken, diced
- ½ cup mixed veggies
- ½ cup enchilada sauce
- ¼ cup cheese, shredded

DIRECTIONS:

» Preheat oven to 375°F (190°C).
» Fill tortillas with chicken and veggies, roll up.
» Top with sauce and cheese, bake for 30 minutes.

Nutrition (per serving): Calories: 360 | Protein: 22g | Carbs: 40g | Fat: 12g | Fiber: 6g

---

CAULIFLOWER GRATIN WITH WHOLE GRAIN CRUMBS

Servings: 2
Preparation Time: 35 minutes

INGREDIENTS:

- 2 cups cauliflower florets
- ½ cup low-fat cheese sauce
- 2 tbsp whole-grain breadcrumbs

DIRECTIONS:

» Preheat oven to 375°F (190°C).
» Place cauliflower in baking dish, pour cheese sauce over top.
» Sprinkle with breadcrumbs and bake for 25 minutes.

Nutrition (per serving): Calories: 180 | Protein: 10g | Carbs: 18g | Fat: 8g | Fiber: 5g

---

DASH BAKED EGGPLANT PARMESAN

Servings: 2
Preparation Time: 40 minutes

INGREDIENTS:

- 1 eggplant, sliced
- 1 cup marinara sauce
- ¼ cup mozzarella cheese
- ¼ cup Parmesan cheese

DIRECTIONS:

» Preheat oven to 400°F (200°C).
» Layer eggplant slices with marinara and cheeses in baking dish.
» Bake for 30 minutes.

Nutrition (per serving): Calories: 300 | Protein: 14g | Carbs: 25g | Fat: 16g | Fiber: 8g

---

DASH TUNA NOODLE CASSEROLE

Servings: 2
Preparation Time: 35 minutes

INGREDIENTS:

- 4 oz whole-grain noodles
- 1 can tuna, drained
- ½ cup peas
- ½ cup cream of mushroom soup
- ¼ cup whole-grain breadcrumbs

DIRECTIONS:

» Preheat oven to 375°F (190°C).
» Mix noodles, tuna, peas, and soup.
» Place in baking dish, top with breadcrumbs.
» Bake 25 minutes.

Nutrition (per serving): Calories: 320 | Protein: 20g | Carbs: 40g | Fat: 8g | Fiber: 5g

DASH SAUSAGE PEPPERS FLATBREAD

Servings: 2
Preparation Time: 25 minutes

INGREDIENTS:
- 2 whole-grain flatbreads
- 4 chicken sausages, sliced
- 1 cup sliced bell peppers
- ½ cup marinara sauce
- ¼ cup mozzarella cheese

DIRECTIONS:
» Preheat oven to 400°F (200°C).
» Spread marinara on flatbreads, top with sausage, peppers, and cheese.
» Bake for 15 minutes.

Nutrition (per serving): Calories: 360 | Protein: 18g | Carbs: 35g | Fat: 16g | Fiber: 4g

CREAMY POLENTA ROASTED TOMATOES

Servings: 2
Preparation Time: 30 minutes

INGREDIENTS:
- 1 cup cooked polenta
- 1 cup cherry tomatoes
- 2 tbsp olive oil
- ¼ cup Parmesan cheese

DIRECTIONS:
» Roast tomatoes in olive oil at 400°F (200°C) for 15 minutes.
» Serve over warm polenta topped with Parmesan.

Nutrition (per serving): Calories: 290 | Protein: 8g | Carbs: 35g | Fat: 14g | Fiber: 3g

DASH MINI CHICKEN POT PIES

Servings: 2
Preparation Time: 40 minutes

INGREDIENTS:
- 1 cup cooked chicken, diced
- ½ cup mixed veggies
- ½ cup low-sodium broth
- ¼ cup whole-grain biscuit dough

DIRECTIONS:
» Preheat oven to 375°F (190°C).
» Combine chicken, veggies, and broth in ramekins.
» Top with biscuit dough and bake for 25 minutes.

Nutrition (per serving): Calories: 310 | Protein: 20g | Carbs: 28g | Fat: 12g | Fiber: 4g

DASH BAKED CHICKEN WILD RICE

Servings: 2
Preparation Time: 40 minutes

INGREDIENTS:
- 2 chicken breasts
- 1 cup cooked wild rice
- ½ cup mushrooms, sliced
- ¼ cup low-sodium broth

DIRECTIONS:
» Preheat oven to 375°F (190°C).
» Place chicken, rice, mushrooms in baking dish, add broth.
» Bake for 30 minutes.

Nutrition (per serving): Calories: 340 | Protein: 30g | Carbs: 30g | Fat: 10g | Fiber: 3g

BAKED SPAGHETTI ZUCCHINI NEST

Servings: 2
Preparation Time: 35 minutes

INGREDIENTS:
- 4 oz whole-grain spaghetti, cooked
- 1 zucchini, spiralized
- ½ cup marinara sauce
- ¼ cup mozzarella cheese

DIRECTIONS:
» Preheat oven to 375°F (190°C).
» Mix spaghetti and zucchini with marinara, place in baking dish.
» Top with mozzarella, bake 25 minutes.

Nutrition (per serving): Calories: 320 | Protein: 14g | Carbs: 42g | Fat: 10g | Fiber: 5g

DASH SHEPHERD'S PIE WITH TURKEY

Servings: 2
Preparation Time: 40 minutes

INGREDIENTS:
- 8 oz ground turkey
- 1 cup mixed veggies
- 1 cup mashed sweet potatoes
- Salt, pepper, herbs

DIRECTIONS:
- Preheat oven to 375°F (190°C).
- Brown turkey in skillet, mix with veggies.
- Top with mashed sweet potatoes, bake 25 minutes.

Nutrition (per serving): Calories: 340 | Protein: 22g | Carbs: 35g | Fat: 12g | Fiber: 6g

DASH VEGAN LENTIL MEATBALLS

Servings: 2
Preparation Time: 35 minutes

INGREDIENTS:
- 1 cup cooked lentils
- ¼ cup breadcrumbs
- 1 tsp Italian seasoning
- Marinara sauce for serving

DIRECTIONS:
- Combine lentils, breadcrumbs, seasoning; form meatballs.
- Bake at 375°F (190°C) for 25 minutes, serve with sauce.

Nutrition (per serving): Calories: 280 | Protein: 12g | Carbs: 40g | Fat: 6g | Fiber: 10g

DASH MUSHROOM SWEET POTATO BAKE

Servings: 2
Preparation Time: 40 minutes

INGREDIENTS:
- 2 cups diced sweet potatoes
- 1 cup sliced mushrooms
- 2 tbsp olive oil
- Salt, pepper, rosemary

DIRECTIONS:
- Preheat oven to 400°F (200°C).
- Toss sweet potatoes and mushrooms with olive oil, season.
- Bake for 30 minutes.

Nutrition (per serving): Calories: 260 | Protein: 6g | Carbs: 35g | Fat: 12g | Fiber: 5g

DASH CREAMY VEGETABLE BAKE

Servings: 2
Preparation Time: 35 minutes

INGREDIENTS:
- 2 cups mixed vegetables
- ½ cup low-fat cream sauce
- ¼ cup breadcrumbs

DIRECTIONS:
- Preheat oven to 375°F (190°C).
- Mix veggies and cream sauce in baking dish.
- Top with breadcrumbs, bake for 25 minutes.

Nutrition (per serving): Calories: 240 | Protein: 8g | Carbs: 30g | Fat: 10g | Fiber: 6g

LIGHT BBQ PULLED CHICKEN SLIDERS

Servings: 2
Preparation Time: 30 minutes

INGREDIENTS:
- 1 cup cooked chicken, shredded
- ¼ cup BBQ sauce
- 4 whole-grain slider buns

DIRECTIONS:
- Mix chicken with BBQ sauce, heat through.
- Serve on slider buns.

Nutrition (per serving): Calories: 320 | Protein: 20g | Carbs: 35g | Fat: 6g | Fiber: 4g

DASH VEGGIE TAMALE PIE

Servings: 2
Preparation Time: 40 minutes

INGREDIENTS:
- 1 cup cornmeal
- ½ cup black beans
- ½ cup diced tomatoes
- ¼ cup corn kernels
- ¼ cup cheddar cheese

DIRECTIONS:
- Preheat oven to 375°F (190°C).
- Mix cornmeal with beans, tomatoes, and corn.
- Place in a baking dish, top with cheddar cheese.
- Bake for 30 minutes.

Nutrition (per serving): Calories: 320 | Protein: 12g | Carbs: 45g | Fat: 10g | Fiber: 7g

DASH LOW-SODIUM BAKED BURRITOS

Servings: 2
Preparation Time: 35 minutes

INGREDIENTS:
- 2 whole-grain tortillas
- ½ cup cooked brown rice
- ½ cup beans
- ½ cup diced veggies

- Salsa for topping

DIRECTIONS:

» Fill tortillas with rice, beans, and veggies.
» Roll tightly, place seam-side down in baking dish.
» Bake at 375°F (190°C) for 25 minutes, top with salsa.

Nutrition (per serving): Calories: 340 | Protein: 12g | Carbs: 55g | Fat: 6g | Fiber: 10g

---

ROASTED BROCCOLI CHEDDAR QUICHE

Servings: 2
Preparation Time: 45 minutes

INGREDIENTS:

- 4 eggs
- 1 cup roasted broccoli
- ¼ cup cheddar cheese
- Salt and pepper

DIRECTIONS:

» Preheat oven to 375°F (190°C).
» Whisk eggs, mix in broccoli and cheese.
» Pour into baking dish, bake for 35 minutes.

Nutrition (per serving): Calories: 300 | Protein: 20g | Carbs: 8g | Fat: 20g | Fiber: 3g

---

DASH CHICKEN ZOODLE ALFREDO

Servings: 2
Preparation Time: 30 minutes

INGREDIENTS:

- 2 cups zucchini noodles
- 1 cup cooked chicken, diced
- ½ cup low-fat Alfredo sauce

DIRECTIONS:

» Cook zoodles until tender.
» Mix with chicken and Alfredo sauce, heat through.

Nutrition (per serving): Calories: 260 | Protein: 20g | Carbs: 10g | Fat: 14g | Fiber: 2g

---

DASH TUNA BEAN MELT

Servings: 2
Preparation Time: 25 minutes

INGREDIENTS:

- 1 can tuna, drained
- ½ cup white beans
- ¼ cup cheddar cheese
- 2 slices whole-grain bread

DIRECTIONS:

» Mix tuna and beans, spread on bread slices.
» Top with cheese and bake at 375°F (190°C) for 15 minutes.

Nutrition (per serving): Calories: 300 | Protein: 22g | Carbs: 30g | Fat: 8g | Fiber: 6g

---

DASH EGGPLANT AND CHICKPEA BAKE

Servings: 2
Preparation Time: 40 minutes

INGREDIENTS:

- 1 eggplant, diced
- 1 cup chickpeas
- 1 cup marinara sauce
- ¼ cup mozzarella cheese

DIRECTIONS:

» Preheat oven to 400°F (200°C).
» Mix eggplant and chickpeas with marinara.
» Top with cheese, bake for 30 minutes.

Nutrition (per serving): Calories: 320 | Protein: 12g | Carbs: 45g | Fat: 8g | Fiber: 10g

---

DASH SWEET POTATO BLACK BEAN TACOS

Servings: 2
Preparation Time: 30 minutes

INGREDIENTS:

- 2 whole-grain tortillas
- 1 cup diced sweet potato, roasted
- ½ cup black beans
- ¼ cup avocado slices
- Salsa for topping

DIRECTIONS:

» Fill tortillas with roasted sweet potato, beans, avocado.
» Top with salsa and serve.

Nutrition (per serving): Calories: 350 | Protein: 10g | Carbs: 50g | Fat: 12g | Fiber: 12g

---

DASH CHICKEN CORNBREAD CASSEROLE

Servings: 2
Preparation Time: 40 minutes

INGREDIENTS:

- 1 cup cooked chicken, diced
- ½ cup mixed veggies
- ½ cup cornbread batter

- Salt and pepper

DIRECTIONS:

» Preheat oven to 375°F (190°C).
» Mix chicken and veggies in baking dish, top with cornbread batter.
» Bake for 30 minutes.

Nutrition (per serving): Calories: 380 | Protein: 20g | Carbs: 45g | Fat: 12g | Fiber: 4g

DASH ZUCCHINI NOODLE LASAGNA

Servings: 2
Preparation Time: 40 minutes

INGREDIENTS:

- 2 cups zucchini noodles
- 1 cup marinara sauce
- ½ cup ricotta cheese
- ¼ cup mozzarella cheese

DIRECTIONS:

» Layer zoodles, marinara, and cheeses in baking dish.
» Bake at 375°F (190°C) for 30 minutes.

Nutrition (per serving): Calories: 280 | Protein: 15g | Carbs: 18g | Fat: 14g | Fiber: 4g

DASH CHICKPEA STEW WITH ROOT VEGGIES

Servings: 2
Preparation Time: 35 minutes

INGREDIENTS:

- 1 cup chickpeas
- 1 cup diced root vegetables
- 2 cups low-sodium broth
- Salt and pepper

DIRECTIONS:

» Simmer chickpeas, veggies, and broth for 30 minutes.
» Season with salt and pepper.

Nutrition (per serving): Calories: 290 | Protein: 10g | Carbs: 45g | Fat: 6g | Fiber: 10g

DASH MOZZARELLA TOMATO FLATBREADS

Servings: 2
Preparation Time: 25 minutes

INGREDIENTS:

- 2 whole-grain flatbreads
- ½ cup cherry tomatoes, halved
- ¼ cup mozzarella cheese
- Basil, salt, and pepper

DIRECTIONS:

» Top flatbreads with tomatoes, cheese, basil, salt, pepper.
» Bake at 400°F (200°C) for 15 minutes.

Nutrition (per serving): Calories: 310 | Protein: 12g | Carbs: 35g | Fat: 12g | Fiber: 4g

DASH CHEESY BROCCOLI QUINOA BAKE

Servings: 2
Preparation Time: 35 minutes

INGREDIENTS:

- 1 cup cooked quinoa
- 1 cup broccoli florets
- ½ cup cheddar cheese

DIRECTIONS:

» Mix quinoa and broccoli in dish, top with cheese.
» Bake at 375°F (190°C) for 25 minutes.

Nutrition (per serving): Calories: 320 | Protein: 14g | Carbs: 40g | Fat: 10g | Fiber: 6g

DASH BAKED CHICKEN NUGGETS

Servings: 2
Preparation Time: 30 minutes

INGREDIENTS:

- 8 oz chicken breast, cubed
- ½ cup whole-grain breadcrumbs
- 1 egg, beaten
- Salt and pepper

DIRECTIONS:

» Preheat oven to 400°F (200°C).
» Dip chicken cubes in egg, coat with breadcrumbs, season.
» Bake for 20 minutes.

Nutrition (per serving): Calories: 280 | Protein: 30g | Carbs: 15g | Fat: 10g | Fiber: 2g

DASH LOW-SODIUM JAMBALAYA

Servings: 2
Preparation Time: 35 minutes

INGREDIENTS:

- ½ cup cooked brown rice
- ½ cup chicken sausage, sliced
- ½ cup shrimp
- ½ cup diced veggies

- ½ cup low-sodium broth

DIRECTIONS:

» Cook sausage, shrimp, veggies in broth until cooked.
» Stir in rice, simmer 10 minutes.

Nutrition (per serving): Calories: 340 | Protein: 24g | Carbs: 30g | Fat: 10g | Fiber: 4g

DASH TURKEY SPINACH STUFFED SHELLS

Servings: 2
Preparation Time: 40 minutes

INGREDIENTS:

- 6 jumbo pasta shells
- ½ cup cooked ground turkey
- ½ cup spinach
- ¼ cup ricotta cheese
- ½ cup marinara sauce

DIRECTIONS:

» Stuff shells with turkey, spinach, and ricotta.
» Place in dish, top with marinara, bake at 375°F (190°C) for 25 minutes.

Nutrition (per serving): Calories: 320 | Protein: 20g | Carbs: 35g | Fat: 10g | Fiber: 5g

DASH SLOPPY LENTIL JOES

Servings: 2
Preparation Time: 30 minutes

INGREDIENTS:

- 1 cup cooked lentils
- ½ cup tomato sauce
- 2 whole-grain buns

DIRECTIONS:

» Simmer lentils with tomato sauce for 15 minutes.
» Serve on buns.

Nutrition (per serving): Calories: 280 | Protein: 14g | Carbs: 45g | Fat: 4g | Fiber: 10g

DASH CAJUN PASTA WITH TURKEY SAUSAGE

Servings: 2
Preparation Time: 35 minutes

INGREDIENTS:

- 4 oz whole-grain pasta
- 2 turkey sausages, sliced
- ½ cup diced veggies
- 1 tbsp Cajun seasoning

DIRECTIONS:

» Cook pasta according to package instructions.
» Sauté sausage and veggies, add Cajun seasoning.
» Toss pasta with sausage and veggies.

Nutrition (per serving): Calories: 340 | Protein: 20g | Carbs: 40g | Fat: 10g | Fiber: 5g

Appendices

Weekly Meal Planner

DAY	BREAKFAST	LUNCH	DINNER	SNACKS	NOTES MEAL PREP SUGGESTIONS
Monday	DASH Avocado Toast	Mediterranean Chickpea Quinoa Bowl	DASH Chicken Alfredo Casserole	Carrot sticks, hummus	Prep quinoa and chicken casserole Sunday evening.
Tuesday	Berry Yogurt Parfait	DASH Turkey Chili Mac	Sweet Potato Lasagna	Almonds, fresh fruit	Cook turkey chili Monday evening.
Wednesday	Spinach Mushroom Omelette	Lentil Kale Anti-Inflammatory Bowl	DASH Baked Fish and Chips	Greek yogurt with berries	Slice veggies in advance.
Thursday	DASH Smoothie Bowl	DASH Falafel Couscous Bowl	DASH Eggplant Parmesan	Edamame, mixed nuts	Bake eggplant slices in advance.
Friday	Overnight Oats with Fresh Fruit	DASH Grilled Shrimp Avocado Bowl	Creamy Mushroom Lentil Pot Pie	Apple slices with peanut butter	Prepare overnight oats Thursday night.
Saturday	DASH Veggie Omelette	DASH Tuna Bean Melt	Roasted Broccoli Cheddar Quiche	Whole-grain crackers, cheese	Prepare quiche filling Friday evening.
Sunday	DASH Peanut Butter Banana Toast	DASH Chickpea Stew with Root Veggies	DASH Spaghetti Squash Marinara Bake	Celery sticks, peanut butter	Roast spaghetti squash and veggies Saturday afternoon.

28 Days Meal Plan

DAY	BREAKFAST	LUNCH	DINNER	DESSERT
1	Raspberry Yogurt	Tuna Salad-Stuffed Tomatoes With Arugula	Mexican Chicken	Banana Delight
2	Southwest Tofu Scrambles	Eggplant Parmigiana	Chicken Breast With Red Onion And Cabbage	Caramelized Apricot
3	Blueberry Waffles	Honey Crusted Chicken	Mackerel Fillets With Roasted Peppers	Stylish Chocolate Parfait
4	Super-Simple Granola	Salmon With Turmeric	Beef Stroganoff	Sautéed Bananas With Orange Sauce
5	Simple Cheese And Broccoli Omelets	Penne Pasta With Arrabbiata Sauce	Chicken With Curry	Chocolate Avocado Pudding
6	Creamy Apple-Avocado Smoothie	Fajita Chicken Wraps	Cod With Cherry Tomatoes, Olives And Capers	Simple Brownies
7	Steel-Cut Oatmeal With Plums And Pear	Pork Medallions With Pear-Maple Sauce	Pesto Tilapia	Mango Sweet Mix
8	Salmon And Egg Scramble	Sliced Beef With Artichokes	Turkey Skewer And Beer Sausages	Cinnamon Apples
9	Creamy Avocado And Egg Salad Sandwiches	Hake Fillets With Quinoa Salad	Chicken With Walnut Pesto And Red Salad	Coconut Mousse
10	Banana Cinnamon Oatmeal	Herbed Seafood Casserole	Fusilli With Cherry Tomatoes, Capers And Crispy Crumbs	Baked Apple Slices
11	Blueberry-Vanilla Yogurt Smoothie	Baked Chicken Thighs	Grilled Salmon Fillet With Chili And Avocado Puree	Mousse Vanilla Banana
12	Chia Seeds Breakfast Mix	Buckwheat Spaghetti With Prawns	Salmon With Red Wine And Broccoli	Rainbow Salad
13	Breakfast Fruits Bowls	Pasta Alla Carrettiera	Pork Sausage With Fennel Salad Garnish	Blueberry Cream

DAY	BREAKFAST	LUNCH	DINNER	DESSERT
14	Red Velvet Pancakes With Cream Cheese Topping	Tuna Salad	Sirloin Steak In A Bed Of Rocket	Gentle Blackberry Crumble
15	Steel-Cut Oatmeal With Plums And Pear	Penne Pasta With Arrabbiata Sauce	Chicken With Walnut Pesto And Red Salad	Simple Brownies
16	Banana Cinnamon Oatmeal	Sliced Beef With Artichokes	Pesto Tilapia	Sautéed Bananas With Orange Sauce
17	Simple Cheese And Broccoli Omelets	Hake Fillets With Quinoa Salad	Chicken Breast With Red Onion And Cabbage	Cinnamon Apples
18	Raspberry Yogurt	Honey Crusted Chicken	Tuna Salad-Stuffed Tomatoes With Arugula	Rainbow Salad
19	Chia Seeds Breakfast Mix	Pasta Alla Carrettiera	Turkey Skewer And Beer Sausages	Banana Delight
20	Southwest Tofu Scrambles	Baked Chicken Thighs	Grilled Salmon Fillet With Chili And Avocado Puree	Coconut Mousse
21	Creamy Avocado And Egg Salad Sandwiches	Tuna Salad	Chicken With Curry	Mousse Vanilla Banana
22	Blueberry Waffles	Buckwheat Spaghetti With Prawns	Beef Stroganoff	Mango Sweet Mix
23	Red Velvet Pancakes With Cream Cheese Topping	Eggplant Parmigiana	Mackerel Fillets With Roasted Peppers	Caramelized Apricot
24	Blueberry-Vanilla Yogurt Smoothie	Pork Sausage With Fennel Salad Garnish	Fusilli With Cherry Tomatoes, Capers And Crispy Crumbs	Gentle Blackberry Crumble
25	Super-Simple Granola	Salmon With Turmeric	Mexican Chicken	Stylish Chocolate Parfait
26	Breakfast Fruits Bowls	Fajita Chicken Wraps	Sirloin Steak In A Bed Of Rocket	Chocolate Avocado Pudding

DAY	BREAKFAST	LUNCH	DINNER	DESSERT
27	Creamy Apple-Avocado Smoothie	Pork Medallions With Pear-Maple Sauce	Cod With Cherry Tomatoes, Olives And Capers	Blueberry Cream
28	Salmon And Egg Scramble	Herbed Seafood Casserole	Salmon With Red Wine And Broccoli	Baked Apple Slices

www.ingramcontent.com/pod-product-compliance
Lightning Source LLC
Chambersburg PA
CBHW081358070526
44583CB00020B/2591